American Indian Image
Makers of Hollywood

ALSO BY
FRANK JAVIER GARCIA BERUMEN

*Latino Image Makers in Hollywood: Performers,
Filmmakers and Films Since the 1960s*
(McFarland, 2014)

American Indian Image Makers of Hollywood

Frank Javier Garcia Berumen

McFarland & Company, Inc., Publishers
Jefferson, North Carolina

Library of Congress Cataloguing-in-Publication Data

Names: Berumen, Frank Javier Garcia, author.
Title: American Indian image makers of Hollywood / Frank Javier Garcia Berumen.
Description: Jefferson, North Carolina : McFarland & Company, Inc., Publishers, 2020 | Includes bibliographical references and index.
Identifiers: LCCN 2019042168 | ISBN 9781476678139 (paperback) ∞
  ISBN 9781476636474 (ebook)
Subjects: LCSH: Indians in motion pictures. | Indian motion pictures—United States—History. | Indian motion picture actors and actresses—United States | Indian motion picture producers and directors—United States | Motion pictures—United States—History.
Classification: LCC PN1995.9.I48 B47 2020 | DDC 791.43/652997—dc23
LC record available at https://lccn.loc.gov/2019042168

British Library cataloguing data are available

ISBN (print) 978-1-4766-7813-9
ISBN (ebook) 978-1-4766-3647-4

© 2020 Frank Javier Garcia Berumen. All rights reserved

No part of this book may be reproduced or transmitted in any form or by any means, electronic or mechanical, including photocopying or recording, or by any information storage and retrieval system, without permission in writing from the publisher.

Front cover image of Graham Greene in *Dances with Wolves*, 1990 (Orion Pictures Corporation/Photofest)

Manufactured in the United States of America

McFarland & Company, Inc., Publishers
Box 611, Jefferson, North Carolina 28640
www.mcfarlandpub.com

For:

My mother, who from childhood educated me about our *Huichol* roots, traveled with me to numerous pre-Columbian sites, and informed me about the numerous achievements and cultures of indigenous America.

My native ancestors and their legacy of respecting Mother Earth, honoring the Great Spirit, and being grateful for every gift, in every stage in the circle of life.

The Native American activists of the 1970s, who led us out of the recesses of oblivion and into a rediscovery of ourselves.

Rita Padmore, a dear colleague and friend, whose support in one of my darkest hours blessed me with her support and friendship.

Leonard Noriega, a close friend in the journey of life, who walked on from the road too soon.

Table of Contents

Acknowledgments   ix

Introduction   1

1. Native American History and the Genesis of Native American Images (1492–1880)   5
2. The Representation of Indigenous Women in U.S. Films   9
3. Celluloid Native American Film Images (1880–1919)   16
4. The Noble Savage and the White Man's Enemy (1920–1929)   31
5. In the Way of Progress (1930–1939)   60
6. Native Americans as Part of the Nation's Family (1940–1949)   95
7. New Images and Consciousness (1950–1959)   124
8. The Winds of Change (1960–1969)   156
9. The American Indian Movement and the Reel Invisibility (1970–1979)   171
10. Dashed Expectations (1980–1989)   197
11. A Quincentennial of Misappropriation (1990–1999)   205
12. Native Voices and Native Images (2000–2010)   237
13. The Return to Invisibility (2011–Present)   254
14. Looking Back and Looking Forward   260

Chapter Notes   261

Bibliography   269

Index   271

Acknowledgments

No man stands alone unto himself. Like history and life, we emanate and partake from others—their stories in the journey of life, their inspiration in difficult times, and their wisdom acquired in the turbulence of life.

This book would not have been possible if many other scholars, both Native American and non-native, had not documented and written parts and pieces of the more than one hundred years of the Native American presence in U.S. cinema. To them all, I am grateful and indebted. They were the pioneers of a new field of study within the discipline of Native American studies, scholarship, and inquiry. Their work has enlightened, informed, and enabled the further evolution of the study of native film images and contributions.

Among these groundbreaking scholars and writers are the following:

Eva Marie Garroutte's *Real Indians: Identity and the Survival of Native America* (Berkeley: University of California Press, 2003), particularly her focus on the connections between ethnic identity and community survival;

Angela Aleiss' *Making the White Man's Indian: Native Americans and Hollywood Movies* (Westport, CT: Praeger, 2005)—her study on the presence of native people in the early part of the 20th century in the Hollywood film industry has been especially illuminating;

M. Elise Marubbio's *Killing the Indian Maiden: Images of Native American Women in Film* (Lexington: University Press of Kentucky, 2006), and her research on gender and sexuality in the depiction of native women in films;

Roxanne Dunbar-Ortiz's landmark book *An Indigenous Peoples' History of the United States* (Boston: Beacon Press, 2014), which has helped reshape the new periodization of U.S. history.

Several books written by American Indian Movement (AIM) leaders have been especially illuminating regarding the native struggle for renewal, sovereignty, and self-determination:

Russell Means with Marvin J. Wolf, *Where White Men Fear to Tread: The Autobiography of Russell Means* (New York: St. Martin's Griffin, 1995);

Leonard Peltier, *Prison Writings: My Life Is My Sun Dance* (New York: St. Martin's Griffin, 1999);

Dennis Banks with Richard Erdoes, *Ojibwa Warrior: Dennis Banks and the Rise of the American Indian Movement* (Norman: University of Oklahoma Press, 2004).

There have been many other books about Native American, United States, Mexican, Mexican American and Chicano, and Latin American history that have contributed to my understanding about both the past and the present, though sadly not all can be highlighted in the space available here.

I have included numerous film reviews as sources in this book. They contribute a time-based perspective on the way people viewed Native Americans, as well as race relations in the nation. I have also included more recent film reviews by prominent contemporary critics and authors of the Native American experience. It is interesting to compare and contrast the different views of the same film from different eras. I wish to thank the following newspapers and media sources for the use of some of their film reviews: *New York Times, Los Angeles Times, San Francisco Chronicle, Washington Post, Variety, Hollywood Reporter, Chicago Sun-Times, Boston Globe, Chicago Reader, New York Herald, The Observer, Bright Lights Journal, Daily Kos, Of magazine, Fortnight, Reader, Focus on Film, Rolling Stone, Esquire, Newsweek, Film Daily, Films and Filming, Time, Playboy, TV Guide, ABC News, Photoplay, Saturday Review, Cue magazine, Los Angeles Herald-Examiner, Men with Guns Press Kit* (Sony Pictures), U.S. Bureau of the Census, *Screen Actors' Guild Report,* Ultimate Movie Ranking website, Indian Country website, Powhatan website, *Daily Beast,* Native News Online website, Alibi website, Tom Laughlin website, IMDb, and many others.

I wish to thank the Academy of Motion Picture Art & Sciences (particularly the Margaret Herrick Library and staff) for hard-to-find film photos, newspaper clippings, and other materials, and Larry Edmund's Bookstore for rare film photos. I would also like to express my thanks to Sean Hathwell and Jeff Mantor of Larry Edmund's Bookstore for many years of assistance in searching for hard-to-find movie photos.

Bianca E. Hernández is likewise owed many thanks for her extraordinary work of inserting hundreds of Spanish accent marks and correcting grammar in the text.

There are numerous persons (my parents, friends, relatives, acquaintances, and persons in academia) with whom I have conversed and exchanged thoughts, opinions, analysis, and conversations about the Native American experience, both in the United States and Mexico, in reservations and in cities. These personal exchanges have provided me with a multitude of different opinions and perspectives on numerous subjects related to this topic.

Last, but not least, I have watched thousands of films in the United States, Canada, Mexico, and other parts of Latin America related to Native American film images. I have digested these images and narratives over a lifetime and contrasted them with the real history of native people in the Americas. Most of these films were emotionally painful and difficult to watch, especially during my childhood. These film images had an incalculable effect on the evolution of my ethnic identity, self-worth, life goals, and social consciousness.

The goal of this book is to provide a history of Native American images and history in U.S. cinema. I have provided a brief overview of the pre–Columbian world and the history of the United States to contextualize and to inform readers. I have also traced the evolution of Native American images created by Europeans upon their arrival in the Americas, images that in turn were transplanted into the infant cinema industry.

I have presented the history of Native American film images decade by decade, providing an overview of the major historical events in native history during each decade, along with the representation and/or misrepresentation of these events in the contemporary cinema. This approach allowed me to present the prevailing film images, key representative films, and native filmmakers and performers. I hope that this format will enrich the readers' understanding of this subject.

The history of Native Americans in television is beyond the scope of this book. However, most of the native performers and filmmakers listed here have worked in both feature films and television. Their television credits are included in their respective biographies.

Of course, no book could ever include all contributors to this extensive history. There are omissions of individuals and films, due to the limits of any book, despite its ambition and scope.

I have avoided using the word *America* as a substitute for the United States of America. America is two continents, not only one nation or country. The American continents comprise 35 nations and/or nation-states. I have used the terms *American Indian*, *Native American*, *First Nations*, and *indigenous* to describe the first inhabitants of the Americas. There is no consensus among indigenous people regarding a general term to describe the entire group. Many indigenous people identify themselves by their tribal affiliation. There is also the fact that Columbus assumed that he was in India, the ancient Far East civilization, when he arrived on the American shores in 1492. As a consequence, the term *American Indian* has become a permanent descriptor for the indigenous peoples of the Americas. I have used this term in the title of this book.

There are two other terms that I wish to address. Both are used in the United States, and they often confuse and confound people when it comes to Native Americans: *Latino* and *Hispanic*. The term *Latino* is one designated by the community itself. In its narrower definition, it includes the heterogeneous peoples who were formerly under the colonial dominion of Spain and Portugal. For example, Angel R. Oquendo writes, "It calls to mind the Latino/a struggle for empowerment in the United States.... The adoption of the term 'Latino' could be regarded as part of a broader process of self-definition and self-assertion.... It accentuates the bond between the Latino/a community and the Spanish language."[1]

There also the term *Hispanic*, which was first used by the U.S. Census in 1980 to count persons of Spanish and Hispanic origin. The term *Hispanic* connotes a link to the Spanish Empire in Latin America. However, Suzanne Oboler notes, "Like other ethnic labels currently used to identify minority groups in this country, the term Hispanic raises the question of how people are defined and classified in this society and in turn how they define themselves in the United States. It points to the gap between the self-identification of people of Latin American descent and their definition through the label created and used by others."[2]

The more modern *Latino* label is not without difficulty and controversy. Latinos come in different hues of skin color: brown, black, white, and everything in between. The current Latino mosaic includes Native Americans, mestizos, mulattos, and others. Some Latinos in the United States and in Latin America speak Native American languages and dialects; others speak Spanish and Spanglish, while still others speak French and Portuguese, and even English. All of these people are the products of their diverse history.

However, the inclusion of Native Americans in the Latino mosaic is contradictory and confounding. The term *Latino* totally obliterates the ethnic origin of the native peoples of the Americas, who were here thousands of years before the arrival of Europeans and others. Mexico, for example, was home to 80 percent of the Native American population at the time of the first European contact. The actual number of Spaniards after the conquest in 1519 was relatively small (around 200,000, according to some estimates) compared to the overall indigenous population. Immigration to Mexico was almost nonexistent until the 1930s, with the arrival of Spanish refugees (fleeing Franco's fascist dictatorship) and others after World War II. The images of light-skinned, blonde, and European-looking newscasters and actors present in Telemundo and Televisa news programs and *telenovelas* are misleading; they do not represent most Mexicans (either in Mexico or in the United States). The vast majority of Mexicans are indigenous or mestizos. In addition, many countries in Latin America still have indigenous-majority populations: Guatemala, Perú, Bolivia, El Salvador, Honduras, and Nicaragua. Many of these indigenous peoples continue to live in traditional native cultures. For these individuals especially, the term *Latino* is irrelevant and even offensive.

The Caribbean nations (Cuba, Puerto Rico, Haiti, and the Dominican Republic, among others) and those nations on the rim of the southern part of the Americas (Venezuela, Panamá, Colombia, and Brazil) have predominantly or significantly Spanish and African cultural roots. Many of the indigenous peoples of these regions became extinct or greatly diminished in the wake of European diseases and the genocidal tendencies of conquistadores. As a result, three nations in South America (Brazil, Argentina, and Chile) are the product of the immigration of millions of Italians and Germans to those regions.

In summary, history, conquest, geography, and the push and pull of economics have created the current Latino mosaic. It is a cultural experiment in progress. The term *Latino* is useful and convenient for the sake of cultural unity, political expediency, and economic cohesiveness. However, the undeniable fact remains that the number of people with indigenous origins and cultures remains in the tens of millions in the United States, Mexico, and the rest of the Americas. However, this fact goes largely unremarked in the current (and ethnocentric) immigration debate.

It is my objective in this book to inform Native American–origin peoples and nonnative peoples about the long and arduous evolution of native images in film. I hope that it will fire the imaginations of young people, motivate them to write their own stories, and share them through cinema and/or the arts. Through our culture and history, endurance and resilience, and humanity, we can enrich the world.

Before 1492, tens of millions of Native Americans lived in the Americas, from the north to the furthermost south. Over the course of some five hundred years, most of their collective history has been destroyed, mislaid, or marginalized.

We stand on the shoulders of our ancestors, and we must speak on their behalf to tell their stories through oral history, literature and film. To remember is to relive, and to relive is to reconnect to the tree of life and to history.

Introduction

The primary purpose of this book is to document the history of Native American film images and filmmakers in U.S. motion pictures, from the late 1800s to the present. A secondary purpose is to celebrate the contributions of Native Americans in U.S. cinema.

I have carried this book inside me since my childhood, when I watched my first motion picture. From the beginning I knew that these film images were at odds with my history and culture. And the more I learned about my history and culture, the more I became aware of the great divide between the dominant white culture and the native culture.

The writing of this book has been a journey of rediscovering the lives and accomplishments of many native people. Through my extensive research, I became aware of the thousands of Native Americans in the film industry who have contributed anonymously, devoid of awards or wealth, and of the hundreds of historical events in Native American history and stories that have never reached the screen.

The arrival of Europeans in the Americas had (and continues to have) an incalculable impact on the lives of all native peoples throughout the Americas: economically, socially, politically, and culturally. Many tribes became extinct (like the Taíno in the Caribbean islands), and others were substantially reduced in numbers. Numerous languages and traditions that had survived for thousands of years were obliterated. The massive and forced movement of millions of native peoples from and to reservations resulted in cultural disorientation. The rape and violation of native women created the mestizo and other ethnic mixtures. Military-like boarding schools, Christian schools, and the public schools of nation-states forcefully assimilated millions of native children. They were robbed of their culture, language, religion, dress, and self-identity. For some, a deep-rooted sense of inferiority, denial, and self-hatred became ingrained in their psyches.

Miraculously, many native peoples, against almost insurmountable odds, clung to and maintained their respective cultures: oral history, traditions, language, religion, and self-identity. The rest became lost and marginalized in the evolution and formalization of nation-states. In the United States, the federal government determined who was indigenous and who was not—what tribes were recognized as First Nations and which were not. In the rest of the Americas, different ways were formulated in order to dilute the presence of native peoples in individual countries. For instance, Mexico continues to have the largest native population in the Americas; however, even Mexico's government has developed revisionist demographics.[1]

Movies have exercised a powerful influence on how Native Americans have been viewed. The film images have obliterated both the truth and the history. In the 1962 John Ford film *The Man Who Shot Liberty Valance*, there is a phrase that expresses the revisionism of U.S. history. In one scene, a politician asks a reporter whether he plans to print the truth. The reporter responds, "When the legend becomes fact, print the legend!" This statement summarizes the written and cinematic history of the nation. For more than one hundred years, movies have been perpetuating myths and legends about Native Americans.

Many U.S. films have represented Native American genocide as entertainment. The film image of native people as savages—bloodthirsty, cruel, and uncivilized—is an indelible one. Thousands of films have depicted them as an impediment to progress and civilization. Conversely, Europeans and Euro-Americans have always been portrayed on film as perpetual victims rather than invaders or perpetrators. Films have depicted stagecoach and railroad passengers, covered wagon pioneers, and besieged U.S. Cavalry units shooting down hundreds upon hundreds of screaming indigenous warriors as a sporting entertainment. U.S. films have recycled and glorified macho white men as professional "Indian fighters" (another name for Native American exterminators). No other ethnicity has had this genocidal term created for them. Native women have fared no better, being inevitably portrayed as scheming and treacherous, promiscuous, and objects of ridicule. According to these movies, native women are always lusting for the stalwart white protagonist, even at the expense of their own people.

The vast majority of these indigenous characters, until recently, have been portrayed by white performers. Euro-American performers were smeared with brown grease to darken their appearance, and they spoke a bizarre series of invented languages. The Hollywood film industry created a one-size-fits-all type of native attire, pseudo-rituals, and psychopathic cultural traits. None of the Euro-American film characters could ever understand why native peoples were resisting their home invasion, diseases, and extermination. Movies are entertainment, but they are also a mirror of how a society wishes to see itself. In addition, films are artifacts of anthropology, for they reveal what a society believes, how it behaves, and what it chooses to remember to (or to forget).

Popular culture has often perpetuated the worst of society's prejudices and mores. The first images of native peoples were born at the moment when Europeans landed on the continent and saw the indigenous residents as darker, different, and exotic. The diaries, ships logs, and reports that these Europeans conveyed to their brethren across the ocean became the first stereotypes and images of native peoples. Later, the official documents of genocide and conquest chronicled the justification (i.e., paganism, uncivilized, etc.) of the misdeeds committed by the Spanish, Portuguese, French, English, and other invaders and conquerors. These images were in turn immortalized in church documents, colonial correspondence, government archives, newspapers, novels, Wild West shows, and plays. At the end of the 1800s, these stereotypes and derogatory images were transplanted into the infant art of cinema.

Euro-American mythology and revisionism has become so ingrained that even well-meaning individuals have succumbed to it. For example, in his first inaugural speech (January 20, 2009), the first African American president, Barack H. Obama, stated, "For us, [the Euro-American immigrants] packed their few worldly possessions and travelled across oceans in search of a new life. For us, they toiled in sweatshops *and settled the West*, endured the lash of whip and plowed the hard earth."[2] President Obama did not mention the fact that the Americas were already occupied by Native Americans and that it was not an empty and vacant land space. A few days later, Obama, in an interview in Dubai, stated, "We have not been perfect. But if you look at the record, as you say, America was not born as a colonial power."[3]

1

Native American History and the Genesis of Native American Images (1492–1880)

The genesis of Native American images began with the arrival of the first Europeans in the Americas. The history of pre–Columbian America and the subsequent history of the European conquest is beyond the scope of this book. However, a brief overview is necessary for context.

The pre–Columbian world was a unique entity, not perfect or a paradise, but a place untarnished by many of the socio-economic ills besetting Europe at the time.[1] The Americas were populated by tens of millions of people living in North, Central, and South America. Historian Roxanne Dunbar-Ortiz noted, "The total population of the hemisphere was about one hundred million at the end of the fifteenth century, with about two-fifths in North America, including Mexico. Central Mexico [Meso America] alone supported some thirty million people."[2] It is estimated that Mexico was home to some 80 percent of the native population at the time that the Europeans arrived.[3] Today, Mexico continues to have the largest Native American population in the Americas.[4]

Thousands of roads crisscrossed the Americas, bustling with trade and commerce. Dunbar-Ortiz wrote, "Influences from the south powerfully shaped the indigenous peoples to the north (in what is now the United States) and Mexicans continue to migrate as they have for millennia but now cross the arbitrary border that was established in the US war against Mexico in 1846–48."[5] Alvin M. Josephy, Jr., likewise wrote, "In pre–Columbian days that division [the present U.S.–Mexico border] had no meaning ... the diffusion of ideas and skills from Mexico, including the knowledge of maize agriculture, moved north ... affecting with varying degrees of intensity the lives and cultures of Indian nations from the present-day American Southwest to Canada."[6]

Mexico was the center of the pre–Columbian Native American world, due to the massive populations of the Toltecs, Aztecs, Mayans, and other native societies. Josephy noted, "Until the coming of the Europeans, Indian Mexico in many ways was the vital hearth of the continent, radiating out from its center the traits and influences of its native civilizations.... The area was a dynamic one with millions of people representing diverse tribal backgrounds and languages."[7] The Aztecs and Mayans boasted highly developed societies, especially in the areas of medicine, astronomy, engineering, agriculture, commerce, and mathematics (the Mayans, for example, had invented the concept of zero). They also had large cities with populations larger than many in Europe.

North of Mexico lay hundreds of native nations. Over the years 850 to 1250 CE, the Anasazi (the Navajo word for "ancestors") developed in the Four Corners region of Utah, Colorado, Arizona, and New Mexico. They built large cities in Chaco Canyon (Pueblo Bonito), Mesa Verde, Azteca, and Casas Grande, among others. This highly developed native society established hundreds of miles of paved roads, agricultural irrigation, and ceremonial centers, and it traded with central Mexico, the Caribbean, and Canadian native nations.

Further north, in the 1200s, the great city-state of Cahokia developed along the Mississippi River, populated by tens of thousands. Along the West Coast, in what today is California, more than 200,000 native peoples (living in the most populous region north of Mexico) practiced agriculture, fishing, and trade. In the great plains of North America were the nomadic peoples of the Lakota, Blackfoot, Comanche, and others, who subsisted on the buffalo. Along the East Coast of the present-day United States, dozens of tribes lived under confederations with written constitutions and flourished in agriculture, fishing, and trade. In the southeast lived the Creeks, Cherokee, Choctaw, and Seminole in prosperous agricultural and trading communities.

In the southern part of the Americas lay the highly developed society of the Quechua-speaking peoples of the Andean regions (which the Spanish called the Inca Empire)[8] and numerous agricultural and nomadic tribes (especially in the Amazon region). The people known as the Incas had developed advanced engineering, mathematics, astronomy, medicine, and agriculture.

The first victims to feel the brutality of the European conquest were the native peoples of the Caribbean islands (Taínos, Arawak, Caribs, and others). In 1492, Christopher Columbus led three Spanish ships into their world. Soon thereafter, the Spanish thirst for gold and silver resulted in enslavement of these densely populated areas. Bartolome de las Casas, a Catholic missionary who accompanied Columbus, commented on the treatment of Native Americans by the latter: "It was a general rule among the Spaniards to be cruel; not just cruel but extraordinarily cruel so that harsh and bitter treatment would prevent Indians from daring to think of themselves as human beings or having a minute to think at all."[9] Twenty years later, most of these native people had become extinct.

The next focus of Spanish conquistadores was Mexico in 1519. The expedition was led by Hernán Cortés. He forged an alliance with the Aztecs' adversaries in Meso America (including, critically, the Tlascalans). Aided by the invisible weapon of diseases that were previously nonexistent in the Americas, as well as muskets, gunpowder, horses, and dogs, the conquerors were able to subdue the Aztecs in 1621. The Spanish burned the Aztec capital of Tenochtitlán, covered Lake Texcoco, and built the modern-day Mexico City. The conquerors then imposed a system called *la encomienda*, essentially feudal peonage, which was no better than slavery, for the next three hundred years.

From central Mexico, the Spanish conquistadores headed north in search of more gold and silver. However, they were never able to subdue semi-nomadic tribes such as the Yaqui, Tarahumara, Apache, and others. Wherever the Spanish conquered, they forcefully imposed their Catholic religion and, in the wake of their constant pillage and plunder, left thousands of indigenous victims through murder, disease, rape, and torture.[10] Not to be outdone, Portugal manifested its military and political ambitions in the Americas, with its arrival in 1500 along the shores of what would later become Brazil.

Later came the British and French, who fought the French and Indian War (1754–

1763) for the destiny and control of North America. The English victory in this conflict paved the way for the subsequent consolidation of the Thirteen Colonies. By 1781, these colonies had won independence and became the United States of America. However, the new nation's aspirations to expand all the way to the opposite coast were already in motion. They quickly discarded the British Proclamation of 1763, which prohibited European settlement east of the Appalachian Mountains. The removal of this law set in motion the westward expansion without any pretense of legality. The ideological justification was that of Manifest Destiny. It was the widespread Euro-American belief that God had ordained that the United States would extend "from sea to shining sea," and if God had ordained it, everything that was done along the way to make it happen was morally justified.

The nation's westward expansion was clothed in a series of documents that appeared benevolent and considerate of native peoples, such as the Northwest Land Ordinance of 1787, which stated, "The utmost good faith shall always be observed toward the Indians: their lands and property shall never be taken from them without their consent and in their property rights and liberty they never shall be invaded or disturbed unless in just and lawful wars authorized by Congress; but laws founded in justice and humanity shall, from time to time be made for preserving wrongs being done to them and for preserving peace and friendship with them."[11] However, this document's words were contradicted by the misdeeds of the new republic's leaders in enacting a federal policy of Native American annihilation.

During his first administration, George Washington was frustrated by his slow takeover of the Ohio Valley, which remained strong under Native American alliances. As a consequence, Washington's secretary of war, Henry Knox, ordered the U.S. army commander of Fort Washington (present-day Cincinnati), "No other remedy remains, but to extirpate, utterly, I possible, said Banditti."[12]

Between 1781 and 1881, the U.S. Congress approved exactly 371 treaties with Native American nations, as required by the U.S. Constitution. However, there were many other treaties that were signed by the president of the United States but not ratified by the U.S. Congress. As a result, there are some 600 treaties that indigenous tribes consider bona fide and legal.[13] During this period of treaty making with the United States, some two million acres were taken from native tribes through coercion, fraud, or outright broken promises.[14]

In the next 150 years, the United States would carry out numerous "Indian Wars" in all directions, against "hostile Indian tribes." Roxanne Dunbar-Ortiz wrote, "Nearly all the population areas of the Americas were reduced by 90 percent following the onset of colonizing projects, decreasing the targeted Indian populations of the Americas from one hundred million to ten million. Commonly referred to as the most extreme demographic disaster—framed as natural—in human history."[15] The genocide included massacres, rapes, diseases, forced removals, the destruction of food and animal husbandry, scalping, and slavery.[16]

The last indigenous tribe to resist the U.S. government militarily was the Apache. Their resistance ended on September 4, 1886, when Geronimo surrendered. After so many years of fighting, he had been reduced to only a handful of warriors. He also traveled with women and children, whom he had to protect, clothe, and feed. He and his men were granted prisoner-of-war status but denied their right be set free. In turn, Geronimo, his men, and even the Apache scouts who had worked with the U.S. Army were sent as prisoners to Fort Pickens in Pensacola, Florida (Geronimo's family was removed to Fort Marion in the same state). Thereafter, he and his people were sent to Fort Sill, Oklahoma, where Geronimo died as a prisoner of war on February 17, 1909.[17] He spent twenty-eight years as a prisoner of the U.S. government.

The "Indian Wars" officially ended with the U.S. Cavalry massacre of unarmed men, women, and children in 1890 at Wounded Knee (today part of the Pine Ridge Oglala Reservation, in South Dakota). However, there would be many other tragedies that Native Americans would go on to endure.

After the Indian Wars ended, Christian churches and missionaries founded the Native American boarding schools. Prototypes of these Euro-American-administered schools had actually begun in the 1630s. But the proliferation of Indian boarding schools really began with the founding in 1879 of the Carlisle Indian Industrial School by the U.S. Army in a former military installation in Pennsylvania. Soon this school became the model for other boarding schools established by the Bureau of Indian Affairs (BIA). By 1902, there were some twenty-five federally funded Indian boarding schools in fifteen states and territories, far removed from the reservations of the respective children.

The primary objective of these schools was to assimilate native children into white culture and to remove any vestige of their indigenous identity. Native children were subjected to punishment for speaking their native languages, practicing their religion, and having any outward appearance of being indigenous. The Indian boarding schools inflicted untold mental, physical, and cultural trauma on these children. By the 1960s, growing Native American activism and tribal complaints about the boarding schools led to their slow decline and transition into community colleges. The passage of the Indian Self-Determination and Education Assistance Act of 1975 ushered in a new era of Native American education. However, for the hundreds of thousands of native people who had experienced the boarding schools, their impact would last a lifetime.

In 1919, U.S. citizenship was granted to Native Americans who had been called to service during World War I. More than 10,000 native persons had served in the armed forces, and large numbers had fought and died.

On June 2, 1924, President Calvin Coolidge signed the Indian Citizenship Act into law. It officially made all Native Americans born within the United States and its territories U.S. citizens. However, the law did not cover or include the hundreds of thousands of Mexican indigenous people who had lived in the Southwest before the Mexican-American War (1846–1848) or who had moved to the United States since that time. In addition, the act did nothing to classify these individuals as legitimate indigenous people.

During this time, Charles Curtis, who was part Osage, Kaw, Potawatomi, and European, was elected Republican congressmen (1893–1907) and then U.S. senator (1907–1913 and 1915–1929) for the state of Kansas. Curtis believed in assimilation and, during his term of office in the U.S. Congress, helped pass the Curtis Act of 1898. The latter act extended the Dawes Act to the Five Civilized Tribes, thus ending self-government and communal land and allowing the surplus land to be sold to non–Native Americans. Curtis would go on to serve as vice president of the United States under Herbert Hoover from 1929 to 1933. He was the first and only person with significant indigenous blood to serve in such positions of political power and influence.

2

The Representation of Indigenous Women in U.S. Films

Historically, the representation of Native American women in U.S. films has been both demeaning and stereotypical. Most indigenous roles in U.S. films have been in westerns. The western genre, until recently, has celebrated Manifest Destiny (which propelled the nation's western expansion) with relish and gusto. These films were told from a strictly Euro-American point of view. However, the Native American point of view is quite different. For native peoples, the Euro-American expansion west resulted in genocide and the appropriation of the entire continent of North America.

Western films replicated that biased history on the big screen. In U.S. history and in film, indigenous peoples were always subordinate in the narrative, and the native characters were always deemed inferior. If indigenous males were portrayed as raving savages and uncivilized, native women roles did not fare any better. Often, they were worse.

The early part of the 20th century witnessed the greatest number of Native American roles in U.S. cinema. Indigenous roles came in all types: good, bad, and indifferent. Some films were sympathetic to native people, while others were outright racist and demeaning. During this period in film history, there were more native women film roles than at any other time. From the 1920s onward, however, native women protagonists have been reduced to incidental, decorative, or small roles. As a consequence, the scholarship on the film images of native women has been recent and long overdue.[1]

The invasion and conquest of the Americas was first undertaken by the Spanish, who did not bring their women or their families with them on their expeditions. They proceeded to murder, loot, pillage, and rape on a massive scale. Other European powers soon joined the competition to claiming an empire in the Americas. The English, unlike the Spanish, brought their women and families. However, in the end, all European powers brutalized, enslaved, and violated native women. Motion pictures have replicated this history of conquest, albeit from an ethnocentric perspective.

M. Elise Marubbio suggests that there have been two types of native women stereotypes: the early Celluloid Princess and later the Sexualized Maiden: "The Celluloid Princess emerges during the silent period in romantic tragedies that set the stage for subsequent figures.... In the earlier works, she appears as a helper figure—a young girl—who saves the white hero from attack by savage Indians but dies in the cross fire of battle."[2] Angela Aleiss observed, "In Walt Disney's *Pocahontas*, a warrior is about to decapitate John Smith when a young maiden flings herself between them. 'If you kill him, you'll have to kill me, too!' she sobs. Her offer of sacrifice, her curvaceous figure and her virginal stature have come to symbolize America's Indian heroine."[3]

Marubbio proposes that the Sexualized Maiden stereotype began in the 1930s but came to the forefront in the 1940s. She notes, "The character's scanty clothing accentuates her pinup girl figure, which in turn strains to control a volatile psyche. The underlying theme in these films equates the women's sexual taint with a disease carried through her Indian bloodline. She represents a great danger from within civilized society."[4]

I have selected and analyzed twenty-three films, from the 1920s to the present, in order to address the issue of representing Native American women in U.S. motion pictures. Fourteen of these films feature interracial unions between Euro-American males and indigenous women. Eight of the films depict indigenous relationships between native couples, and one shows an indigenous woman and an African American male.

The 1920s was a time when independent white women celebrated liberating social mores and financial independence. However, that was not the case for indigenous women, whether in real life or *reel* life. *The Squaw Man* was based on a popular play that has been filmed three times (in 1914, 1918, and 1931). All three versions were directed (or co-directed) by Cecil B. DeMille. The narrative is set in the late 1800s and early 1900s. In the story, Naturich (or Nat-U-Ritch) is a Native American woman who rescues Captain James Wingate, an expatriate Englishman. Later, she kills another white man to save Wingate. They marry and have a child. However, Naturich increasingly becomes docile and subservient to Wingate. Later, she kills herself when she is about to be arrested for the murder she committed earlier in the film.

Helen Hunt Jackson's novel *Ramona* was published in 1884. It has been the subject of four film adaptations: three in the silent era, released in 1910, 1916, and 1928 (the only version in which an indigenous actress, Dolores Del Río, played Ramona), and one talking film in 1936. The story is set in California, just before the 1848 takeover by the United States. Ramona is a mestiza (half Scottish and half Native American). She is loved by two men: Felipe, the Spanish son of the *haciendado*, and Alessandro, an indigenous suitor. Ramona goes with Alessandro, whom she marries, and then flees to the mountains to escape the Euro-American arrivals, who are resorting to ethnic cleansing. Alessandro is killed, and Ramona eventually is rescued by Felipe, and they return to what is left of the hacienda. Both Naturich and Ramona are strong women who have agency in their lives. However, the racism of the times destroys their lives and their relationships.

In *Red Skin* (1928, Paramount), the narrative depicts the trials and tribulations of a college-educated Navajo named Wing Foot (Richard Dix) who becomes acculturated. Throughout his ups and downs, however, his indigenous girlfriend Corn Blossom (Julie Carter) both supports him and fights alongside him to protect their reservation and their people. Both have experienced prejudice, and both have something in common to fight for. In the end, they succeed.

The 1930s brought the Great Depression and more gripping film narratives. In *They Call Her Savage* (1932), Clara Bow played a half-breed who is destructive, prone to violence, and promiscuous in the white world. The film proposes that her indigenous blood is to blame for her behavior and lifestyle. At the end of the movie, she returns to her home to live with Moonglow (Gilbert Roland), another half-breed like herself.

In the film *Massacre* (1934, Warner Bros.), Joe Thunderhorse (Richard Barthelmess) is a cocky and arrogant Wild West performer. He is adored and loved by white socialists, who see him as an "exotic savage." However, it is not until he returns to the reservation to visit his dying father that he finally realizes the magnitude of the poverty and racism facing his people. He is informed further by the college-educated Lydia, a Native American and a Bureau of Indian Affairs secretary. She has seen the widespread federal corruption at the reservation. Both characters dedicate themselves to exposing the fraud and graft. As in *Red Skin*, their relationship ends well.

In *Laughing Boy* (1934, MGM), Laughing Boy (Ramón Novarro), a Navajo, falls in love with Slim Girl (Lupe Vélez). She has been raised by whites and is shunned by the Navajos for her promiscuity and hard-living lifestyle. Although Laughing Boy proposes marriage, Slim Girl is unable to leave her sordid lifestyle behind. It ultimately results in her accidental death. Many films had depicted indigenous people as contaminated with evil and depravity. In an interesting turnaround, however, both *They Call Her Savage* and *Laughing Boy* attribute the indigenous women's loss of morality to living in the white world.

The 1940s brought World War II and a loosening of some film taboos in the postwar period. The key film (and the only film in which a Native American woman is the lead character) is *Duel in the Sun* (1946, Selznick). Pearl Chávez (Jennifer Jones) is a half-breed. Her father has been hanged for killing her promiscuous and adulterous mother and her mother's lover. Pearl is sheltered by a wealthy, though distant, white family in Texas of the late 1800s. Pearl becomes a promiscuous woman, like her mother. Even worse, she is attracted to an abusive and racist wastrel named Lewt (Gregory Peck). In the end, they kill each other in a bizarre ritual of sexual attraction and hatred. Pearl Chávez reflects the self-fulfilling prophecy of a sense of inferiority and self-hatred. She is unable to fit in, either in the native world or in the white world. She thus destroys herself and everybody around her. Aleiss noted, "Duel's half-breed Pearl rattled the rigid guidelines of religious and local censorship organizations and reminded audiences that Indian women could also possess an appetite for sexuality."[5]

Black Gold (1947, Allied Artists) features a supporting role for Katherine DeMille, the adopted daughter of director Cecil B. DeMille; she also became the first wife of Anthony Quinn. In the film, Anthony Quinn and Katherine DeMille Quinn play an indigenous couple (Charlie Eagle and Sarah Eagle) who raise horses and barely survive, eking out a marginalized existence. Like other movies, this film depicts the life of an indigenous couple that triumphs over the adversities in their lives by struggling together for the same things.

With the exception of the 1920s, the 1950s is perhaps the decade with more Native American women roles, although all were played by non-indigenous actresses. In *Broken Arrow*, Tom Jeffords (James Stewart) makes an effort to establish peace with Cochise (Jeff Chandler) and the Apaches. In the process, Jeffords falls in love with Sonseeahray (Debra Paget). Jeffords agrees to meet the time requirements, customs, and traditions in order to wed his beloved. However, white settlers violate the signed treaty and intrude upon Apache land. They kill Sonseeahray, and Jeffords is devastated. He tries to convince Cochise to abandon the treaty. However, it is Cochise who maintains his integrity and stands by the agreement. Thus Sonseeahray is sacrificed for the sake of peace.

In *Across the Wide Missouri* (1951, MGM), a rugged trapper named Flint Mitchell (Clark Gable) marries Kamiah (María Elena Márquez), a Blackfoot princess. She is subsequently killed in a skirmish between the whites and the Blackfoot. However, her son (the narrator) recounts that her death cemented peace between the two groups. *The Far Horizons* (1955, Paramount) featured a fictional love story between Sacajawea (Donna

Clark Gable as the rugged trapper and María Elena Márquez as his Blackfoot wife in *Across the Wide Missouri* (1951, MGM).

Reed) and Lieutenant William Clark (Charlton Heston). At the end, however, he abandons her for the sake of Manifest Destiny. *Broken Lance* (1954, 20th Century–Fox) depicted the interracial marriage of white cattle baron Matt Devereaux (Spencer Tracy) and Señora (Katy Jurado), a Native American woman. However, she is despised by the sons of his first marriage and the white residents of the town. The couple lives a cloistered and segregated life—the price for their interracial union.

In *Apache* (1954, United Artists), Massai (Burt Lancaster) is an escaped Apache from the forced removal. He kidnaps Nalinle (Jean Peters) from the impoverished San Carlos Reservation and continues a one-man war against the whites. However, when she bears him a child, he renounces war in order to become a farmer and feed his family. Nalinle becomes his retribution for all the pain and suffering that the Apaches have endured. *Run of the Arrow* (1957, Universal) features the narrative of a defeated and traumatized Confederate soldier (Rod Steiger) who flees to the west. There, he is accepted by the Lakota as a member of the tribe and marries Yellow Moccasin (Sarita Montiel). However, their interracial union is threatened—not by the indigenous people, but rather by the coming of more white settlers.

White Feather (1955, 20th Century–Fox) is set in Wyoming in the 1870s and depicts the U.S. Army's forced removal of the Cheyenne because white settlers have moved in to search for gold. Army surveyor Tanner (Robert Wagner) falls in love with Appearing

Day (Debra Paget), the sister of Little Dog (Jeffrey Hunter). However, she is already the fiancée of American Horse (Hugh O'Brien). Appearing Day goes to live with Tanner at the fort, and conflict arises as a result between the Cheyenne and the whites. In the end, Tanner convinces the Cheyenne chief to let American Horse and himself settle the conflict and maintain peace. Here, the woman Appearing Day rejects her world for the white world, though she is unwilling to sacrifice her own happiness for peace. It is her white lover who takes the initiative to keep the peace.

Although the 1960s brought significant political, economic, and cultural changes, the images of indigenous people were frozen in time. A minuscule number of films included Native American female roles, and even fewer had a lead character. John Ford's *Cheyenne Autumn* (1964, Warner Bros.) focused on the epic journey of the northern Cheyenne's return to their homeland in Yellowstone during 1878–1879. The most important indigenous character is Spanish Woman (Dolores Del Río), the aged woman who has seen all the horrors of Manifest Destiny directed at her people. However, she desperately wants peace. Even when her hot-headed son Red Shirt (Sal Mineo) is killed by the Cheyenne chief in order to prevent violent conflict with the U.S. Cavalry, she is resigned to not give in to more violence. *Tell Them Willie Boy Is Here* (1969, Universal) tells the true story of a young Paiute Willie Boy (Robert Blake), who flees with his indigenous girlfriend Lola (Katherine Ross) after killing her father in self-defense. Unfortunately, a posse gives relentless chase to the pair. As their pursuers are closing in, Lola dies of a bullet wound. The narrative leaves unclear whether she killed herself in order to prevent her capture and the duress of interrogation or whether Willie shot her in order to spare her the ordeal. Either way, the character of Lola is willing to sacrifice herself so that her unjustly accused lover can make his escape.

In *100 Rifles* (1969, 20th Century–Fox), Raquel Welch (née Raquel Tejada) plays Sarita, a member of the Yaqui people, who are desperately fighting to stop their forced removal from Sonora to Yucatán. Sarita is fearless, tenacious, and highly admired for her courage. She is assisted in her efforts by Yaqui Joe (Burt Reynolds), who is being pursued by an African American sheriff known as Lyedecker (Jim Brown). Yaqui Joe is wanted for stealing $6,000 from a U.S. bank in order to purchase 100 rifles for the Yaqui resistance. Sarita becomes involved in an interracial relationship with Lyedecker. However, he ultimately returns to the United States, and she continues her struggle on behalf of her people.

It was not until the 1990s that U.S. films featured any significant indigenous female characters. The groundbreaking *Dances with Wolves* (1990, Orion) featured Tantoo Cardinal as Black Shawl, a strong-willed and independent-minded Lakota woman. She is not above voicing her opinions and/or disagreement to the Lakota warriors and to her husband Kicking Bear (Grahame Greene). Black Shawl has authority and is an equal of the tribal elders.

The film *Smoke Signals* (1998, Shadow Catcher) represented the first contemporary film that was written (Sherman Alexie), directed (Chris Eyre), and acted by a predominantly indigenous cast. The film is set in the Coeur d'Alene Indian Reservation in Plummer, Idaho. Suzy Song (Irene Bedard) is the indigenous woman who contacts Arlene (Tantoo Cardinal) regarding the death of her former husband Arnold (Gary Farmer). The latter had a long history of alcoholism, domestic abuse, and child abandonment, in addition to causing the fire at the beginning of the film. Arnold's son Victor (Adam Beach) and his friend (Evan Adams) journey to retrieve his father's ashes. Victor is resentful,

100 Rifles (1969, 20th Century–Fox), starring Jim Brown as the Arizona lawman Lyedecker and Raquel Welch (née Tejeda) as Sarita, the Yaqui woman fighting against the forced removal of her tribe by dictator Porfirio Díaz in the early 1900s.

embittered, and desolate about his father's behavior. However, it is Suzy who educates him about his father's undying love for him and his regret for abandoning his son. She also teaches Victor about the power of healing that comes from forgiveness and renewal.

The film *Grey Owl* (1999, Largo) depicts the life of Archibald "Grey Owl" Belaney, an Englishman who took on a Native American identity and gained fame as an environmentalist. However, it is his indigenous girlfriend Anahareo (Annie Galipeau) who endures his masquerade and then provides him with a purpose (environmentalism) and retribution in his empty life.

In the 2000s, a few films provided indigenous female roles. In *Imprint* (2007, Linn Prods.), Shayla Stonefeather (Tonantzín Carmelo) is an acculturated Lakota lawyer with political ambitions in the white world. However, her visit to see her dying father and overwhelmed mother leads to an epiphany. The marginalized existence of her people in the Pine Ridge Reservation and the wisdom of the Lakota shaman provide her with an illuminating consciousness of obligation on behalf of her people. *Thunderheart* (1992, TriStar) focused on a young FBI agent named Ray Levoi (Val Kilmer), a mixed blood who is sent to investigate a militant Native American organization in South Dakota. He is attracted to Maggie Eagle Bear, a single mother and activist. She educates him about the dire state of indigenous people in the reservation and the machinations of corporations to plunder the natural resources. However, Levoi is too acculturated, naïve, and committed to "law and order." It is only when Maggie is murdered that he realizes the magnitude of the hard realities facing the reservation.

Out of the previous 23 films, fourteen featured interracial unions and eight indigenous unions. Most of the interracial unions featured in these films ended in domestic abuse, alcoholism, and destructive promiscuity. The indigenous unions fared better, although one union had the same result of alcoholism, domestic abuse, and child abandonment. One speculation might be that interracial unions (between white males and indigenous women) involve an unequal balance of economic, educational, and societal power, which favors white protagonists. In all these interracial unions between white males and indigenous women, the latter were clearly at a disadvantage. In the eight films that featured indigenous relationships, the narratives involved a cohesion of native culture, a commonality of purpose, and proactive behavior.

In conclusion, although film reflects life, it is not always identical. Nevertheless, in an overview of eight decades of U.S. film, the cinematic representation of indigenous females has been most often negative, stereotypical, and denigrating.

3

Celluloid Native American Film Images (1880–1919)

The first Native American images in celluloid occurred early in the evolution of motion pictures. Euro-American filmmakers and audiences were fascinated by these "noble savages." They found Native Americans exotic, primitive, and, as a cultural curiosity, worthy of anthropological and biological study.

The Native Images and Films (1900–1910)

Native Americans have long been the object of interest (and at times fascination) by Euro-Americans. At the time of the arrival of Europeans in the Americas, native peoples were dehumanized in word and deed. Later, as the United States expanded westward, the native image evolved from subhuman savages who occupied what Europeans desperately desired to the "noble savage." After the end of the Indian Wars, reformers, clergy, and some government officials proposed assimilation as a policy for those whom they deemed the "vanishing race."

The Dawes Act of 1887 (also known as the Dawes Severalty Act) was passed by the U.S. Congress in 1887 and signed by the president of the United States. Its purpose was to detribalize native communities and turn their land into individual plots, just like those of Euro-American farmers. Mother Earth was no longer a sacred place that belonged to the entire tribe, but rather a commodity to be sold in the capitalist market like any other product. The tribal council was seen as the glue that created the backwardness of native people. The traditional role of leadership was removed from the tribal council and entrusted in the white government, making native people completely dependent on it for their survival.

The act proposed that those native people who lived in the individual allotments and apart from their respective tribes would be granted U.S. citizenship. In addition, the act stated that the U.S. government would "classify" as "excess" any reservation land after the allotments were designated and sell them in the marketplace to Euro-American immigrants and settlers. The so-called Five Civilized Tribes (Seminoles, Chickasaw, Cherokee, Choctaw and Creek/Muscogee) located in the southern part of the nation would lose some 90 million acres during the implementation of this law. The Office of Indian Affairs (later changed to the Bureau of Indian Affairs in 1947) had been established on March

11, 1824, and its purpose was (and still is) to hold in trust all land on behalf of Native American tribes.

By the early 1900s, as Euro-Americans appropriated more land, the contact between the two peoples became more pronounced. As a result, other issues became sources of conflict: miscegenation, education, alcohol, law enforcement, employment, and politics. For white citizens, natives were no longer, faraway exotic people huddled in remote reservations or depicted only in history books, but rather living in their midst. Conversely, motion pictures capitalized on the tenuous contact between the two different cultures. Melodramatic movie scenarios were created about the "noble savage" of the past and the "exotic bronze people" of the present, who would not assimilate.

At the very beginning of the movie industry, numerous short films were made about the Native American way of life: traditional dances, arts and crafts, reservation life, and religious practices. Today, they serve as the anthropology of the history of film. In 1894, Thomas Edison became the first U.S. filmmaker to capture Native Americans on film. This was in a short film titled *Sioux Ghost Dance*, produced by Edison, which depicted the novelty of native people performing a traditional dance. The dancers were part of Buffalo Bill's Wild West Show. The Library of Congress has preserved this short film, and it is available to view on YouTube.

In 1903, Edison produced *The Great Train Robbery*, written, directed, and produced by Edwin S. Potter. It became the first U.S. film to tell a story. In the same year, *Kit Carson* (1903, Biograph) created the first (and indelible) image of savage native warriors attacking white soldiers (the 21-minute-long film was shot in the Adirondack Mountains of New York). The primary Native American image was formally transferred into motion pictures: savage, violent, ruthless, and raving.

Beginning in 1910, the film industry moved from the highly urbanized centers of New York and New Jersey to California. Then as now, the Southwest was home to large populations of Native Americans and Mexicans. This circumstance aroused even more interest in these darker peoples. It was therefore inevitable that native peoples would become the subject of hundreds of good, bad, and indifferent film narratives.

During the period from 1900 to 1909, several important directors and film companies specialized in making Native American–themed films that proved popular at the box office. The French film company Pathé Frères (or Pathé) constructed a film studio in New Jersey in 1908. They specialized in one and two reels (one reel was 15 minutes in silent film, and two reels were 30 minutes), particularly dramas, westerns, and comedies. The studio had been founded in France by the Pathé Brothers in 1896 and soon became the largest film production company in the world. In 1908, they invented the newsreel and expanded their business to the United States.

In 1910, Pathé Frères produced a key film that focused on Native Americans: *The Red Girl and the Child*, a western produced by James Gordon Young Deer. This film featured a native woman as an unconventional heroine. Young Deer boasted Winnebago roots, and soon he won accolades for his dedication to detail and authenticity in Native American–themed films.

Young Deer became a creative force in developing new images of native peoples in the film medium. According to Angela Aleiss, "Young Deer created some unusual tales. Many of his films were idyllic Indian love triangles or tragic stories of an Indian's heroic sacrifice, but others proved to be more daring and rather unconventional."[1] His films during this time featured strong, independent, and resourceful native women who took agency in their lives, such as *The Yaqui Girl* (1910, Pathé Frères), *For the Squaw* (1911, Pathé Frères), and *The Squaw's Mistaken Lover* (1911, Pathé Frères), among others.

Two other important film pioneers would feature numerous Native American characters in their films: D. W. Griffith and Cecil B. DeMille.

David Wark Griffith (1875–1948) was an important film director, screenwriter, and producer for most of the silent period of U.S. motion pictures. He directed some 518 films during 1908–1931. He is credited with creating numerous film techniques, like the close-up. Griffith directed some thirty short films that featured important Native American characters. Although Griffith showed sympathy for native people, he tended to view them from a "noble savage" perspective. His main theme in these films was that of the racist "white man's government" and the oppression of Native Americans. These Griffith films offered images completely at odds with his own racist stereotypes of African Americans, which would be featured later in *Birth of a Nation* (1915).

In 1908, Griffith featured his first Native American lead character in *The Red Man and the Child* (Biograph). A year later, in 1909, he directed *The Red Man's View* (Biograph),[2] which focused on the forced removal of a native tribe. In 1910, he directed *In Old California* (Biograph), set in 1822, during the Spanish era, and presented his first glimpses of Native Americans during this historical period.[3] However, his most important film with a Native American narrative and characters was *Ramona* (1910, Biograph).

Cecil B. DeMille (1851–1959) was another noted director and producer, who worked from the silent period into the era of talking films. His key Native American films were *The Squaw Man* (1914) and, to a lesser extent, his second version of the same film in 1918 (now lost). He featured Native American characters throughout his silent film period. However, it was not until the 1930s and 1940s that DeMille directed several westerns with important Native American characters.

Ramona (1910, Biograph)

Helen Hunt Jackson's famous novel *Ramona* was first filmed in 1910. The novel had been a huge success and, indirectly, had the effect of creating a mythical-like image of California that brought millions to live in the state.

The 1910 version of *Ramona* was directed by famed director D. W. Griffith. The screenplay was written by Stanner E. V. Taylor and Griffith himself. The impressive cinematography was undertaken by G. W. Bitzer. The film was only 17 minutes in length.

The caption at the beginning of the film reads, "The story of white man's injustice to the Indians." The narrative is set in southern California during the mid–1840s as the state passes into U.S. control in the aftermath of the Mexican-American War (1846–1848). Ramona is a mestiza adopted by a wealthy Spanish land-owning family. She receives a proposal of marriage from Felipe, the oldest son of the *Californios*. However, Ramona is in love with Alessandro, a Native American. The arrival of thousands of Euro-Americans results in the destruction of the old way of life. Alessandro is banished from the hacienda and, later, discovers that his village has been destroyed by white settlers. Ramona and Alessandro marry and have a child and then flee to the San Joaquín Mountains. Later, Alessandro is killed by white settlers, and the baby subsequently dies. At the end of the movie, Ramona is found by Felipe, who takes her to his devastated hacienda.

The film proved a critical and commercial success for Griffith. Today, more than a century later, the film appears well meaning in depicting the destruction of the native people of California in the aftermath of the U.S. takeover. However, it is also melodramatic and emoted in an acting style that long ago went out of fashion. Nevertheless, it portrays an important time period in the history of Native Americans.

The title role was played by the popular Mary Pickford (1892–1979), who was on her way to becoming "America's Sweetheart" and a legendary film star. The rest of the cast hailed from Griffith's stock company of players. Henry B. Walthall played Alessandro, and Francis J. Grandon was Felipe. There were no Native Americans and/or Mexicans in the cast; as a result, authenticity is lacking.

The film is available on YouTube for viewing. A copy of the film print is preserved at the U.S. Library of Congress.

Native American Film Images in the 1910s

The vast majority of silent films have been lost. What remains is a minuscule and incomplete amount of actual footage. Much the history of U.S. film from the 1880s to the late 1920s has been mislaid as well. However, several film historians have recently undertaken a vast amount of research to recover that period of film history. Thanks to them, we have a much fuller understanding of the history of that time period. One film scholar in particular, Angela Aleiss, has been responsible for reconstituting and documenting the history of Native Americans in U.S. film from the late 1800s to the late 1920s.

During the decade that spanned the years of 1911–1919, there continued to be great interest in Native Americans as the subject of motion pictures. Indigenous protagonists remained popular, as were native-themed films. One popular subject was the focus on the alleged tainted characteristics of mixed-race individuals and/or half-breeds. Other films during this period centered on the issues of miscegenation, acculturation, and assimilation of native characters.

The subject of mixed-race people fascinated filmmakers and filmgoers. These characters were portrayed as contaminated human beings, with a proclivity for treachery, duplicity, and obsessive desire for white women. Unusually, *The Half-Breed's Courage* (1911, Champion) displayed a half-breed's capacity for sacrifice on behalf of a white maiden. In other films, half-breeds were depicted as incapable of forming mixed-race unions; these movies included *The White Man Takes a Red Wife* (1910, Kalem), *Lo, the Poor Indian* (1910, Kalem), and *The Blackfeet Halfbreed* (1911, Kalem).

Some studios and filmmakers pushed for the authenticity of native performers in native roles. For example, the Bison Company promoted an attractive actress named Princess Mona Darkfeather. Although Darkfeather denied that she had native ancestry, the Bison Company continued to publicize her as such, and she appeared in dozens of western and indigenous-themed films during this decade.

Action-packed and melodramatic westerns were popular. The Bison and Ince studios were the most prolific studios in the western genre. Some of these films were sympathetic to native characters. In the film *The Massacre* (1912, Biograph), for example, the narrative points to white greed and violence as the cause for the decimation of a Native American village. However, *Custer's Last Fight* (1912, Ince) and *Blazing the Trail* (1912, Ince) blamed Native American duplicity for their own downfall.

Mixed-race relations were depicted as inevitable tragedies of one sort or another, as seen in *His Squaw* (1912, Ince), *The Hour of Reckoning* (1914, Ince), and *The Battle of Elderbush Gulch* (1914, Griffith), among others.

The key Native American–themed film of the decade was *The Squaw Man* (1914, Lasky), which was co-directed by Cecil B. DeMille. It focused on a doomed mixed marriage set in the West. Its commercial and critical success cemented the view that native and white relationships always resulted in tragedies and failure.

Douglas Fairbanks, Sr., starred in the film *The Half-Breed* (1916, Fine Arts), which featured an interracial romance. Later, films like *The Vanishing American* (1925, Paramount), *Braveheart* (1925, Paramount), and many others would repeat the doomed outcome of such unions. One exception to this view was Cecil B. DeMille's *The Women God Forgot* (1917, Paramount). Here the film narrative focused on the relationship between a captain (Wallace Reid) in Hernán Cortés' invading army and the daughter (Geraldine Farrar, the legendary opera star) of the Aztec emperor Moctezuma. Angela Aleiss noted, "The couple's final union, however, carefully eschews any cultural compromise: following Montezuma's [sic] defeat, the two flee the arid desert and retreat to the secluded forest. The movie concludes with an uneasy alliance between its two protagonists ... a symbol of their separate cultural identities."[4]

The period of 1911–1919 marked the height of an era of Native American–themed films and protagonists. Hundreds of films were made with indigenous characters at the center of the narratives, and hundreds of Native American actors were employed. Great effort was put into making the way of life of indigenous peoples authentic and evocative. At this time, filmgoers were genuinely fascinated by the indigenous peoples of North and South America. However, as the United States became a highly industrialized nation and a world power, the indigenous history receded into the past. The Hollywood film industry would never again give Native Americans and their way of life so much importance and screen time.

Representative Films

The Squaw Man (1914, Lasky)

The Squaw Man was a popular film that focused on the relationship between a Euro-American and a Native American woman. It was based on a Broadway play written by Edwin Milton Royle, and the story and screenplay (or scenario) were by Beulah Maria Dix. The film was produced by Cecil B. DeMille and Jesse L. Lasky.

Many years later, in his autobiography, Cecil B. DeMille would remember the film as follows: "It was a good story too, virile and exciting. Its dramatic value had been tested on the stage. Its title was known to that part of the public which followed the theatre."[5]

The narrative focuses on two wealthy Englishmen: James Wynnegate (Dustin Farnum) and Henry (Monroe Salisbury). Both have been made trustees of an orphan fund. However, when Henry loses money on a derby race, he embezzles funds from the trust. Unfortunately, it is James who is blamed by the authorities and is forced to flee to Wyoming. During his flight, he happens to rescue Nat-U-Ritch (Lillian St. Cyr), a daughter of the Utes' chief, from the clutches of outlaw Cash Hawkins (William Elmer). Hawkins vows revenge on James, but when he attempts to carry out his threat, he is killed by Nat-U-Ritch. She rescues James again when he is lost in a snowstorm. They fall in love and have a son.

3. Celluloid Native American Film Images (1880–1919)   21

The Squaw Man (1913, Lasky), starring Lillian St. Cyr and Dustin Farnum. St. Cyr was the first Hollywood Native American film star.

In the meantime, Henry is killed in an accident in the Alps. Before dying, however, he writes a confession of his embezzlement, clearing James of the crime. Henry's widow, Lady Diana (Winfred Kingston, Farnum's real-life wife), who had always been attracted to James, tracks him down in Wyoming to inform him of the good news. The town sheriff subsequently recovers the gun used by Nat-U-Ritch to kill Hawkins inside the couple's house and proceeds to arrest her. James and Nat-U-Ritch send their son with Lady Diana for safety. Afterward, Nat-U-Ritch kills herself, unable to bear losing her husband and son.

The Squaw Man was co-directed by Cecil B. DeMille and Oscar Apfel (1878–1938), an actor, director, and producer. This film marked DeMille's directorial debut. He was a former theater actor and became one of the founding fathers of the Hollywood film industry. DeMille directed some seventy films: fifty-one silent films and nineteen talking films. He directed every type of genre (i.e., epics, westerns, dramas, etc.). However, he is most associated with biblical epics such as *The Ten Commandments* (1923, Lasky); *King of Kings* (1927, Pathé Exchange); *The Sign of the Cross* (1932, Paramount); *Cleopatra* (1934, Paramount); *The Crusades* (1935, Paramount); *Samson and Delilah* (1949, Paramount); and *The Ten Commandments* (1956, Paramount).

DeMille personally chose Lillian St. Cyr to play the female lead of Nat-U-Ritch.[6] In his autobiography, DeMille wrote, "Our stars, Dustin Farnum squiring his new bride

Winifred Kingston ... the Indian girl Red Wing whom I had cast in preference to an experienced actress because I wanted a real Indian to play her part—they were all there, with the rest of the cast, to see themselves in the Lasky Company first feature play."[7] Lillian St. Cyr is now recognized as the first Native American film star in the Hollywood industry.

During this time, anti-miscegenation laws existed throughout the United States (including California). They primarily targeted marriages between whites and blacks. Nevertheless, marriages between Native Americans and whites (although legal in California) continued to arouse widespread scorn. It was not until 1948 that the California Supreme Court, in *Perez v. Sharp*, determined that the California anti-miscegenation statute violated the Fourteenth Amendment.[8] As a result, California became the first state since Ohio in 1887 to rule anti-miscegenation laws unconstitutional.

DeMille professed to have been supportive of authentic native portrayals when making the first version of *The Squaw Man* in 1914. However, his sound westerns—*The Squaw Man* (1931, MGM); *The Plainsmen* (1936, Paramount); *Union Pacific* (1939, Paramount); *North West Mounted Police* (1940, Paramount); and *Unconquered* (1947, Paramount)—are filled with offensive Native American stereotypes.

The Squaw Man was made when the original play was hugely popular. However, today it comes across as stagey and overacted at times. Dustin Farnum was a widely popular and rugged leading man during the 1910s and is effective as the male lead. Lillian St. Cyr is a revelation: natural, graceful, self-reliant, and attractive. However, Joseph Singleton plays Nat-U-Ritch's alcoholic father in a typical stereotypical performance.

The Squaw Man was financially successful and motivated DeMille to create two remakes: another silent version in 1918 (now a lost film), and a talking version in 1931. The second remake, however, is not even mentioned in DeMille's autobiography. The original 1914 version of *The Squaw Man* was thought to have been the first film shot in Hollywood, California, until the rediscovery of D. W. Griffith's *In Old California* (1910).

The Half-Breed (1916, Fine Arts)

The Half-Breed is a film that depicts an interracial relationship between a destitute Native American and a white woman. It was directed by the veteran Allan Dwan (1885–1981), who is thought to have directed some 1,400 films (including one reelers) from 1909 to 1961, working in all film genres.

The Half-Breed was based on a short story by Bret Hart titled "In the Carquinez Woods." The screenplay was written by the legendary Anita Loos (1888–1981), who authored the book *Gentlemen Prefer Blondes*. She was a trailblazer for women screenwriters in the Hollywood film industry and is credited with 139 film credits between 1912 and 2008 (some posthumously).

However, the main creative impetus for *The Half-Breed* was the pioneer filmmaker and superstar, Douglas Fairbanks, Sr. (1893–1939). His paternal grandparents were German Jewish immigrants. Fairbanks arrived in Hollywood film industry in 1915 and rose quickly to stardom with his awe-inspiring athletic ability. During the first part of his career, he starred in action-packed social comedies and later his legendary swashbuckling films. He co-founded United Artists in 1919, along with Charlie Chaplin, D.W. Griffith and his then-wife Mary Pickford.

The Half-Breed tells the story of a Native American mother who realizes that her white lover has betrayed her, leading her to take her own life. Her son Lo Dorman (played by Fairbanks) becomes an orphan and lives in the trunk of a tree in the forest. Eventually, Lo develops a tenuous romance with a white maiden named Nellie (Jewel Carmen), the preacher's daughter. However, Lo's efforts anger Sheriff Dunn (Sam De Grasse), who has courted the young lady. In the meantime, Teresa (Alma Rubens), a Mexican lady, attacks her double-crossing lover with a knife and then flees into the sanctuary of the forest. She inadvertently ends up living in the same tree that is Lo's home.

Nellie searches for and finds Lo in the forest, hoping to renew her relationship with him. However, the racist climate in the town makes her realize that her relationship with the half-breed Lo is doomed. In the meantime, the sheriff pursues Teresa into the forest and finds evidence that he himself is actually Lo's father. In the end, a horrific forest fire kills several people, and Lo leaves to find a home in a remote forest.

It is interesting to speculate on why Fairbanks made *The Half-Breed*, a film that went against the tide of the kind of films being made about Native Americans and/or Mexicans. The sting of discrimination endured by his German Jewish grandparents must have rooted in him a sense of social consciousness and understanding of the plight of other minorities. In 1915, D. W. Griffith's *The Birth of a Nation* (Griffith Corp.), a controversial film that depicted the Ku Klux Klan as heroes, had caused race riots across several cities. Despite Fairbanks' friendship and partnership with Griffith, he did not share his contemporary's racial politics. The following year, the William S. Hart western *The Aryan* (1916, Triangle) depicted association with people of mixed blood as a sign of the degeneration of the white race. Earlier in the 1910s, a series of Mexican Greaser films had been made, which proposed that Mexicans could never overcome their innate traits of violence and sexual debauchery. However, Fairbanks had, since the beginning of his film stardom, developed a stock company of vaqueros, stuntmen, and doubles, mostly made up of Mexican and Native American men. Among these was Charles Stevens. These experiences certainly broadened Fairbanks' consciousness even more.

Unfortunately, *The Half-Breed* was not a commercial success. Some filmgoers must have seen this as a rebuke to Fairbanks' position on race and ethnicity. However, the bulk of his films display many actors of color playing prominent roles: Lupe Vélez in *The Gaucho* (1927, United Artists) and Anna May Wong and African American actor Noble Johnson in *The Thief of Bagdad* (1924), among others. Fairbanks, to his credit, remained undeterred by the commercial failure of *The Half-Breed*, and his films continued to have a liberal bent.

The Half-Breed also featured uncredited bit parts by the legendary marshal and gunfighter Wyatt Earp and Elmo Lincoln, the first U.S. movie Tarzan.

Native Film Stars

Chief John Big Tree

Chief John Big Tree was a Native American character actor who was featured in some fifty-nine films between 1915 and 1950. He was born Isaac Johnny John on June 2, 1887, in Buffalo, New York, and was a member of the Seneca Nation.

Big Tree made his film debut in 1915 with a bit part in *Author, Author*. He gradually moved up to play supporting roles. He made both B-westerns and big-budget films. His films include *The Spirit of '76* (1917, Continental Prod. Co.); *A Fight for Love* (1919, Universal Manuf. Co.); *The Avenging Arrow* (1921, Pathé Exchange); *The Iron Horse* (1924, Fox Film Corp.); *The Frontier Trail* (1926, Charles R. Rogers Prods.); *Winners of the Wilderness* (1927, MGM); *Sioux Blood* (1929, MGM); *The Big Trail* (1930, Fox Film Corp.); *The Last of the Mohicans* (1932, Mascot Pictures); *The Singing Vagabond* (1935, Republic); *Daniel Boone* (1936, RKO); *Lost Horizon* (1937, Columbia); *Stagecoach* (1939); *Destry Rides Again* (1939); *Drums Along the Mohawk* (1939, 20th Century–Fox); *North West Mounted Police* (1940, Paramount); *Hudson's Bay* (1941, 20th Century–Fox); *Western Union* (1941); *Unconquered* (1947, Paramount); *She Wore a Yellow Ribbon* (1949, Argosy Pictures); and *Devil's Doorway* (1950, MGM), in which he played Chief Thundercloud.

He was one of the three Native American chiefs used as a model by artist James Fraser for the famous profile of the "Indian head nickel" minted from 1913 to 1938. Big Tree appeared in the March 1964 cover of the magazine *Esquire*, which commemorated the Indian head nickel.

He died on July 6, 1967, in the Onondaga Indian Reservation, New York (where he is buried).

Dark Cloud

Dark Cloud was a Native American actor active in silent films. He was born Elijah Tahamont on September 20, 1855, in Odanak, Quebec, Canada. He belonged to the Abenaki, part of the Algonquin First Nations people of the northeastern part of North America. He attended Carlisle Indian Industrial School and later became a chief of the Algonquins.

Dark Cloud became known first as a lecturer on native culture, and later he served as a model for the painter Frederic Remington, who specialized in Native American images.

He entered film in 1910 and worked in the Biograph and American Mutoscope Studios in New York City. He made his film debut in *The Broken Doll* (1910). In 1912, he moved to the West Coast with D.W. Griffith's film company.

Dark Cloud appeared in some thirty-four films (most of them westerns) between 1910 and 1918. He was at times billed as William Dark Cloud or Chief Dark Cloud. His films include *An Indian's Loyalty* (1913, Biograph Corp.); *The Penitentes* (1915, Film Arts Prods.); *The Birth of a Nation* (1915, D. W. Griffith Corp.); *Intolerance: Love's Struggle through the Ages* (1916, Triangle Film Corp.); *The Spirit of '76* (1917, Continental Prod. Co.); *A Fight for Love* (1919, Universal Film Manuf.); *What Am I Bid?* (1919, Universal Film Manuf.); and *The Woman Untamed* (1920, Pyramid Photo Play). In 1917, he also collaborated in a movie with the popular Francis Ford (the older brother of director John Ford) based on *John Ermine of Yellowstone*.

Dark Cloud married Margaret Camp, an actress known as Dove Eye in silent films. Their daughters Bessie and Beulah acted in silent films.

Dark Cloud died on October 17, 1918, in Los Angeles, California, from bronchopneumonia, apparently connected to the Spanish influenza pandemic. Some of his films were released after his passing.

Beulah Dark Cloud

Beulah Dark Cloud was one of the early Native American actresses of silent films. She was born Beulah T. Filson on March 28, 1887, in New York. She was one of the two daughters of Native American actor Dark Cloud.

Beulah began her career in films in 1912 and worked with director D. W. Griffith. She is best known for two films: *Desert Gold* (1919, Zane Grey Pictures) and *The Crimson Challenge* (1922, Lasky).

She died on December 29, 1945, in Thermolite, California.

Lillian St. Cyr (Red Wing)

Lillian St. Cyr was the first Native American to become a Hollywood film star. Although she is forgotten today, she deserves credit for facing overwhelming odds and making her mark in the early silent film industry.

She was born on February 13, 1873, in the Winnebago Reservation, Nebraska. She was educated at the Carlisle Indian Industrial School in Pennsylvania. She later moved to Washington, D.C., and worked as a domestic servant for Senator I. Long (a Republican from Kansas who served from 1903 to 1909).

St. Cyr married Younger Johnson (James Young Deer) on April 9, 1906. Johnson claimed that he was of mixed Delaware (Naticoke tribe), European, and African American ancestry.[9] Later, however, the question of his ethnicity would become the subject of controversy.

St. Cyr and her husband traveled throughout New York and Philadelphia, performing a western act. She made her cinematic debut in 1908 in film short titled *The White Squaw* (Kalem Co.), following it up with *The Falling Arrow* (Lubin Manuf. Co.), another short film released that same year. During 1909, both she and her husband worked as technical advisors (and later extras) for director D. W. Griffith. St. Cyr became well known when she played Princess Red Wing in Vitagraph's *Red Wing's Gratitude* (Vitagraph Co.). During this time, she also made films for the Bison studio.

In 1914, she played the female lead in *The Squaw Man* (Lasky), produced and co-directed by Cecil B. DeMille and Oscar Apfel. It was a historic film for several reasons. First, St. Cyr, an authentic Native American, played the lead of a native woman (under the name of Red Wing). Second, it was DeMille's directorial film debut. Last, but not least, *The Squaw Man* was one of the first feature films shot in Hollywood, California. St. Cyr and Young Deer worked to make the native characters authentic and sympathetic, along with the costumes they wore. *The Squaw Man* proved to be a commercial success, and St. Cyr reached her height of popularity.

In 1914, she starred in the western *In the Days of the Thundering Herd* (Selig Polyscope Co.), with the popular Tom Mix, and then in *Fighting Bob* (1915, Rolfe Photoplays). However, by 1916, her career was in decline. In that year she played the supporting role of the mother of the title character of the film *Ramona* (Cline Producing Co.). Her last film role was in *White Oak* (1921, William S. Hart Prod. Co.). During the period of 1908–1921, St. Cyr made some thirty-five western film shorts. She had a total of 67 film credits. She retired from films in the 1920s and went to live in New York City.

Lillian St. Cyr has been the subject of much interest and research in the past few years. Angela Aleiss, who has completed extensive research on the early Native American presence in silent films, commented, "Lillian's Hollywood career spanned approximately 15 years, but she worked hard to promote Native culture throughout most of her 90-year life. Relatives recall Lillian as short and stout with dark brown-black hair and a real warmth around her."[10]

St. Cyr died at the age of 101 in New York City on March 13, 1974. She was buried in the Roman Catholic St. Augustine Cemetery, in Thurston County, Nebraska, not too far from the Winnebago Indian Reservation.

NON-NATIVE ACTORS MASQUERADING AS NATIVE AMERICANS

Over the course of more than a century of U.S. cinema, numerous non–Native American performers have portrayed native roles in films. For most of these decades, the nation's deep-rooted racism and prejudice prevented native actors from playing their own people.

In the Golden Age of the Hollywood film industry (1920–1950), major white film stars and supporting players were regularly assigned to native roles by the studios as part of the tradition of film casting. However, there were also non-native actors who knowingly appropriated a native identity, which was not their own, for their entire career. Even today, non-native actors often say that they "have some Native American roots somewhere!" For some, being native is like a hobby or an exotic habit, but they don't have to experience the lifelong, marginalized existence and prejudice that comes with a true native identity.

For better or worse, the following performers appropriated a Native American identity in both film and their personal lives.

Iron Eyes Cody

Perhaps the best-known character actor to play Native American film roles from the 1930s to the 1970s was Iron Eyes Cody, who was not of native ancestry. He was born Espera Oscar de Corti on April 3, 1904, in Kaplan Vermillion Parish, Louisiana. Espera was the second son of Antonio de Corti and his wife, Francesca Salpietra, both Italian immigrants from the island of Sicily. The father left his family and moved to Texas, where he anglicized his name to Tony Corti. His wife subsequently married Alton Abshire and had a family of five with her second husband.

The three original sons (including Espera) left for Texas when they were adolescents, taking up the surname of Corti. The brothers subsequently moved to Hollywood, where they began working in the growing film industry. It was at this time that they changed their surname to Cody. Two brothers, Henry Cody and Joseph W. Cody, moved on to other employment, but Espera continued working in films.

Espera Cody would play Native American roles in more than one hundred film and television roles throughout his career. He made his film debut in 1926's *The Scarlet Letter* (MGM). His work included both big-budget and low-budget features: *Fighting Caravans* (1930, Paramount); *Massacre* (1934, Warner Bros.); *Union Pacific* (1939, Paramount); *Kit Carson* (1940, United Artists); *My Gal Sal* (1942, 20th Century–Fox); *The Paleface* (1949, Paramount); *Broken Arrow* (1950, 20th Century–Fox); *Ace in the Hole* (1951, Paramount);

The Big Sky (1952, RKO); *Sitting Bull* (1954, Tele-Voz S.A.); *Alias Jesse James* (1959, United Artists); *Nevada Smith* (1966, Paramount); *A Man Called Horse* (1970, Cinema Center Films); *Grayeagle* (1977); and *The Spirit of '76* (1990, Black Diamond Prods.). He also played Native American roles in scores of popular television shows: *The A-Team, Fantasy Island, Bonanza, Maverick, Here's Lucy, Gunsmoke, Wagon Train, Daniel Boone, Rawhide, Cheyenne, Sugar Foot*, and *The Legend of Wyatt Earp*, among many others.

Cody earned national fame in 1970 as the "crying chief" in the "Keep America Beautiful" public service announcement. Throughout his career, he insisted that he was Native American (claiming to have Cherokee-Cree roots) and kept changing the place of his birth.

Cody married Bertha Parker, who actually had Native American ancestry. They adopted two children who were of Dakota-Maricopa ancestry. After his wife died in 1978, Cody married Wendy Foote, but they divorced the following year. In 1996, his half-sister revealed that Cody had Italian ancestry, not Native American roots.

Cody earned several honors for his film career. He was honored by Native Americans in the film industry for his contributions, although they pointedly indicated his non–Native American ancestry. In 1999, he was honored with a Golden Palm Star on the Walk of Stars in Palm Spring, California.

Cody died on January 4, 1999, in Los Angeles, California, at the age of ninety-four.

Mona Darkfeather

One of the popular leading ladies of the 1910s was an attractive actress known as Mona Darkfeather. There is contradictory evidence regarding whether she was truly Native American.

She was born Josephine M. Workman on January 13, 1883, in Los Angeles (in the Boyle Heights area, which is also known as East Los Angeles). Her parents were Joseph Manuel Workman and Josephine Mary Belt. Her father is said to have been English but with Pueblo Native American ancestry (from the Taos, New Mexico, area). Her mother was Chilean and Scottish.

Beginning in 1909, Josephine became famous as Princess Mona Darkfeather for Bison Motion Pictures. However, she told newspapers of the time that she was not of native ancestry. Nevertheless, the movie studio continued promote her as a member of the Blackfoot Nation. She made her film debut in *A Cheyenne's Love for a Sioux* (Bison).

She became a very popular actress with such films as *A Blackfoot's Conspiracy* (1912, Bison); *The Massacre of the Fourth Cavalry* (1912, Bison); *A Red Man's Love* (1912, Bison); *A White Indian* (1912, Bison); *Justice of the Wild* (1913, Nestor Film Corp.); and *The Hidden Danger* (1917, Universal Film Corp.), her last film. All of her 107 features were short films.

Darkfeather married Frank Montgomery, a prolific director of the era, who directed some of her most successful films. After her divorce from Montgomery, she went on to marry two more times. She died on September 3, 1977, in Los Angeles, from a stroke at the age of ninety-four.

Buffalo Child Long Lance

Buffalo Child Long Lance enjoyed unprecedented fame and renown in the early 1910s. He cultivated an identity as a Plains indigenous person and was a favorite of white artistic circles, who saw him as an "exotic" addition. People were baffled when he committed suicide on March 30, 1932, in Los Angeles, California.

The secret he bore lay in the fact that he was not Native American. He was born Sylvester Clark Long in Winston-Salem, North Carolina. His father Joe Long was a former slave. His wife Sallie Long was seven-eighths Caucasian and one-eighth Croatan Native American. The Long family was classified by the authorities as "colored."

At the age of 13, Long joined a Wild West show, fabricating a story that his mother was half Croatan and his father was half Cherokee. The masquerade allowed him to pass as an "Indian." It also facilitated his entry into the famous Carlisle Indian Industrial School in Pennsylvania. He then proceeded to change his name to Sylvester Long. His academic success eventually resulted in his being admitted to St. John's Military School in Manlius, New York.

With the advent of World War I, Long enlisted in the Canadian army and was wounded in 1917. Upon being discharged, he settled in Calgary, Alberta, and became a reporter for the *Calgary Herald* for three years. By this time, he claimed to be a Cherokee from Oklahoma. He wrote numerous articles about the native people of western Canada in Canadian newspapers and, later, in U.S. magazines like *Good Housekeeping* and *Cosmopolitan*. In 1922, he was formally adopted by the Blood Indian tribe, members of the Blackfoot Confederacy of southern Alberta. After this, he also presented himself as Blackfoot and became known as "Buffalo Child," the honorary name he had been given by the Canadian tribe.

Banking on his newfound fame, Long moved to New York in 1927. He went on to publish his autobiography, titled *Long Lance*, which soon became a huge success. In the book he fabricated his "Blackfoot boyhood." In 1930, he was cast in the role of an Ojibwa brave named Baluk who leads a starving tribe out of their fatal predicament in the landmark Native American film *The Silent Enemy* (Paramount). The film was hailed as a masterpiece by many, and Long earned wide acclaim for his performance. However, it was during the making of this film that studio employees became suspicious of his true ethnic identity, and soon the truth came to be known. Long was subsequently dropped by high society and shunned by most of his celebrity friends, as well as others. His invented life was about to completely unravel.

More than twenty-two years after having disappearance from his family, Long one day, by chance, ran into his brother Walter. He was informed that his father was deathly ill and that he needed money for his medical needs. Long sent money home but soon became the victim of his own fateful creation. He would not (or could not) return home, or the charade would be exposed.

His inability to resolve his predicament apparently led to his suicide. Some have called Long a victim of Jim Crow and the vicious racism of the time, which compelled him to masquerade as a member of another ethnic community. Others, however, see him as the tragic captain of his own fate.

James Young Deer

For most of the 20th century, film historians claimed that James Young Deer was the first Native American filmmaker and producer in the Hollywood film industry. However, recent research has revealed that he was not in fact Native American. For years, film historians and native tribes have tried to unravel Johnson's murky past and origins.

After intense research, film historian Angela Aleiss wrote, "In the 1900 census, Young Deer is clearly black.... Century-old military personnel file buried within the National Personnel Center describe Young Deer as mulatto with brown hair and brown eyes. He had a short 5-foot 3¼ inch frame at 114 pounds with defective lower teeth and a scar on his right wrist and right neck."[11]

His real name was James Young Johnson, and he was born around April 1, 1878, in Washington, D.C., to mulatto parents Emma Margaret Young and George Durhan Johnson. Despite these origins, he always claimed that he was Winnebago.

Johnson enlisted in the U.S. Navy in 1898 during the Spanish-American War. He was consigned to manual duties, and, at 5-foot 3¼ inches, he was accused of being insolent whenever he spoke out against his mistreatment. He left the navy in 1901, apparently determined to craft a new identity.

He changed his name to Young Deer and invented a history as a "Plains Indian." In 1906, he married Lillian St. Cyr (Winnebago), the first genuine Native American film star in the Hollywood film industry. In 1909, D.W. Griffith hired the couple as technical advisors for the New York Motion Picture "Indian films."

Lillian St. Cyr and Young Deer performed in western shows such as the "Pioneer Days: A Spectacle Drama of Western Life," which reenacted battles between natives and white soldiers at New York's Hippodrome Theatre. Soon the media and motion picture studios became enamored of the famous couple as "perfect types of their race." Shortly thereafter, the two were appearing in films as Young Deer and Red Wing (St. Cyr). Young Deer made his debut as an actor in *The Falling Arrow* (Lubin) in 1909, in which Red Wing starred.

In 1910, the French film studio Pathé Frères opened a movie facility in New Jersey. French director Louis J. Gasnier discovered Young Deer's skills for daredevil stunts and cast both him and his wife in in such films as *The Indian and the Maid* (1910, Pathé Frères) and *The Red Girl and the Child* (1910, Pathé Frères). Both husband and wife strove for authenticity in their films, casting authentic native performers and genuine settings in the Southwest. Soon Young Deer became both a screenwriter and a director.

However, in May 1913, allegations of Young Deer's involvement in a white slave ring became public. Later, a 15-year-old girl accused him of statutory rape. He jumped bail and headed to New York. He then sought refuge in England, where he found employment as a film director and writer. There he made several successful films, such as *The Black Cross Gang* (1914, British & Colonial), *The Water Rats of London* (1914, British & Colonial), and *The World at War* (1914, Monograph). The last film he directed and wrote was *Lieutenant Daring RN and the Water Rats* in 1924 (MacDowell Co.). His last acting credit was in *Man of Courage*, a U.S. film, in 1922.

Upon returning to Los Angeles, he discovered that the accusing females had vanished, but the motion picture industry had also changed. Feature films of five reels became the norm, instead of the short films that Young Deer produced. Soon thereafter, his marriage to Lillian St. Cyr unraveled. Young Deer and St. Cyr separated in 1915 after growing friction and apparently never reconciled.

For the rest of his life, Young Deer became a roaming jack of all trades, working as a boxing promoter, comedy writer for Mack Sennett, and acting teacher, among others. He married his second wife Helen Gilchrist (a Scottish immigrant who was some twenty years younger than he) in 1930. She died of breast cancer in 1937 at the age of thirty. Later, it would be discovered that while Young Deer and Lillian St. Cyr had separated in 1915, they were never officially divorced.

Aleiss quoted Louis Mofsie, the great nephew of Lillian St. Cyr, as saying, "Lillian had really nothing good to say about him.... I had a sense that he got into Hollywood and found being American Indian profitable. He wasn't a very good person. She was glad to be rid of him, to say the least."[12]

Young Deer's last years were ones of vanished fame and fortune. Toward the end of his life, he shared an apartment with his widowed sister Minnie in New York City. His former wife Lillian St. Cyr lived in the nearby area.

He died of stomach cancer on April 6, 1946, and was buried in the Long Island National Cemetery under the name James Young Johnson, a veteran of the Spanish-American War. There is no mention on his grave of his past achievements in the film industry.

Despite his mishaps, Young Deer was a pioneer and a talented filmmaker. He made 33 film shorts as an actor and had 10 writing credits and 34 credits as a director. Many years after his passing, he was finally recognized for his considerable achievements. In 2008, the Library of Congress brought to its National Film Registry one of his last surviving films: *White Fawn's Devotion* (1910).

4

The Noble Savage and the White Man's Enemy (1920–1929)

During the 1920s, the preeminent film image of Native Americans was that of the "noble savage" and the white man's enemy. Of course, films and film images are created by the times in which they took place.

The 1920s was affectionately dubbed "the Roaring Twenties." It was a time of unprecedented material prosperity and energy in the United States. It appeared that the nation was vigorous and dynamic in every conceivable endeavor and task, including the innovative assembly-line Model T; the prolific literature of the "lost generation" of Hemingway, Fitzgerald, and others; the galvanized passions and emotions elicited by the trial of Sacco and Vanzetti and the "Red Scare"; the dubious and colorful escapades of bootleggers and gangsters of the Prohibition; the dawning of professional sports, as epitomized by Jack Dempsey and Babe Ruth; and last, but not least, the beginning of Hollywood's Golden Age (1920–1950). The decade even ended with a bang. It came with Black Tuesday on October 29, 1929, the day of the infamous stock market crash and the beginning of the Great Depression.

Across the ocean, while the nation was preoccupied with prosperity, two obscure ex-socialists in Germany and Italy planned fascist movements and Japanese militarists dreamed of a great empire. In the Americas, the U.S. Marines had been withdrawn (during August 1924) from Nicaragua, but they returned one year later, when they were confronted by a nationalist leader, César Augusto Sandino, fighting against foreign occupation. However, Secretary of State Frank B. Kellog perceived the conflict in apocalyptic proportions and warned of a menacing Mexican-Soviet-Nicaraguan conspiracy to violently establish a "Mexican-fostered Bolshevist hegemony" that threatened the Panama Canal.[1]

The U.S. film industry had originally begun in the East Coast (New York and New Jersey) but was transplanted (bit by bit) to the obscure town called Hollywood, California, early in the century. The main reasons for the change were the local Californian weather (perpetual sunshine most of the year) and a diverse geography of deserts, mountains, forests, and beaches—perfect for filming. The Hollywood-based film industry flourished after 1910, and by the 1920s motion pictures had become the fifth largest industry in the nation.

The two foundations of the film industry were the studios and the star system. The autocratic movie moguls of the new art form were alternatively paternal and dictatorial, seeking to retain control of the film stars who were created and maintained by the studios in order to attract filmgoers to the box office. All major studio stars were under some type of long-term contract that even included "morality clauses." In truth, however, it was the stars that made a studio. They gave birth to the era and, in the end, contributed to the demise of the studio system (though this system would define the Golden Age of Hollywood films from 1920 to 1950).

By 1910, the star system had begun to alter the budgeting and marketing of movies. *Variety* (November 21, 1913) noted, "The stars are scrapping for the spotlight."[2] The spotlight augmented the recognition of a film's performers and dictated lucrative salaries (and, at times, an inordinate share of a motion picture's gross profits). Fan magazines, autographed photos, fan mail and fan clubs flourished. The "film star" phenomenon had arrived. Ken Wlaschin noted, "The stars of the silent cinema were popular and influential to a degree that is almost impossible to imagine today. In the days before rock and pop stars and TV and radio celebrities, all the dreams and fantasies projections of the mass public were focused on the movie star."[3]

From the very beginning, motion pictures were a collaborative art form, involving thousands of culturally and ethnically diverse contributors from throughout the world. The film stars themselves represented a wide range of ethnic diversity. The big stars of the 1920s included Charlie Chaplin (British), Pola Negri (Polish), Rudolph Valentino (Italian), and Sessue Hayakawa (Japanese), among others. They also included the first group of Mexican film stars: Ramón Novarro (José Gil Samaniegos), Dolores Del Río (Dolores Asunsolo y López y Negrete, Novarro's cousin), Gilbert Roland (Luis Antonio Damaso de Alonso), Lupe Vélez (María Guadalupe Vélez de Villalobos), and Lupita Tovar. In addition, Novarro, Del Río, Vélez, and Tovar all had Mexican Native American ancestry.

The only bona fide Native American film star in the 1920s who was born in the United States was Monte Blue, who specialized in romantic leading roles in both dramas and adventure tales. Other native performers included Charles Stevens, who claimed to be the grandson of the legendary Apache warrior Geronimo, and scores of bit players. Among the bit players who rose to long-term prominence was Iron Eyes Cody, who passed himself off as Native American but was in fact of Italian origin (as detailed in the previous chapter).

The most prominent director of mixed native roots was Edwin Carewe. He is credited with discovering Dolores Del Río and guiding her through some of her biggest film successes in the 1920s.

However, at the core of the new art form was the ethos of the nation's history. The United States was portrayed as exceptional, democratic, benign, compassionate, and inclusive. Motion pictures of the time pretended that the hard truths of the nation's history had never happened: Native American genocide, Manifest Destiny, racism, imperialism, the forced removal of native peoples, reservations, native boarding schools, slavery, segregation, and prejudice. As a consequence, Native Americans, Mexicans, African Americans, and Asians, as well as women, were consigned to portrayals based on the prevailing prejudices and attitudes of the dominant Euro-American perspectives.

The predominant image of Native Americans in the films of the 1920s was that of marauding savages who obstructed the U.S. Manifest Destiny in its westward march. This image was emphasized in two of the most important films of the decade, both of which were epic westerns: *The Covered Wagon* (1923) and John Ford's *The Iron Horse* (1924, Fox Corporation). Nevertheless, in this decade of widespread economic and material prosperity, there were films with a progressive bent. These included a group of films that documented the historic injustice perpetuated against Native Americans: *The Vanishing American* (1925, Paramount Pictures), *Ramona* (1928, United Artists), and *Redskin* (1928, Paramount Pictures).

The 1930 U.S. Census listed 332,000 persons of Native American ancestry; in 1940, it had 334,000 counted as Native Americans. Both censuses included those living in the reservations and off the reservations, and living in the forty-eight states. According to the Bureau of the U.S. Census, the federal government spent some $38 million a year on the Native American community in the latter part of the 1920s. During 1933, it indicated that federal spending fell to $23 million, but by 1940 it had risen back to $38 million.

Representative Films

The 1920s produced thousands of films. The following is a summary of the representative overview of Native American–themed films and/or those films that featured indigenous characters.

Robert J. Flaherty's groundbreaking *Nanook of the North* (1922, Pathé Exchange) provided a cultural window into the world of the Inuit in a semi-documentary style. *North of 36* (1924, Paramount) was an epic western about a 600-cattle drive across some 1,000 miles through Indian Territory (north of the 36th parallel) to Abilene, Kansas. The film featured dozens of attacks by one-dimensional Native American warriors.

D. W. Griffith's grand-scale *America* (1924, Griffith) was, according to the film's opening titles, "The story of sacrifice made for freedom in the American Revolution, in the Civil War between two groups of English people: one group, the Americans [Euro-Americans], being merely Englishmen on the American continent." This film depicted most the important events of the U.S. War of Independence interspersed with a love story. Lionel Barrymore played the villainous real-life character of Captain Walter Butler (an Indian agent of King George III), who conspired with the Iroquois Confederacy to prevent the independence of the new nation. On November 1778, Butler led British Loyalists and the Iroquois in the Cherry Valley Massacre, which killed an estimated 32 Euro-American settlers. As in other movies, the indigenous characters were portrayed as one-dimensional savages. The film *America* was a commercial failure and ended Griffith's tenure as the preeminent filmmaker in the nation.

John Ford's *The Iron Horse* (1924, Fox Film Corp.) celebrated the building of the transcontinental railroad and the spread of Euro-American civilization.

The Scarlet West (1925, 1st National Pictures) was an independent film produced by Frank J. Carroll and headlined by the popular Clara Bow. It was shot on location in Dolores, Colorado. This film was unusual in that it focused on the Battle of the Little Big Horn with a unique plot twist. The film's narrative told the story of Cardelanche (Robert Frazer), an educated Lakota and son of a chief, who is turned away by his tribe. He joins the U.S. Cavalry and rises in rank after he rescues a detachment attacked by native warriors. He also falls in love with Miriam (Clara Bow), the daughter of the Euro-American fort commandant. However, a jealous Lt. Parkman becomes involved in a fight with Cardelanche after he learns of Custer's defeat by the Lakota. As a result, Cardelanche undergoes a profound reevaluation of his life. He leaves Miriam and returns to his own people. *The Scarlet West* is now considered a lost film.

General Custer at the Little Big Horn (1926, Sunset Productions) depicted the well-known battle between Custer's 7th Cavalry and the Lakota. This film portrayed Custer in traditional heroic mode, at the expense of the indigenous people. The three leading Native American roles were played by several native actors who had short careers in cinema: Running Deer (Sitting Bull), Felix Whitefeather (Chief Gall), Young Eagle (Chief Little Bear), and Black Hawk (Little Bear). One sole print of this film is being preserved at the Library of Congress.

However, there were films that diverged from the traditional narrative of indigenous people as an impediment to white progress. *Braveheart* (1925, Prod. Dist. Corp.) depicted the efforts of a college-educated indigenous lawyer who fights for the land rights of his people. *The Vanishing American* (1925, Paramount) also focused on a college-educated native youth who returns to the reservation and encounters a culture shock regarding the traditional way of life. *The Devil Horse* (1926, Hal Roach) was directed by Fred Jackman. The film features a boy named Dave (initially played by Fred Jackman, Jr., the director's son), who survives the death of his parents in a wagon train attack by Native Americans. He is captured by the natives and befriends a young colt. Many years later, Dave (played as an adult by Yakima Canutt, the legendary stuntman and actor) is a soldier in the U.S. Cavalry and is recaptured by indigenous people. He is then asked to help them tame the devil horse—the colt he previously befriended.

Sitting Bull at the Spirit Lake Massacre (1927, Sunset Productions) was actually made in 1925, though it was not released until July 15, 1927. The film was thought lost for many decades but has recently been rediscovered. Native actor Chief Yowlachie played the role of Sitting Bull. The narrative revolved around the 1857 Spirit Lake Massacre in Iowa.[4] The film also featured a young Bob Steele (real name Bob Bradbury, Jr.), the legendary B-western film star.

In turn, *Ramona* (1928, United Artists) depicted the destructive impact of Manifest Destiny and the California Gold Rush upon indigenous people. *Redskin* (1929, Paramount) was the story of a college-educated Navajo and his difficult reintegration into his tribe.

Braveheart (1925, Producers Dist. Corp.)

The 1925 film *Braveheart* focuses on the proactiveness of Native Americans in the Northwest with regard to their fishing rights, environment, and way of life. It is a progressive film in both intent and content.

This film was one of only a few directed by the iconic character actor Alan Hale, Sr. (1892–1950), a strapping Irish American who became more famous as Errol Flynn's sidekick in thirteen of his films in the 1930s and 1940s. It was produced by Cecil B. DeMille and written by Mary O'Hara (adapted from a play by William C. DeMille, the older brother of Cecil).

Native American actor Nipo T. Strongheart was asked to rewrite the screenplay. He included the Yakima Nation and their struggle to protect their treaty rights of fishing. He subsequently was cast in the role of the Medicine Man.

The narrative focuses on Braveheart (Rod La Roque), a Native American college football star and law school student in a prestigious university back east. There he once again meets Dorothy Nelson (Lillian Rich), the daughter of the president of a canning company, who is attempting to take over native land. Both young people are smitten with each other. However, Braveheart is accused of throwing an important football game for money by a jealous white player and is ejected from the team. In shame, he returns to the reservation, where he becomes an outcast.

Despite his dejection, Braveheart litigates a legal case, challenging the takeover of native land by a powerful canning company that seeks to strip the tribe of their fishing rights. Chief Standing Rock (Tyrone Power, Sr.), the father of Braveheart, is caught between those Native Americans who want to repay violence with violence, like Ki-Yote (Frank Hagney), and others like Braveheart, who proposes a legal alternative. In the end, Braveheart wins the case and the land is returned to the tribe. He also averts an uprising led by Ki-Yote when he apprehends him and turns him over to the authorities. Braveheart is sought by Dorothy, but he realizes that their love is impossible. He tells her, "I'm am red, and you are white!" He explains to her that he will always love her, but they can never be together.

The lead role of Braveheart was played by the very popular Rod La Roque (1898–1969), an actor of French-Irish ancestry. La Roque came to fame and stardom with lead roles in two Cecil B. DeMille films: *The Ten Commandments* (1923, Paramount) and *The Golden Bed* (1925, Paramount). The female lead in *Braveheart* was played by British actress Lillian Rich as Dorothy Nelson. Her most famous role had been the scheming vamp in DeMille's *Golden Bed*. Tyrone Power, Sr. (1869–1931), the famous Irish American theater and film actor, played Standing Rock. Power was also the father of the famous matinee idol Tyrone Power (1914–1958).

The film made a sincere effort to depict the plight of and prejudice against Native Americans. *Braveheart* was one of a few native-themed films that had a contemporary setting. Rod La Roque offered a convincing portrayal of the character Braveheart, and his athleticism added to the realism of the football scenes. Actor and medicine man (in real life) Nipo T. Strongheart, as a native, consulted contributed to the authenticity of native life and culture in the depiction of the Yakima Nation. Hundreds of Yakima were employed to play extras and bit roles. The striking cinematography by Faxon M. Dean highlights the beauty of the unspoiled land held by the Yakima.

Native American actors in the film included Jean Acker (who was one-quarter Cherokee) in the role of Sky-Arrow and Nipo T. Strongheart as the Medicine Man.

The Vanishing American (1925, Paramount Pictures)

The film *The Vanishing American*, based on a novel by the popular Zane Grey (whose books were the subject of many Hollywood films), begins with a Darwinist prologue depicting the history of human life in the Southwest through different evolutionary stages: cave dwellers, slab house people, cliff dwellers, and pueblo societies. The arrival of the Spanish in the 1500s from the south and other Europeans (i.e., Kit Carson) from the east is also depicted.

The narrative revolves around Nophaie (Richard Dix), a Navajo who was kidnapped by well-meaning white women from the reservation as a boy and sent to a special Indian school. There, he became acculturated and Christianized. He earns a college degree and fame as a great athlete. He then returns to the reservation and becomes a tribal leader but, due to his upbringing, is unable to articulate his tribal concerns.

Nophaie falls in love with a white schoolteacher named Marian (Lois Wilson), further confusing his allegiance to his people. The reservation is riddled with corruption under the auspices of Booker (Noah Beery), the assistant to the official Indian agent,

Halliday (Charles Crockett), an ineffectual bureaucrat. After Nophaie defends Marian against sexual assault by Booker, he is forced to flee into the desert. He is followed by Marian, who informs him about the outbreak of World War I. Nophaie and other Indian youth join the army, thinking, "Maybe if we fight and die for our country, things will be better for our people."

After the war has ended, Nophaie returns a hero, only to find that Booker has become the new Indian agent (Halliday has been transferred to service in Washington, D.C.). The Pueblo war veterans likewise discover that their best land has been taken away by unscrupulous white farmers, with the elders living in squalor and misery, bereft of hope. The veterans organize a revolt against the reservation authorities and besiege them in an old building. Nophaie tries to convince the rebels to lay down their arms and resolve the injustice in a peaceful manner. However, the Pueblo men have had enough and ignore him.

At this point in the original novel, Nophaie dies of a flu. Hollywood, however, has Nophaie dying in the arms of Marian, killed by Booker's new weapon—a war-surplus machine gun—as he tries to reconcile the opposing groups. During the course of the movie, Nophaie has abandoned his native traditions and religion and become a Christian. Ironically, he is shot in the chest through the little Bible that Marian had given him. As he dies, he tells her that he now understands that "one who finds life will lose it and one who loses it will find everlasting life."

After portraying hundreds of Native American stereotypes (especially in numerous B-westerns), the Hollywood film industry at last made a dramatic shift with a sympathetic depiction of native peoples in *The Vanishing American*. However, although the film is well meaning (and has earned recognition over the decades for its positive aspects), it is filled with historical inaccuracies and paternalism.

The film promotes the idea of the noble but doomed native and arouses sentimental sympathy. It frees the audience from a direct sense of responsibility, as the demise of the native culture is said to be a consequence of Darwinist evolution. In the melodramatic style of many silent films, the evil committed by the villain Booker is punished, and good is rewarded by the seeming sense of peace between whites and natives. In the end, the film perpetuates the myth that the injustice against Native Americans is attributed to individuals, not to the institutional policies of plunder and genocide.

In addition, *The Vanishing American* depicts the Anasazi, the extraordinary ancestors of the native peoples of Arizona, New Mexico, and northern Mexico, in a stereotypical fashion as indolent and lazy. Numerous scenes depict them as slovenly and sleeping throughout the day. Nothing could be further from the historical truth. Roxanne Dunbar-Ortiz has noted that "the Anasazi constructed more than four hundred miles of roads radiating out of Chaco ... connected some seventy-five communities. Around the thirteenth century, the Anasazi people abandoned the Chaco area and migrated, building nearly a hundred smaller agricultural city-states along the northern Rio Grande valley and its tributaries."[5]

The Spanish conquistador Francisco Vásquez de Coronado (1510–1554), who led an expedition into the Southwest during 1540–1542, is portrayed within the film as a benevolent and fearless military leader, accompanied by relatively few men. In reality, Coronado had thousands of men, heavily armored and armed with guns, attack dogs, and hundreds of Mexican Native American servants. He brought disease, brutality, and destruction to the Pueblo and other natives. He also never traveled to the Grand Canyon, as depicted in the film, or that far north in the area.

In one scene in the film, one Pueblo leader says of the Spaniards, "They are gods!" He then states that the Pueblo cannot defeat them, at which point he and hundreds of warriors prostrate themselves before the Spaniards. This is patently a distortion of history, as the Pueblo people and all other Native Americans continuously fought against Spanish control. In 1680, the Pueblo Revolt of 1680 was a testament to their profound desire to be free. For example, David Roberts wrote, "The Pueblo Revolt had cost its perpetrators many lives. But it had succeeded as no other rebellion by natives in North America against a European oppressor ever had, or ever would in the centuries to come."[6] In 1847, there was another Pueblo revolt against the U.S. takeover, led by both Pueblo natives and Mexicans. Many of the rebels were subsequently executed.

Another gross distortion depicted in the film is the glorification of Christopher Houston "Kit" Carson (1809–1868), the Indian fighter and "scalper." He is portrayed in *The Vanishing American* as the "friend of the Navajo." In reality, he led a genocidal war against the Navajo during 1863–1864, murdering women and children indiscriminately; burning homes, crops and animals; and devastating the land so that it could never be productive again. Carson led similar wars of extermination against other native tribes.

Film reviewers of the time were less sentimental about *The Vanishing American*. *Variety* (October 2, 1925) wrote, "The story itself calls attention to the vanishing of the real America, the Indian, off the face of the North American continent."[7]

The film met with significant critical and commercial success. Its success was aided by the rising popularity of the square-jawed, muscular film star Richard Dix (1894–1949), who would enjoy continued stardom until his death, usually playing noble but doomed heroes. Dix would go on to play another Navajo role in *Redskin* (1929, Paramount). Charles Stevens (who was purported to be Geronimo's grandson) also had a substantial role as Shoie, a Navajo who leaves with Nophaie to fight in World War I and returns to lead the uprising against Booker.

The film's director, George B. Seitz (1888–1944), would go on to direct several native-themed features: *The Last of the Mohicans* (1936, United Artists), *Kit Carson* (1940, Edward Small Prods.), and *Pierre of the Plains* (1944, MGM). The film's striking cinematography was undertaken by Harry Perry and Charles Edgar Schoenbaum. It was shot on the Navajo Reservation in the Four Corners region near Monument Valley, the Grand Canyon, and several Anasazi cliff dwellings.

The Iron Horse (1924, Fox Film Corp.)

One of the most important native-themed films of the decade was *The Iron Horse*. This film was directed by the Irish American John Ford, who would become the filmmaker most closely associated with the western genre. *The Iron Horse* was an unofficial sequel to the 1923 western epic *The Covered Wagon*.

The Iron Horse has a threadbare narrative, though there is a love story between Davy Brandon (George O'Brien) and Miriam Marsh (Madge Bellamy). Brandon is a surveyor who aspires to build a railroad to the west, and Miriam is contractor who is not totally convinced that it is feasible. Both set out to survey the route. Along the way, they are obstructed in their engineering endeavors by Native American war parties that attack them. The backdrop of the narrative is the building of the first transcontinental railroad. The climax of the film is the driving of the gold spike at Promontory Summit, which took place on May 10, 1869.

The brilliant cinematography was done by George Schneiderman. The screenplay was drafted by a trio of writers: Charles Darnton, John Russell, and Charles Kenyon. The film was some 150 minutes long—a rare length for a silent film. The budget is said to have been $280,000 (a huge amount at that time). The film was shot in the iconic area of Monument Valley, which Ford would use for the rest of his westerns. Ken Nolley has noted, "Not only was John Ford canonized by the first wave of auterist critics, but his stubborn attachments to the central myths of Westerns culture in general and American culture specifically also made his work seem for decades to be commercial Hollywood's principal representation of the American experience."[8]

The Iron Horse celebrated Manifest Destiny and the westward expansion of the United States. Native Americans are portrayed as the main impediment to civilization and progress. It is populated by the familiar array of western characters, some historical and others fictional. For example, there is Colonel William "Buffalo Bill" Cody (George Waggnor), President Lincoln (Charles Edward Bull), and a Cheyenne chief (Chief John Big Tree). There is also the standard assortment of heroic military officers, a harried judge, and numerous villains.

The *New York Times* (August 29, 1924) wrote, "This is an instructive an inspiring film, one which should one which should make every American proud of the manner of men who were responsible for great achievement in the face of danger, sickness and fatigue."[9]

In 2011, *The Iron Horse* was included in the National Registry by the Library of Congress. The National Registry stated, "A classic silent film, '*The Iron Horse*' introduced to American and world audiences a reverential elegiac mythology that has influenced subsequent Westerns."[10]

Ramona (1928, United Artists)

One of the most famous Native American stories in both novel and film form was *Ramona*. The author of the original best-selling novel, Helen Hunt Jackson (1830–1885), was an outspoken feminist and activist who campaigned against the genocide of native peoples. She also wrote the popular book *A Century of Dishonor* (1881), which denounced government complicity in the violation of treaties, the corruption of government agents and military leaders, and the ongoing dispossession of native lands. Jackson called for reforms in the treatment of native peoples.

Later, while on a visit to California, Jackson became aware of the plight of mission natives. Under Mexican rule, the missions had been secularized, and native peoples were free to occupy the former mission lands. However, when the United States had taken over, the new authorities disregarded the former laws. By the time Jackson visited southern California, only around 4,000 native people remained on the former mission lands, having been pushed out by the government and white settlers. In 1884, Jackson published *Ramona*, whose characters were based on real people, trying to survive the onslaught of foreigners. The novel went on to become a huge international success. Ironically, it also had the effect of luring even more residents to the enchanted land of California.

The story is set in California in the 1850s, when the United States appropriated the Southwest at the end of the Mexican-American War (1846–1848). Ramona (Dolores Del Río) is a mestiza (part Native American and Scottish), who is in love with Alessandro (Warner Baxter), a Native American.

The film documents the Ramona's efforts to make a life with Alessandro after she has been promised in marriage to Felipe (Roland Drew), a rich *Californio*. As more Euro-Americans flood into California, their world is turned upside down. Thousands of gold seekers enter previously isolated areas looking for the gold dust. Campaigns of extermination are carried out against Native Americans; native women are raped, bounties are offered as incentives, and there is even legalized slavery of natives due to a shortage of agricultural workers. California had originally been home to some 200,000 Native Americans, the largest number north of Mexico. By the end of the 1800s, the native population had been narrowed down to some 20,000.[11]

Amid all this tumult, Ramona and Alessandro flee to the San Jacinto Mountains, near the town of Hemet. There they can be together—even if only for a short time. Later, Alessandro is killed when he is mistaken for a horse thief.

As detailed in the previous chapter, the first film version of *Ramona* was released in 1910, directed by D.W. Griffith, and the title role was played by Mary Pickford, while Henry Walthall played Alessandro. The third version was made in 1936 by 20th Century–Fox and shot in Technicolor; Euro-American film stars Loretta Young and Don Ameche played Ramona and Alessandro, respectively.

The second and best film version of *Ramona* was directed by Edwin Carewe, a part Chickasaw Native American filmmaker. Most of the roles (except for bit parts) were played by non-native actors. However, the role of Ramona was played by a Mexican actress, Dolores Del Río, who had Native American ancestry.

The film received generally excellent reviews and proved to be a box-office success. It had synchronized music score and sound effects, but no spoken dialogue. The screenplay was written by director Crewe's older brother Finis Fox. The excellent cinematography was done by Robert Kurle. The song "Ramona" was written by L. Wolfe Gilbert and Mabel Wayne (later Dolores Del Río would record the popular song for RCA, to great success).

At the heart of the film is Dolores Del Río's extraordinary performance as Ramona. She evolves movingly from a naïve young girl to a woman passionately in love with Alessandro to a resigned, bittersweet bride living as a fugitive and outcast. Mordaunt Hall wrote in the *New York Times* (May 15, 1928), "This current offering is an extraordinarily beautiful production intelligently directed and, with the exception of a few instances, splendidly acted.... Dolores Del Río is an excellent choice for the part of Ramona.... Miss Del Río's interpretation of Ramona is an achievement. Not once does she overact."[12]

The 1928 version of *Ramona* was for years thought to have been lost. However, a copy of the film was discovered in the Narodni Filmovy Archive in Prague, Poland. The restored version of had a world premiere at the Billy Wilder Theater at the University of California, Los Angeles, on March 29, 2014. There are plans to release the film on DVD in the near future.

Redskin (1929, Paramount Pictures)

The film *Redskin* was released at the end of the silent era with synchronized sound effects, music score, and Technicolor sequences. It was directed by Victor Schertzinger (1888–1941), who was a director, composer, producer, and screenwriter. The film was based on a screenplay by Elizabeth Picket. The striking cinematography was undertaken by Edward T. Estabook, Ray Rennahan, and Harry Hallenberger (uncredited).

The film was shot on location in northern New Mexico, much of it on the Acoma Pueblo (one of the oldest of the pre–Columbian pueblos); Canyon de Chelly, in Arizona; and Gallup and White Sands, in New Mexico. Paramount warned Schertzinger that he was spending too much money on the color process. Improvising under duress, he decided to be creative, using black and white film for the harsh white world and Technicolor sequences for the reservation. Much effort went into authentically portraying life in the reservation and pueblos.

The film depicts the contemporary life of Native Americans, thankfully avoiding the historical distortions and mythology that plagued *The Vanishing American.* The narrative focuses on Wing Foot (played by Richard Dix as an adult), a Navajo who, as a child, is forced to attend a government Indian boarding school. While at the school, he and other native children are beaten for speaking their language and keeping their traditions. Wing Foot is consoled by Corn Blossom (played by Lorraine Rivero as a child) when he is beaten by John Walton (Larry Steers), a Bureau of Indian Affairs official, for not saluting the U.S. flag. Judith Stearns (Jane Novak), one of the schoolteachers who abhors such treatment, breaks off her relationship with Walton as a result of this incident.

Wing Foot becomes acculturated in order to survive in the harsh white society, where people often refer to him as "redskin." Although he becomes an outstanding track and field runner, he encounters harsh racism from other college students. Nevertheless, Wing Foot dreams of becoming a doctor and returning to help his people. His girlfriend Corn Blossom (played as an adult by Gladys Belmont, who later changed her name to Julie Carter) gets a job to be near him when he wins an athletic scholarship.

When Wing Foot returns to his reservation, he suffers rejection by some. He has been conditioned to reject traditional native medicine, which destroys his relationship with his father Notani (George Regas), a chief. Wing Foot is subsequently exiled from the Navajo Reservation and lives in the desert, an outcast from both cultures. Later, he encounters two white men exploring the reservation, where oil has been discovered. Wing Foot confronts them and realizes that one of them is John Walton, who beat him as a child at the Indian school for refusing to salute the U.S. flag. Wing Foot tells him, "You are to blame for what I have become, neither Navajo nor white!" Overcome by guilt, Walton apologizes.

Wing Foot learns that Corn Blossom has been promised to marry another man in the Acoma Pueblo. He climbs the rugged mesa where the ancient pueblo is located but fails to rescue her. Later, Corn Blossom feigns suicide and escapes. In the meantime, Wing Foot's old teacher Judith reunites with John Walton, who expresses remorse for his actions at the school. Wing Foot's father is then killed by Corn Blossom's groom-to-be, and an armed conflict between the Navajo and the Acoma Pueblo appears imminent. However, Wing Foot resolves the conflict by promising to share the earnings of the oil claim he has filed with both the Acoma Pueblo and the Navajo. At the end of the movie, Wing Foot reconciles with the Navajo and agrees to be their medicine man.

The film's title of *Redskin* has long been an offensive word to Native Americans. Nonetheless, little has changed since this film was made about educating the general public about this term or its history. Dunbar-Ortiz noted, "The settler gave a name to the mutilated and bloody corpses they left in the wake of scalp-hunts: redskins."[13]

Reviewers of the film were generally positive. Mordaunt Hall in the *New York Times* (January 29, 1929) wrote:

Once again Richard Dix is to be seen as a man of copper hue. The last time he played an Indian was in "*The Vanishing American.*" This time he appears as a Navajo, a fine athletic and agile person, who becomes smitten with the undeniable charms of a Pueblo maiden name Corn Blossom.... There seems to be an erroneous conception in the sequences where Wing Foot goes to college, for the students there are made to look down on the redskin. This, in itself, is an incredulous notion and in in a measure necessary it is a pivotal point in the story. Certainly no white student would have been seen scornful of Wing Foot, who proved himself to be the fleetest of the fleet at the college.[14]

Redskin proved to be a commercial and critical success. This was due to the excellence of the film and also to the box-office appeal of star Richard Dix, who was nearing the peak of his career and would make an easy transition into talking films. Like the majority of films until recent years, white performers were cast in the roles of Native Americans. In this case, Dix, a Euro-American, was cast as the lead role of Wing Foot, just as he had been in *The Vanishing American*. He was dramatically impressive (although not ethnically convincing). However, the important role of Grandmother Yani was played by Agustina Lopez (1843–1932), a Yaqui. Both Navajo and Pueblo native people played bit parts and extra roles.

The early Technicolor footage of the native way of life—the centuries-old pueblos, customs, language, geography, and authentic native people—gives this film a powerful sense of authenticity.

NATIVE FILM STARS AND FILMMAKERS

Jean Acker

Jean Acker was born Harriet "Hattie" Ackers on October 23, 1893, in Trenton, New Jersey. Her father, Joseph Ackers, was reputed to have been part Cherokee, and her mother was Irish.

Young Jean grew up on a farm and became an expert horse rider. She attended St. Mary's Seminary in Springfield, New Jersey. Thereafter, her family moved to Lewiston, Pennsylvania. She performed in vaudeville and moved to California in 1919. In Hollywood, she became the lover and protégé of the famed Alla Nazimova, a dancer and actress.

She played second leads in the silent era; with the coming of sound films, her film career collapsed. She was reduced to bit roles by the early 1930s. Acker made her film debut in 1913 in *The Man Outside* (IMPC). Other films include *In a Woman's Power* (1913, IMPC); *Brewster's Millions* (1921, Lasky); *Her Own Money* (1922, Lasky); *Braveheart* (1925, CCA); *The Nest* (1927, Excellent Pictures); *San Francisco* (1936, MGM); *My Favorite Wife* (1940, RKO); *Spellbound* (1945, Selznick Int.); *The Perils of Pauline* (1947, Paramount); *The Mating Season* (1951, Paramount); *Something to Live For* (1952, Paramount); and *How to Be Very, Very Popular* (1955, 20th Century–Fox).

Acker married film star Rudolph Valentino in 1919 for a brief time. She was apparently bisexual and became involved in highly publicized affairs with men and women.

She died on August 16, 1978, in Los Angeles, California, at the age of 84.

Monte Blue

One of the most popular film stars of the 1920s and box-office draw was Monte Blue, who was part Native American. He was born Gerard Montgomery Bluefeather on January

11, 1887, in Indianapolis, Indiana. His father was half French and half Osage or Cherokee. Upon the death of his father, his mother had a difficult time rearing her five children. As a result, Monte was sent to the Indiana Soldiers' and Sailors' Children's Home. He later attended Purdue University in West Lafayette, Indiana.

Monte Blue's imposing athletic physique (6 feet and 3 inches) led to several physically grueling jobs: football player, coal miner, lumberjack, cowboy, circus rider, fireman, and day laborer at the film studios of famous director D. W. Griffith. He entered the film industry without any sort of acting experience. He made his debut in Griffith's *Birth of a Nation* in 1915 (Griffith Corp.) as an extra and then got a small part in Griffith's *Intolerance* (1916, Triangle Film Corp.). He graduated to supporting roles in several films directed by Cecil B. DeMille and D. W. Griffith.

Blue's big opportunity came when he got the role of Danton in *Orphans of the Storm* in 1922 (Griffith Prods.). Thereafter, he earned romantic leading man status in dozens of popular films, including *Peacock Alley* (1921); *Loving Lies* (1924); *Hogan's Alley* (1925, Tiffany Prods.); *Across the Pacific* (1926, Warner Bros.); *The Greyhound Limited* (1929, Warner Bros.); *Tiger Rose* (1929, Warner Bros.); *Isle of Escape* (1930, Warner Bros.); and *Those Who Dance* (1930, Warner Bros.). His rugged looks and acting ability earned him leading roles with some of the most glamorous female stars of the time, like Gloria Swanson, Clara Bow, and Norma Shearer.

Blue was able to make a graceful transition into talking films. His biggest success and most memorable role came in MGM's *White Shadows in the South Seas* (1928), also starring Raquel Torres and shot on location in the South Pacific. He played an alcoholic doctor trying to prevent the destruction of the native way of life with the arrival of European missionaries and sailors.

At this point, Blue and his wife Tova Janson (the second of two wives) decided to take a trip around the world. When he returned in 1931, he was shocked to learn that he had lost all of his investments and wealth in the stock market crash of 1929.

Now, looking middle-aged (he was 43 years of age at that time) and heavyset, Blue could no longer get leading man roles. Coming to terms with the loss of his stardom, he returned to film acting, playing supporting roles in B-films and bit parts in A-films. Blue had been a money-making star at First National Pictures, which later became Warner Brothers Studios. The head of the studio, Jack Warner, an old friend, came to his assistance. Warner made sure that Blue would always have employment at Warner Brothers. Another benefactor was director Cecil B. DeMille, for whom Blue had made several successful films.

Blue went to do scores of films, some of them forgettable, but some classic films. His films include *Come On, Marine* (1934, Paramount); *G-Men* (1935, Warner Bros.); *Desert Gold* (1936, Paramount); *Juarez* (1939, Warner Bros.); *Sullivan's Travels* (1941, Paramount), *Across the Pacific* (1942, Warner Bros.);

Monte Blue was a leading man in the 1910s and 1920s and a character actor in the 1930s and 1940s.

Passage to Marseilles (1944); *Key Largo* (1948, Warner Bros.); and *The Iroquois Trail* (1950. Small Prods.), in which he played a Native American. His last film role was that of Geronimo in *Apache* (1954, United Artists). He also ventured into the television medium in the 1950s. In total, Blue had 292 film and television credits over his long career.

Monte Blue was an advance man for the Hamid-Morton Shrine Circus and busy as a Freemason. While making his annual circus appearance in Milwaukee, Wisconsin, he suffered a fatal heart attack on February 18, 1963.

Edwin Carewe

Although forgotten today, Edwin Carewe was an important film director, producer, screenwriter, and actor during the 1920s and 1930s. He was born Jay John Fox on March 22, 1883, in Gainesville, Texas. His father, Frank Fox, was Caucasian, and his mother Sallie (Priddy) Fox was Chickasaw. Carewe and his two brothers, Wallace Carewe and F. Finis, were enrolled under their real names as members of the Chickasaw Nation as $1/16$ Chickasaw.

Carewe studied briefly at the Universities of Texas and Missouri. After leaving his studies, he joined some regional theater groups. In 1910, he moved to New York City, where he joined the Dearborn Stock Company. He changed his name to Edwin Carewe in honor of the famed actor Edwin Booth (the brother of John Wilkes Booth).

In the 1910s, Carewe left acting and took up directing in the Hollywood film industry, though he still occasionally took on acting roles. The first film he directed was *Across the Pacific* (Blaney Prods.) in 1914. Carewe's brother Wallace became a director and producer in films, and his other brother Finis Fox became a screenwriter.

Carewe directed some fifty-seven films, including *Her Great Price* (1916, Rolfe Photoplays); *A Question of Honor* (1922, Mayer Prods.); *The Girl of the Golden West* (1923, Carewe Prods.); *Joanna* (1925, Carewe Prods.); *High Steppers* (1926, Carewe Prods.); *Pals First* (1926, Carewe Prods.); *Resurrection* (1931, Carewe Prods.), a remake; and *Are We Civilized?* (1934, Raspin Prods.). He also produced some nineteen films during the 1920s and 1930s.

In the 1920s, Carewe achieved his greatest critical and commercial successes. One of his finest moments was his discovery of actress Dolores Del Río, whom he met on a visit to Mexico and convinced to try her luck in films. Both Del Río and Carewe earned critical and commercial success with *Resurrection* (1927, Universal), *Ramona* (1928, Inspiration Pictures), and *Evangeline* (1929, Carewe Prods.), all of which Carewe produced.

However, after the coming of sound in 1927, Carewe's directorial career began to wane. He made several remakes of his silent films. He ended his career directing low-budget and religious films. He directed his last film, *Are We Civilized?*, in 1934.

He was married three times (twice to Mary Akin).

Edwin Carewe died of a heart condition on January 22, 1940, and was buried at the Hollywood Forever Cemetery.

Chief Standing Bear

Luther Standing Bear had a brief career in films during the 1920s and 1930s. Born with the name of Plenty Kill in December 1868 at Fort Robinson, Nebraska, he was of the Oglala Lakota tribe. As a youth, he was one of the first students at the Carlisle Indian Industrial School in Pennsylvania.

He worked numerous jobs before focusing on acting: dancer, interpreter, and later in Buffalo Bill's Wild West Show as a horseback performer. This employment allowed him to travel throughout the country at the turn of the century.

Standing Bear made his film debut in *Ramona* (1916, Clune Film). His films include *Bolshevism on Trial* (1919, Mayflower Photoplay); *The Santa Fe Trail* (1930, Paramount); *The Conquering Horde* (1931, Paramount); *Texas Pioneers* (1932, Trem Carr Pictures); *Massacre* (1934, Warner Bros.); *Laughing Boy* (1934, MGM); *Murder in the Private Car* (1934, MGM); *The Miracle Rider* (1935, Mascot Pictures), a serial; *The Circle of Death* (1935, Willis Kent Prods.); and *Fighting Pioneers* (1935, Resolute Pictures).

Standing Bear was a man of many talents. Among other achievements, he wrote three important books: *My People the Sioux* (1928), *Land of the Spotted Eagle* (1933), and *Stories of the Sioux* (1934). These books won wide acclaim and continue to sell to this day. In addition, he founded the Indian Actors Association in 1936, a nonprofit organization with the mission of establishing a pool of authentic Native American actors for motion pictures, equal pay, and the improvement of indigenous images in films.

In 1939, he invited noted sculptor Korczak Ziolkowski to build a memorial of the legendary Lakota leader Crazy Horse in the Black Hills of South Dakota. The sculptor accepted; work on the giant statue is still ongoing to this day. This event was the subject of the documentary titled *Dreaming in Stone* (2010, Volvo).

Standing Bear died on February 20, 1939, in Huntington Park, California, on the set of the film *Union Pacific*. His death was attributed to the flu. He was 70 years of age. He was buried at the Hollywood Forever Cemetery, Los Angeles. Standing Bear was widely admired, respected, and beloved by both indigenous people and others.

Chief White Eagle

Chief White Eagle was born on May 5, 1892, in Phoenix, Arizona. He made his film debut in the film short titled *The Last Ghost Dance* in 1914 (Miller Bros.) under the name White Eagle. His films include *The Heart of Wetona* (1919, Talmadge Film Corp.); *Fighting Caravans* (1931, Paramount); *Trails of the Golden West* (1931, West Coast Pictures); *Oklahoma Jim* (1931, Trem Carr Pictures); and *End of the Trail* (1932, Columbia).

In 1939, he played himself in the *Western Cabaret Series* in episodes one and two. It was an early effort in the medium of television.

He died on April 4, 1984, in Los Angeles, California, at 91 years of age.

Chief Yowlachie

Chief Yowlachie enjoyed a long film career in motions pictures from the silent era to the 1960s.

He was born Daniel Simmons in Yakima, Washington, on August 15, 1891. He was a member of the Yakima tribe.

He began his career as an opera singer but gradually transitioned into a long career in motion pictures. He made his film debut in *Kentucky Days* in 1923 (Fox Film Corp.). Most of his roles were in westerns. He often played native villains or amiable characters.

His films included *Ella Cinders* (1926, McCormick Prods.); *The Scarlet Letter* (1926, MGM); *Sitting Bull at the Spirit of the Lake Massacre* (1927, Sunset Prods.); *The Girl of the Golden West* (1930, First National); *Man of Conquest* (1939, Republic); *North West*

Mounted Police (1940, Paramount); *Canyon Passage* (1946, Wranger Prods.); *Red River* (1948, United Artists); *The Paleface* (1948, Paramount); *Yellow Sky* (1948, 20th Century–Fox); *Ma and Pa Kettle* (1949); *My Friend Irma* (1949); *Ma and Pa Kettle Go to Town* (1950, Univ. Inter.); *Winchester '73* (1950, Univ. Inter.); *Annie Get Your Gun* (1950, MGM); *Lone Star* (1952, MGM); *Hollywood or Bust* (1956, Paramount); *The Spirit of St. Louis* (1957, Warner Bros.); *The Buccaneer* (1958, Paramount); *The FBI Story* (1959, Warner Bros.); *Yellowstone Kelly* (1959, Warner Bros.); *Heller in Pink Tights* (1960, Paramount); and his last, *Nevada Smith* (1966, Paramount). His many television appearances included *The Tall Men*, *The Stories of the Century*, *The Lone Ranger*, *The Cisco Kid*, *Death Valley Days*, *The Range Rider*, and *The Virginian*.

Yowlachie died on in Los Angeles, California, on March 7, 1966.

Gertrude Chorre

Gertrude Chorre was a Native American actress. She had two children, Sonny Chorre and Marie Chorre, who also became actors in the 1930s.

She was born on April 30, 1885, in the La Jolla Indian Reservation in California. She made her film debut in *Frozen Justice* in 1929 (Fox Film Corp.).

Her films included *In Old California* (1929, Audible Pictures); *The Outlaw Tamer* (1935, H&H Prods.); *Lawless Riders* (1935, Darmour Prods.); *Ramona* (1936, 20th Century–Fox); *Join the Marines* (1937, Republic); *Navajo Kid* (1945, Alexander-Stern); *The Sea of Grass* (1947, MGM); *We Were Strangers* (1949, Columbia); *Raw Edge* (1956, Univ. Inter.); and *The First Traveling Saleslady* (1956, RKO). Her television appearances include *The Adventures of Rin Tin Tin* in 1958.

Chorre died at the age of 87, on September 3, 1972, in Riverside County, California.

Dolores Del Río

Dolores Del Río was the first Mexico-born female film star to triumph in Hollywood during the 1920s. Her Mexican Native American ancestry stemmed from the state of Durango in northern Mexico. She was the cousin of film star Ramón Novarro.

She was born Dolores Asunsolo y López Negrete in Durango, Mexico, on August 3, 1905. She was the daughter of Jesus Asunsolo, director of the Bank of Durango and part of a wealthy family from Chihuahua, Mexico. Her mother, Antonia López Negrete de Asunsolo, came from a wealthy family from Durango, Mexico. The Mexican Revolution of 1910 compelled the family to leave Durango; her father moved to the United States, while the rest of the family went to Mexico City, where they later reunited. In Mexico City, Dolores attended the French convent of Saint Joseph, where all the courses were taught in the French language.

At the age of fifteen, Dolores married a wealthy lawyer, Jaime Martínez Del Río, who was some eighteen years her senior. In 1925, the noted painter Adolfo Best Maugard introduced her husband to the visiting Hollywood director Edwin Carewe. The latter then persuaded Dolores to try a career in film. She was encouraged by her husband, and both came to live in Hollywood.

Dolores Del Río made her film debut in a small part as a Spanish countess in Carewe's *Joanna* (1925, Carewe Prods.). Studio publicity introduced her as a "Spanish actress." However, she made sure that the studio refuted this ethnic origin and insisted that she be known as a Mexican actress. Her breathtaking beauty and charisma made an impact in her first film. Carewe placed Del Río under a personal contract and cast her in a variety of roles: *High Steppers* (1926, Carewe Prods.); *The Whole Town Is Talking* (1926, Universal); *Pals First* (1926, Carewe Prods.); and the lead in *Upstairs* (1926, Carewe Prods.).

However, it was the role of French country girl Charmaine, a loving and self-sacrificing coquette in Raoul Walsh's *What Price Glory?* (1926, Fox Film Corp.), opposite Victor McLaglen and Edmund Lowe, that won Del Río film stardom. The film was an adaptation of the Lawrence Stallings–Maxwell Anderson play and chronicled the World War I adventures and constant bickering of Sergeants Flagg (McLaglen) and Quirt (Lowe). It was an enormous success. Carewe then cast Del Río in the adaptation of Leo Tolstoy's *Resurrection* (1927, Carewe Prods.), with Rod La Roque as Prince Dimitri. Her performance provided an impressive range: from an innocent peasant to a prostitute, subsequently reduced to a derelict, and then a lost woman redeemed by love. Other films during this time included *The Loves of Carmen* (1927, Fox Film Corp.), *Gateway to the Moon* (1928, Fox Film Corp.), and *The Trail of '98* (1928, MGM).

In 1928, Dolores played Ramona the mestiza in the Edwin Carewe–directed version of Helen Hunt Jackson's best-selling novel *Ramona* (Inspiration Pictures). The film was set in the turbulent California of the 1850s, when Euro-American immigrants invaded and almost wiped out the state's last remaining Native Americans. This film provided Dolores with one of her most memorable roles.

Dolores Del Río (center) was a Mexican indigenous film star who played a native maiden in *Bird of Paradise* (1932, RKO). She personified the indigenous woman in numerous Mexican films.

4. The Noble Savage and the White Man's Enemy (1920–1929)

During the 1920s, Dolores Del Río became an icon for native and Mexican women and others who were not Caucasian. She epitomized the liberated and sophisticated successful woman who happened to be native looking and captivating. She followed up her role in *Ramona* with another impressive film, *Evangeline* (1929, Carewe Prods.), based on Longfellow's poem of the same name. During this time Del Río headlined other successful films: *No Other Woman* (1928, Fox Film Corp.); *The Red Dance* (1928, Fox Film Corp.); and *Revenge* (1928, Carewe Prods.).

These were years of transition for Del Río. She realized that she had to learn English, as talking films would soon take over the film industry. Her private life also took a turn when she divorced her first husband and married MGM art director Cedric Gibbons in 1930.

Del Río made her talking film debut in Edmund Carewe's *The Bad One* in 1930 (Schenck Prods.). Her transition into sound films was successful. The microphone picked up her accent, but her career flourished. However, from then on she was often typecast as exotic or foreign-sounding women, as in *The Sculpture's Dream* (1929, Tellegen) and *The Girl of the Rio* (1932, RKO). She had one of her best roles as Luana, a Polynesian native girl who falls in love with a white adventurer (Joel McCrea) in King Vidor's *Bird of Paradise* (1932).

During this period, her films included *Flying Down to Rio* (1933, RKO); *Wonder Bar* (1934, Warner Bros.); *Madame Du Barry* (1934, Warner Bros.); *In Caliente* (1935, Warner Bros.); *I Live for Love* (1935, Warner Bros.); *The Widow from Monte Cristo* (1935, Warner Bros.); *The Devil's Playground* (1937, Columbia); *The Accused* (1937, United Artists); *Lancer Spy* (1937, 20th Century–Fox); *Ali Baba Goes to Town* (1937, 20th Century–Fox), a cameo role; *International Settlement* (1938, 20th Century–Fox); and *The Man from Dakota* (1939, MGM), in which she received lowly third billing.

By the mid–1930s, her film career began to decline, as she was assigned to less distinguished pictures. It was also during this time, in the midst of the Depression, that the Mexican Repatriation took place, in which more than a million Mexican nationals and Mexican Americans were repatriated to Mexico. Some blamed Mexicans for "stealing jobs," and other were gripped by anti–Mexican racism.

After finishing the excellent *Journey into Fear* (1942, RKO), directed by Orson Welles (and a failed affair with the director), Dolores Del Río left Hollywood for her native Mexico. There, a cultural renaissance was taking place in art, music, and film.

Her return to Mexico began a long collaboration with director/screenwriter Emilio "Indio" Fernández, film star Pedro Armendáriz, and cinematographer Gabriel Figueroa. Fernández asserted the Native American identity of Mexico in film and was influenced by the great nationalist muralists (Orozco, Rivera, etc.) and writers of the era. Fernández's films celebrated the native faces, cultural traditions, and land in striking and vigorous cinematography. Its men and women were passionately alive, resilient, and three dimensional.

In all her films directed by Fernández, Del Río would play strong and resilient Native American women, often mired in poverty, ethnic taboos, and prejudice. Her first two films for Fernández were *Flor Silvestre* (1943, Films Mundiales) and *María Candelaria* (1943, Films Mundiales). Both films earned international acclaim for the Mexican cinema. Two more Fernández-directed films followed: *Las Abandonadas* (1944, Films Mundiales) and *Bugambilia* (1944, Films Mundiales).

After *La Selva de Fuego* (1945, Grovas) and *La Otra* (1946, Mercurio), director John

Ford requested Del Río's services. Ford's film *The Fugitive* (1947, Argosy) was based on Graham Greene's novel *The Power and the Glory*, which documented the *Cristero* era of the 1920s in Mexico. The film co-starred Pedro Armendáriz and Henry Fonda, and it was shot on location in Mexico.

Del Río's film career flourished in Mexican cinema: *Historia de Un Mala Mujer* (1948, Sono Film), an Argentine film based on Oscar Wilde's *Lady Windermere's Fan*; *La Malquerida* (1949, Cabrera Films), directed by Emilio Fernández; *Casa Chica* (1949, Filmex); *Dona Perfecta* (1950, Cabrera Films); *Deseada* (1951, Sanson); *Reportaje* (1953, ANDA); and *El Niño y la Niebla* (1953, Grovas).

In 1956, Del Río made her stage debut in English in *Anastasia*, which played in New England. She also did *Lady Windermere's Fan* throughout the Mexican Republic and in Argentina. She continued to have mass appeal throughout Mexico and the Spanish-speaking world, where she was highly respected and admired. In 1959, she married for the third time, this time to documentary filmmaker Lewis A. Riley.

In the 1950s, she performed in both Mexican and U.S. television shows. In 1959, she worked with actor/director Emilio Fernández on *La Cucaracha* (Rodríguez Pictures), which focused on the Mexican Revolution. Other films of during this period included *Señora Ama* (1955, Diana Films); *¿A Dónde Van Nuestros Hijos?* (1956, Filmex); Don Siegel's *Flaming Star* (1960, 20th Century–Fox), in which she played the Native American mother of Elvis Presley; and John Ford's *Cheyenne Autumn* (1964, Warner Bros.), about epic trek of the Cheyenne Nation, in which she played Spanish Woman.

During the next two decades, her film output dwindled: *Casa de Mujeres* (1966, Brooks Prods.); *Río Blanco* (1967, Gavaldón); *More Than a Miracle* (1967, Cinecitta); *La Dama de Alba* (1966, Rovira); *Salsa* (1977); and *The Children of Sanchez* (1978, CONACINE), based on the Oscar Lewis book of the same name, with her compatriot Anthony Quinn.

Dolores Del Río died on April 11, 1983, of natural causes in her home in Newport Beach, California.

Over her lifetime, Del Río was honored with many awards and recognition. More than any other actress in Mexican film history, she created an indelible and enduring imprint of Mexican Native American women in the national cinema.

Ramón Novarro

Ramón Novarro was the first Mexico-born male actor to become a Hollywood superstar in the film industry. His native roots went back to Aztec lineage.

He was born José Gil Samaniegos on February 6, 1899, in Durango, Mexico, the oldest of thirteen children. His father was a successful dentist who had graduated from the University of Pennsylvania and spoke English fluently. His mother's family, the Gavilans, claimed to be descendants of the Aztec emperors. He was the second cousin of Dolores Del Río, who was also born in Durango.

He was educated in Mexico City, where he studied English, French, and music. While visiting relatives in El Paso, Texas, in 1916, he left for Hollywood with dreams of the movies and stardom. After the death of his father, his family accompanied him in Los Angeles in the early 1920s.

Novarro worked as a waiter-singer and performed with the Los Angeles Majestic Stock Company. Between 1917 and 1921, he worked as an extra and bit player in dozens of silent films: *The Jaguar's Claws* (1917, Lasky); *The Little American* (1917, Pickford

Prods.); *The Woman God Forgot* (1917, Artcraft Pictures); *The Hostage* (1917, Lasky); *Joan the Woman* (1917, Paramount); *The Goat* (1918, Lasky); *The Four Horsemen of the Apocalypse* (1922, Metro); and *Man-Woman-Marriage* (1921, Holubar), among many others.

Finally, in 1921, vaudeville dance director Marion Morgan (in whose troupe he had performed since 1919) had Novarro tested for a novelty dance in the full-length comedy titled *Small Town Idol* (1921, Mack Sennett) with Ben Turpin and Phyllis Haver. Novarro followed it up with a featured role in *Mr. Barnes of New York* (1922, Goldwyn) and then the lead role in a small independent film, *The Rubaiyat of Omar Khayyam*, which was not released until 1925.

The young actor is said to have crashed into director Rex Ingram's office at Metro Pictures to request a screen test for the title role of Prince Rupert of Henzau in *The Prisoner of Zenda* (1922, Metro) opposite Barbara La Marr. His bravado in making an impromptu audition with Ingram earned him the role, as well as film stardom (billed under his own name). Film critic Herbert Howe of *Photoplay* would write that Novarro had won the film public "with one flip of the monocle."[15] At the suggestion of Ingram, his screen name was changed to Novarro (one of his maternal names).

Novarro was almost immediately compared to Rudolph Valentino, who had just reached stardom in Ingram's *The Four Horsemen of the Apocalypse* (1922). Hollywood films created the stereotype of the "Latin Lover," and a group of leading men quickly became popular playing those roles (even though several were not of Latin American extraction, like Ricardo Cortez). However, the vogue became an endangered species with the coming of sound. Hollywood's ethnic antipathy was also quickly apparent. Howe wrote in the April 1923 issue of *Photoplay*, "It is hard to write about one of these outstanding, whole-wheat boys. My sympathies are all with the criminal classes. And Ramón Novarro is not one of these, even though he is a Hollywood resident and a Mexican. Not that I mean any disparagement of Mexicans."[16]

Novarro signed a personal contract with director Rex Ingram (at $125 per week) and played a tragic hero in *Trifling Women* (1922, Metro), reuniting him with the popular Barbara La Marr. Novarro was quickly signed by Metro Studios (in 1925, the studio would merge and become Metro-Goldwyn-Mayer [MGM]) under a lucrative contract. There, he made three films opposite Alice Terry, Ingram's wife: *White the Pavement Ends* (1923), playing a native in love with a missionary's daughter; Rafael Sabatini's swashbuckling *Scaramouche* (1923), taking on the title role; and *The Arab* (1924), filmed in North Africa and inspired by Valentino's *The Sheik*. By that time the studio had raised Novarro's salary to $10,000 per week.

Novarro's signature role was that of Judah Ben-Hur in the epic film *Ben-Hur* (1925, MGM), based on the novel by Lew Wallace. The film became both a critical and a commercial success. *Photoplay* (March 1926) wrote of the film, "*Ben-Hur* is not a flat picture upon the screen. It is a thing of beauty and joy for ten years at least. It is truly a great picture. No one, no matter what age or religion, should miss it."[17] The film was re-released in 1931 with synchronized sound. It would go on to become a classic in U.S. cinema.

Now at his peak of his stardom, Novarro displayed his versatility in all his roles. He played a Spaniard in *Lovers?* (1927, MGM), opposite Alice Terry, and a Spanish cavalier in *The Road to Romance* (1927, MGM) with Marceline Day. He also played a young Austrian prince in love with a working-class waitress in Ernst Lubitsch's *The Student Prince* (1927, MGM). In addition, Novarro played a seaman in search of revenge in *Across to Singapore* (1928, MGM) opposite Joan Crawford; *A Certain Young Man* (1928, MGM) with

Ramón Novarro (Ramón Samaniegos, right; others unidentified) was a film star who could claim Aztec ancestry. Among other famous roles, he played the native icon Juan Diego, who sees the *Virgen de Guadalupe* in *La Virgen Que Forjó Una Patria* (1942, Films Mundiales).

the ailing Renee Adoree; a Ruritanian king in *Forbidden Hours* (1928, MGM); and a U.S. naval cadet in *The Flying Fleet* (1929, MGM).

In 1929, Novarro scored another massive hit playing a South Seas native in W.S. Van Dyke's *The Pagan* (MGM). The film was music-scored, but otherwise a silent film. He sang impressively "The Pagan Love Song," which became a big hit. He made a smooth transition into sound films with *Devil May Care* (1929, MGM), in which he sang four songs. Although he had an accent, it did not affect his continuing popularity among moviegoers. In his next two films, he displayed his talent for singing and dancing. He played a Spanish troubadour *In Gay Madrid* (1930, MGM) and a romantic Spanish captain in *Call of the Flesh* (1930, MGM). Novarro also made history by becoming the first Mexican-born filmmaker to direct and co-direct two Hollywood Spanish and French versions of the same movie: *La Sevillana/Sevilla de mis Amores* (1930, MGM) and *Le Chanteur de Séville* (1930, MGM), both foreign-language version of *Call of the Flesh*.

The advent of the Great Depression in 1929 brought a vicious jingoism and ethnic backlash against Mexicans in the United States. More than one million and a half Mexicans (both Mexican nationals and U.S. born) were rounded up and sent to Mexico in what became the Mexican Repatriation. Novarro, along with his cousin Dolores Del Río and others, conducted fundraisers to assist their compatriots. During this period, Novarro, Del Río, and Lupe Vélez were smeared with Communist affiliations.[18]

The early 1930s brought a series of important changes to Novarro's life and career. He began to have increased conflict with his studio. He also took up drinking on a regular

4. The Noble Savage and the White Man's Enemy (1920–1929)   51

basis. (Eventually his drinking would become a lifelong addiction, which would destroy his stardom and tarnish his health.) The causes closest to his heart appeared to be his devout Catholicism and his gay lifestyle. Actress Anita Page (1910–2008), whose real name was Anita Evelyn Pomares (of Spanish ancestry), co-starred with Novarro in the film *The Flying Fleet* (1929, MGM). She became enamored of Novarro. Many years later, Page revealed that Novarro had asked her to marry him. She unintentionally laughed at his request, apparently hurting him.[19] Their relationship ended soon thereafter.

There were also numerous reports that Novarro intended to give up his wealth and fame for the priesthood. His friend, Mexican singer and actor José Mojica, would do so in the early 1940s. Some would say later that Novarro had a lifelong regret of not leaving for the priesthood when he was young enough to do so.

His career throughout the 1930s remained in high gear. He starred in two excellent films for famed French director Jacques Feyder: *Daybreak* (1931, MGM) and *Son of India* (1931, MGM). He scored another big hit playing the Russian pilot in love with the famous German spy (Greta Garbo) in *Mata Hari* (1932, MGM). He also played a Yale football player in *Huddle* (1932, MGM); a cameo role in the film short *The Christmas Party* (1932, MGM); and an Oriental prince in the *Son-Daughter* (1932, MGM).

Novarro played a sheik masquerading as an Egyptian guide in Sam Wood's sparkling *The Barbarian* (1933, MGM) with Myrna Loy. Elsewhere, he played a contemporary Navajo in love with Slim Girl (Lupe Vélez) in W.S. Van Dyke's *Laughing Boy* (1934, MGM), based on Oliver La Farge's Pulitzer Prize–winning novel of the same name. He also played a Balkan prince in love with a singer (Evelyn Laye) in the excellent *The Night Is Young* (1935, MGM). After this film, he left MGM abruptly and freelanced at other studios.

He wrote, produced, and directed the Spanish-language film *Contra la Corriente* (1936, RNS Prods.), a love story set against the backdrop of the 1932 Olympics in Los Angeles. He played a sheik again in Irving Pichel's *The Sheik Steps Out* (1937, Republic Pictures) with Lola Lane, which was a satire on his former image. He followed this movie with the excellent *A Desperate Adventure* (1938, Republic Pictures), which told the story of a painter trying to recover his lost masterpiece.

At this point, Novarro's life and career appeared adrift. His drinking increased, and he was arrested several times for drunk driving. However, Novarro was always a person who welcomed a new challenge. In 1939, he left for Rome to film *La Comédie de Bonheur* (Discina) with Micheline Presle, but the film was abandoned when World War II erupted. The film's director, Marcel l'Herbier, left for Paris, and Novarro finished directing. The film, which was released in 1940, proved to be a classic French film, widely popular and admired. In the same year, the Italian version of the film *Ecco la felicità* (Discina) was also made (with the same cast) and subsequently released.

In 1942, Novarro left for Mexico to film *La Virgen Que Forjó Una Patria* (Films Mundiales), which was directed by Julio Bracho (a second cousin). Novarro played Juan Diego, the revered Native American who witnessed the apparition of *La Virgen de Guadalupe*, Mexico's most important and revered religious icon. The film proved to be a huge commercial and critical success throughout Latin America. It revived Novarro's stature and career, and he received numerous offers to both act and direct in Mexican films. This was the beginning of Mexico's Golden Age of Film. His cousin Dolores Del Río had recently moved to Mexico to start a second career. Like her, Novarro might have had a second career as both director and film star. However, Novarro returned to the United States, where his drinking increased and he became a near-recluse throughout most of the 1940s.

Although wealthy, Novarro still hungered for the limelight of acting. After almost a decade of retirement, he returned to films in John Huston's *We Were Strangers* (1949, Columbia), in which he played a Cuban revolutionary and earned rave reviews. The media and the public warmly welcomed him back. He went on to play a sly Mexican police detective in Don Siegel's offbeat film noir *The Big Steal* (1949, RKO), earning the best reviews for the film. He next played a corrupt Latin American general in Robert Wise's *Crisis* (1950, MGM), opposite Cary Grant, Paula Raymond, and contemporaries Gilbert Roland and Antonio Moreno. *Crisis* marked his first film at his old studio in fifteen years. He played a swashbuckling caballero in the western *The Outriders* (1950, MGM) alongside Joel McCrea and Arlene Dahl.

As time went by, he appeared to mellow about his past demons and career. He commented about this period of his career, "A character role is much more enjoyable than a starring role. It's not your picture and you are not blamed if anything goes wrong. By not having to look good you can concentrate more on your acting."[20] About contemporary films, he noted, "They have progressed technically but have died artistically."[21]

He then disappeared from the limelight again, except for a few stage performances. However, unable to leave the art form that had made him famous, he returned for his last role in George Cukor's offbeat western *Heller in Pink Tights* (1960, Paramount Pictures) with Anthony Quinn and Sophia Loren.

Novarro made his television debut in the 1950s. Toward the end of the decade he appeared in several popular television shows, such as *Dr. Kildare*, *Bonanza*, *Combat*, and *Thriller*, among others.

On October 31, 1968, Ramón Novarro was murdered at his Hollywood home by two brothers with a long criminal record. It was a tragic ending for the legendary leading man. The *New York Times* (November 1, 1968) eulogized him as follows: "Although Mr. Novarro was hailed as a lover, he often drew praise for injecting a touch of humor into his roles, a difficult thing to achieve in a medium where every line was spoken by gesture alone. He never considered acting as the end-all life."[22]

Novarro (along with his cousin Dolores Del Río) was a pioneer for Mexican Native Americans in the Hollywood film industry. His impact has often been underestimated by film historians. However, he served as an important reference point in the evolution of Native American film images.

Will Rogers

One of the most popular film stars of the 1920s and 1930s was Will Rogers. He was a well-known humorist, vaudeville performer, radio personality, and movie star.

Rogers was born on November 4, 1879, in Oologah, Cherokee Nation Indian Territory (presently Oklahoma). His parents were Mary America Schrimsher and Clement Vann Rogers, both of whom were part Cherokee. That made Will Rogers about one-quarter Cherokee. He was the youngest of eight siblings (only three of whom survived into adulthood). His father was a Cherokee judge, served as a delegate to the Oklahoma Constitutional Convention, and won two terms in the Cherokee Senate.

Rogers attended school in Neosho, Missouri, and then went on to the Kempler Military School at Boonville, Missouri. He was said to have been a good student, but he dropped out during the 10th grade. For the next few years, he worked at odd jobs in Argentina as a cowboy and in South Africa breaking horses. He worked as a trick roper in Texas Jack's Wild West Circus in the United States and in the same capacity in Australia. He returned to the United States in 1904 and performed at the St. Louis World's Fair, and then he delighted audiences with his roping skills in vaudeville throughout the country.

His increasing popularity led Rogers to make his film debut in *Laughing Bill Hyde* (1918, Goldwyn Pictures), shot in New Jersey. He met with immediate success and moved to Los Angeles, California, where he founded his own film production company. Although silent films denied him the opportunity to showcase his unique verbal wit, Rogers' humble demeanor and riding and rodeo skills earned him millions of fans.

He made forty-eight silent films. However, it was the arrival of sound films that allowed him to develop his full array of talents, specifically his wit and homespun humor. He rapidly became one of the top film stars in the early 1930s and remained so until the time of his death.

His silent films include *Almost a Husband* (1919, Goldwyn); *Hollywood* (1923, Goldwyn), in a cameo role; *Two Wagons Both Covered* (1923, Hal Roach), a short film; *Uncensored Movies* (1923, Hal Roach), a film short; *The Cowboy Sheik* (1924, Hal Roach), a film short; *Our Congressman* (1924, Hal Roach), a film short; *A Truthful Liar* (1924, Hal Roach), a film short; *Tip Toes* (1927, British National); and *A Texas Steer* (1927, Sam E. Rork), among others.

Between 1927 and 1929, he made no feature films. However, during this time he made twelve travelogue film shorts for Pathé Exchange that were based on his European travels: *In Dublin* (1927); *In Paris* (1927); *Hiking Through Holland* (1927); *Roaming the Emerald Isle* (1927); *Through Switzerland and Bavaria* (1927); *In London* (1927); *Hunting for Germans in Berlin* 1927); *Prowling Around France* (1927); *Winging Round Europe* (1927); *Exploring England* (1927); *Reeling Down the Rhine* (1927); and *Over the Bounding Blue* (1928).

The advent of talking films resulted in film studios competing with each other to sign Rogers for a long-term contract. However, it was Fox Film Corporation (soon to be 20th Century–Fox) that contracted him for all of his talking films. He became the highest-paid film star during the early decade. Rogers made his talking film debut in *They Had to See Paris* (1929, Fox). Most of his talking films cast him in rural settings as a small-town banker, a simple farmer, a down-to-earth politician, or an easygoing steamboat captain. Filmgoers during the harsh economic downturn responded to his down-to-earth persona and sense of the average man.

Rogers made a total of twenty-one talking films. They include *Happy Days* (1929, Fox); *So This Is London* (1930, Fox); *Lightnin'* (1930, Fox); *Young as You Feel* (1930, Fox); *Ambassador Bill* (1930, Fox); *A Connecticut Yankee* (1931, Fox); *Down to Earth* (1932, Fox); *Too Busy to Work* (1932, Fox); *Business and Pleasure* (1932, Fox); *State Fair* (1933, Fox); *Doctor Bull* (1933); *Mr. Skitch* (1933, Fox); *David Harum* (1934, Fox); *Handy Andy* (1934, Fox); *Judge Priest* (1934, Fox); *The County Chairman* (1935, Fox); *Life Begins at 40* (1935, Fox); *Doubting Thomas* (1935, Fox); *In Old Kentucky* (1935, 20th Century–Fox); and his last film, *Steamboat Round the Bend* (1935, 20th Century–Fox).

Rogers married Betty Blake (1879–1944), and they remained together until his death. The union produced four children: Will Rogers, Jr., Mary Amelia, James Blake, and Fred Stone (who died of diphtheria at the age of two).

Rogers wrote a weekly syndicated newspaper column between 1922 and 1935 for the *New York Times*, as well as several humor-laced books meant to inspire people out of pessimism. He was tireless in his efforts to provide biting social commentaries on the state of the nation and the world. He promoted common sense in government policies and expounded on the virtue of helping others. He gave numerous lectures and fundraisers for floods, earthquakes and charities.

During the Great Depression, Rogers' humor became more biting on the subjects of do-nothing politicians and government waste and inefficiency. He became a goodwill ambassador to Mexico, and he also served briefly as the mayor of Beverly Hills. As the depression worsened, he joined a fundraising tour with the Red Cross. Enormous crowds greeted him wherever he went, anxious for some words of encouragement and humor in the difficult times.

Ironically, despite his many appearances in film, Will Rogers never played a Native American role.

He died in a plane crash on August 15, 1935, in Point Barrow, Alaska, along with his friend and famous aviator Wiley Post.

Charles Stevens

Charles Stevens was a familiar character actor for more than half a century, recognizable but not famous. His Native American features were undeniable and his roles indelible in a more than a hundred films and television appearances.

Stevens claimed to be the grandson of the great Apache leader and patriot Geronimo and bore a striking physical resemblance to the Apache chief, though there is no evidence to support a familial relationship. Given the available documentation, there is a strong likelihood that he was of Yaqui ancestry, on his mother's side, as her family was from the Mexican state of Sonora. Stevens was born in Solomonville, Arizona, on May 26, 1893. As a young man, he worked in the Miller Bros. 101 Ranch Wild West Show and then traveled to the growing film industry in Hollywood, California. He made his film debut in D.W. Griffith's *Birth of a Nation* (Griffith Corp.) in an uncredited role as a "volunteer" in 1915. It would be the first of almost two hundred film appearances. He was married in 1918 to Lila Stevens until his passing.

He befriended the rising star Douglas Fairbanks, Sr., and quickly became part of Fairbanks' stock company of players. Between 1915 and 1962, Stevens amassed 222 film and television credits. He played scores of bit parts and later supporting roles, typically as a villainous Native American, Mexican, or Asian. His roles in Douglas Fairbanks' films (most for the Douglas Fairbanks Corporation) included *Wild and Woolly* (1917, Fairbanks); *The Mollycoddle* (1920, Fairbanks); *The Mark of Zorro* (1920, Fairbanks); *The Three Musketeers* (1921, Fairbanks); *Robin Hood* (1922, Fairbanks); *The Thief of Bagdad* (1924, Fairbanks); *Don Q. Son of Zorro* (1925, Elton Corp.); *The Gaucho* (1927, Elton Corp.); and *The Iron Mask* (1929, Elton Corp.), among others. In the film *The Vanishing American* (1925, Paramount Pictures), Stevens played one of the leading Native American roles and was able to display his true acting talent in a fully developed character, instead of the usual one-dimensional roles he was often assigned.

Stevens' other film credits included *Lives of a Bengal Lancer* (1935, Paramount); *Swing High, Swing Low* (1937, Paramount); *The Mark of Zorro* (1941, 20th Century–Fox); *Blood and Sand* (1941); *San Antonio* (1945, Warner Bros.); *My Darling Clementine* (1946, 20th Century–Fox); *Sinbad the Sailor* (1947, RKO), with Douglas Fairbanks, Jr.; *The Last Command* (1955, Republic); and *The Ten Commandments* (1956, Paramount). His last film was *The Outsider* (1961, Univ. Inter.), the story about Ira Hayes, the Native American U.S.

James Griffith and Charles Stevens in *Indian Territory* (1950, Gene Autry Prods.).

Marine who was one of the men who raised the flag at Iwo Jima. His television appearances included *The Range Rider* (1952), *My Friend Flicka* (1956), *Sugarfoot* (1958), and *Rawhide* (1961), among others.

Stevens died on August 22, 1964, and was buried in the Valhalla Memorial Park Cemetery in an unmarked grave.

Lupe Velez

Lupe Vélez, who in Mexico is widely recognized as having indigenous heritage, was the second Mexican actress (the first was Dolores Del Rio) to achieve stardom in the Hollywood film industry. Since her death in 1944, U.S. film historians and websites have most often focused on alleged sexual escapades and tales of promiscuity, instead of her considerable achievements in motion pictures.

A film stereotype has been developed and perpetuated about Lupe Vélez, which is misleading. The fact remains that her film roles were remarkably versatile at different times in her career. Ana M. Lopez noted, "Vélez's position in Hollywood was defined not by her acting versatility, but by her smoldering ethnic identifiability. Although as striking as Del Rio's, Vélez's beauty and sexual appetite were aggressive, flamboyant, and stridently ethnic. Throughout the '30s she personified this hot-blooded, thickly accented Latin temptress with insatiable sexual appetite."[23] Film historian Allen L. Woll wrote, "Lupe retained that hellish quality throughout her seventeen-year Hollywood career, and her exuberance dwarfed all Latin competitors. She became the 'Hot Baby of Hollywood' and 'The Mexican Spitfire.' Like Carmen Miranda, she had an aggressive, almost mannish quality, which drove her co-stars mad in her films about hot-blooded Latin women."[24] One wonders if these perspectives are attributed to Lupe Vélez because she was an assertive and strong woman of color in her films, breaking the gender stereotype of the proverbial docile and submissive woman.

She was born Maria Guadalupe Vélez de Villalobos in San Luis Potosi, Mexico, on July 18, 1908, to a middle-class family. Her father Colonel Villalobos, was actively involved in the Mexican Revolution. She was stage-struck since childhood and began working in Mexico City theatre at the young age of thirteen. In 1926, the veteran stage actor Richard Bennett saw her in the Mexican musical play *Rataplan* in Mexico City. He was looking for new talent to cast for his new play *The Dove*. However, by the time she arrived in Hollywood the role had already been cast and she earned a livelihood dancing in a Hollywood nightclub revue. While Vélez was dancing in the Music Box Revue, Fannie Brice saw her and sent Flo Ziegfeld a most enthusiastic telegraph. Ziegfeld in turn replied by telegraph, requesting Lupe come to New York for a tryout. However, on the very day of her scheduled departure MGM signed her to a film contract.

Vélez made an impressive debut in the comedy short *What Women Did for Me* (1927, Hal Roach) with Charley Chase; and then followed it with the two-reel comedy *Sailor Beware* (1927, Hal Roach) with the formidable Stan Laurel and Oliver Hardy. At the same time, Douglas Fairbanks, Sr., was casting for *The Gaucho* (1927, United Artists) for an actress (after Dolores Del Rio had declined) to fill the role of the heroine who was "as willing to fight a man as love him." Fairbanks went to see Vélez and was instantly impressed with her vitality and personality. As a consequence, he borrowed her from MGM. In the film, Fairbanks played the leader of a band of *gaucho* outlaws attempting to overthrow an evil tyrant. Vélez matched the veteran star in kinetic energy and dynamic charisma. Upon the film's release, she (at the age of 17) became a star. United Artists bought her contract from MGM.

For the next sixteen years, she played a wide assortment of nationalities and ethnicities: Mexican, Native American, Hindu, French, Chinese, Swedish, Eskimo, Japanese, and Malayan. While some of her films were not critically acclaimed, they were for the most part, commercial successes, and a testament to her box-office appeal. She displayed her multi-talented skills in drama and comedy, as well as singing and dancing. She held her own against some of the most able, charismatic and talented film stars of the era: Douglas Fairbanks, Sr., John Barrymore, Gary Cooper, Ramón Novarro, Lon Chaney, Sr., Edward G. Robinson, Walter Huston, Jimmy Durante, and Stan Laurel and Oliver Hardy, among many others.

Her next films were *Stand and Deliver* (1929, DeMille Prods.) with Rod La Roque; and *Masquerade* (1929, United Artists) with William Boyd. This was the last film directed by D.W. Griffith. She played a Mexican maiden who lives in Taos, New Mexico, who falls in love with a Euro-American immigrant (Gary Cooper) in the 1840s in Victor Fleming's silent film *Wolf Song* (1929, Paramount). During the film Vélez and Cooper began a torrid love affair, which apparently left profound feelings for each for the rest of their lives. The relationship did not survive, due to their temperamental differences.

More films followed: Vélez played the daughter of a murderer (Lon Chaney, Sr.) in Tod Browning's excellent *Where East Is East* (1929, MGM) set in Indo-China. She also made a Spanish-language version called *Oriente es Occidente* (1930, Universal). She played the woman seduced by a prince in Edwin Carewe's version of Leo Tolsoy's novel *Resurrection* (1931). She made the Spanish-language version entitled *Resurrecíon* (1931, Universal) with Gilbert Roland (billed as Luis Alonso). She was reunited with Gilbert Roland for another Spanish-language film *Hombres de mi Vida* (1932, Columbia).

Vélez played another native women in *Tiger Rose* (1929, Warner Bros) with Monte Blue; another Cuban maiden in Henry King's *Hell Harbor* (1929, Inspiration); an indigenous maiden in William Wyler's *The Storm* (1930, Universal); a Native American maiden in Cecil B. DeMille's remake of his own *The Squaw Man* (1931, MGM) with Warner Baxter; and a Cuban girl discarded by a U.S. Marine (played by opera singer Lawrence Tibbett) and befriended by Jimmy Durante, in MGM's *The Cuban Love Song*. The Cuban government formally protested the stinging stereotypes in the film.

Vélez co-starred with Melvyn Douglas and Leo Carrillo in *Broken Wing* (1932, Paramount) set in Mexico; and played the victim of mad and partially paralyzed man who controls an area in Africa in the horror film *Kongo* (1932, MGM) with Walter Huston.

During this low point in her film career, Jimmy Durante persuaded her to star with him in two Broadway successes: *Hot-Cha* (1932) and *Strike Me Pink* (1933). She made a triumphant return to comedy in the hilarious *The Half-Naked Truth* (1932, RKO). She played "Princess Exotica," a publicity-seeking actress, with the madcap Lee Tracy. Vélez then played a boisterous Latina bombshell in the fourth and weakest of the Quirt and Flagg (Victor McLaglen, Edmund Lowe) buddy films, *Hot Pepper* (1933, Fox), which was set in World War I. Vélez sang the title song, "Hot Pepper." She made a cameo appearance in Ed Sullivan's theatre extravaganza called *Mr. Broadway* (1933, Malcomar Prods.).

Vélez made another comedy, *Palooka* (1934, United Artists), inspired by the Hans Fisher comic boxer, in which she played a Spanish vamp, reuniting her with Jimmy Durante in a fast-paced and funny film, her last under her United Artists contract.

In 1934, Vélez was signed by MGM for two entirely different films. The first was *Laughing Boy* (1934, MGM) with Ramón Novarro, directed by the highly respected W.S. Van Dyke. It was based on Oliver La Farge's Pulitzer Prize–winning novel of the same name. The narrative focused on an indigenous couple in love who are destroyed by the pressures of racism and acculturation. It was one of the rare sympathetic films about native people of the era. Vélez played herself in the comedy *Hollywood Party* (1934, MGM) in which she was reunited with Oliver & Hardy, as well as Jimmy Durante. It also included Ted Healy and the Three Stooges.

Her next assignments were weak entries: *Strictly Dynamite* (1934, RKO) with Jimmy Durante; the British effort *The Morals of Marcus* (1935, Gaumont) in which she played a harem girl; and another British film, titled *Gypsy Melody* (1936, British Artists), in which she played a Gypsy girl stranded in London.

At this moment of a career decline, Vélez scored a personal triumph with an excellent comedic performance in the last of the Bert Wheeler and Robert Woolsey films, *High Flyers* (1937, RKO) wherein she upstaged everyone and did hilarious imitations of famous figures, including her rival Dolores Del Rio.

Vélez went to Mexico next to make Fernando De Fuentes popular *La Zadunga* (1937, Films Selectos) with Mexico's new heartthrob, Arturo De Cordova. She made a third British film, *He Loved an Actress* (1938, BL) playing a struggling showgirl pretending to be a cattle heiress in order to star in a film. The film was known as *Stardust* in the United States. It co-starred one of the greatest silent film comedians, Harry Langdon (1884–

1944), whose career had been destroyed by sound. Langdon was desperate for a comeback. *Variety* (May 25, 1938) noted that the "film is doomed to the sluff sports, too slow for a satisfactory musical as this country sees them." The film failed to resurrect Langdon's career. He faded into obscurity, reduced to doing supporting roles in shorts.

The film that made her a box-office draw again was *The Girl from Mexico* (1939, RKO), her first of eight *Mexican Spitfire* films. She played the temperamental Carmelita, and it featured the facially mobile Leon Errol. It was the first time that a Mexican or Latina actress starred in a film franchise. *Variety* (May 24, 1939) commented, "This Lupe Vélez starrer, with a dandy cast, excellent direction and general good production, will exceed its cost despite a mediocre story. It'll redeem, too, Miss Vélez's earlier less successful tries despite the fact that for her comeback she's been given a yarn off the cob, with only slight variations...."

Vélez was very pleased with her unexpected success, and to celebrate built a mansion ranch in Laurel Canyon; in her bedroom she stocked 75 canaries. She scored another hit with *Mexican Spitfire* (1939, RKO). *Variety* (December 13, 1939) noted that it was a "net concoction of comedy situations, running though many old, but still good Mack Sennett routines in a zippy and zestful unwinding...." While the subsequent Spitfire films fell into a predictable formula, they were continuous moneymakers. *Mexican Spitfire out West* (1940, RKO) was less successful.

Six Lessons from Madam Zonga (1941, RKO) used the *Mexican Spitfire* cast again, but had different characters and was set in Cuba; it was not a good film. Of *Mexican Spitfire's Baby* (1941, RKO) *Variety* (September 10, 1940) reported that the film "strains to catch up laughs and only mildly achieves that aim...."

Vélez was teamed with the fading but still brilliant John Barrymore in the very funny *Playmates* (1941, RKO). *Variety* (September 12, 1941) noted, "It's good entertainment. Lupe Vélez, as a femme bullfighter, helps the plot. She does the conga to 'Que Chica.'" Returning to her film franchise in *Mexican Spitfire at Sea* (1942, RKO) the film had Carmelita going to Hawaii to get and advertising contract for her husband (Buddy Rogers). It received a cool critical reception. *Variety* (January 7, 1942) commented that the "production is chockful of stock two-reel comedy gags, all easily recognizable."

The sixth film in the series was *Mexican Spitfire Sees a Ghost* (1942) and focused on the efforts of enemy agents to build a powerful bomb, which acknowledged World War II. The film's box office success brought the seventh film of the series *Mexican Spitfire's Elephant* (1942, RKO), of which *Variety* (August 5, 1942) wrote, "solid laugh entertainment and the best of the group.... Miss Vélez is the same explosive gal of previous issues of the series."

At this point, Vélez took a much-need respite from her film franchise with *Honolulu* (1941, Columbia) set in Hawaii and in which she played a singer going from a risqué nightclub act to becoming a beauty queen. She was reunited with her former co-star Leo Carrillo in this film.

In her next film she was teamed with the talented newcomer Eddie Albert, in *Ladies' Day* (1943, RKO). Albert played a useless baseball player who is in the throes of a love affair with Vélez. The eight and last of the *Mexican Spitfire* films was *Mexican Spitfire's Blessed Event* (1943, RKO). *Variety* (July 15, 1943) commented, the "finale of the series displays the usual complications on light framework for displays of broadcast farce and horseplay." Another comedy followed, *The Redhead from Manhattan* (1943, Columbia), in which she played twins.

4. The Noble Savage and the White Man's Enemy (1920–1929)

Lupe Vélez's final film was the Mexican film *Nana* (1944, Grovas Prods.), based on the famous novel by Emile Zola of the same name, about the life of a prostitute in the 19th century. It was directed by the noted Mexican film director Roberto Gavaldón.

Miss Vélez's private life was apparently unhappy, despite her wide popularity and success. On December 14, 1944, she was found dead, an apparent suicide due to an overdose of sleeping pills. The motive, according to police reports, was a three-month pregnancy and a broken relationship. She was buried in Mexico City, next to Lucha Reyes, a legendary *ranchera* singer who had committed suicide the year before. All the notables of Mexican cinema were present: Dolores Del Rio, Arturo De Cordova (a previous love), Cantinflas, and Jorge Negrete, among others. From Hollywood, came her former husband (1933 to 1938), Olympic star and "Tarzan" film icon Johnny Weissmuller, along with Gilbert Roland. It was a sad ending to one so full of the love of life. Her legacy, however, remains forever in film.

5

In the Way of Progress (1930–1939)

The 1930s was the apex of Hollywood's Golden Age (1920–1950). During the early part of the decade, the film industry underwent the transition from silent to talking film, an evolution of film stars and filmmakers, and changes in public tastes and trends. In the first all-talking film *The Jazz Singer* (1927, Warner Bros.), Al Jolson boasted to the audience, "You ain't seen nothing yet!" For Native Americans (and Mexicans), however, their film images would get predictably worse and more derogatory.

For the most part, the Hollywood films of the 1930s provided escapist entertainment and reflected little of the tumultuous political and social issues of the time (at least not in a serious manner). Abroad, dark clouds began to gather, as fascism and militarism were on the rise. Adolf Hitler became chancellor in Germany; Benito Mussolini consolidated his fascist state in Italy; Francisco Franco seized control of the Spanish Republic; and in Japan, militarists rose to power and invaded Manchuria. In the Americas, the U.S. Marines finally were finally removed from Nicaragua in 1933. In Mexico, President Lázaro Cárdenas nationalized the U.S.– and British-owned oil fields. In the meantime, U.S. foreign policy coddled three dictators out of self-interest: Anastasia Somoza of Nicaragua, Rafael Leónidas Trujillo of the Dominican Republic, and Fulgencio Batista of Cuba.

In the United States, the Great Depression had reached its worst point by 1933, by which time "one-third of the nation" (at least officially) of the labor force was unemployed, living in makeshift communities christened "Hoovervilles." Others, like the Okies of Oklahoma, became perpetual migrant workers in a devastated land. Prohibition was finally repealed by Congress with the Twenty-First Amendment. The U.S. labor movement continued to organize and press for the right to unionize (National Labor Relations Act) and the eight-hour day (Fair Labor Standards Act).

Race relations in the nation worsened during the Great Depression. Segregation continued to be the law of the land, *de jure* in the South and *de facto* in the elsewhere. Native Americans, Mexicans, African Americans, and Asians were the primary victims. Mexicans became the object of a nativist backlash that resulted in the repatriation of more than one million Mexicans (both U.S. born and Mexican born).[1]

NATIVE AMERICAN FILM IMAGES IN THE 1930S

The dominant film image of Native Americans in the 1930s remained that of people who obstructed Euro-American progress. Historical and western films portrayed native people as getting in the way of Manifest Destiny and the westward expansion. Films set in the present depicted native peoples as backward and objects of mockery.

During the 1930s, Native American roles were overwhelmingly segregated in western movies, both big-budget and B-films. The key image of native peoples in westerns was that of screaming, violent savages. One movie, *Annie Oakley* (1935, RKO), chronicled the adventurous life of sharpshooter Annie Oakley (Barbara Stanwyck), a member of Buffalo Bill's Wild West Show. The film documented Oakley's real-life friendship with Sitting Bull (Chief Thunderbird), who adopted her as a daughter in 1884. However, it also romanticized the imprisonment and suffering of the great native leader. *The Texas Rangers* (1936, Paramount) depicted the 1800s adventures of the famous law enforcement group, in which Native Americans are routinely compared to "rotten apples."

Wells Fargo (1937, Paramount) celebrated the fictional life of a man named Ramsay (Joel McCrea) who develops banking and transportation business endeavors, despite the inexplicable resistance of violence-prone Native Americans. John Ford's *Drums Along the Mohawk* (1939, 20th Century–Fox) presented an ethnocentric perspective of indigenous resistance to the encroachment of European settlers in the 1700s. These images and scenarios were established and perpetuated by the key westerns of the decade: *Cimarron* (1931, RKO); *The Plainsman* (1936, Paramount); *The Last of the Mohicans* (1936, United Artists); *Union Pacific* (1939, Paramount); and *Stagecoach* (1939, Republic). In addition to these, the studios produced hundreds of both A- and B-westerns too numerous to list here.

Infrequently in the 1930s, some films demonstrated a passing sympathy for the plight of Native Americans. In the B-western titled *The Fighting Cowboy* (1933, Superior), the cowboy action star Buffalo Bill, Jr. (real name Jay Wilsey), while investigating a murder, is assisted by Squaw Mary (Marin Sais) in resolving the crime. The film *Neath Arizona Skies* (1934, Lone Star) features a young John Wayne as the guardian of a half-indigenous girl (Sheila Jean Rickert). Wayne helps the girl search for her white father and cash in on a $50,000 oil lease from her deceased mother. In the film *Behold My Wife!* (1934, Paramount), a wealthy white man (Gene Raymond) marries an Apache woman (a miscast Sylvia Sidney) to seek revenge on the affluent family who destroyed his marriage. (Another film version had previously been made in 1920.) This film featured the legendary Native American athlete Jim Thorpe as a chief and Charles Stevens as an Apache herder.

In *Dodge City* (1938, Warner Bros.), Wade Hatton (Errol Flynn) and his men apprehend a notorious outlaw (Bruce Cabot) for illegally slaughtering buffalos for their hides and murdering Native Americans. *Susannah of the Mounties* (1939, 20th Century–Fox) featured the survivor of a native attack, the titular Susannah (Shirley Temple), who subsequently develops a deep friendship with Little Chief (played by Blackfoot actor Martin Goodrider) and helps to bring the white and indigenous communities together. The friendship depicted in the film was replicated in real life when the Blackfoot tribe made Shirley Temple an honorary member of their tribe and named her "Bright Shining Star." *Juárez* (1939, Warner Bros.) was a film about the much-revered Benito Juárez, the first Mexican Native American (Zapotec) president, who fought a war against French intervention in the 1860s. It was the first Hollywood film about an authentic Mexican national hero.

A handful of films depicted native people in an urban environment. *Massacre* (1934, Warner Bros.) documented the dramatic arc of a Lakota who leaves the reservation, becomes famous as a Wild West show marksman, and returns to his place of origin. The film *Call*

Her Savage (1931, Fox Film Corp.) depicted the plight of a young mixed-blood woman who falls prey to all the vices of the white world. Cecil B. DeMille's third remake of *The Squaw Man* (1931, Paramount) was set in the early 1900s and explored the trials and tribulations of miscegenation. In turn, *Laughing Boy* (1934, MGM) documented the love story of a native couple destroyed by prejudice and vice in the Euro-American world.

Also of note from this decade were two semi-documentary films: the film *Eskimo* (1934, MGM), set in remote areas of Alaska, and *The Silent Enemy* (1931, Burden-Chanler Prods.), which was set in the pre–Columbian Ojibway world, around the Great Lakes area.

Native American actors made numerous efforts to improve their working conditions in the film industry. In 1936, Luther Standing Bear (a Lakota activist, writer, and actor discussed in the previous chapter) founded the Indian Actors Association. This organization sought to educate the public about the misrepresentation of indigenous peoples on the screen, achieve equal pay, and establish a "pool" of authentic native actors. The group also provided support and funding for unemployed native actors. They raised money through powwows, membership dues, and performances. Standing Bear led the group until 1939. Thereafter, Bill Hazlet and Many Treaties took on leadership roles.

Standing Bear's younger brother, Henry Standing Bear, also organized an activist group named the Society of American Indians, which produced pageants and plays. These events highlighted native performers and the richness and truth about Native Americans. The National League for Justice to American Indians (NLJAI) likewise worked to lobby and educate film studios about the indigenous talent and the efforts of the Indian Actors Association. A later group, the Indian Actors Workshop was founded by actor Jay Silverheels in 1963, for the purpose of training actors for films and television. These and other groups testified to the sense of agency within the Native American community and their determination to improve their lives.

Representative Films

The Big Trail (1930, Fox Film Corporation)

Raoul Walsh's *The Big Trail* was an epic film chronicling a caravan of Euro-American settlers moving westward. It emphasized how Native Americans were the main impediment of this westward movement.

The film was directed by the legendary Raoul Walsh (1887–1980), a former actor who helmed scores of films from 1913 to 1964. Five writers were assigned to this film: Hal G. Evans (story) and screenwriters Florence Postal, Maria Boyle, Fred Sersen, and Jack Peabody. The impressive cinematography was undertaken by Arthur Edeson and Lucien Ardriot.

The Big Trail cost an estimated $1,250,000—an enormous amount at that time, especially considering that it had no major film stars to attract moviegoers. The film was shot in a widescreen format using 70-mm film that was dubbed "70 mm Grandeur film." It had first been used in the *Fox Movietone Follies of 1929*. It was one of several widescreen processes invented by the major studios with the advent of sound at the end of the 1920s and in the early 1930s. However, the process proved costly for theaters, especially in light of the Great Depression. As a result, *The Big Trail* was a financial failure, and the film drifted into obscurity. The widescreen process would not be brought back by Hollywood studios until the film *The Robe* (20th Century–Fox) in 1953.

The leading parts were played by newcomer John Wayne (who had been recommended by director John Ford) and Marguerite Churchill. Wayne was only twenty-three years old at that time. For Wayne, the film's financial failure resulted in his relegation into scores of B-westerns until John Ford's 1939 film *Stagecoach* (United Artists). Well-known stage actor Tyrone Power, Sr. (in his only talking film), played the villainous trapper Red Flack. He was the father of later matinee idol Tyrone Power.

Native American actors were cast in small parts, including Chief John Big Tree, Nino Cochise (a grandson of the legendary Apache chief Cochise), and Charles Stevens.

The narrative is set between 1837 and 1845 and involves the westward movement of Euro-American settlers in a wagon train along the Oregon Trail. Breck Coleman (Wayne) is a fur trapper looking for Red Flack (Tyrone Power, Sr.), who he suspects killed an older trapper who was his friend. While returning to Missouri, Coleman is approached by white settlers about leading their wagon train to the Oregon area. He agrees to lead the group because doing so allows him to search for Flack.

Along the way, Coleman becomes romantically involved with Ruth Cameron (Churchill). Flack and his friend Thorpe (Ian Keith) also join the group with the intention of killing Coleman to silence him. The journey ends in the Willamette Valley in Oregon. The villains end up getting the typical frontier justice, and Coleman and Ruth make a life together.

The Big Trail was an ambiguous film. Among other things, the character of Coleman (John Wayne) has lived with Native Americans. In one scene Coleman tells a group of admiring children, "The Indians are my friends."

The film generally received positive reviews. Mordaunt Hall wrote in the *New York Times* (November 2, 1930), "The spectacular side of this production is accomplished with true artistry a fine sense of contrasts…. The juvenile roles are played by Marguerite Churchill and John Wayne. It is not, however, a picture in which a few participants count for much."[2]

The Silent Enemy (1930, Burden-Chanler Prods.)

The film *The Silent Enemy* was the first U.S. movie made with an all–Native American cast. Except for a spoken introduction at the beginning, it is a silent film.

The Silent Enemy was directed by H.P. Carter (1856–1972). This was the only film Carter directed, although he was part of the crew of the 1932 French film *A Father Without Knowing It*. The story for *The Silent Enemy* was written by W. Douglas Burdern, and the scenario was by Richard Carver and Julian Johnson. It was produced by W. Douglas Burden and William C. Chanler, who banded together to create Burden-Chanler Productions. The film was distributed by Paramount Pictures. The stunning cinematography was the work of Marcel Le Picard. The film's length was 84 minutes (the original version is reputed to have been some six hours long).

The film begins with the spoken introduction from Chief Chauncey Yellow Robe, who portrays the old Ojibway chief Chetoga. The narrative follows the plight of a group of Ojibway and their struggle to subsist and survive in the harsh environment of northern

Ontario, Canada. The film depicts the everyday activities of fishing, gathering, and hunting. The silent enemy is defined as hunger.

One of the unique things about *The Silent Enemy*, among several, is that it captured in an anthropological manner the culture of the Ojibway people in their original homeland before it was destroyed further by Euro-American intrusion. This film has often been compared to Robert J. Flaherty's *Nanook of the North* (1922), a documentary film about the Inuk in the Canadian Artic.

The all–Native American cast was headed by Chief Buffalo Child Long Lance as the highly respected hunter Baluk; Mary Alice Nelson Archanbaud as Neewa, the mother; Cheeka as Cheeka, the young boy; and Yellow Robe as Chetoga. Unfortunately, Yellow Robe contracted pneumonia while in New York City and died on April 6, 1930, before *The Silent Enemy* was released four months later on August 2.

The film received glowing reviews. Mordaunt Hall wrote in the *New York Times* (May 20, 1930), "An engrossing silent film study of the Ojibway Indian's struggle for food before the coming of Columbus.... The performances of the other Indians are all remarkably natural. Some of them had never beheld a motion picture camera until they found themselves acting before one."[3]

The Squaw Man (1931, MGM)

The Squaw Man was a perennial film for almost three decades. It was the last film that Cecil B. DeMille made at MGM before working exclusively for Paramount Pictures. This was also the third time DeMille had worked on *The Squaw Man*, as he had co-directed the first film version in 1914 and helmed the second in 1918.

The film's narrative was based on the popular play by Edwin Milton Royle (see the 1914 film entry for more information). It focused on the tribulations of an Englishman, James Wingate, wrongly accused of embezzling money from an orphanage trust. He is forced to flee to a remote corner of the world (in this version to Arizona), where he is befriended by a Native American woman named Naturich (Lupe Vélez), who kills Cash Hawkins (Charles Bickford), a villainous thug. James and Naturich fall in love and have a son (Dickie Moore). When Lady Diana (Eleanor Boardman) and Sir John Applegate (Roland Young) arrive to tell James that he has been exonerated, the couple's life is thrown into turmoil. In addition, the sheriff and a vigilante group are going to arrest Naturich for the killing of Hawkins. Diana, who has always loved James, is crushed.

Sir John convinces James that his son's "cultural heritage" will be lost in the native world, and the latter agrees to send him to be educated in England as a gentleman. Naturich subsequently kills herself when she realizes that she has lost her son and she will soon be apprehended.

The third version of *The Squaw Man* has mixed results. There is a palpable downbeat feeling of doom throughout the film. However, two performances enrich it. One is the performance of the much-maligned Mexican Native American actress Lupe Vélez. She provides a refreshing, sensitive, heartwarming, and touching performance far removed from the frantic mannerisms of her Mexican Spitfire roles. However, as written, the role is limited by the image that native women must be docile and meek.

The second performance that stands out is that of the luminous Eleanor Boardman (1898–1991) as Lady Diana. She brings the inner despair of a hopeless love that is utterly wrecked at the end of the film. Boardman was one of the top film stars of the 1920s and perhaps best remembered for King Vidor's *The Crowd* (1926). An acrimonious divorce from Vidor compelled her to flee the spotlight and retire early from films.

Warner Baxter, a huge film star at the time, was the male lead. As always, his acting is good, but as the role is written, there is a pervasive inner sadness and depression that limits his performance. James is already a broken man who is revived briefly when he falls in love with Naturich, only to lose both his wife and son soon thereafter. The film's direction appears uncertain and wayward at times. It lacks Cecil B. DeMille's typical vigorous and boisterous style.

The film was shot on location in Arizona, but there is little of the beautiful landscape that shaped its people and history. Reportedly, the shooting costs escalated beyond $722,000 and resulted in loss of some $150,000 upon release.[4] However, to be fair, the film was released during one of the worst years of the Great Depression. In addition, the film's downbeat story and ending contributed to its commercial failure. DeMille's directorial career hit a downturn with the film. However, his fortunes would change with *The Sign of the Cross* (1932, Paramount), an epic film set in Nero's Rome.

The *New York Times* review by Mordaunt Hall (September 19, 1931) noted, "The seams of age shine through; it is agreeable and expert melodrama.... The other principle parts are more than adequately played by the lovely Eleanor Boardman as the English peeress, Lupe Vélez as the Indian Girl.... Warner Baxter's performance is delivered with his customary ease and sense of fitness."[5]

A recent review by Felicia Feaster on the Turner Classic Movies website noted, "The original two *Squaw Man* productions had been cast with Native American actors, according to DeMille's wishes, to generate authenticity. By the time of ... 1931 the more standard Hollywood practice was to use non–Native Americans to play such roles, including Mexican actress Velez as Naturich."[6]

Cimarron (1931, RKO Radio Pictures)

One of the most popular westerns of the early decade was *Cimarron*, based on the best-selling novel by Edna Ferber. Ferber would later write another sprawling novel called *Giant*, which would go on to become another important film success.

The film was directed by the highly regarded Wesley Ruggles (1889–1972), who directed such films such as *Bolero* (1934, Paramount Pictures) and *True Confession* (1937, Paramount Pictures). The screenplay was written by Louis Sarecky and Howard Estabrook. RKO Radio Pictures invested some $1.5 million in this film in the midst of the Great Depression.

The cast was headlined by the then very popular Richard Dix, who had played native heroes in *The Vanishing American* (1925, Paramount Pictures) and *The Redskin* (1929, Paramount Pictures). The female leads were played by the fast-rising Irene Dunne and the fading Estelle Taylor, who had been popular in the silent era. This film was one of the few westerns to win the Academy Awards for Best Picture (contemporary critics feel it was undeserving); Best Writing, Adaptation (Howard Estabrook); and Best Art Direction (Max Ree). Both Dix and Dunne were nominated for Best Actor and Best Actress, respectively.

Playwright and novelist Edna Ferber (1885–1868) wrote stories characterized by strong-willed women who have agency over their lives, challenging the traditional role assigned to women. In *Giant*, the character of Leslie challenges the male oil barons and the neglect of the impoverished Mexican population. In *Cimarron*, Sabra becomes the prime mover of her family when her husband Yancey disappears for years at a time. She stays with him despite the highs and lows of their lives.

Cimarron is set during the Oklahoma Land Rush of 1889 (created by the infamous Homestead Act of 1862 and the Indian Appropriations Act of 1889), which allowed native land to be taken away and given to white settlers. In the film, Yancey Cravat (Richard Dix) and his new wife Sabra (Irene Dunne) and son Cim (Junior Johnson) become part of the mass of Euro-Americans who join the large land rush. In the process, Dixie Lee (Estelle Taylor), a prostitute, is able to grab the land that Yancey had aspired to claim.

Later, Yancey and his family moves to the town of Osage, where he establishes the *Osage Wigwam*, a newspaper that seeks to fight corruption and injustice. Yancey is compelled to kill Lon Yountis (Stanley Fields), a notorious outlaw who had murdered a previous newspaper publisher. When the town is peopled by a gang of thugs, Yancey also kills the Kid (William Collier, Jr.), a former friend, in order to save the town. Guilt ridden by the killings, Yancey leaves his family. In the meantime, Sabra raises her children, becomes the newspaper's publisher, and is elected as the first female congresswoman.

The Oklahoma Territory becomes a state in 1907 and undergoes an oil boom. Native American tribes also gain, and Yancey (having returned) strongly advocates for their right to benefit from the economic upturn. Yancey disappears again for several years, which fractures his marriage to Sabra. When he reappears again, their son has become romantically involved with a Native American woman, though his wife opposes the interracial relationship. Once more, Yancey disappears for several years.

Yancey returns one last time and reunites with his wife. Later, after an explosion, Yancey saves the lives of several oil men. However, he dies in the process.

The film *Cimarron* received high praise from most critics of the time. The *Motion Picture Magazine* (March 4, 1931) wrote, "A great and worthy effort, this transcription of early Oklahoma life will be hailed as one of the high-spots of the year." Most critics especially praised the spectacular cinematic re-creation of the land rush scenes.

However, seen today, the film appears condescending to Native Americans and outdated in its perspective of the monumental land grab. Yancey appears to be a person of integrity, if at times vastly irresponsible as the patriarch of a family. His wife is a strong-willed but flawed woman deeply prejudiced against native people. She reprimands her young son Cim for playing "with those dirty Indians." Later, when he is about to marry a native woman, she is strongly against him doing so. By contrast, Yancey refuses to become involved in a scheme to deny Native Americans of their rightful land once oil is discovered there. He uses his newspaper to educate others about the plan and also advocates for U.S. citizenship on behalf of native peoples. He likewise supports his son's marriage to a Native American woman when his wife is strongly opposed. However, what the film lacks are native characters who take the initiative and agency over their lives. Here, it is white characters who intercede for them and are the movers of their history.

This film also contains a stinging stereotype of a black servant (played by Eugene Jackson). He is depicted as a slow-witted and shuffling figure throughout the film. The portrayal of the Jewish tailor Sol Levy (played by George E. Stone) is presented with exaggerated mannerisms and behavior that is insulting.

Despite the fact that the story was set in heart of native land, the Native American characters and performers were minimal. They included Clara Hunt (a full-blooded Chippewa) in the role of an Indian girl and Apache Bill Russell, among the very few.

End of the Trail (1932, Columbia)

End of the Trail was an unusual B-western starring the popular western film star Tim McCoy. This film took a progressive and sympathetic view of Native Americans. It was directed by D. Ross Lederman (1894–1972), a former second unit director in the silent era who (after the coming of sound) directed scores of B-westerns and television westerns, and written by Stuart Anthony, who specialized in scripting B-westerns. The script was based on a story by Zane Grey. The film is only 61 minutes in length.

The film's star, Tim McCoy (1891–1978), had served in World War I and would go on to serve in World War II. He had a very sympathetic view of Native Americans and one time was made "High Eagle" by the Arapaho tribe from the Wind River Reservation in Wyoming. He also became an expert in indigenous sign language. McCoy starred or co-starred in 93 films between 1925 and 1965. His westerns were action-packed films, often using the very best stuntmen of the era. By the time he made *End of the Trail*, he was already 41 years of age, considerably older than most of the B-western stars of the time. His face has a withered quality of resolve and regret that adds to his convincing portrayal.

The narrative is set in the Old West of the 1800s. Captain Travers (McCoy) and his U.S. Cavalry platoon are unexpectedly attacked by a war party of Native Americans. Travers is the only survivor of the battle. Later, he learns that Major Jenkins (Wheeler Oakman) has betrayed him. Travers is framed and accused of selling guns to the Native Americans and dishonorably dismissed from active duty. However, before he leaves, he makes a moving speech denouncing the numerous treaties (including the Treaty of Fort Laramie) that the U.S. government has broken and the victimization of Native Americans.

Together with his young son, Travers leaves the fort and, on the way, is joined by another soldier. A cavalry patrol later mistakes the trio for a war party, and the boy is killed. Travers goes to live with the native people and is welcomed by Chief Grey Bear (Chief White Eagle). He learns to respect them as human beings. He also falls in love with the native maiden Luana (Luana Walters).

Travers is subsequently captured by Jenkins and taken to a fort. Native warriors then attack the fort. Colonel Burke (Lafe McKee), the commanding officer, realizes that they will be overwhelmed and defeated. He goes to Travers and asks him to help him make peace with the attacking natives.

The leading native role of Chief Grey Bear was played by Chief White Eagle. Many Arapahos were hired as extras. The film was shot on location in the areas of Lander and Little Wind River, Wyoming.

Two endings were shot for the film: one apparently was a downbeat and tragic ending to the narrative, while the other was more conventional. Both endings are reported to still exist.

Call Her Savage (1932, Fox Film Corporation)

The film *Call Her Savage* is an unusual film in that the main protagonist is a mixed-race woman who is the object of continued calamity (both sexual and criminal) and personal misfortune.

This film was made before the Motion Picture Production Code censorship (also called the Hays Code) was enforced in mid–1934 to regulate the content of U.S. films. *Call Her Savage* was directed by John Frances Dillon and written by Edwin J. Burke, based on the novel by Tiffany Thayer.

The title role was played by Clara Bow (1905–1965), a very popular film star in the 1920s. She became a sex symbol and represented the resilient, independent, and sexually liberated woman of the Roaring Twenties. However, her career declined with the advent of talking films. *They Call Her Savage* was intended to be her comeback film, but it failed to resurrect her career.

The narrative takes place in Texas and revolves around a rebellious young woman named Nasa Springel, who is of mixed Native American and Caucasian heritage (though at first she is unaware of her ancestry). She begins a love-hate relationship with her father's ranch foreman Moonglow (Gilbert Roland), another mixed blood. Her father sends her to Chicago in hopes of taming her wild and careless ways. There she marries a useless wastrel Lawrence Crosby (Monroe Owsley) out of convenience. Crosby in turn dumps her for a new girlfriend (Thelma Todd). Nasa goes through his money and lives a loose and promiscuous lifestyle. In the meantime, she has become pregnant with Crosby's baby.

After her father disowns her, Nasa is reduced to poverty, and she resorts to prostitution to survive. Later, her child dies in a fire in her boarding house. She returns to Texas when her mother is dying and finally learns that she is a "half-breed." The narrative promotes the idea that her Native American genes are why she has had such carnal and savage impulses. She concludes that only a relationship with Moonglow, a half-breed—someone like herself—can bring her happiness.

The film was a box-office success, though it did not salvage Clara Bow's film career. Critics of the time gave her good reviews. Mordaunt Hall, writing in the *New York Times* (November 25, 1932), said, "Miss Bow does quite well by the role of this fiery-tempered impulsive Nasa, but whether the flow of incidents makes for satisfactory entertainment is a matter of opinion."[7]

They Call Her Savage was daring film for the era in that it depicts miscegenation, homosexuality, prostitution, and promiscuity. However, the film perpetuates the stereotype that indigenous people are noble savages, doomed to failure and unhappiness due to their culture and bloodline.

Massacre (1932, Warner Bros.)

This film chronicles the tale of Joe Thunderhorse (Richard Barthelmess), a Sioux and graduate of the federal Indian school at Carlisle, Pennsylvania. He is a popular star of the Wild West Show at the 1933 Chicago World's Fair. Joe is financially successful, self-assured, and a sophisticated bachelor who wears monogrammed, white, double-breasted suits, as well as a huge Stetson hat, and drives a custom-built roadster. He is popular with white socialites. One of them remarks, "I'd be that chief's squaw any day."

Joe maintains two different personas: the full regalia native in the Wild West Show and that of the white-assimilated counterpart. He is totally removed from his people's pressing problems.

It is only when Joe pays a visit to his dying father in the reservation that he finally becomes aware of the widespread injustice and rampant corruption. With the assistance of his new native girlfriend (Ann Dvorak) and Franklin D. Roosevelt's commissioner for Indian Affairs, he takes an active role in bettering his people's circumstances. The film documents numerous instances of prejudice and injustice in the everyday life in the reservation. The injustices inflicted on Native Americans in *The Vanishing American* were attributed to the evil of a few men and their ambition, while this film makes the point that the impoverished status of modern-day natives is a result of corrupt government and capitalist interests (lumber, oil, etc.).

Joe becomes a fugitive due to his efforts to enforce change, traveling to Washington, D.C., with the police on his heels. There he voices his newfound consciousness before a U.S. Senate committee: "You used to shoot 'em Indian down, now you cheat and starve him and kill him off by dirt and disease. It's a massacre any way you look at it."

The film ends in the idealism of FDR and the New Deal in the midst of the Great Depression. It proposes that the injustices faced by natives will be alleviated by the "new administration in Washington."

Massacre is one of two key films of the 1930s to portray modern-day Native Americans sympathetically. The other film was *Laughing Boy* (1934, MGM), based on the Pulitzer Prize–winning novel by Oliver La Farge and starring Ramón Navarro and Lupe Vélez. Despite its flaws, *Massacre* is a radical film within the context of other Hollywood products of its time. It is part of a body of work in the 1930s of socially conscious films, most of them produced by Warner Brothers. These films included *Wild Boys of the Road* (1933, Warner Bros.), about homeless youth in the Depression; *Our Daily Bread* (1934, United Artists), about a socialist commune; *Black Legion* (1937, Warner Bros.), about a domestic terrorist group similar to the Ku Klux Klan; and *I Am a Fugitive from a Chain Gang* (1932, Warner Bros.), about brutal prison conditions.

One of the prime movers of the film *Massacre* was its star Richard Barthelmess (1895–1963). Although he is almost forgotten today, he enjoyed enormous popularity between 1917 and 1935. Well known in Hollywood for his progressive politics, his best work remains the socially conscious films that he made in the late 1920s and early 1930s. Besides *Massacre*, they include *The Patent Leather Kid* (1926, First National), about an ambitious working-class boxer and World War I soldier; *Heroes for Sale* (1933, Warner Bros.), about drug-addicted World War I veterans; *The Last Flight* (1931, Warner Bros.), about a group of self-destructive and traumatized World War I pilots; *The Dawn Patrol* (1930, Warner Bros.), an anti–World War I film; and *A Modern Hero* (1934, Warner Bros.), about a ruthless big business tycoon.

Massacre was directed by Alan Crosland. It was based on a novel by Robert Gessner. The screenplay for *Massacre* was penned by Sheridan Gibney (b. 1908), who had written *I Am a Fugitive from a Chain Gang* and earned an Academy Award for *The Story of Louis Pasteur* (1938, Warner Bros.). The evocative cinematography was done by George Barnes and the film was produced by Robert Presnell.

Massacre, previously forgotten by film historians, has recently been rediscovered and reassessed. John E. O'Connor noted of the film, "In *Massacre*, Warner executives found a set of ideas around which they could create a successful movie. At the same time, they popularized the problems of the Indians and raised the public consciousness."[8] Upon its initial release, *Variety* (January 2, 1934) commented, "Persecution of the redskin under the white administrators of Indian Affairs in the southwest is the not-so timely subject of '*Massacre*.' Film attempts to modernize the tepid subject by setting the action at the time of the last Chicago World's fair. Richard Barthelmess stars as an Indian with Broadway playboy ideas, and upon his shoulders rests the assignment of drawing about all '*Massacre*' will get."[9]

Eskimo (1934, MGM)

Eskimo was the first Hollywood film completely spoken in a Native American language. It was shot on location in Alaska and introduced one of the early Native American film stars, Ray Mala.

The film was directed by the noted W. S. Van Dyke (1849–1943), who had previously directed the highly acclaimed *White Shadows in the South Seas* (1928, MGM), a film about the impact of Europeans on a South Seas island, and numerous other critical and commercial successes. The screenplay was the work of John Lee Mahin, based on the book *Der Eskimo and Die Flucht ins weisse Land* by Peter Freuchen (a noted Danish writer and explorer). The impressive cinematography was done by Clyde De Vinna, who had won an Academy Award for his work on *White Shadows in the South Seas* and who went on to a long film career.

Eskimo used the Inupiat language for the first time in film. Both Van Dyke and producer Hunt Stromberg wanted to use Inupiat instead of English. In the end, they decided to use the native language with English subtitles. The film took some seventeen months to complete.

The studio cast authentic Eskimos for the roles, the majority of whom had never seen a camera or a film. Ray Mala played the lead role of Mala; Lulu Wong was Aba; Lotus Long was Iva; and Iris Yamaoka was the Second Wife. Van Dyke himself was cast as Inspector White.

The narrative was set in Alaska and depicted the events of everyday life in Eskimo culture. The film documents the epic 500-mile journey of Mala (Ray Mala) and his wife Aba (Lulu Wong) and family through the Alaskan tundra. Mala intends to trade furs with a European whaling ship that is exploring the region in Tjarnak. However, the ship captain (Edward Hearn) turns out to be a conniving individual who to wants to take advantage of Mala. The captain's malevolence results in his rape of Mala's wife, and Mala is compelled to kill him. The Royal Canadian Mounties are alerted, and they organize a manhunt to capture Mala. They apprehend him, but he escapes. Against all odds, Mala is able to return to his family deep in the tundra. (There is one factual error in the narrative: namely, the Royal Canadian Mounties do not operate in Alaska.)

Eskimo received excellent reviews, but its large budget of $955,000 and its subject matter resulted in a box-office failure. The film won the first Academy Award for Best Film Editing (Conrad A. Nervig). Mordaunt Hall, in the *New York Times* (November 15, 1933), wrote, "It is an exciting and often grim melodrama.... It is a remarkable film, one that often awakens wonder as to how the camera men were able to photograph some of the scenes and record the impressive sounds."[10]

The Plainsmen (1936, Paramount) and *Union Pacific* (1939, Paramount)

After Cecil B. DeMille had completed his third version *The Squaw Man* in 1931, he turned his attention to several historical epics and dramas. He directed and produced two epic westerns focusing on Manifest Destiny and the westward march of the United States: *The Plainsmen* and *Union Pacific*.

The Plainsmen was a big-budget western centering on the interplay between three legendary white characters of the Old West: Wild Bill Hickok, Calamity Jane, and William

5. In the Way of Progress (1930–1939)

"Buffalo Bill" Cody. The screenplay was written by Lynn Riggs, Waldemar Young, and Harold Lamb, based on the *Wild Bill Hickok* stories by Frank J. Wilstach.

DeMille played fast and loose with the history of the era. Adding to this was the fact that by the time of Hickok, Jane, and Cody had all died, numerous dime novelists (most of them Easterners who had never been out west) had already misrepresented the true history and created a mythology of the Old West.

The narrative is set in the Great Plains several years after the Civil War. After his discharge from the Union Army, William Hickok (Gary Cooper) heads back to the Great Plains, where he has a chance encounter with his friend, former army scout Buffalo Bill Cody (James Ellison), and Cody's new wife. They meet Calamity Jane (Jean Arthur), the driver of the stagecoach that takes them to Hays City, Kansas. There Hickok discovers that John Lattimer (Charles Bickford) is selling repeating rifles to Cheyenne warriors and reports the news to General Armstrong Custer (John Miljan).

Subsequently, Hickok and Jane are captured by the Cheyenne. Yellow Hand (Victor Varconi) informs them that his people have gone to war because white settlers have taken over their land and are annihilating the buffalo. Yellow Hand promises to release them if they tell him where the ammunition train is located. When the Cheyenne ambush said train, Hickok and Jane are trapped with a group of soldiers. General Custer rescues them. Eventually, Hickok tracks down Lattimer in Deadwood and kills him (after Custer is defeated at the Little Big Horn battle). In the end, however, Hickok is shot in the back by a Lattimer informant named Jack McCall (Porter Hall) while playing cards with his killer.

The backdrop to the film was the then popular stereotype of Native Americans as the main impediment to the settling of the west by Euro-Americans. There is one scene, however, that humanizes the native people. This is when Yellow Hand (Paul Harvey) tells Hickok and Jane that his people have been compelled to fight whites because they have stolen their land and slaughtered the buffalo, despite the signed treaties. However, the truth does not move any of the white protagonists to alter their behavior.

The film's large cast did not feature any indigenous actors in any important roles. The only native performers were cast in bit parts. They included Anthony Quinn, in his first speaking role, as a Cheyenne warrior; Monte Blue in an uncredited role; Sonny Chorre as Indian #2 with Painted Horse; Charles Stevens as Indian Charley; and Greg Whitespear as Indian #4 with Painted Horse. The character of Painted Horse was played by a white actor, Victor Varconi, and Yellow Hand was played Paul Harvey.

DeMille's epic western *Union Pacific* focuses on the building of the transcontinental railroad and the political chicanery behind the scenes of the undertaking. At this time, big-budget westerns had been pretty much dead on arrival at the box office. Raoul Walsh's *The Big Trail* (1930), which introduced a young John Wayne, had proven to be a box-office disaster (even with a widescreen format). *The Plainsmen* in 1937 had revived interest in the genre. However, 1939 would become the true turning point for the western genre. That year saw the release of a series of memorable films—Michael Curtiz's *Dodge City* (Warner Bros.); Henry King's *Jesse James* (20th Century–Fox); George Marshall's *Destry Rides Again* (Universal); and John Ford's *Stagecoach* (United Artists)—which had brought back the western in a big way. DeMille's *Union Pacific* came out a few months later.

DeMille chose two big stars to star in his railroad epic: Barbara Stanwyck as the headstrong Irish American Mollie Monahan, and Joel McCrea as the rough and ready Captain Jeff Butler. He rounded out his cast with Brian Donlevy as the villainous Sid Campeau, newcomers Robert Preston and Anthony Quinn as two Campeau henchmen, and an assortment of capable character actors like Akim Tamiroff, Lynne Overman, Robert Barrat, and newcomer Evelyn Keyes.

Native American actors were reduced to bit parts: Monte Blue (an Indian—uncredited); Sonny Chorre (an Indian—uncredited); Ray Mala (Indian Finding Cigar Store Indian); Charles Stevens (Indian Shooting Mollie); Chief Thundercloud (an Indian); and George Whitehorse (an Indian). Several non-native actors played other Native American bit parts, including Iron Eyes Cody.

The narrative is set in 1862, the year when President Abraham Lincoln signed the Pacific Railroad Act, thus beginning the unification of the nation by the transcontinental railroad system. Corrupt banker Asa Barrows (Henry Kolker) and Sid Campeau (Brian Donlevy), a crooked gambler, along with assorted henchmen, see the opportunity for graft and self-interest and move to take advantage of this historic event.

Captain Jeff Butler (Joel McCrea) leads a crusade against Barrows' minions, including Dick Allen (Robert Preston). Butler has fallen in love with Mollie Monahan (Barbara Stanwyck), the daughter of the engineer (J.M. Kerrigan), but Allen attempts to destroy the relationship. Oddly, the corrupt Barrows is never held accountable for his misdeeds or his henchmen. He is instead made to walk some twenty miles by Butler. In the end, his only physical discomfort is that he is compelled to hit a spike into the track of the transcontinental railroad!

Like its predecessor *The Plainsmen*, this film portrays Native Americans as savage obstructers of the settling of the west. In one scene, after natives wreck the train, they see a cigar store Indian, and they are obligated to respond with childish awe and disbelief. Then they go on to tie women's corsets around their horses' necks. The film is packed with gunfights, robberies, and the standard Native American attack and battle.

Union Pacific proved to be a box-office success and helped to revitalize big-budget westerns. *Variety* (May 3, 1939) wrote, "Paramount and DeMille have a boxoffice winner in 'Union Pacific.' ... On its size and scope it is undeniable film fare.... Basically, it's a super-western, cowboys and injuns backgrounded by the epochal building of the Union Pacific."[11] Frank S. Nugent wrote in the *New York Times* (May 11, 1939), "Mr. DeMille's little opus is a mighty fine movie, colorful, spectacular and of distinguished ancestry. 'The Iron Horse' sired it."[12]

DeMille undertook to parallel the unification of the United States in the 1860s by means of the transcontinental railroad with the situation in 1939, as the nation began to overcome the Great Depression and the clouds of war started appearing over Europe and Asia.

Ramona (1936, 20th Century–Fox)

This was the third film based on Helen Hunt Jackson's novel *Ramona*, a love story between a Native American (Alessandro) and a mestiza (Ramona). It is set in southern California amid the near annihilation of Native Americans in the late 1800s. The 1936 versions follows Jackson's novel in a short 84 minutes. (Please see the entries for the earlier *Ramona* film releases for the narrative.)

The studio lavished some $600,000 for the film's budget and shot it in three-strip Technicolor; Alfred DeGaetano was responsible for the impressive cinematography. It was directed by Henry King (1886–1982), whose distinguished film career spanned from 1916 to 1962. Among his notable films were *Tol'able David* (1921), *Jesse James* (1939), *The*

Song of Bernadette (1943), and *Twelve O'Clock High* (1949. The screenplay was written by the highly respected Lamar Trotti (1900–1952). Four other writers were also credited: Sonya Levien, Stuart Anthony, Lillian Wurtzel, and Paul Hervey Fox.

Despite the high quality of the collaborators, the film's main weakness was the miscasting of the lead characters. The popular and talented Loretta Young, who often specialized in romantic dramas, played the mestiza Ramona. Don Ameche, an excellent actor of both cheerful comedies and somber dramas, was given the role of Alessandro. However, they were both totally unconvincing as native people. Their black wigs and brown grease paint did not make them any more authentic. The rest of the cast included Kent Taylor (Felipe Moreno), Pauline Frederick (Señora Moreno), Jane Darwell (Aunt R. Hyer), and Katherine DeMille (the native girl Margarita).

Native American roles were small, and only a few were played by native performers: Chief Thundercloud was cast as Pablo, while Sonny Chorre, Big Eagle Penna, I. R. Swift Eagle, and Elmo Red Fox played bit roles.

The film critic Frank S. Nugent wrote in the *New York Times* (October 7, 1936), "Loretta Young, the most appealing of the screen's ladies, wears a black wig, photographs beautifully…. As Alessandro, her Indian brave, Don Ameche is stalwart, protective but a bit too Oxonian to convince us the he is related even distantly, to Chingachgook, Uncas, Sitting Bull and their ilk."[13]

Stagecoach (1939, United Artists)

One of the most famous westerns ever made was John Ford's *Stagecoach*. This film focuses on a group of disparate characters in a stagecoach headed for the west. On the way, they are continuously accosted by scores of faceless, screaming, and violent Native American warriors.

John Ford had not made a western since *The Last Outlaw* (1936—RKO). The screenplay was written by the highly respected (and future Ford collaborator) Dudley Nichols. It was based on the short story titled "The Stage to Lordburg" (published in *Colliers* on April 10, 1937) by Ernest Haycox. Once Ford bought the rights to the story, he shopped the project around to different studios but had difficulty finding a taker. Big-budget westerns were then out of fashion. Further, Ford kept insisting that the little-known B-western star John Wayne play the lead. Wayne had spent most of 1930s making low-budget westerns and was not a "name" for a big-budget film.

Independent producer Walter Wranger finally provided $250,000 (more than the film's budget) to make the movie, although he kept insisting that Gary Cooper and Marlene Dietrich play the leads. Ford insisted on Wayne. Even though Wranger ultimately gave in to Ford's demand, he convinced him to give Claire Trevor first billing (instead of Wayne).

Stagecoach was shot mostly in the Four Corners region, especially in the iconic Monument Valley; the town scenes were filmed at the RKO ranch.

The narrative is set in 1880. The main characters are passengers on a stagecoach from Tonto, Arizona Territory, to Lordsburg, New Mexico Territory. They include a prostitute, Dallas (Claire Trevor); a whiskey salesman, Samuel Peacock (Donald Meek); an alcoholic, Doc Boone (Thomas Mitchell); a pregnant army wife, Lucy Mallory (Louise Platt); a bank embezzler, Henry Gatewood (Henry Gatewood); and young cowboy who has just broken out of jail, the Ringo Kid (John Wayne).

Their lives are complicated by the sudden news that Geronimo (Chief White Horse) has broken out of the reservation. Afterward, they are attacked constantly by Apache warriors. Throughout the film, derogatory remarks are made about Native Americans. Doc Boone states that "Geronimo is a butcher!" Upon their arrival at a waystation run by Chris (Chris-Pin Martín), Peacock suddenly screams "Savage! Savage!" when he sees Yakima (Elvira Rios), Chris' Apache wife.

Through their journey, we learn about each of the passenger's characters when under stress. However, Native American characters remain only as the props of terror. Even the Indian scout (Chief Big Tree) who accompanies the U.S. Cavalry is an outsider in the white community.

John Ford assembled a stock company of players that would endure for the rest of his career, including actors from both his silent and his talking films; among these were Frances Ford (his brother, who had been a western star in the silent era); George Bancroft; popular B-western star Tom Tyler; Tim Holt (son of Jack Holt); comic relief Andy Devine; villainous John Carradine; stuntman-actor Yakima Canutt; and many others. The Native American actors cast in *Stagecoach* included Chris Pin Martín, Elvira Rios, Chief Whitehorse (Geronimo), and Chief John Big Tree. Hundreds of Navajo extras were hired to play the marauding native warriors.

This film became a landmark western. It was nominated for seven Academy Awards: Best Picture, Best Director (John Ford), Best Art Direction (Alexander Toluboff), Best Cinematography, Black and White (Bert Glennon), Best Film Editing (Dorothy Spencer and Otho Lovering); Best Supporting Actor (Thomas Mitchell); and Best Music Score (John Leipold, Richard Hageman, and Leo Shuken), ultimately winning the latter two.

Stagecoach thrust the Irish American John Ford into realm of the director best associated with the western genre, despite the fact that most of his films were not westerns. The film also catapulted John Wayne into stardom and helped make him a mythical figure in the western genre. However, for Native Americans, *Stagecoach* froze in stone the stereotype of the screaming, violent, and heartless savage obstructing Manifest Destiny.

The Last of the Mohicans (1936, United Artists)

The Last of the Mohicans (directed by George S. Seitz and written by Philip Dunne) was based on the 1826 novel by James Fenimore Cooper (1789–1851), one of the earliest works of literature in the United States. Both the novel and the film focus on Hawkeye, a white colonist who becomes acculturated to the native way of life. It is a theme that would be repeated numerous times: a white outcast living with native people after rejecting the Euro-American way of life. Later films, such as *A Man Called Horse* and even the *Rambo* character, would be directly influenced by this theme.

The Last of the Mohicans is one of the few films that had numerous Native American characters (as in the book). One great disappointment of this film and many others is that the vast majority of the native characters are played by white actors (and unconvincingly so): Phillip Reed plays Uncas; Robert Barrat is Chingachgook; and William V. Mong is Sachem. The only exceptions to this rule are Bruce Cabot, who was part Cherokee and played Magua, and White Dove, cast as an Indian.

The narrative is set during the misnamed French and Indian War in the Northeast. The plot focuses on the trip of Alice and Cora Monro (Binnie Barnes, Heather Angel), daughters of the British Colonel Munro (Hugh Buckler), from Albany to reunite with their father. They are accompanied by Major Duncan Hayward (Henry Wilcoxon), who is in love with Alice, and Magua (Bruce Cabot), a native scout who wants revenge against the British. When Magua becomes involved in an ambush against the party, Hawkeye (Randolph Scott), a colonial scout who has decided to live with Native Americans, rescues them. He is helped by the Mohicans Uncas (Phillip Reed) and Chingachgook (Robert Barrat), the last of their tribe. What follows is a series of battles between the British and the French (with native allies) and a burgeoning romantic relationship between Hawkeye and Alice.

Cooper's novel has several cultural inaccuracies. He based his cultural aspects on the Mohegan tribe, an Algonquin tribe that lived in eastern Connecticut. The Mohicans (or Mahicans) are an Algonquin Native American tribe. They lived in the upper Hudson River Valley (New York and Vermont presently) and endured Euro-American invasions and forced removals. Today they occupy a federally recognized reservation known as the Stockbridge-Munsee Community in Wisconsin.

The film depicts native characters, especially Magua (played by Bruce Cabot), as utterly cruel and violent. There is no backstory of how Europeans launched a campaign of annihilation against native peoples from the very beginning and created a native resistance that responded in kind. In absence of this background, native characters are one-dimensional props, present only to justify the territorial ambitions of Europeans.

Cooper introduced the notion that Native Americans would disappear. By doing so, he perpetuated the stereotype of the "vanishing race" and "the noble savage." He set his novel in a time of transition (the French and Indian War), when England and France fought for the destiny of North America. Missing is the human and environmental impact caused by the intruders. At the end of *The Last of the Mohicans*, Cora and Uncas are buried and Hawkeye acknowledges Chingachgook's trust and friendship. Then Tamenund makes a prophetic comment: "The pale-faces are masters of the earth, and the time of the red-men has yet to come again." Nevertheless, indigenous peoples have survived.

The 1936 film received mixed reviews upon its release. The *New York Times* (September 3, 1936) said, "Bruce Cabot's Magua is as evil a Huron as ever you pictured him and his misdeeds.... The massacre of Fort William Henry is by far the bloodiest, scalpingest morsel of cinematic imager ever produced, and we were consequently about ready to overlook the lessons made necessary in fitting the novel to the screen when Hollywood permitted Hawkeye to fall in love."

Laughing Boy (1934, MGM)

Laughing Boy was one of only two studio-produced films in which the protagonist was a Native American (the other was *Massacre*). This film paired two of the most popular Mexican-born film stars (both of whom had Native American roots) of the era: Ramón Novarro and Lupe Vélez. MGM brought together all of the elements to make an important film.

The film was directed by the noted W.S. Van Dyke (1889–1943), who had helmed many important films. One of his most important works was *White Shadows in the South Seas* (1928, MGM), which had focused on the annihilation of Pacific Islander culture. Other key films included *The Pagan* (1929, MGM) with Ramón Novarro; *Tarzan, the Ape Man* (1932, MGM); *The Thin Man* (1936, MGM); and *San Francisco* (1936, MGM), among many others.

Laughing Boy was based on the Pulitzer Prize–winning novel of 1929 of the same name by Oliver La Farge. He was both a highly respected writer and an anthropologist who made major discoveries regarding Mexican, Central American, and Southwest native peoples. He was a dedicated advocate for native issues and concerns. La Farge had also been the president of the Association on American Indian Affairs, one of the oldest native advocacy groups. The film was written by John Colton (1887–1946), a playwright, and John Lee Mahn (1901–1963), a veteran MGM writer and producer.

The narrative revolves around Slim Girl (Lupe Vélez), a Navajo who was raised by Euro-Americans. Her promiscuous lifestyle makes her an outcast in the Navajo community. She seduces Laughing Boy (Ramón Novarro), a silversmith, who becomes smitten with her. Slim Girl becomes enamored of him when he loses a horse race and gets revenge by beating his rival Red Man (Pellicana) in a wrestling match.

Slim Girl also renews her old relationship with George Hartshone (William B. Davidson), who is a wealthy miner. However, the latter's violent nature causes her to abandon him. She searches out Laughing Boy, and they become lovers. Laughing Boy expresses his desire to marry Slim Girl. However, one day when she goes into town to sell his silverware products, Laughing Boy follows her. She encounters Hartshone, who is adamant that she return to him. As she struggles to be free of him, Laughing Boy is consumed by anger and jealousy. He attempts to shoot an arrow at Hartshone but mistakenly hits Slim Girl, who dies.

The film was shot on location in the Navajo Reservation and nearby Flagstaff and Cameron. During the shooting, Ramón Novarro and Bud Barksy (the production manager) were made honorary Navajo chiefs. The film provided numerous roles for native actors: Chief Thunderbird (as Laughing Boy's father), Deer Spring, White Dove, Alphed Elk, White Flower, Chief Standing Bear, Kuuks Walks-Alone, and Pellicana.

Before the film's release, the New York censor board deemed some parts of the film objectionable and deleted them for screenings in the state. One of the scenes thus removed was when Laughing Boy and Slim Girl camp out together. The deletions brought the film's running length to only 75 minutes.

Despite all the talent involved in the making of this film, *Laughing Boy* was only a mixed success. The most evocative scenes were those set in the Navajo Nation, especially those involving Novarro and Vélez with native actors. These scenes capture a sense of authenticity. Many have criticized the casting of Novarro and Vélez in the lead roles. However, the key flaw of the film is the lack of effective direction by W.S. Van Dyke, though he had previously captured evocative authenticity in *White Shadows in the South Seas* and *The Pagan*. Both films had been set among the indigenous peoples of the South Pacific.

Laughing Boy, like other native-themed films

Lupe Vélez was a Mexican Native American film star. She played numerous native women in U.S. films, including in *Laughing Boy* (1934, MGM) with Ramón Novarro.

of the decade, was not a commercial success. Nevertheless, it must be seen as a sincere effort to document the Native American experience.

Geronimo (1939, Paramount)

This film about Geronimo was a B-western. Its main selling point was the cinematic depiction of numerous acts of violence against white settlers. The film promoted a strictly good (white settler) versus evil (Native Americans) scenario.

Geronimo was directed and written by Paul Sloane (1893–1963), a reliable (if unremarkable) director whose career spanned from 1916 to 1952. The cinematography was done by Henry Sharpe (1992–1966), who had shot several important films like *Don Q. Son of Zorro* (1925), *The Crowd* (1928), *Duck Soup* (1933), and *Ministry of Fear* (1944). Many of the action scenes were pulled from numerous other western films.

The threadbare story line involved the U.S. Army's campaign to capture Geronimo, who is accused of leading his warriors in murdering and attacking peaceful white settlers. The film focuses on Lieutenant John Steele, Jr. (William Henry), who is estranged from his father General Steel (Ralph Morgan) and involved in a family feud. The nominal leads are played by the veteran Preston Foster (Captain Starrett), who is in love with Ellen Drew (Alice Hamilton). The role of Geronimo is played by Chief Thundercloud. Native American actors play bit parts: Monte Blue plays an interpreter; Charles Stevens appears as an Indian; and Chief Eskiminzu plays Chief Thunderbird. The tagline for the film was "THRILL to the thundering courage of a boy and a girl who risked their very lives for love … who dare the ruthless wrath of the war-mad-demon, Geronimo!"

Geronimo is an utterly forgettable film in all respects. It is remembered as a film with one of the worst Native American stereotypes and its depiction of a native resistance fighter as the incarnation of pure evil.

Juárez (1939, Warner Bros.)

The beginning of World War II in September 1939 increased U.S. concern for hemispheric unity, and the film industry responded in kind. For the duration of hostilities, Mexican and Latino film stereotypes diminished and/or softened. In addition, the president's Good Neighbor Policy toward Mexico and Latin America contributed to those objectives.

Benito Juárez (1806–1872) was a Zapotec (from the southern state of Oaxaca) who became Mexico's first Native American president, serving from 1858 to 1872. He was a progressive reformer who fought against the political power of the *criollo* class that controlled Mexico. He came to power in a turbulent era in Mexican history, at the time of the War of Liberal Reform (1858–1860) and the invasion of France (1862–1867). During his time as president, Juárez curbed the power of the Catholic Church (which included nationalizing the wealth of the clergy), restricted the intervention of the military in politics, passed laws to eliminate prejudice against indigenous people, and began an ambitious attempt at land reform. He died of a heart attack at the age of 66. Both Abraham Lincoln and Benito Juárez admired each other and shared similar humble beginnings.

The film *Juárez* had three interlocking stories: the intrigues related to Napoleon III's efforts to annex Mexico as part of the French empire; the doomed love story between Maximilian (the Hapsburg prince and younger brother of Emperor Franz Joseph) and

Carlotta; and Benito Juárez's struggle to oppose foreign rule and establish a constitutional democracy. France's invasion of Mexico in 1862 compelled Juarez to leave Mexico City and fight a guerrilla war that eventually forced France to withdraw its troops. Subsequently, Maximilian depended on common mercenaries and Mexican collaborators. While his wife Carlotta left to plead for French aid, Juárez's army captured Maximilian and defeated his army. Maximilian was executed as a warning to all foreign powers with similar ambitions.

Warner Brothers lavished on *Juárez* some $1,750,000, which was the largest budget for the studio up to that time. A variety of historical sources were utilized to develop the screenplay, including Bertita Harding's *The Phantom Crown* and Franz Werfel's play *Juárez and Maximilian*, as well as Juarez's private letters and official correspondence, contemporary newspapers, and congressional debates.

The highly respected actor Paul Muni was cast in the role of Benito Juárez. Producer Hal Wallis and director William Dieterle traveled to Mexico for further research at the request of President Lázaro Cárdenas. Muni interviewed aged survivors of the Juarista army, General Velásquez and Colonel Gabriel Moreno, and inquired about Juárez's personality, such as his mannerisms. Muni decided to underplay Juárez and etched out the inner man, stoic and indomitable, as well as the outer man. His makeup included the high indigenous cheekbones, the straight black hair, and body padding to emphasize the massive shoulders. The actor was effective and convincing, but the brevity of Juárez in the overall canvas of the film undermined his effort to craft a more fully developed role.

The studio rounded out the cast with prominent actors, such as John Garfield, who portrayed the ambitious Porfirio Díaz (although Garfield's New York accent was at odds with his role). Brian Aherne played Maximilian and won an Academy Award nomination for Best Supporting Actor. Gilbert Roland (the only Mexican in a major role) played the treacherous Colonel Miguel López. The role of Carlotta was played by Bette Davis, whose hysterical type of acting was, for once, appropriate to the role.

The studio arranged a special screening for President Cárdenas, and the film premiered in Mexico's national theater in Bellas Artes. The Mexican response was positive, unlike the one for MGM's stereotypical *Vival Villa* (1934). *Variety* (April 26, 1939) noted, "To the list of distinguished characters whom he has created in films, Paul Muni now adds a portrait of Benito Pablo Juárez, Mexican patriot and liberator. With the aid of.... Brian Aherne giving an excellent performance as the ill-fated Maximilian, and a story that paints up the parallels of conflicting political though of today and three-quarters of century ago."[14] A related film, *The Mad Empress* (1939, Miguel Contreras Torres), was bought by Warner Brothers in order to avoid competition.

Juárez was a well-meaning effort within the context of hemispheric understanding and unity in the midst of the dark clouds of World War II. Although it was the first time that a Hollywood film had presented a Mexican historical figure in a positive light, it was a flawed image. For example, *Variety* (April 26, 1939) discerned, "There is frequent mention of the Monroe Doctrine, of one-man rule over the lives and destinies of millions, and the rights of common man to possess land and work out his own salvation."[15] Latin Americans, especially Mexicans, hardly had a rosy view of the Monroe Doctrine, as presented in the film, since it had been the justification for a long history of U.S. intervention in Central America. There is also a persistent claim throughout the film that it was the fear of U.S. intervention that deterred the return of the French troops to Mexico, rather than the numerous military defeats that Juárez's army had already inflicted on the French army. In addition, the constant juxtaposition of Lincoln's portrait and Juárez's face every time Juárez is confronting a crisis was a subtle perpetuation of the idea of Mexicans as ideological disciples, unable to think for themselves even with regard to their national self-determination.

In conclusion, while *Juárez* is a flawed film, it nevertheless raised the expectation that Mexican and Native American images would change for the better. It was a hope that was temporary, and ultimately premature.

NATIVE FILM STARS AND FILMMAKERS

Chauncey Yellow Robe

Chauncey Yellow Robe was a widely respected and renowned Native American social activist, educator, lecturer, and (for a very brief moment) film actor.

He was born Chauncey Yellow Robe ("Kills in the Woods") Canowicakte in the Sichangu Oyate in the Lakota Nation, southern Montana, in 1867. His father Chief Yellow Robe (Tsinagi) was a descendent of two important Lakota leaders and patriots, Iron Plume and Sitting Bull. Yellow Robe's mother was Tachcawin (Deer Woman). She bore seven children and was also a niece of Sitting Bull.

During his childhood, Yellow Robe grew up in the Rosebud Reservation in South Dakota. He was immersed in the great history of his people—the chiefs, shamans, warriors, and traditions. He was sent to the Carlisle Indian Industrial School, where he excelled academically and as a young leader. After graduating with honors, he worked with the Bureau of Indian Affairs (BIA) and later as a teacher and basketball coach at the Rapid City Indian School. He was a co-founder of the Society of American Indians (1911–1923), which was the first national Native American civil rights organization administered by indigenous people.

More and more, Yellow Robe became a vocal critic of the injustice perpetuated against indigenous peoples, alcohol addiction, and the exploitation of native performers by Buffalo Bill's Wild West Show, and he demanded that citizenship be granted to Native Americans.

In his personal life, Yellow Robe married Lillian (Lillie) Belle Springer (who was of German-Swiss ancestry) in 1905. Lillian had been a volunteer nurse at the Rapid City Indian School. The union produced three daughters: Rosebud, Evelyn, and Chauncina. Soon after the death of his wife in 1927, Yellow Robe took a leave of absence from his teaching and when to New York to visit his daughter Rosebud. During the visit, he was approached about a playing the native chief in the film *The Silent Enemy* (1930).

Yellow Robe distrusted Wild West shows and films because they had stereotyped and demonized native people. After much hesitation, he finally agreed to play the lead role. Besides playing the chief, he also served as technical director, researcher, and uncredited writer.

He traveled to New York City after the shooting of his prologue. During his visit, he caught pneumonia. Chauncey Yellow Robe died on April 6, 1930 (on the third anniversary of his wife's death). *The Silent Enemy* was released after his passing. He was buried beside his wife in the Mountain View in Rapid City, South Dakota.

Chief Thundercloud

One of the busiest Native American performers during the 1930s and 1940s was Chief Thundercloud (real name Victor Daniels). He made scores of B-westerns and several big-budget films in different genres.

He was born on April 12, 1899, in Muskogee, Indian Territory (present-day Oklahoma), although his Social Security number lists his birthplace as Arizona. His parents were Jesus Daniels and Tomoca Daniel. There have been conflicting reports that he had Irish, German, and Scottish blood. In addition, there are also claims that his father was Joseph Mahawa.

Thundercloud attended the University of Arizona, where he distinguished himself in both boxing and football. Thereafter, he worked in various jobs: boxer, rodeo rider, cowboy, and mining foreman. His athletic build helped him enter films as a stuntman in 1929.

He made his film debut in 1935's *Rustlers of Red Dog* (Universal). Like most native actors of the time, he was cast in villainous native roles. His films include *The Farmer Takes a Wife* (1935, 20th Century–Fox); *Ramona* (1936, 20th Century–Fox); *The Plainsmen* (1936, 20th Century–Fox); *Union Pacific* (1939, Paramount); *Man of Conquest* (1939, Republic); *The Cat and the Canary* (1939, Paramount); *North West Mounted Police* (1940, Paramount); *Hudson's Bay* (1941, 20th Century–Fox); *The Fighting Seabees* (1944, Republic); *Buffalo Bill* (1944, 20th Century–Fox); *Nob Hill* (1935, 20th Century–Fox); *Unconquered* (1947, Paramount); *The Senator Was Indiscreet* (1947, Univ. Inter.); *Mrs. Mike* (1949, United Artists); *Ambush* (1950, MGM); *I Killed Geronimo* (1950, Eagle-Lion Pictures); and *The Searchers* (1956, Warner Bros.).

The high point in Thundercloud's film career came when he played the title role in the 1939 film *Geronimo* (Paramount). He was also the first actor to play the role of Tonto in two Republic Pictures serials: *The Lone Ranger* (1938, Republic) and *The Lone Ranger Rides Again* (1939, Republic). He appeared in several television shows, such as *Death Valley Days*, *My Little Margie*, *The Gene Autry Show*, *Buffalo Bill, Jr.*, and *The Adventures of Rin Tin Tin*.

Later in his life, Thundercloud performed in live western shows, along with other western stars. He died on December 1, 1955, of stomach cancer following surgery. He is interned at Forest Lawn Memorial Park in Glendale, California.

Chief White Eagle

White Eagle was born Basil F. Heath on March 18, 1917, in the Iroquois Indian Reservation in Canada. He was educated at McGill University in Montreal, Quebec, Canada, and also at Oxford University in England. After moving to the United States, he was a liaison officer in the U.S. Office of War Information during World War II. He also volunteered for the U.S. Army's 101st Airborne Division.

He held numerous odd jobs, such as welder, iron worker in skyscrapers, and eventually a film stuntman. He made his film debut in *Northwest Passage* (MGM), which was shot during 1939 but released one year later. His films included *Stagecoach* (1939, Republic); *Last of the Redmen* (1947, Columbia); *Red River* (1948, United Artists); *She Wore a Yellow Ribbon* (1949, RKO); *How the West Was Won* (1962, MGM); and *McLintock* (1963, United Artists).

During the 1960s, he hosted the television program *Totem Club* in Chicago, over the WTTW (a public broadcasting station). In order to supplement his income, he did numerous radio and television commercials.

He was married to Roberta "Bear" Heath on June 29, 1977, and the union lasted until his passing.

He died on January 24, 2011. He was immortalized in the Potawatomi Trail of Death Association with a memorial.

Chief White Horse

Chief White Horse was a Native American actor and horseman. He was born on January 2, 1864, in Georgetown, Missouri.

He began his professional career as a jockey, later working as a steeple chase rider. His horsemanship and skills soon earned him a job with the Ringling Circus and then the Burgess Pawnee Indian Show. He performed in vaudeville and was later employed by the Universal Film Company between 1912 and 1918. White Horse was contracted to work in Fox westerns (mostly with William Farnum) for a year; he then worked with William S. Hart for three years and later with Leo Maloney during the late 1920s.

His numerous films include *Rough Going* (1922, Malobee Prods.), a film short; *Lost, Strayed and Stolen* (1923, Malobee Prods.), a film short; *Double Clinched* (1923, Malobee Prods.), a film short; *Leatherstocking* (1924, Pathé Exchange), a film serial; *The Perfect Alibi* (1924, Stenier Prods.); *The Trouble Buster* (1925, Steiner Prods.); *Without Orders* (1926, Maloford Prods.); *The Devil's Twin* (1927, Maloney Prods.); *The Wagon Master* (1929, Myanard Prods.); and *Stagecoach* (1939, United Artists), in the role of Geronimo. He died in 1955.

Marie Chorre

Marie Chorre was a Native American actress. She was the daughter of Gertrude Chorre and sister to Sonny Chorre. Both were native actors.

She was born Rosalu Chorre on January 21, 1919, in Los Angeles, California. Her film credits include *White Fang* (1936, 20th Century–Fox) and *Ramona* (1936, 20th Century–Fox). She passed away on June 8, 1980, in San Bernardino, California.

Sonny Chorre

Sonny Chorre was a Native American actor. He was born Joseph Vance Chorre on November 14, 1914, in Los Angeles, California. He was the son of Gertrude Chorre and brother to Marie Chorre, both native performers.

Sonny was also a wrestler who used the name Suni Warcloud. He made his film debut in *Wolf Rider* in 1935. Other films included *Rose Marie* (1934, MGM); *Ride, Ranger, Ride* (1936); *The Plainsmen* (1936, Paramount); *Ebb Tide* (1937); *Flaming Frontiers* (1938); *Hawk of the Wilderness* (1938); *Union Pacific* (1939, Paramount); *Man of Conquest* (1939); *Western Union* (1941, 20th Century–Fox); *Son of Fury: The Story of Benjamin Blake* (1942, 20th Century–Fox); *The Paleface* (1948, Paramount); *Jim Thorpe—All-American* (1951,

Warner Bros.); and *Tip on a Dead Jockey* (1957, MGM), among others. His television credits include *Stampede Wrestling* (1957).

Sonny Chorre passed away on June 14, 1987, in Los Angeles, California.

Molly Spotted Elk

Molly Spotted Elk was born Mary Alice Nelson on November 17, 1903, in the Penobscot Indian Island Reservation in Maine. She was the oldest of eight siblings. Her father was Horace Nelson, an important Penobscot leader, and her mother, Philomene Saulis Nelson, was a highly respected woman noted for her arts and crafts.

Molly became involved in show business at a young age. She attended the University of Pennsylvania, although she obtained no degree. She attracted much attention as a performer in the Miller Brothers 101 Ranch while touring. She also won a Native American dance competition in Oklahoma. She made such an impression that the Cheyenne tribe adopted her with the name of Spotted Elk.

During the 1920s, Molly Spotted Elk became a popular attraction in chic New York City nightclubs. In 1930, she was cast as the Native American female lead in the landmark film *The Silent Enemy* and won wide praise. However, it would be her only lead role in a film. The economic downturn of the Great Depression and moviegoers' lack of interest in a film about Native Americans resulted in the film's commercial failure.

Despite the failure of *The Silent Enemy*, Spotted Elk was in high demand as an artist's model and as a dancer. During the 1930s, she moved to Paris, France, where a host of expatriate artists from different countries lived and created music, literature, and dance. These expatriates included Frida Kahlo, Ernest Hemingway, Josephine Baker, and many others. Spotted Elk was in a high demand with her traditional Native American dances and wardrobe. She subsequently married Jean Archambaud, a French journalist and vocal critic of the rising fascism in Europe.

The coming of the Great Depression devastated the French economy, and the purchasing power for entertainment declined dramatically. Archambaud was fired from his job and thereafter freelanced, though at a lower salary. Consequently, Spotted Elk was reduced to doing menial jobs in order to survive. She returned to the United States in 1934, where she resumed dancing. She was cast in several bit parts in a few Hollywood films: *The Last of the Mohicans* (1936, United Artists); *The Charge of the Light Brigade* (1936, Warner Bros.); *The Good Earth* (1937, MGM); and *The Lost Horizon* (1937, Columbia). Soon thereafter, she gave birth to her daughter, Jean Alice.

At the end of the 1930s, Spotted Elk and her daughter returned to Paris, where she was reunited with her husband. She researched and collected numerous Native American stories and found a publisher that was enthusiastic about publishing a book on her work. However, World War II soon broke out in Europe during September 1939. Less than a year later, in June 1940, France fell to Nazi Germany. The war forced Spotted Elk to flee with her daughter over the Pyrenees Mountains into Spain, from which point she managed to escape to the United States. Amid the chaos and tragedies of World War II, she lost touch with her husband and never saw him again.

Perhaps traumatized by the events of the war, Spotted Elk declined physically and mentally. At one point, she was confined briefly to a mental institution. She continued to write children's stories and also made traditional Native American dolls. She would spend the rest of her life in her native land, the Penobscot Reservation in Maine.

Molly Spotted Elk died on February 21, 1977, in the Penobscot Indian Island.

Ray Mala

Ray Mala became widely known for his lead role in the film *Eskimo*. He was the first Eskimo to become a Hollywood star.

Ray Mala was born Ray Wise on December 27, 1908, in Candle, Alaska. His father was a Russian Jewish immigrant, and his mother a native Alaskan. At the time of Mala's birth, Alaska was still only a territory of the United States; it would not become a state for another fifty years.

At the age of 14, Mala made his film debut in *Primitive Love*, made by an explorer named Captain Frank Kleinschmidt. In addition to acting in the film, Mala served as the cameraman. He later accompanied another explorer, the Danish Knud Rasmussen, on the trip that became known as "The Great Sled Journey" during 1921–1924. The purpose was to collect Inuit legends and songs. One of Mala's tasks was once again serving as a cameraman.

In 1925, Mala went to Hollywood, where he worked as a cameraman with the Fox Film Corporation (later 20th Century–Fox). Soon thereafter, he won the lead role in the film *Igloo* (1932, Scott Artic Prods.). The success of that film led to him being cast in the starring role in *Eskimo* (1933, MGM). In his native land, Mala earned widespread respect and admiration.

His third lead role came in *Last of the Pagans* (1935, MGM), which was filmed and set in Tahiti. Although the movie was a moderate success and Mala earned acclaim for his acting ability, the Hollywood film industry had limited opportunities for native Inuits. Thereafter, he would only be cast in supporting or small roles.

Mala's films include *Robinson Crusoe of Clipper Island* (1936, Republic Pictures); *The Jungle Princess* (1936, Paramount Pictures); the serial *The Great Adventures of Wild Bill Hickok* (1938, Columbia Pictures), chapters 5–6; *Hawk of the Wilderness* (1938); *Call of the Yukon* (1939, Republic Pictures); *Union Pacific* (1939, Paramount); *Mutiny on the Blackhawk* (1939, Republic Pictures); *Coast Guard* (1939, Universal); *Green Hell* (1940, Universal); *Zanzibar* (1940, Universal); the serial *Flash Gordon Conquers the Universe* (1940, Universal), chapters 7–9; *South of Pago Pago* (1940, Edward Small Prods.); *Girl from God's Country* (1940, Republic); *North West Mounted Police* (1940, Paramount Pictures); *The Devil's Pipeline* (1940, Universal); *Hold Back the Dawn* (1941, Warner Bros.); *Honolulu Lu* (1941, Columbia Pictures); *Son of Fury: The Story of Benjamin Blake* (1942, 20th Century–Fox); *The Mad Doctors of Market Street* (1942, Universal); *The Girl from Alaska* (1942, Republic); *The Tuttles of Tahiti* (1942, RKO Radio Pictures); and *Red Snow* (1952, All American Film Corp.) Mala was usually cast as an exotic from the South Pacific, a Native American, and/or a Mexican.

In addition to his acting career, Mala became a respected cinematographer. His credits include such films as *Shadow of a Doubt* (1943, Universal); *Happy Land* (1943, 20th Century–Fox), uncredited; *Laura* (1944, 20th Century–Fox), uncredited; *Thunderhead—Son of Flicka* (1945, 20th Century Fox), uncredited; *Doll Face* (1945), uncredited; *The Fan* (1949, 20th Century–Fox), uncredited; and *Meet Me After the Show* (1951, 20th Century–Fox), uncredited.

He was married to Galina Liss and had one child.

Mala made his last film appearance in *Red Snow* (1952) with Guy Madison. During the making of the film, he died on the set as a result of heart problems. He was only 45 years of age.

Ray Mala was a unique talent who left his mark as a First Nations actor and cinematographer.

Chris-Pin Martín

Chris-Pin Martín was a popular actor in scores of films from the silent era to the talking era. He was born Ysabel Ponciana Chris-Pin Martín Paiz on November 19, 1893, in Tucson, Arizona. His Native American origin appears to have been from the Yaqui people of southern Arizona and northern Sonora (Mexico) area.

Throughout his long film career, he was variously listed under different names, including Chris King Martin, Ethier Crispin Martini, Cris-Pin Martín, and Chris-Pin Martin, among others. His film persona was that of a rotund, happy-go-lucky, comedic and/or dramatic character. He made more than one hundred films, half of which were westerns.

Martín is perhaps best remembered and recognized for his role as the Cisco Kid's sidekick Gordito and/or Pancho in nine films. Developed by O. Henry (1962–1910), the noted short story writer, the Cisco Kid was based on the real-life social bandit Joaquin Marietta, active in California in the aftermath of the gold rush of 1849. Chris-Pin Martín worked with three actors playing the Cisco Kid: Warner Baxter, César Romero, and Gilbert Roland.

Martín made his film debut in Charlie Chaplin's *The Gold Rush* (1925, United Artists) as a man in the dance hall. He eventually moved from bit parts to supporting roles. His numerous film appearances included *Border Vengeance* (1925, Harry Webb Prod.); *The Gaucho* (1927, United Artists), with Douglas Fairbanks; *The Crowd* (1928, MGM); *Across to Singapore* (1928, MGM); *The Squaw Man* (1931, MGM); *The Cisco Kid* (1931, Fox Film Corp.), as Gordito opposite Warner Baxter; *Viva Villa!* (1934, MGM); *Bordertown* (1935, Warner Bros.); *The Bold Caballero* (1936, Republic Pictures); *A Star Is Born* (1937); *The Hurricane* (1937); *Too Hot to Handle* (1938, MGM); *Return of the Cisco Kid* (1938, 20th Century–Fox), as Gordito opposite Warner Baxter; *The Fighting Gringo* (1939); and *The Cisco Kid and the Lady* (1939, 20th Century–Fox), as Gordito opposite César Romero. During the 1940s, Martín played Gordito in four more films with Romero: *Viva Cisco Kid!* (1940, 20th Century–Fox); *Lucky Cisco Kid* (1940, 20th Century–Fox); *The Gay Caballero* (1940, 20th Century–Fox); and *Romance of the Rio Grande* (1941, 20th Century–Fox). Other films included *The Mark of Zorro* (1940, 20th Century–Fox); *The Ox-Bow Incident* (1943, 20th Century–Fox); *San Antonio* (1945, Warner Bros.); *Robin Hood of Monterey* (1947, Monogram Pictures), as Pancho opposite Gilbert Roland; *King of the Bandits* (1947), as Pancho opposite Gilbert Roland; *The Fugitive* (1947, Argosy Pictures); *Captain from Castile* (1947, 20th Century–Fox); *A Millionaire for Christy* (1951, 20th Century–Fox); and *Mesa of Lost Women* (1953, Howco Productions). He also appeared on *The Lone Ranger* television series during 1950.

Chris-Pin Martín passed on June 27, 1953, in Montebello, California.

Anthony Quinn

Film star Anthony Quinn was at times thought to be Irish, Greek, and/or some other ethnicity due to his numerous ethnic performances. However, he was in fact of Mexican Native American heritage.

Quinn was born Antonio Rodolfo Oaxaca Quinn in Chihuahua, Mexico, on April 21, 1915. He wrote about his background in his second autobiography: "My mother,

Manuela was born of misplaced passion. Her mother was an Indian [Tarahumara], who as a child worked for one of the wealthiest landowners in Mexico.... Soon after her birth ... they lived for several years in the Sierras, among the Taraumares [*sic*] Indians."[16] Of his father, Quinn wrote, "My father, Francisco Quinn, spoke Spanish with a brogue. His father came from Ireland to work for the Union Pacific railroad, laying tracks from New York to Los Angeles."[17]

The early 1900s was a turbulent time for Mexico. The Mexican Revolution broke out in 1910 and transformed the primarily Native American nation forever. Quinn wrote, "In Pancho Villa, they [his parents] both saw a man who would stand up to the rich *federales*.... By 1913, when Villa allied with Emiliano Zapata in Mexico City, he spoke with the voice of the working class man, and my father listened ... one of the things my father was fighting for was an identity. My mother, too."[18]

The Quinn family later moved to El Paso and then to Los Angeles (in what is now known as Boyle Heights and/or East Los Angeles). At that time Boyle Heights was home to diverse ethnicities: Mexican, Russian, Croatian, Japanese, and others. However, it was primarily a low-income Mexican majority population. The young Anthony Quinn worked in an assortment of jobs to help his family: newspaper boy, shoeshine boy, factory worker, and boxer.

Quinn as a young man was more than six feet and two inches, athletic and graceful. He lied about his age to work as a professional boxer at the famous Spring Street Gym. He won the first ten fights before his manager Jim Foster agreed to train him for better things. He worked out at the famous Main Street Gym, where he trained with former champion Mushy Callahan and Newsboy Brown. At times Quinn sparred with world heavyweight champion Primo Carnera when he was in town.

In one fight held in Long Beach, California, Quinn was matched with a young black boxer. He recalled in his autobiography one particular boxing match in which he hit his African American opponent with his left and send him backward. He then followed up with a right to the stomach, and then a left hook. Quinn noted, "The crowd starting chanting, 'Kill the nigger! Kill the nigger!' But I was unable to respond.... By the sixth round, the crowd had turned for my opponent. They would sooner root for a tentative black kid than a yellow Mexican." Quinn lost the fight by knockout. He recalled, "But there would be no other fights. Foster said ... 'You don't belong in the game unless you're a killer.'"[19] At that time, Quinn was sixteen years of age.

Regarding trying to get a break in films, Quinn recollected, "There were a few uncredited bits in forgettable 'B' movies, but I worried I would never land a speaking role. I was either too dark, or too Mexican, or too unusual-looking."[20] His first speaking role came in Cecil B. DeMille's western *The Plainsmen* (1936, Paramount). Quinn was cast as Native American brave in the film, which focused on Wild Bill Hickok (played by Gary Cooper) and Buffalo Bill Cody (James Ellison). The scene called for Quinn to ride up on a horse to a campfire left burning in the forest. However, he purposely turned and hid in the forest. DeMille was furious with the young actor. Quinn told him, "You think an Indian doesn't know the difference between a white man's fire and an Indian fire? The fire's still burning, someone's around, somewhere, and you want me to stand there all that time? What kind of Indian would just stand there, waiting, without hiding to protect himself?"[21] Cooper interceded for the young actor, telling DeMille that Quinn had a good point. The director finally agreed.

Quinn was paid for three days' work and offered a studio contract at $250 a week.

During the making of the film, Quinn also met Katherine DeMille (the director's adopted daughter), whom he would later marry in October 1937. However, in a sad comment on the prejudiced film industry, Quinn's family was not invited to his wedding. The long and chilly relationship with his famous father-in-law is reflected indirectly in DeMille's autobiography: "But the actor in *The Plainsman* whose association with me was to be most consistent and most intimate was a young man whose part is listed in the cast only as 'Northern Cheyenne Indian': his name is Anthony Quinn and, as well as being a highly talented and popular star today, he is also my son-in-law, the husband of my daughter Katherine."[22] It was the only one of three times DeMille would mention Quinn in his four-hundred-plus-page autobiography.

Despite having Cecil B. DeMille as a father-in-law, Quinn settled into small and supporting roles as an ethnic villain: Mexican bandits, Italian gangsters, Chinese criminals, and the like. He struck up a friendship on the Paramount lot with the legendary film star Carole Lombard, who tried to lobby for him at the head office. One day, she gave him a candid and blunt reality check: "You'll never be an actor here.... These assholes will never take you seriously.... You're a goddam Indian, Tony. That's what people see. You're an Indian, or a Mexican, or a sleazy racketeer. You're not a leading man."[23]

Quinn toiled in relative anonymity for most of the studios—20th Century–Fox, Paramount Pictures, and others. Among his better roles were a brash dancer in *City of Conquest* (1941, Warner Bros.) with James Cagney; the ambitious bullfighter Manolo in *Blood and Sand* (1941, 20th Century–Fox) with Tyrone Power and Rita Hayworth; Crazy Horse in Raoul Walsh's *They Died with Their Boots On* (1941, Warner Bros.) with Errol Flynn; the one-eyed pirate in *The Black Swan* (1942, 20th Century–Fox) with Tyrone Power and Maureen O'Hara; the Filipino guerrilla fighter in *Back to Bataan* (1945, RKO) with John Wayne; a Native American chief in *Where Do We Go from Here?* (1945, 20th Century–Fox); the wicked emir in *Sinbad the Sailor* (1947, RKO) with Douglas Fairbanks and Maureen O'Hara; and the Latino engineer in *Tycoon* (1947, RKO) with John Wayne.

In 1947, Quinn finally had the lead in a small-budget film called *Black Gold* (Allied Artists) alongside his wife, Katherine DeMille. He wrote about the film, "For me as an actor, *Black Gold* was an important breakthrough—or at least it might have been, in more perfect world. For the first time, I was cast as the male lead, and my career was riding on whether I could carry the picture."[24]

In 1947, at the age of thirty, Quinn decided to leave films and stretch his acting talent on the New York stage. In his very first play, *The Gentlemen from Athens*, he won critical acclaim. He would say later, "In Hollywood, all I could play were gangsters and Mexican bandits, but here in New York I could play anything at all. My God, what freedom! What an abundance!"[25]

On Broadway, he starred in several successful plays. His most acclaimed achievement was serving as the understudy to Marlon Brando while playing Stanley Kowalski in *A Streetcar Named Desire* (1948). In 1950, Quinn replaced Brando in the famous role. To this day, there some who argue that Anthony Quinn was as good as (or even better than) Brando in the legendary role.

In 1952, Quinn was cast in *Viva Zapata!* (20th Century–Fox) as Eufemio Zapata, the brother of Native American Mexican revolutionary Emiliano Zapata (played by Marlon Brando). The film was directed by Elia Kazan and co-starred Jean Peters. Quinn would write later about the role, "If ever an actor was born to a role, it was I to Eufemio Zapata, brother to the famed peasant revolutionary ... and [I] convinced myself that the transformation of Eufemio, from swaggering sidekick to power-mad drunk, made for a more interesting characterization."[26] Quinn went on to win an Academy Award for Best Supporting Actor for his role in *Viva Zapata!*—the first Mexican-born film actor to win the coveted award.

In the early 1950s, Quinn traveled to Italy, where he made several films. Among other roles, he played the strongman in Federico Fellini's *La Strada* (1954, Trans Lux Inc.). He would comment later about the film, "*La Strada* vaulted me from respect as a supporting player to international recognition. It might have made me a rich man—if I had held on to my piece of the picture. I had no idea the movie would have such an impact."[27]

Anthony Quinn (Antonio Oaxaca Quinn) was a Tarahumara from Chihuahua, Mexico. He played numerous Native American roles, as well as many other ethnicities, during his long career.

After his Academy Award win, Quinn began to gradually move up to bigger parts in better pictures. He had finally hit big-time stardom in a series of top-quality films and diverse roles: Robert Rossen's *The Brave Bulls* (1951, Columbia), as the tormented bullfighter; *Against All Flags* (1952, Universal), as the villainous pirate, with Errol Flynn; *Ride, Vaquero* (1953, MGM), as the Mexican *bandido*, with Robert Taylor; and *Ulysses* (1953), as one of Penelope's suitors, with Kirk Douglas and Rossana Podesta. He also played a gangster in Victor Saville's film noir *The Long Wait* (1954, United Artists); another bullfighter in Budd Boetticher's *The Magnificent Matador* (1955, 20th Century–Fox) with Maureen O'Hara; and a Spanish conquistador in *Seven Cities of Gold* (1955, 20th Century–Fox) with Richard Egan.

In 1956, Quinn won his second Best Supporting Actor Academy Award for his role as the painter Paul Gauguin in Vincente Minnelli's outstanding *Lust for Life* (MGM). The role of Vincent Van Gogh was played by the equally brilliant Kirk Douglas. Quinn later played an illiterate Mexican gunfighter in the offbeat western *Man from Del Rio* (1958, United Artists) with Katy Jurado; a man tormented by his past in the crime-drama *The River's Edge* (1957, 20th Century–Fox) with Ray Milland; Quasimodo in *The Hunchback of Notre Dame* (1957, Allied Artists) with Gina Lollobrigida; and part of George Cukor's love triangle *Wild Is the Wind* (1957, Paramount) with Anna Magnani. For his role as the jilted husband, Quinn was nominated for an Academy Award as Best Actor. He became the first Mexico-born actor so honored.

In 1958, Quinn directed his first and only film after his father-in-law became ill while shooting the film *The Buccaneer* (Paramount Pictures). The film starred Charlton Heston as Andrew Jackson and Yul Brynner as the pirate Jean Laffite. The cast also boasted Charles Boyer and Claire Bloom. The star of the film, Charlton Heston, said of Quinn, "I found Tony Quinn a stimulating director, a talented man, and a very sincere artist ... even though the film didn't turn out well. I believe it was difficult for him to work for DeMille, as it was probably difficult for DeMille not to direct a picture."[28] After the shooting finished, DeMille took the film and edited himself without Quinn's knowledge or permission. When DeMille called him to the screening room, Quinn "sat for two hours, barely recognizing the picture I was watching. It was like nothing like the film I had shot.... I walked away thinking, I might have known."[29]

Soon thereafter, DeMille's health declined, and Quinn went to visit him: "As we spoke, I was overcome by a warmth I had never felt for the man. I began to understand about him, to feel sorry for him, to forgive.... It took saying it to recognize that I had needed a man like DeMille, a father figure, to guide me."[30]

Quinn's career continued with such films as Martin Ritt's *The Black Orchid* (1959, Paramount) with Sophia Loren; Edward Dmytryk's complex western *Warlock* (1959, 20th Century–Fox) with Henry Fonda and Dorothy Malone; John Sturges' western *Last Train from Gun Hill* (1959, Paramount); George Cukor's western *Heller in Pink Tights* (1960, Paramount) with Ramón Novarro (in his last role) and Sophia Loren; Ross Hunter's glossy soap opera *Portrait in Black* (1960, Universal) with Lana Turner; Nicholas Ray's *The Savage Innocents* (1960, Paramount), in which Quinn played an Eskimo; and Lee J. Thompson's World War II classic *Guns of Navarone* (1961, Columbia) with Gregory Peck and David Niven.

During the 1960s, the Chicano movement (i.e., the Mexican American civil rights movement) came into being. The social movement was led by several charismatic individuals and highlighted by a series of pivotal events: César Chávez and Dolores Huerta organized the United Farm Workers union to empower impoverished and exploited farm workers (mostly made up of Mexicans). In New Mexico, Reies Tijerina and the Alianza Federal de Mercedes organized to recover stolen land grants in the aftermath of the U.S. takeover of the Southwest in 1848. In Texas, José Ángel Gutiérrez and other activists founded the Raza Unida Party in order to politically empower urban Mexican Americans. It was an era of change throughout the nation and the world.

During Ronald Reagan's first term (1967–1970) as governor of California, Quinn was approached by a group of influential Mexican American Democrats and asked to consider running for governor against Reagan in the next election. Quinn recalled, "I had been active in the Screen Actors Guild politics opposite Reagan, but I had never contemplated a political career ... it was never felt that Reagan would amount to much of a statesman ... Bill Holden was always seen as the more skilled politician."[31]

Quinn went on an exploratory tour of California in order to test the feasibility of running for political office. He met with Mexicans, Filipinos, Greeks, Jews, Native Americans, Chinese, Japanese, and other ethnic communities and leaders. He found that most of the people he met identified with him and believed that he could give Reagan a good challenge.

Though Quinn was open to the possibility of giving up his acting career (and the big money he was making), he remained skeptical, so he decided to go talk to his friend César Chávez (whom he had known since the 1940s). Quinn recollected, "He was a wonderful man, who cared deeply about the rights of California fruit pickers, but a reluctant leader. He was never comfortable with the symbol he had become.... I trusted his instincts, and knew that he was probably the only man in a position to accurately assess my prospects."[32]

Quinn visited Chávez in his house in Tehachapi and told him of his exploratory candidacy and his hopes in the political arena. Chávez told him, "Listen to me, Tony.... Politics is not for you. It's about making deals. You're a man of principle. You're not a man to make deals. But do this and you will be making deals every day ... and one day you'll be flat on your ass and know that you can't get back up."[33] Gradually, Quinn let go of the idea of going into politics, although he wondered thereafter what might have been.

In 1960, Quinn triumphed on Broadway in *Becket* (October 1960–May 1961), opposite no less than Laurence Olivier, and *Tchin-Tchin* (October 1962–May 1963) opposite Margaret Leighton. Two years later, in 1962, he gave three of his greatest performances on film in three completely different roles. He played the over-the-hill heavyweight boxer Mountain Rivera in *Requiem for a Heavyweight* (1962, Columbia) with Mickey Rooney and Jackie Gleason; the biblical thief in Richard Fleischer's religious epic *Barabbas* (1962, Columbia) opposite Silvana Mangano; and the warlord Auda Abu Tayi in David Lean's epic *Lawrence of Arabia* (1962, Columbia) with Alec Guinness, Jack Hawkins, and newcomer Peter O'Toole. Quinn gave superb performances in all three films and unbelievably was not nominated for an Academy Award!

Quinn's film career met with more successes. He played an obsessed policeman in Fred Zinnemann's drama of the aftermath of the Spanish Civil War titled *Behold a Pale Horse* (1964, Columbia) with Gregory Peck and Omar Sharif, and he also appeared in the drama *The Visit* (1964, 20th Century–Fox) with Ingrid Bergman. These were followed by *Zorba the Greek* (1964, Columbia), the film adaptation of Nikos Kazantzakis' novel about an aging Greek laborer and his love for life. This role won Quinn another nomination for an Academy Award for Best Actor, but he lost. However, he won the National

Board of Motion Pictures Review for Best Actor, among many other accolades. Quinn would go on to perform the role of Zorba in theater for many years throughout the world to both critical and commercial success.

His next two films were anticlimactic and lesser work. *A High Wind in Jamaica* (1965, 20th Century–Fox) was a pirate tale with James Coburn, and *Lost Command* (1966, Columbia) was an ambitious but flawed film set in revolutionary Algeria in the late 1950s, co-starring Michelle Morgan.

On a personal level, Quinn divorced Katherine DeMille in 1965 and married Jolanda Addolori (whom he had met on the *Barabbas* film location). Their union produced several offspring (Francisco, Lawrence, and Daniele).

In the late 1960s, Quinn's career experienced a series of ups and downs. He played, variously, a Romanian peasant in *The 25th Hour* (1967, 20th Century–Fox) with Virna Lisi; a kidnapped mobster in *The Happening* (1967, Columbia) with Martha Hyer and Faye Dunaway; a wayward captain in the routine *The Rover* (1967, Selmur) with Rita Hayworth; and a Mexican mestizo patriot in the uneven *Guns for San Sebastián* (1968, MGM) with Silvia Pinal. He was excellent as a Russian pope in the superb *Shoes of the Fisherman* (1968, MGM) with Laurence Olivier. He also played the intellectual wizard in the complicated *The Magus* (1968, 20th Century–Fox) with Candice Bergen and Michael Caine.

Quinn scored a critical and financial success with Stanley Kramer's *The Secret of the Santa Vittoria* (1969, United Artists), set in a World War II Italian village with Virna Lisi and Anna Magnani; played an urban Greek American in *A Dream of Kings* (1969, NG) with Ingrid Stevens and Irene Papas; and guest-starred in the excellent documentary *King: A Film Record: Montgomery to Memphis* (1970), about Martin Luther King. In 1972, Quinn narrated and appeared in another documentary, *The Voice of La Raza*, about the plight of the Chicano community.

In 1972, he published his first autobiography, titled *The Original Sin*; he followed it up in 1995 with his second, *One Man Tango*. Both books were highly praised and well received.

As he aged, Quinn developed heart problems. During February 1989, he underwent bypass surgery for a blockage of three arteries in his heart, and in February 1990, he underwent a successful coronary bypass operation.

In the meantime, Quinn scored several more commercial and critical successes: *Mohammad, Messenger of God* (1976); *The Greek Tycoon* (1976); *The Children of Sanchez* (1978); *The Lion of the Desert* (1981, UFD); *Revenge* (1990); *Only the Lonely* (1991); and *A Walk in the Clouds* (1995).

As he grew older, he found it difficult to be insured for leading roles and settled for guest-star roles and/or cameo roles. Many of the films he made abroad in leading roles failed to cross over into the U.S. film market or were critical and commercial failures. His later work included *A Walk in the Spring Rain* (1970, Columbia); *R.P.M.* (1970, Columbia); *Flap* (1970, Warner Bros.); *Across 110th Street* (1972, United Artists); *Deaf Ears and Johnny Ears* (1973, MGM); *The Don Is Dead* (1973, Universal); *The Destructors* (1974, United Artists); *High Risk* (1981, AC); *The Con Artists* (1981, SJI); *The Old Man and the Sea* (1990), a TV film; *Jungle Fever* (1991); *Mobsters* (1991); *Last Action Hero* (1993); *This Can't Be Love* (1994); *Somebody to Love* (1994); *Seven Servants* (1996); *The Fine Art of Separating People from Their Money* (1996), a documentary; *Il Sindicato* (1996); *Gotti* (1996); and *Oriundi* (1999). His last role was in the 2002 film *Avenging Angelo*.

Quinn returned triumphantly to Broadway to star in the musical revival of *Zorba* from October 16, 1983, to September 2, 1984. Thereafter, he traveled throughout the United States on a long and successful run of the show.

Quinn had appeared on television infrequently beginning in 1949, in *The Philco Playhouse*, and several interview programs. In 1971, he starred in the one-season television series *The Man and the City* (1971–1972), in which he played the Mexican American mayor of a Southwestern city. In 1972, he played the part of Julius Caesar in *The Assassination of Julius Caesar*, filmed in Rome for Mexican television. He also played Caiaphas in Franco Zeffirelli's masterful six-hour mini-series *Jesus of Nazareth* (1977, ATV) with a large international cast.

In addition to his film, theater, and television work, Quinn developed into a highly respected painter and sculptor. His work has been exhibited throughout the world in many galleries. When asked why he continued to work so hard, he responded, "To me working is something physical, like digging ditches. Acting, writing, painting, sculpting is child's play."[34] Regarding his long career and success, he commented, "I love making movies, but they don't satisfy me completely. That's why I also write, sculpt and paint…. It's the spirit of the man to keep looking for the whys. I'm really rather satisfied. No, I don't think I'm lucky. I don't believe in luck or astrology."[35]

Anthony Quinn died on June 3, 2001, of respiratory problems.

Elvira Ríos

Elvira Ríos was Mexican Native American actress in U.S. and Mexican films, as well as a well-known singer. She was born María Elvira Gallegos Ríos on November 16, 1913, in Mexico City. She was born in the Lagunilla barrio, one of the poorest in the capital city. Her mother was Maria Guadalupe Ríos Rodríguez, and her father was José María Gallegos Villalobos. She was the oldest of three siblings.

Elvira was a striking indigenous beauty, with luminous eyes, black hair and dark skin. She began singing at an early age, specializing in the *bolero*, foxtrot, and waltz genres. She won acclaim as the one of the best interpreters of Agustín Lara's songs. She came to widespread attention while performing for the XEW radio station in Mexico City and soon was contracted by the RCA Victor, Orfeón, and Musart music labels. She earned worldwide fame (the first Mexican singer to do so) and performed in nightclubs and on records, radio, tours, and film. Among her greatest successes were such songs as "Ausencia," "Flores negras," and "Noche de ronda." Many of her biggest hits were compositions by Agustín Lara. Elvira Ríos' music continues to be popular long after her death.

Ríos made her Mexican film debut in *¡Esos hombres!* (1937). She came to the attention of Manuel Riachi, an assistant at Paramount Pictures, and was contracted for the film *Tropic Holiday* (1938, Paramount Pictures) with the popular Tito Guízar. In the film she sang with Guízar and played his sister. She then came to the attention of director John Ford, who cast her in the role of Yakima, the Apache wife of Chris-Pin Martín in *Stagecoach* (1939, United Artists).

Her films included *Cupid Rides the Range* (1939, RKO), a film short; *The Real Glory* (1939, Paramount Pictures) with Gary Cooper; *Sombra Rey* (1942, Lumiton), an Argentine film; *Murallas de pasión* (1944, Plata Films), a Mexican film; *El tango vuelve a Paris* (1954, Argentina Sono Film), an Argentine film; and *Melodias inovidables* (1959, Producciones Rosas Priego).

Elvira Ríos passed on January 13, 1987, in Mexico City, of bladder cancer and subsequent kidney failure.

Jim Thorpe

Jim Thorpe was a legendary athlete of the 20th century who competed in several sports: track and field, football, baseball, and basketball. He was baptized Jacobus Franciscus Thorpe in the Catholic Church and generally assumed that he was born on May 22, 1887, in Prague, Indian Territory (today Oklahoma), though his birth certificate has never been found. His native name was Wa-Tho-Huk, which means "path lit by great flash of lightening." His mother, Charlotte Vieux, was born to a French father and a Potawatomi mother descended from Chief Louis Vieux; his father, Hiram Thorpe, had a Sac and Fox mother and an Irish father.

Thorpe attended the Sac and Fox Indian Agency School located in Stroud, Oklahoma. His twin brother Charlie accompanied him to school but died of pneumonia at the age of nine. After the loss of his brother, Thorpe ran away from school several times. His father then sent him to the Haskell Institute, a Native American boarding school located in Lawrence, Kansas. Two years later, Thorpe's mother died of childbirth complications. He underwent periods of deep depression, which became even more complicated by his quarrels with his father. He left home to work on a ranch and find his way in life.

In 1904, Thorpe returned to live with his father and then attended the Carlisle Indian Industrial School in Pennsylvania. At the age of sixteen, he became widely recognized for his athletic ability. He was mentored by Glenn Scobey "Pop" Warner, a celebrated football coach of the early 1900s.

The extraordinary athletic accomplishments of Jim Thorpe are beyond the scope of this book. However, the highlights of his legendary deeds are necessary. At Carlisle, Thorpe played several positions in football: defensive back, placekicker, punter, and running back. He was chosen All-American for 1911 and 1912.

In the 1912 Olympics held in Stockholm, Sweden, he took part in the pentathlon and the decathlon, for a combined total of 15 events (of which he won 8). Thorpe was awarded gold medals for both the pentathlon and the decathlon. However, in early 1913, controversy arose over the revelation that Thorpe had previously played baseball for a small payment. He was deemed a "professional athlete" instead of an "amateur," and the International Olympic Committee (IOC) stripped him of his Olympic medals, records, and awards.

As was typical at the time, ethnic slurs were often used in relation to people of color. Thorpe's deeds of athletic brilliance were the subject of derogatory and stereotypical reporting, such as "Indians Scalp Army 27–6" and "Jim Thorpe on Rampage." For example, news of Thorpe's intention to qualify for the 1912 Olympics was headlined "Indian Thorpe in Olympiad; Redskin from Carlyle Will Strive for Place in American Team."[36] Throughout his athletic career, the stereotypical characteristics of being Native American were highlighted for publicity and/or marketing purposes.

After the 1912 Olympics, Thorpe played professional football, baseball, and basketball. He played the position of outfielder for the New York Giants baseball team (1913–1915 and 1917–1919), the Cincinnati Reds (1917), and the Boston Braves (1919). In football, he played halfback for the Canton Bulldogs (1915–1920 and 1926), Cleveland Indians

(1921), Oorang Indians (1922–1923), Rock Island Independent (1924), New York Giants (1925), and Chicago Cardinals (1928). He retired from professional sports at the age of 44. Thereafter, he found it difficult to make a living or care for his family.

In 1931, Thorpe made his film debut in *Touchdown!* He went on to appear in scores of films, most of them B-westerns, in which he was cast as a Native American warrior or chief. His roles were bit parts, in which he had little dialogue, but his muscular build and charisma were unmistakable. He also worked at the major studios like Warner Brothers and Paramount Pictures and in several of their big-budget films. For example, he was cast in two Errol Flynn films: *The Green Light* (1937, Warner Bros.) and *They Died with Their Boots On* (1941, Warner Bros.). According to some, Thorpe is said to have bested the former boxer, Flynn, in a real bar fight. However, they later become drinking buddies.[37] During his years in movies, Thorpe worked actively to have real Native Americans cast in native roles.

Thorpe married three times and had eight children, one of whom died at an early age. At the end of his sports career, he underwent financial woes. He made an entry into films and supplemented his income by working as a security guard, bouncer, and construction worker. In 1945, he had a short stint in the U.S. Merchant Marine. He struggled with alcoholism during the last years of his life.

In 1951, Warner Brothers paid Thorpe for his manuscript about his life, and a film was made (*Jim Thorpe—All-American*), in which Thorpe was portrayed by Burt Lancaster. Thorpe earned approximately $15,000 and an annuity of $2,500. The film resurrected Thorpe's fame, and the Associated Press honored him as the "greatest athlete" of the first 50 years of the 20th century. The Pro Football Hall of Fame would later induct him in the inaugural class of 1963.

In 1950, Thorpe was diagnosed with lip cancer. However, he was financially broke. As a result, he was treated as a charity patient. His wife Patricia at that time told the press, "We're broke.… Jim has nothing but his name and his memories. He has spent money on his own people and has given it away. He has often been exploited."[38]

Jim Thorpe died of heart failure on March 28, 1953. He was only sixty-five years old. Sadly, he continued to be the object of injustice and controversy even after his death. Following his funeral, Thorpe's third wife Patricia, without the permission of the rest of the family, sent Thorpe's remains to Pennsylvania. Jack Thorpe, Jim's son, would later argue that she had made a deal with officials for monetary considerations. The newly named Jim Thorpe borough, where he was buried, would later erect a museum in his honor. Over the years Thorpe's family attempted numerous times to move his remains back to his native Oklahoma. His son Jack brought legal proceedings for the return of his father's remains, arguing on the basis of the Native American Grave Protection and Repatriation Act. His suit was unsuccessful, and the younger Thorpe died in 2011. On October 23, 2014, the U.S. Court of Appeals for the Third Circuit ruled that the Jim Thorpe borough is not a museum and therefore does not fall under the federal statute, meaning it was under no obligation to return Thorpe's remains. On October 5, 2015, the U.S. Supreme Court refused to hear the issue, ending all legal remedies.

The efforts to reinstate Thorpe's Olympic titles took several decades. In October 1982, the IOC Executive Committee reinstated Thorpe's status as an amateur athlete and his Olympic standing. On January 18, 1983, the IOC held a ceremony in which two of Thorpe's children, Bill and Gale, were presented with commemorative medals. Although Thorpe is now listed as the Olympic medalist, his results have not been restored to the

1912 Olympic official records. His medals were held by several museums over the years, but they have since been stolen and have never been recovered.

Jim Thorpe made his film debut playing himself in a documentary short titled *The Giants-White Sox Tour* in 1914 and followed it up with another appearance in *The Baseball Revue of 1917*. His film career took place after the end of his athletic career, mainly out of financial necessity. He was often cast in bit parts in both big-budget films and B-films (most of them westerns).

Thorpe appeared in 71 films: *Touchdown!* (1931); *Battling with Buffalo Bill* (1931, Universal), a serial of 12 episodes; *The Dark Horse* (1932, Warner Bros.); *My Pal, the King* (1932, Universal); *Hold 'Em Jail* (1932, RKO); *Off His Base* (1932, Educ. Corp.), a film short, as himself; *White Eagle* (1932, Columbia); *Always Kickin'* (1932, Educ. Corp.), a film short; *The Golden West* (1932, Fox Film Corp.); *Air Mail* (1932, Universal); *Wild Horse Mesa* (1932, Paramount); *King Kong* (1933, RKO-Pathé); *Sweepings* (1933, RKO); *The Red Rider* (1934, Universal); *Behold My Wife!* (1934, Paramount); *Rustlers of Red Dog* (1935, Universal), a serial; *Under Pressure* (1935, Fox Film Corp.); *One Run Elmer* (1935, Educa. Films Corp.), a film short; *The Miracle Rider* (1935, Mascot Pictures), a 12-part serial; *Code of the Mounted* (1935, Conn Pictures Corp.); *Alibi Ike* (1935, Warner Bros.); *The Arizonian* (1935, RKO); *She* (1935, RKO-Pathé); *The Daring Young Man* (1935, Fox Film Corp.); *The Farmer Takes a Wife* (1935, Fox Film Corp.); *Wanderer of the Wasteland* (1935, Paramount); *It's in the Air* (1935, MGM); *Barbary Coast* (1935, Samuel Goldwyn); *The Last Days of Pompeii* (1935, RKO); *Fighting Youth* (1935, Universal); *Moonlight on the Prairie* (1935, Warner Bros.); *The Ivory-Handed Gun* (1935, Buck Jones Prods.); *La Fiesta de Santa Bárbara* (1935, MGM), a film short; *Captain Blood* (1935, Warner Bros.); *Klondike Annie* (1936, Paramount); *Sutter's Gold* (1936, Universal); *Silly Billies* (1936, Hal Roach); *Hill-Tillies* (1936, RKO), a film short; *Under Two Flags* (1936, 20th Century Corp.); *Treachery Rides the Range* (1936, Warner Bros.); *Wildcat Trooper* (1936, Conn Pictures Corp.); *The Phantom Rider* (1936, Universal), a 15-part serial; *Yellow Stone* (1936, Universal); *Trailin' West* (1936, Warner Bros.); *Green Light* (1937, Warner Bros.); *Pick a Star* (1937, Hal Roach); *San Quentin* (1937, Warner Bros.); *Big City* (1937, MGM), as himself; *52nd Street* (1937, Walter Wranger Prods.); *Born to the West* (1937, Paramount); *Trial* (1937); *Cattle Raider* (1938, Columbia); *Start Cheering* (1938, Columbia); *Frontier Scout* (1938, Franklyn Warner Prods.); *The Man from Texas* (1939, Edward F. Finney Prods.); *Man of Conquest* (1939, Republic Pictures); *Henry Goes Arizona* (1939, MGM); *Arizona Frontier* (1940, Edward R. Finney Prods.); *Knute Rockne, All American* (1940, Warner Bros.); *Prairie Schooners* (1940, Columbia); *Mexican Spitfire Out West* (1940, RKO); *Meet John Doe* (1941, Paramount); *They Died with Their Boots On* (1941, Warner Bros.); *Outlaws of Santa Fe* (1944, Republic); *Outlaw Trail* (1944, Monogram Pictures); *Beyond the Pecos* (1945, Universal); *The Vampire's Ghost* (1945, Republic); *Road to Utopia* (1943, Paramount); *Yes Sir, That's My Baby* (1949, Univ. Inter.); *White Heat* (1949, Warner Bros.); and his last, *Wagon Master* (1950, Argosy Pictures).

6

Native Americans as Part of the Nation's Family (1940–1949)

The key film image of Native Americans during the 1940s was their portrayal as part of the nation's family. Finally, indigenous people were represented in motion pictures as part of the vital fabric of nation.

The advent of World War II compelled the federal government and motion picture studios to create and foster unity of all peoples in the United States as part of nation's fabric. This included Native Americans, Mexican Americans, African Americans, and Asian Americans. President Franklin D. Roosevelt, the armed forces, and all government agencies pushed for solidarity and sacrifice in a time of national crisis.

The goodwill and assistance expressed by federal government in the New Deal programs went a long way to foster better relations with Native American, Mexican American, and African American communities. Communities of color responded in huge numbers by serving in every branch of the armed forces. Native Americans and Mexican Americans served in unsegregated units and won an unprecedented number of war medals. Although African Americans served in segregated units, they also served with distinction. These marginalized communities believed that unless the fascist countries of Europe were defeated, their lives in this nation would never improve.

The advent of the U.S. entry into World War II in December 1941 had a huge impact on Native Americans. Some 44,000 Native Americans enlisted in the U.S. armed forces. This number accounted for one-third of adults aged eighteen to fifty who were said to be "able-bodied."

World War II marked the largest exodus of indigenous peoples since the forced removals to reservations in the 1830s. Plagued by endemic poverty, little or no medical services, poor education, and alcoholism, young Native Americans voluntarily enlisted at a rate of 40 percent greater than those who were drafted. While some of their fellow servicemen held them in high regard due to their legendary exploits as warriors, they often called all native volunteers "chief." Native Americans endured constant discrimination, derogatory name calling, and often the harshest conditions.

Native American soldiers fought and died in some of the most important battles of the entire war: Iwo Jima, North Africa, Australia, the Philippines, Normandy, the Battle of the Bulge, Belgium, and the Battle for Berlin, among many others. In total, Native Americans won more than two hundred military medals (not including many Purple Hearts) and more than thirty Distinguished Flying Cross medals.[1]

Native American servicemen in World War II suffered heavy combat losses. For example, of the 1,200 Pueblo men who served, about half were killed in the war. However, their courage and service in combat were beyond reproach. More than half of the Navajo served as the Navajo "code talkers" in the Pacific theater, and their code was never broken by the Japanese. One of the better-known native U.S. servicemen was Ira Hayes, one of the U.S. Marines who raised the U.S. flag in Iwo Jima.

However, after the war the dreams of good-paying jobs and homeownership proved illusory. In 1940, some 5 percent of Native Americans lived outside the reservations; by 1950, some 20 percent had moved to urban centers. Post-traumatic stress, war injuries, and racism thwarted the hopes and dreams of Native American war veterans.

THE TERMINATION POLICY

From the mid–1940s to the mid–1950s, the federal government began a policy that came to be known as "Indian Termination." This policy was shaped by several laws and policies intended to end the federal government's recognition of tribal sovereignty, the exclusion of state law that was applicable to native peoples, and the termination of trusteeship over reservations. During 1953–1964, the federal government ceased to recognize more than one hundred Native American tribes and bands. As a consequence, more than 2,500,000 acres of trust land lost their protected status, and most of it was sold to non-native persons. The termination policy also included moving thousands of Native Americans to cities with the promise of jobs and housing. This effort was a dismal and heartbreaking failure, as native people found it impossible to find decent-paying jobs and housing due to blatant racism and limited education.[2]

Some tribes fought the termination policy through civil lawsuits. Gradually, important political leaders came out in opposition to the policy. On July 8, 1970, President Richard M. Nixon, in a Special Message on Indian Affairs, stated,

> The first Americans—the Indians—are the most deprived and most isolated minority group in our nation. On virtually every scale of measurement—employment, income, education, health—the condition of the Indian people ranks at the bottom....
>
> Forced termination is wrong, in my judgment, for a number of reasons. First, the premises on which it rests are wrong.... The second reason for rejecting force termination is that the practice results have been clearly harmful.... The third argument I would make against forced termination concerns the effect it has had upon the overwhelming majority of tribes which still enjoy a special relationship with the Federal government.... The recommendations of this administration represent an historic step forward in Indian policy. We are proposing to break away sharply with past approaches to Indian problems.[3]

The protracted litigation lasted until 1980, when it finally was taken up by the U.S. Supreme Court. In that year, the 1974 *Bold Decision* was upheld by U.S. Supreme Court. It recognized that Native American tribes retained treaty rights for such things as hunting and fishing, without state interference.

The rise of Native American activism and numerous acts of civil disobedience and protest put the issues of tribal sovereignty, land rights, and native culture in the forefront of the nation's conscience. In 1973, the U.S. Congress rejected the termination policy with the passage of the Indian Self-Determination and Education Assistance Act. On January

24, 1983, President Ronald Reagan made a policy statement that explicitly repudiated the termination policy: "When European powers began to explore and colonize this land, they entered into treaties with sovereign Indian nations. Our nation continued to make treaties and to deal with Indian tribes on a government-to-government basis. Throughout our history, despite periods of conflict and shifting national policies on Indian affairs, the government-to-government relationship between the United States and Indian tribes has endured. The Constitution, treaties, laws, and court decisions have consistently recognized a unique political relationship between Indian tribes and the United States which this administration pledges to uphold."[4]

HUAC

The majority of the Hollywood films during the 1940s were heavily influenced by two pivotal events. The first was the nation's fight for survival during World War II. The second was the subsequent Cold War, which brought about the House Un-American Activities Committee (HUAC) and its anti–Communist crusade. During the war, escapist films heavily laced with patriotism contributed to the war effort by providing entertainment for the war-weary audiences. During this period, war films and non-war films depicted Native Americans, Mexican Americans, African Americans, Asian Americans, and other minorities as hard-working people and part of the vital fabric of the nation. However, the end of the war saw a return to the regular stereotypes of native people as marauding savages.

The decade was characterized by three distinct political periods. During the years 1939–1941, when the United States was not directly involved in hostilities, the nation focused on preparedness. Beginning on December 7 (the day of the attack on Pearl Harbor), the country became actively involved in World War II. The cessation of hostilities in 1945 soon led to the Cold War with the Soviet Union and the McCarthy era.

The postwar period became a battleground for the Cold War in which heavy-handed and propagandist films like *The Iron Curtain* (1948, 20th-Century Fox) were prevalent. In 1947, the House Un-American Activities Committee (HUAC) appeared in Hollywood in order to investigate alleged Communist influences in the film industry. This investigation coincided with the industry's efforts to address more serious and political issues in film.

HUAC delivered a crippling blow to the film industry, one that devastated a whole generation of actors, writers, and filmmakers and cowed the next generation. A blacklist emerged of "fellow travelers" and "premature anti-fascists" and the disloyal. Naming names and informing on friends, ex-lovers, and associates became a cathartic exercise for many. In addition to the "blacklist," there was a "gray list," which included those who were unnamed but who were unwilling to subscribe to the reigning hysteria.

A group of filmmakers who refused to be "friendly witnesses" became known as the "Hollywood Ten" and were sentenced to prison. They included producer-writer Adrian Scott (*Mr. Lucky*, 1943), director Edward Dmytryk (*Crossfire*, 1947), producer-director Herbert Biberman (*Salt of the Earth*, 1954), and screenwriters John Howard Lawson (*Blockade*, 1938), Albert Maltz (*This Gun for Hire*, 1942), Samuel Ornitz (*Three Faces West*, 1940), Dalton Trumbo (*Thirty Seconds Over Tokyo*, 1944), Alvah Bessie (*Objective

Burma, 1945), Ring Lardner, Jr. (*Woman of the Year*, 1942), and Lester Cole (*The Romance of Rosy Ridge*, 1947).

Many creative talents suffered from the blacklist, while others later recanted but still suffered career damage. The political acrimony and political climate led to the exodus of other talents. HUAC's encore in Hollywood during 1951 further robbed the film industry of its some leading creative and artistic talents.

Native American Film Images in the 1940s

The U.S. concern for hemispheric unity and the president's Good Neighbor Policy contributed to a marked improvement of Native American images—at least temporarily. The record number of Native American enlistment and heroism in the war earned the sympathy and empathy of the federal government and Euro-American population.

Despite all this, however, the 1940s was a mixed decade for indigenous people in terms of the film industry. During the entire decade, only one film (1947's *Black Gold*) was made with Native American man as the leading character. The only film in which a Native American female was the lead character was in *Duel in the Sun* (1946, Selznick). In general, both native protagonists and actors continued to be reduced to supporting roles, usually as the proverbial adversaries to Manifest Destiny in westerns and/or as subsidiary one-dimensional roles in films set in contemporary settings.

The decade brought no new bona fide film stars of native ancestry. The two best-known native stars from the 1920s, Ramón Novarro and Dolores Del Río, all but disappeared during the 1940s. Novarro was semi-retired for most of the decade, and Del Río left for Mexico in 1942 to collaborate with the indigenous director Emilio "Indio" Fernández, going on to make a series of memorable films that celebrated Mexico's indigenous culture. Anthony Quinn, the Tarahumara-origin actor who had made his Hollywood debut in the mid–1930s, was consigned to supporting roles, playing violent Native American warriors, ethnic gangsters, conniving Middle Eastern villains, and pirates. Sometimes he broke the mold, such as when he played a Mexican American G.I. in *Guadalcanal Diary* and/or the native lead in *Black Gold*. For the most part, though, native actors played the usual suspects.

The hard-working and talented native actors working in the film industry during the 1950s included the veterans Monte Blue, Charles Stevens, Chief Yowlachie, and Gertrude Chorre, who had begun in films in the 1920s. Native performers from the 1930s included Marie Chorre, Sonny Chorre, Chief White Eagle, Ray Mala (who also became a respected cinematographer), Chris-Pin Martín, Jim Thorpe (the revered Olympic gold medalist), and Chief Thundercloud. The 1940s brought some new actors of native ancestry, including Linda Darnell; Mexican native performer Rodolfo Acosta; Chief Many Treaties; Tatzumbia Dupea; Mexican director, screenwriter, and actor Emilio "Indio" Fernández; and Jay Silverheels. Many other native actors toiled in anonymity and small roles, which were never enough to provide a long career.

Native American film images evolved from the proverbial marauding warrior and squaw in the early 1940s to that of a more docile and demonstrative red man at the end of the decade. The decade began with several big-budget films that celebrated Manifest Destiny. *Kit Carson* (1940, United Artists) chronicled the deeds and misdeeds of the infa-

6. Native Americans as Part of the Nation's Family (1940–1949)   99

mous trapper and "Indian fighter." Cecil B. DeMille's *North West Mounted Police* (1940, Paramount) chronicled the Riel Rebellion in 1885 in Canada. *They Died with Their Boots On* (1942, Warner Bros.) romanticized the mythology of George Armstrong Custer and the Indian wars. Finally, *Northwest Passage* (1940, MGM) celebrated the frontiersman Robert Rogers and his war against indigenous peoples in the colonial period. All four films proved hugely successful at the box office.

During the war, several films deviated from the proverbial norm of native people as savages and convenient enemies. However, some continued to perpetuate the old mythology. *Apache Trail* (1942, MGM) told the tale of a group of helpless whites besieged by 300 ruthless native warriors in the Old West. In turn, *Frontier Fury* (1943, Columbia), a western headlined by matinee favorite Charles Starrett, deviated from the typical narrative and focused on exposing and arresting corrupt Indian federal agents.

In *The Law Rides Again* (1944, Monogram), two government agents, Hoot Gibson and Ken Maynard, worked to stop the corrupt machinations of an Indian agent who stole from the local native tribe. This movie was the second in a series of eleven films produced from 1943 to 1944, known as the "Trail Blazers" series. Another entry in this series, *Outlaw Trail* (1944, Monogram), starred Hoot Gibson and Bob Steele as government agents investigating the disappearance of a man and the exploitation of a Native American tribe by unscrupulous criminals. This film also featured two native icons: Jim Thorpe and Chief Thundercloud. In the final "Trail Blazers" film, *Sonora Stagecoach* (1944, Monogram), Chief Thundercloud provided crucial help to Hoot Gibson and Bob Steele in order to resolve the robbery of a stagecoach. In the meantime, *Buffalo Bill* (1944, 20th Century–Fox) depicted the ethnic cleansing of the Great Plains in Technicolor.

After the war, it was a return to past stereotypes and mythology. King Vidor's *Duel in the Sun* (1946, Selznick), an epic western, would deliver the key Native American female role of the decade. John Ford's evocative western *My Darling Clementine* (1946, 20th Century–Fox) focused on the legendary gun battle at the OK Corral. This film featured an excellent performance by Linda Darnell as Chihuahua as a Mexican native woman who works in a saloon and is the love interest of the notorious Doc Holliday (Victor Mature). M. Elise Marubbio wrote, "Chihuahua's mixed Indian and Mexican heritage and her actions also relegate her to the position of Indian within the western's structure, in which Indians are synonymous with savagery and the antithesis of white civilization."[5]

Cecil B. DeMille's *Unconquered* (1947, Paramount) was set in the colonial period and depicted native people as the main impediment in the way of progress and white civilization. In the same year, *Captain from Castile* (1947, 20th Century–Fox) subverted the epic genre with some unexpected analogies to the contemporary McCarthy era. *Black Gold* (1947, Allied Artists) provided Anthony Quinn with his first lead role and told the true story of a simple human being of native ancestry.

John Huston's *Treasure of the Sierra Madre* (1948, Warner Bros.) was based on a novel by the enigmatic B. Traven about humanity's insatiable greed. The narrative focused on a trio of Euro-Americans (Humphrey Bogart, Walter Huston, and Tim Holt) reduced to the level of hobos in the oil fields of Veracruz, Mexico. They are consumed by gold fever in the Sierra Madre. Ultimately, one of them steals from his two friends, only to meet with unexpected robbery and death at the hands of indigenous bandits led by Gold Hat (Alfonso Bedoya).

Raoul Walsh's *Colorado Territory* (1949, Warner Bros.) featured a standout performance by the underappreciated Virginia Mayo as the strong-willed and mixed-blood Colorado, aiding and loving the over-the-hill bank robber (Joel McCrea). She is the only one of his friends and acquaintances who does not betray him.

By the end of the 1940s, it seemed that little had changed. John Ford's cavalry trilogy provided a sentimental and romanticized version of how the west was appropriated: *Fort Apache* (1948, Republic); *She Wore a Yellow Ribbon* (1949, RKO); and *Rio Grande* (1950, Republic).

Nevertheless, there were often offbeat films featuring native characters in a positive light. In the film *The Last Roundup* (1947, Autry), the protagonist (played by Gene Autry) works to amicably have Native Americans and ranchers share and benefit from the Mesa City aqueduct. He does so by thwarting the corrupt scheme of the white banker in town who is opposed to the plan. The film *Daughter of the West* (1949, Mooney) depicts the departure of Lolita Moreno (Martha Vickers) from the Juan Capistrano Mission in California to teach in the Navajo Nation. There she falls in love with Navo White Eagle (Phillip Reed), a Navajo. Both work to protect their people from an unscrupulous Indian agent who plans to rob the copper lode. Later, Lolita discovers that she is the daughter of the fabled mestiza maiden Ramona. She then weds Navo, who becomes the new Indian agent.

Alfonso Bedoya as the Mexican Indian Gold Hat and Humphrey Bogart as Fred C. Dobbs in John Huston's *Treasure of Sierra Madre* (1948, Warner Bros.).

Representative Films

They Died with Their Boots On (1942, Warner Bros.)

The most famous film ever made about George Armstrong Custer (1839–1876) and his inglorious defeat at the Battle of the Little Big Horn was *They Died with Their Boots On*. Custer was played by the Australian-born Errol Flynn (1909–1959), and the film was directed by the prolific Raoul Walsh (1887–1980), who, like Flynn, had lived an action-packed life. Walsh's other native-themed films included *The Big Trail* (1930), *Saskatchewan* (1954, Warner Bros.), *The Tall Men* (1955, 20th Century–Fox), and *A Distant Trumpet* (1964, Warner Bros.).

They Died with Their Boots On chronicles Custer's life starting with his arrival at West Point, where he immediately offends everyone with his brash personality. He makes a lifetime enemy of cadet Ned Sharp (Arthur Kennedy), the son of a general. There he also meets his future wife Libby (Olivia De Havilland), the daughter of an important banker.

The film's depiction of Custer's personality is ironically accurate according to different accounts. He is an irresponsible student (graduating last in his class) and often compared to another student, Ulysses S. Grant. He is reprimanded for fighting, gambling, irresponsibility, and skipping guard duty. After finally graduating from West Point, Custer is sent to fight in the Union Army during the Civil War, though only because there is a shortage of trained officers. Custer is promoted by mistake after distinguishing himself in battle, though he also disobeyed orders.

After the war, he is discharged and settles down with his wife. His idleness, however, leads him again to excessive gambling and the prolific consumption of alcohol. Through his wife's intercession, Custer is assigned command of the 7th Cavalry in the Dakotas. However, Sharp, Libby's father, and other railroad associates undermine his command, and Custer is removed when he refuses to become involved in a land scheme in the Black Hills (located in South Dakota).

President Grant forgives Custer's indiscretions and reassigns him to lead the 7th Cavalry. When white settlers make incursions into the Black Hills seeking gold, Custer is sent to fight the united native tribes. At the Little Big Horn, Crazy Horse (Anthony Quinn) and Sitting Bull lead a combined force that defeats Custer and the 7th Cavalry.

They Died with Their Boots On is an epic film in scale, but it is a fictionalized representation of Custer's life and death. The film was made at the height of Hollywood craftsmanship and has the sweep and vigor for which director Raoul Walsh was well known. The cast played their parts with precision, effectiveness, and skill. The screenplay was written by Wally Kline and Aenis MacKensie, and the cinematography was done by Bert Glennon.

The film portrays Custer's personality as reckless, flamboyant, cocky, insubordinate, and arrogant—he is ultimately a seeker of glory. Had the screenplay maintained the character continuity to his ultimate demise, it would have been a subtle commentary on the consequences of his personality disorders. All other films about Custer either maintained his character in a state of underdevelopment (e.g., *Custer of the West*, 1968, Cinerama Releasing Corp.) or featured over-the-top caricatures (e.g., *Little Big Man*, 1970). However, *They Died with Their Boots On* totally subverts the Custer character at the end, becoming contrived and revisionist. Here Custer is portrayed as the solitary defender of the Lakota (Sioux) in the West; yet he obeys the command to fight the Sioux, which is contradictory to the temperament and personality developed through four-fifths of the film. Viewers are asked to believe that a headstrong general would accept meekly an order that runs counter to his principles. Thus the film has Custer fight the Lakota (Sioux) so that the government can sympathize with their plight!

The major indigenous character in the film is Crazy Horse, played convincingly by Anthony Quinn. John E. O'Connor noted that while "no one can doubt that the Indian was the enemy in *They Died with Their Boots On*, the film allowed a grudging respect for Crazy horse (Anthony Quinn) and stressed the fact that white men had broken their treaty and provoked the Indians' final resort to the warpath."[6]

They Died with Their Boots On was both a critical and a box-office success. The film was released just prior to the U.S. entry into World War II, and its glorification of the U.S. military coincided with the mood of the nation. *Variety* (November 17, 1941) commented, "The test of the yarn is not its accuracy, but its speed and excitement. Of these it has plenty … '*Boots*' is a surefire western, an escape from bombers, tanks Gestapo."[7]

John Ford's Cavalry Trilogy: *Fort Apache* (1948, Republic); *She Wore a Yellow Ribbon* (1949, RKO); and *Río Grande* (1950, Republic)

During the late 1940s and early 1950s, John Ford directed three films—*Fort Apache* (1948, Republic), *She Wore a Yellow Ribbon* (1949, RKO), and *Río Grande* (1950, Republic)—that collectively became known as the "cavalry trilogy." All three films had a common theme: the story of the lives of Irish American soldiers in the west, without women or families, and at times with mixed motivations about fighting wars against Native Americans.

All three films were populated by actors from John Ford's stock company of players, many of whom had been in films since the 1910s (like Ford's own brother Francis Ford). This company included John Wayne, Maureen O'Hara, Henry Fonda, Pedro Armendáriz, Harry Carey, Jr., Victor McLaglen, John Agar, Ward Bond, and Ben Johnson, among others. The films were filled with Irish sentimentality, folklore, and songs. All three films were shot on location in Monument Valley, Utah.

Fort Apache tells the story of the glory-seeking Lieutenant Colonel Thursday (Henry Fonda), who is commanded to fight the Apaches. He is at odds with his subordinates Captain York (John Wayne) and Sergeant Buefort (Pedro Armendáriz), who caution him against underestimating the Apaches' skills in warfare. The colonel foolishly goes ahead with his rigid military strategy, getting himself killed in the process.

Ford's depiction of Native Americans in *Fort Apache* is an improvement from the faceless and screaming savages of *Stagecoach*. At one point the film features a parley between the colonel and Cochise (Miguel Inclán), who condemns the U.S. government's policy of land appropriation and extermination of indigenous people. Bosley Crowther, writing in the *New York Times* (June 25, 1948), noted, "But also apparent [is] a new and maturing viewpoint upon one aspect of the American Indian wars. For here it is not the 'heathen Indian' who is the 'heavy' of the piece but a hard-bitten Army colonel, blind through ignorance and passion for revenge."[8]

She Wore a Yellow Ribbon was shot in vivid Technicolor and highlights the striking landscape of Monument Valley and surrounding areas. It is a darker film that dwells on the last days of cavalry service for an aging Captain Brittles (John Wayne), the transportation of helpless women out of harm's way, and Brittles' efforts to prevent another war with native tribes in the aftermath of Custer's military defeat and death. Brittles is filled with remorse and anguish about the loss of life, especially the youth of both sides. He seeks a peace initiative with Chief Pony That Walks (Chief John Big Tree) but fails. Fortunately, a stampede of native horses prevents the war that he fears.

Reviewers of *She Wore a Yellow Ribbon* were generally positive. Bosley Crowther wrote in the *New York Times* (November 18, 1949), "No one could get more emotion out of a thundering cavalry charge or an old soldier's farewell departure from the ranks of his comrades than [director John Ford]."[9] Ford presented a nostalgic rendition of the U.S. Cavalry that borders on pure glorification. The role of Chief Pony That Walks is the only native character with some dimension. The other native characters revert to the roles of faceless, anonymous savages perpetrating violence and destruction.

The third film of John Ford's cavalry trilogy was *Río Grande*, which focuses on Lieutenant Colonel Yorke (John Wayne), based on the Texas frontier and charged with protecting Euro-American settlers from the Apaches during the summer of 1879. His military assignment is to prevent the Apaches from using Mexico as a sanctuary. His life is complicated by the arrival of his estranged wife (Maureen O'Hara), who is visiting his enlisted son (Claude Jarman). The film climaxes with Yorke's daring rescue of white children who have been kidnapped by Apaches. The Native Americans in *Río Grande* are merely used as props to facilitate the military action depicted; there is no effort to humanize them or their behavior.

In conclusion, Ford's cavalry trilogy is an example of his mastery of the art form of film. However, these films, to a great degree, are a rendition of a mythical west, seen strictly from a white perspective.

Northwest Passage (1940, MGM)

The rugged and abrasive *Northwest Passage* was one of the key films depicting the colonial campaigns against Native Americans in the Northeast. It is the most pervasively racist film with regard to Native Americans made during the 1940s.

The film was directed by the legendary director King Vidor (1894–1982), whose impressive films include *The Big Parade* (1925) and *The Crowd* (1926), both socially conscious products of the silent era. Two other directors, W. S. Van Dyke and Jack Conway, also shot parts of the film. The screenplay was written by Talbot Jennings and Laurence Stallings. Other screenwriters are said to have worked on the script, including playwrights Sidney Howard and Robert Sherwood. The screenplay was based on the novel *Northwest Passage* (1937) by Kenneth Roberts. The impressive cinematography (color) was done by Sidney Wagner and William V. Skall, both of whom were nominated for an Academy Award for Best Cinematography.

The narrative begins in 1759 (during the French and Indian War) in Portsmouth, New Hampshire, when Langdon Towne (Robert Young) returns home after having been expelled from Harvard University. His parents and those of his sweetheart (Ruth Hussey) are bitterly disappointed because he has no visible means of making a living, despite his desire to become a painter. Soon thereafter, he is recruited by the rugged military leader Major Robert Rogers (Spencer Tracy), along with his friend "Hunk" Marriner (Walter Brennan), and they become part of "Rogers' Rangers."

The rest of the narrative involves the rangers' march and attack on a settlement of the Abenaki native people in Saint Francis (now Odanak, Quebec, Canada). The justification for this action is that the Abenaki have raided and killed Euro-Americans on the frontier. After the attack, the rangers are decimated due to casualties, hunger, and injuries. They barely make it back to Portsmouth, where the indestructible Major Rogers sets out on another expedition to find the mythical Northwest Passage.

The real Robert Rogers (1731–1795) was less than heroic. He is credited with founding Rogers' Rangers and developing forms of unconventional warfare for England and the United States. However, he was also accused of treason and arrested in 1765 by the British and in 1776 by George Washington on the suspicion of being a British spy. During the American War of Independence, he offered his services to the British. Rogers ultimately died in obscurity, an alcoholic and broke, having lost his family and the respect of many. He was buried in London, England, and his grave is now lost.

Northwest Passage expounds on the virtuous frontiersmen, their toughness, their durability, and their dreams of making a great nation, regardless of consideration for Native Americans. There are derogatory references about native people throughout the film. The attack on the Abenaki settlement is a ruthless slaughter of scalping and brutality. Although women and children are not depicted as victims, the real history of the attack says otherwise. One ranger becomes so enamored of the violence directed at natives that he decapitates a head and carries it as souvenir. Another ranger comments, "You can't judge Indians like white people!" Before the attack, the rangers are advised, "Kill all Indians and kill them good!"

Native American roles were relegated to mostly faceless figures, without words or individuality. The few indigenous actors in the film included George Sky Eagle, Lawrence Porter, and Andrew Pena. Most of the scenes in *Northwest Passage* were shot outdoors, mostly in the rugged areas in Idaho and Glacier National Park. Hundreds of Blackfeet and Nez Perce were used as extras in the film.

Film critics of the time praised *Northwest Passage*. Frank S. Nugent, writing in the *New York Times* (March 8, 1940), remarked that although "somewhat too generously Technicolored and inclined to grow sanctimonious about Indian-fighting hero, Major Roberts of Rogers's Rangers ... it still is a better-than-fair condensation of the first part of the book, still a rich and well-played and vicariously thrilling chapter of pre-national history."[10]

Duel in the Sun (1946, Selznick)

David O. Selznick's epic western *Duel in the Sun* contained the only Native American lead female role of the decade.

The film starts in 1880 Texas, when the gambler Scott Chávez (Herbert Marshall) is hanged for killing his adulterous wife (Tilly Losch) and her lover. His daughter, "Pearl Chávez, the half-breed from along the border," is subsequently adopted by a kindly distant cousin of her father, Laura Belle McCanles (Lillian Gish). Laura's cattle baron husband is Senator McCanles, "who helped build Texas." McCanles is a bigot who treats Pearl with both contempt and disdain. One of his sons, Jesse (Joseph Cotton), is dispatched to pick her up at the stagecoach station and remarks when he sees her, "I'm sorry for not recognizing you. I guess it was the clothes." When the senator finally sees Pearl, he exclaims, "Girl, what are you doing in that get-up?" When she tells him her name, the senator retorts, "They might have better called you Pocahontas or Minnie-ha-ha. Ain't I right?" Her indigenousness is the constant object of derision.

Pearl subsequently becomes romantically involved with Jesse, the attorney of the family, and also with his brother Lewt (Gregory Peck), a vain, egotistical and manipulative wastrel. The senator objects to Lewt keeping company with Pearl. Lewt tells his father, "She looks like a pretty good tamale." "She wouldn't appeal to me," McCanles responds. On another occasion, increasingly disgusted with Lewt's involvement with Pearl, the senator tells him, "I haven't been working on this place for 30 years to turn it into no Indian reservation." Lewt laughingly retorts, "You want me to have a good time, don't you?" Both the father and son share the same hypocritical racism.

A conflict between ranchers and the railroad erupts, as a result of which Jesse also has a falling out with his father. When Jesse rejects Pearl's love because "like mother, like daughter," she seeks solace with Sam Pierce (Charles Bickford), to whom she becomes engaged. Jealous with rage, Lewt kills Pierce and seeks out Pearl for sexual gratification. Lewt then turns down her proposal for marriage: "No woman can tie on to me, least of all a bobcat little half-breed like you!" In a subsequent altercation with Jesse, Lewt wounds his unarmed brother. Nevertheless, his father continues to disregard Lewt's dark side, declaring, "It's that Indian girl." At the end of the film, Pearl tracks down Lewt in the desert in order to prevent him from killing Jesse. There Pearl and Lewt kill each other, dying in each other's arms.

Jennifer Jones as Pearl Chavez and Gregory Peck as Lewt in *Duel in the Sun* (1946, Selznick).

Duel in the Sun was produced by David O. Selznick, who had previously made *Gone with the Wind* (1939, MGM). The film was directed by the famed King Vidor. *Duel in the Sun* was the most expensive film (more than $6 million in 1946 dollars) made until that time. The striking Technicolor cinematography was the work of three distinguished cinematographers. The veteran, Lee Garmes, had been nominated three times for an Academy Award for Best Cinematography. The second, Ray Renahan, had won two Academy Awards for Best Color Cinematography for *Gone with the Wind* (1939, MGM) and *Blood and Sand* (1941, 20th Century–Fox). The third, Harold Rosson, had been nominated for an Academy Award for Best Cinematography five previous times and was honored with an honorary Oscar for the color cinematography work in Selznick's *Garden of Allah* (1936).

For the role of Pearl Chávez, Selznick cast his (then) wife Jennifer Jones (1919–2009), who had previously won an Academy Award for Best Actress for an entirely different type of role in *The Song of Bernadette* (1943, 20th Century–Fox). *Duel in the Sun* was nominated for two Academy Awards: Best Actress (Jennifer Jones) and Best Supporting Actress (Lillian Gish). The film went to become a huge box-office success, grossing $456.5 million domestically when adjusted for inflation.[11]

Sadly, Jones was entirely miscast as Pearl, reducing the character to a blatant stereotype. The character of Pearl epitomized all the denigrating characteristics attributed to Native American/Mexican women in U.S. films, including a singular incapacity to control their primitive sexual passions and an ingrained sense of inferiority. The character was stigmatized with a self-fulfilling prophecy of failure and heartbreak. As part of their portrayals, Jones and Tilly Losch (an Austrian-born dancer and actress who played Pearl's mother) wore the then common brownish skin makeup. Jones' exaggerated sexual gyrations, panting, and facial expressions only added to the stereotype.

M. Elise Marubbio wrote of the tumultuous relationship between Pearl and Lewt, "Their sadomasochistic relationship and their transgressions of social taboos against such actions such as murder, rape, and premarital and interracial sex are linked to their internal psychological darkness.... [Pearl's] Indian heritage already positions her as a savage."[12]

The distinguished London-born actor Herbert Marshall, with his suave English accent, was another casting disaster as Mr. Chávez. In addition, the character of Vashti (played by African American actress Butterfly McQueen) was another stinging stereotype.

Despite the film's large cast and the fact that it was shot on location in the Tucson area in Arizona, there was not a single Native American actor in *Duel in the Sun*.

DeMille's *North West Mounted Police* (1940, Paramount) and *Unconquered* (1947, Paramount)

After the significant commercial successes of his two epic westerns *The Plainsmen* (1936, Paramount) and *Union Pacific* (1939, Paramount), director Cecil B. DeMille returned to explore the western frontier in two films.

North West Mounted Police was a big-budget Technicolor drama set in Canada in the mid-1800s and headlined by big stars—namely, Gary Cooper, Madeline Carroll, Paulette Goddard, Robert Preston, and Preston Foster. This was DeMille's first Technicolor film. The screenplay was written by C. Gardner Sullivan, Jesse Lasky, Jr., and Alan Le May and based on the book *The Royal Canadian Mounted Police* by R.C. Featherstonehaugh. The film won an Academy Award for Best Film Editing (Anne Bauchens, DeMille's lifelong film editor). It was shot on location in both California and Oregon, doubling for Canada.

The threadbare narrative involves the pursuit of an outlaw named Jacques Corbeau (George Bancroft) by Texas ranger Dusty Rivers (Gary Cooper) in the 1880s, during the Riel Rebellion in Canada. In the process of searching for his wanted man, Rivers becomes romantically involved with nurse April Logan (Madeleine Carroll), who is already involved with Mountie Sergeant Jim Britt (Preston Foster). In addition, April's brother, Mountie Ronnie Logan (Robert Preston), is in love with Corbeau's daughter Louvette (Paulette Goddard), a mixed blood, who is determined that her father not be found.

Dusty is finally able to find Corbeau's whereabouts with the help of the Mounted Police. However, Louvette, in order to protect Ronnie, ties him up. He is unable to warn his fellow Mounties about an ambush and is subsequently deemed a deserter. In the end, Dusty and the Mounties prevail, and Dusty rides back with his prey back to Texas, leaving April to Britt.

The Riel Rebellion was led by Louis Riel in 1885 with the support of Native American allies, both Cree and Assiniboine. They joined the rebellion because they felt that Canada had failed to protect their land, culture, and rights. However, after some early military victories, Riel was captured, tried, and hanged.

In the film *North West Mounted Police*, the whole essence of the Riel Rebellion is trivialized and dissipated. The film does not inform viewers about the causes of the rebellion. Native American concerns about the violation of their land, rights, or way of life are never depicted or addressed. The rebels are depicted as a motley crew of violence-prone individuals. The film pays homage to the Royal Mounted Police. DeMille was cognizant of supporting the embattled Britain, already at war with Nazi Germany. That, more than anything, was the purpose of the film. This message was an important factor in the film's incredible commercial success.

Native American actors cast in the film included Chief Thundercloud (Wandering Spirit); Chief John Big Tree (Blue Owl); Monte Blue (an Indian); Sonny Chorre (an Indian); Joe De La Cruz (an Indian); Charles Stevens (Half-breed Archer); Ray Mala (an Indian); Chief Thunderbird (an Indian); William Wilkerson (an Indian); and Chief Yowlachie (an Indian).

The film earned mostly positive reviews and became Paramount's biggest-grossing film of 1940. The film grossed $137.3 million domestically when adjusted for inflation.[13] *Variety* (October 23, 1940) wrote, "He [Cecil B. DeMille] returns with an outstanding and beautifully photographed in gorgeous Technicolor, containing a gory and absorbing melodramatic story in which the tradition of the red-coated constable of the famous brigades are preserved and passed on to younger men."[14]

DeMille's *Unconquered* (1947, Paramount) was his last film set in the era of the U.S. expansion to the west. Like his previous westerns, the director chose to romanticize the era of Manifest Destiny and to demonize Native Americans as the main impediment in the way of progress and white civilization.

Unconquered was an expensive, big-budget (some $4 million, of which $1 million went for actor's salaries). The film was shot in in striking Technicolor by Ray Rennahan and written by Jesse Lansky, Jr., Charles Bennett, Fredric M. Frank, and Jeanie Macpherson (uncredited). Both the screenplay and the adapted story were based on the novel *Unconquered: A Novel of the Pontiac Conspiracy* by Neil Swanson.

The film's narrator (director Cecil B. DeMille) sets the tone of the film: "Civilization lay to the east of the Allegheny Mountains. Conquest, opportunity, and death lay to the west." Set in 1763, the plot focuses on Abby Hale (Paulette Goddard), who is sentenced to death by a British court but spared in exchange for becoming an indentured servant in the British colonies in North America. On board the ship taking her across the Atlantic, her beauty attracts the attention of Captain Christopher Holden (Gary Cooper) and Martin Garth (Howard Da Silva), who bid to purchase her. Holden wins and sets her free, leading Abby to become attracted to him.

In the frontier, however, Garth kidnaps Abby and takes her with him, much to the dismay of Hannah (Katherine DeMille), Garth's native lover. Garth is heavily involved in selling arms and liquor to Native American tribes who desire to free themselves from the expanding Euro-Americans. Eventually, Holden is given the command to stop the arms smuggling; he rescues Abby and puts a stop to the schemes of Garth and his henchmen.

Unconquered received mixed reviews. Bosley Crowther, writing in the *New York Times* (October 11, 1947), said, "Winking broadly at history, Mr. De Mille has easily contrived to suit the Indian uprisings of that period to his own dramatic use."[15] Regardless of its shortcomings, *Unconquered* was Paramount's highest-grossing film of the year. It grossed $14.2 million in actual domestic earnings, which, when adjusted for inflation, comes to a whopping $331.7 million.[16]

The film portrays Native American characters as childish, gullible, and ruthless savages. Remarks are made throughout the film about the cruelty and barbaric traits of native people. The key native characters (played by white actors) speak gibberish and carry out a series of bizarre rituals. Chief Guyasuta (played by a completely miscast Boris Karloff) is the proverbial cartoonish savage, who employs exaggerated mannerisms and rolling eyes. Despite being a leader, Guyasuta is easily outwitted and humiliated by the stalwart white hero. These natives are cardboard, one-dimensional characters without a backstory, meant simply to serve as ploys in the narrative.

Although there were several Native American characters in the film, only a few native actors were cast in small roles. These included Chief Big Tree (an Indian); Rodd Redwing (an Indian); Jay Silverheels (an Indian); and Chief Thundercloud (Chief Kilbuck). The vast majority of native roles were played by Caucasian actors: Boris Karloff (Guyasuta); Katherine DeMille (Hannah); Marc Lawrence (Sioto, the Medicine Man); Iron Eyes Cody, alias Esoera DeCorti (Red Corn); Rus Conklin (Mamaultee); and Robert Warwick (Chief Pontiac), among others.

My Darling Clementine (1946, 20th Century–Fox)

John Ford's *My Darling Clementine* is perhaps the best-known film made about Wyatt Earp and the legendary gun battle at the OK Corral. This film featured only one significant Native American female character: Chihuahua, played by Linda Darnell.

The film's narrative is set in 1882 in Tombstone, Arizona, where Wyatt Earp (Henry Fonda) and his brothers Virgil (Tim Holt) and Morgan (Ward Bond) become marshals after their youngest brother is killed by Old Man Clanton (Walter Brennan) and his sons (John Ireland, Grant Withers). Earp first gains the townspeople's attention and respect when he singlehandedly subdues a drunken Native American (Charles Stevens) and asks the crowd in disgust, "What kind of town is this, serving liquor to Indians?" He warns his humiliated captive, "Stay out of town, Indian!"

Victor Mature as Doc Holliday and Linda Darnell as Chihuahua in John Ford's evocative *My Darling Clementine* (1946, 20th Century–Fox).

Subsequently, the notorious gunfighter and gambler, Doc Holliday (Victor Mature), who runs the town, establishes an accommodation with the Earps. As a result, they overlook his shady dealings. Doc is loved by Chihuahua (Linda Darnell), a beautiful Mexican indigenous *cantinera* (saloon woman) whom he uses for sexual gratification and often mistreats (not unlike the way Lewt treats Pearl Chávez in *Duel in the Sun*). At one point, Doc tells her, "Why don't you go away, squall your stupid little songs and leave me alone?"

Wyatt from the beginning treats Chihuahua with quiet contempt, as he did the drunken Native American (similar to Senator McCanles' treatment of Pearl in *Duel in the Sun*). On one occasion, Earp treats Chihuahua like a pariah in the saloon and then drags her to horse trough and dumps her in, calling her a "wildcat." He then threatens to send her back to "the Apache Reservation." Earp's treatment of Chihuahua contrasts vividly with how he behaves toward the very ordinary and homey Euro-American woman from the East, Clementine (Cathy Downs), Holliday's discarded childhood sweetheart, who has come looking for him. Earp gives Clementine all the courtesy due to a "lady," tipping his hat and calling her "Madam."

Unloved, scorned, and the object of ridicule, Chihuahua takes up with the desperado Bill Clanton, who, in the process of escaping from the Earps, shoots her. Holliday attempts to save her by operating, and at that moment he finally acknowledges his respect and love for her: "You're all right. You're a brave girl." Chihuahua's death finally propels him out of his alcoholic existence, and he seeks redemption for himself at the gunfight at the OK Corral. Marubbio has noted about the character of Chihuahua, "She is 'explicitly erotic, sexually active, and not above a little infidelity.' ... The characterization of Chihuahua goes much further than this, however, engaging overlaps of racial stereotyping that effectively position Chihuahua as a sliding signifier of Mexican inferiority and colonized Native America."[17]

The part of Chihuahua was touchingly played by Linda Darnell. Chihuahua's life of tribulation was the synthesized version of similar experiences endured by Native American and Mexican women in real and reel life.

My Darling Clementine was shot on location in Monument Valley in the Four Corners region of Arizona, New Mexico, Utah, and Colorado.

Captain from Castile (1947, 20th Century–Fox)

The film *Captain from Castile* remains only epic Hollywood film to depict the Spanish conquest of Mexico. Although disguised as a lavish swashbuckler, it reflects a certain ambiguity about history. This is probably due to the fact that the film was released when the old Hollywood began its decline and the new film era began. It was a time when on-location shooting in locales like Mexico compelled U.S. filmmakers to grapple with more historical fact and less historical fiction.

The film was directed by the noted Henry King (1886–1982), who helmed numerous important films, most of them for 20th Century–Fox. The screenplay was written by the distinguished Lamar Trotti, who won an Academy Award for Best Writing, Original Screenplay for *Wilson* (1944, 20th Century–Fox) and was nominated for *There's No Business Like Show Business* (1952, 20th Century–Fox). His script was based on the best-selling novel *Captain from Castile* (1946) by Samuel Shallabarger. The film featured a rousing and evocative musical score by the notable Alfred Newman.

The film's story is set in 1518 and starts off in Jaen, Spain, where a Spanish caballero named Pedro De Vargas (Tyrone Power) assists an escaped Aztec, Coatl (Jay Silverheels). However, his master, Diego De Silva (John Sutton), is a cruel leader of the *Santa Hermandad* (Inquisition). As vengeance for Pedro's act, De Silva has his father, Francisco De Vargas (Antonio Moreno), along with his mother and sister, arrested and tortured. Juan García (Lee G. Cobb), who has just returned from the Americas, knows of De Silva's cruelty, as his mother is tortured as well.

6. Native Americans as Part of the Nation's Family (1940–1949) 111

Juan helps Pedro to rescue his parents. During the escape, Pedro kills De Silva after he makes him renounce God. Juan helps Pedro and Catana Pérez (Jean Peters) escape to the New World. In Cuba, they join Hernán Cortés (César Romero) and his expedition into Mexico in 1519.

In Mexico, Cortés' expedition makes progress through his alliance with several Mexican native tribes against the Aztecs. Padre Bartolomé (Thomas Gómez), who is part of the expedition, has received an order to arrest Pedro. However, he destroys it when he learns of circumstances under which Pedro committed his act. Later, Pedro meets Coatl once more. Coatl condemns the expedition of conquest and brutality against his people. Pedro is sympathetic, but unable to completely comprehend the magnitude of Cortés' crimes.

Later, Pedro is arrested and sentenced to die when De Silva, who was presumed dead, is murdered in the camp. However, Coatl later confesses to Padre Bartolomé that he was the one who took De Silva's life. Catana stabs Pedro to avoid the hanging, only to realize later that he is innocent of De Silvas' death. However, Pedro slowly recovers, and he and Catana (now his bride) follow the Cortés expedition as it nears the Valley of Mexico and the Aztec capital Tenochtitlan.

The fact that *Captain from Castile* was shot on location with Mexican crews and actors went a long way to convince the studio not to document Hernán Cortés' long list of crimes against humanity. Cortés (1485–1547) is perhaps the most famous and infamous (along with Francisco Pizzaro) Spanish conquistador to invade the native Americas. In the film he is portrayed superbly by actor César Romero—charming, astute, ruthless, conniving, sinister, and vain. Cortés is not above disobeying the Spanish king, arresting his emissaries, or terrorizing and enslaving the Mexican native peoples. He is obsessed with both power and gold, and he cares little for the niceties of diplomacy or legality. Cortés use demagoguery to rouse his men in one final battle. As he leads his army into the Valley of Mexico, he proclaims, "Put your faith in me, and in the Almighty, and we will go forward and carry to a glorious conclusion what was so auspiciously begun here."

In turn, Doña Marina, or *La Malinche*, is equally ruthless. Cortés describes her as "a lovely creature, who gives me the voice of these people." Doña Marina later became a much-maligned native woman, seen by many as the embodiment of a cultural sellout and traitor to her own people.[18] In Mexico, a *malinchista* is a person who prefers another culture to one's own.

Doña Marina was Cortés' translator and lover and bore him several children. In *Captain from Castile*, she is depicted as an incredibly strong, articulate, resolute, and attractive woman who is aware that her powers are linked to Cortés' authority. She is clever and conniving as well. When she confers with the Aztec emissaries, she plays the diplomat skillfully while calculating the benefit for her Spanish master. She is as astute as Cortés, knowing full well the value that she brings to his enterprise.

Perhaps the most powerful scene in the film is when Coatl confronts Pedro (who previously helped him escape from Spain). Coatl tells him, "This is my country *señor*, my people, my gods. We cannot tell you to stop loving your gods. We can cannot make you slave. Why you do this, señor?" Pedro responds somewhat unconvincingly, "Well, I'm afraid I don't have any answer for that. It isn't right for men to worship idols. There is only one true God." Coatl counters, "Maybe your God and our God, same God, maybe we call them by different names." Pedro answers, "Perhaps, but we are not enemies, you and I." Coatl then presses him, "I give my life for you, *señor*, but you hurt my people. I fight you." Pedro is evidently at a loss to convince him otherwise: "I can understand that. I suppose that if I was in your place, I would do the same."

The film also references the specter of the House Un-American Activities Committee (HUAC) in the scenes involving the Inquisition, creating a powerful allegory for what was going on in the United States at that time. The HUAC first visited Hollywood in 1947, with the express purpose of rooting out alleged Communists. The character of Diego De Silva is a dead ringer for Senator Joseph McCarthy. Diego asks Pedro's father whether it would be "unpleasant to know that there are those who are defending Christianity by spending themselves to uproot the detestable sin of heresy?" The elder Vargas responds, "I am against any organization, sir, which turns friend against friend, father against son." De Silva also forces information from children about their parents, such as the 12-year-old he tortures to death. When he goes to visit Pedro in prison, he says he is willing to be lenient if Pedro makes a confession of his heresy, language that sounds familiar to the "loyalty oaths" demanded by McCarthyists.

De Silva eagerly smears his enemies. For example, he refers to Coatl as the "escaped heretic, this Indian dog." Nor is De Silva above tracking down his suspects, like Father Bartolomé Romero, who refuses to be a stool pigeon by turning in Pedro.[19] In conclusion, *Captain from Castile* has some profound critical comments about the Spanish genocide against Native Americans, gender and identity, and political dissent. They were both timely and unprecedented, especially for a Hollywood epic film.

Captain from Castile was a huge commercial success. The film grossed $239.2 (when adjusted for inflation) domestically.[20] It also garnered some glowing reviews from critics. *Variety* (November 26, 1947) wrote, "This is a box-office bonanza. A surging, massive, spectacularly iridescent epic."[21] Howard Barnes, in the *New York Herald* (November 26, 1947), perceptively noted, "He [Power] is excellent in the passages describing the flight from the Inquisition, less impressive when he is attempting to tell an Aztec what the Spanish are doing in the New World."[22]

The lavish film was authentic to the last detail, including the pre–Columbian costumes, events and historical characters. The film was shot on location in the states of Michoacán, Guerrero, and Morelia in Mexico. The stunning cinematography was done by Arthur E. Arling, Charles G. Clarke, and Joseph LaCelle (who was uncredited). In addition, the Aztec language of Nahuatl was used extensively throughout the film. The role of Doña Marina (Cortés' translator and lover) was played by the widely respected Mexican actress Estela Inda, herself of native origin. Jay Silverheels played Coatl, in his first significant film role. The film was full of Mexican native actors that included Willy Calles, Gilberto González, and Ramón Sánchez, among many others.

Black Gold (1947, Allied Artists)

The film *Black Gold* is based on a true story written by Caryl Coleman (and screenplay by Agnes Christine Johnson). It was directed by Phil Karlson. Historically, it marked Anthony Quinn's first leading role in a film. It also marked the first and last time that Quinn and his then wife Katherine DeMille would play opposite each other.

The film's narrative focuses on Charley Eagle (Quinn), who while riding one day finds an unconscious Chinese boy named Davey (Ducky Louie), who has been thrown from his horse. The boy's father, who was trying to smuggle them into the United States, was shot in the attempt. Charley takes the boy home, where he and his wife Sarah (Katherine DeMille) set about adopting Davey.

Charley is induced by Dan Toland (Moroni Olson), an unscrupulous manager, to enter his mare in a claiming race, which the horse wins. Charley, though, is unfamiliar with racetrack technicalities and is dazed when Toland claims the mare for $500. With an old friend and horse trainer, Bucky (Raymond Hatton), Charley sneaks the horse away from Toland's paddocks, leaving $500 in its place. Oil is struck on Charley's land the night that his mare gives birth to a colt, and Charley names him Black Gold. Bucky and Davey, Charley's adopted son, team up in training the colt, which Charley eventually enters in the Kentucky Derby. Charley's sudden death is a stunning blow to the boy, who courageously insists on riding Black Gold himself. He wins the Derby, despite Toland's efforts to stop him.

The film was based loosely on the exploits of a Native American who became a millionaire from oil found on his land and also specialized in breeding and training horses. One of his horses named Black Gold (the film's title) won the 1924 Kentucky Derby.

Over the course of his career, Anthony Quinn played every type of ethnic role: Mexicans, Native Americans, Chinese, Greeks, and Spaniards, among others. He played Native Americans in *The Plainsman* (1936, Paramount); *Texas Rangers Ride Again* (1940, Paramount); *They Died with Their Boots On* (1941, Warner Bros.); *Buffalo Bill* (1944, 20th Century–Fox); and *Where Do We Go from Here?* (1945, 20th Century–Fox). In the film *Viva Zapata!* (1952, 20th Century–Fox), Quinn played Eufemio Zapata, the famed revolutionary's brother, and won an Academy Award for Best Supporting Actor. Quinn later played three more Native American roles: *Seminole* (1953, Universal); *The Savage Innocents* (1960, Paramount), as an Eskimo; and *Flap* (1970, Warner Bros.).

Black Gold earned warm reviews but failed to become a box-office success. *Variety* (June 25, 1947) noted, "The Agnes Christine Johnson script, from an original story by Cary Coleman, is commendable in that there is not a single Indian-uttered 'ugh' in the dialog. Plot depicts Charley Eagle, uneducated redskin who loves nature, his horse, and his wife."[23] *Cue Magazine* (September 6, 1947) wrote, "There is much warmth, sincerity and utterly ingratiating quality about this film.... There has been no finer performance this year than Anthony Quinn's in the role of Charley Eagle; in a larger-budgeted picture he would have been certain to win half dozen awards."[24] *The Hollywood Reporter* (June 23, 1947) commented, "Anthony Quinn does a wonderful job as Charley Eagle, marking his characterization with deft touches of fine craftsmanship. He receives beautiful support from Katherine De Mille in an unspectacular but splendidly sincere performance of his Indian wife."[25]

Buffalo Bill (1944, 20th Century–Fox)

Buffalo Bill was an exuberant and colorful film that documented the mythical life and legend of one William F. Cody, better known to history as "Buffalo Bill." The film was directed by the legendary William A. Wellman (1896–1975), who had helmed several important and progressive films such as *The Ox-Box Incident* (1943, 20th Century–Fox), *The Story of G.I. Joe* (1945, United Artists), and *Battleground* (1949, MGM). Wellman is said to have hated the film. The screenplay was written by four writers: Clements Ripley, Cecile Kramer, Aeneas MacKenzie, and Frank Winch. The story was written by John Larkin (uncredited). The impressive cinematography was done by the noted Leon Shamroy, who during his career won four Academy Awards for Best Cinematography and was nominated for 18 others.

The narrative focuses on William F. Cody (Joel McCrea), who becomes famous in 1870s as an Army scout. At one point, he rescues the daughter of a U.S. senator, Louisa Frederick (Maureen O'Hara), whom he eventually marries. Cody later comes into conflict with government officials and politicians as the United States carries out a policy of Manifest Destiny and expansion into the west.

In the film, Cody is presented as a person who respects Native Americans. He becomes friends with Yellow Hand (Anthony Quinn), chief of the Cheyenne. However, business interests and politicians press the government to appropriate native land. Cody is then compelled to fight against the Cheyenne and eventually kills Yellow Hand in battle.

After his exploits are widely reported in the press, Cody becomes friends with Ned Buntine (Thomas Mitchell), whose exaggerated books about Cody make him a national hero. Cody goes on to found the Buffalo Bill Wild West Show, which becomes an international success. At the end of the film, his success is threatened when he takes a position against the mistreatment of Native Americans and the robbery of their lands.

Buffalo Bill won positive reviews by the press. Bosley Crowther, in the *New York Times* (April 10, 1944), wrote, "The film is at its most effulgent when it shows the famous buffalo hunter and Indian scout doing great deeds in the Cheyenne country.... It is least exciting when it puts inconsistent words into his mouth—all about justice for the Indians—and shows him carrying a dreary torch for them back East."[26] Interestingly, many years later in her autobiography, Maureen O'Hara wrote, "I thought the picture was forgettable, but it turned out to be one of the biggest moneymakers 20th Century–Fox had that year. Critics panned the film, except for the positive way in which Native Americans were portrayed."[27] The film grossed $180.8 million domestically when adjusted for inflation.[28]

Buffalo Bill is a feel-good film released in the heat of World War II. It purports to depict William F. Cody (1846–1917) as a decent man caught in the web of Manifest Destiny and ethnic cleansing. However, the real Cody took pride in being an "Indian fighter." Cody slaughtered more than a thousand buffalos in the service of the railroads. He fought without hesitation against native people, who were defending their land and way of life. One scene in the film has Cody overlooking a mass of native corpses in the aftermath of the Battle of Hat Creek (in Nebraska). He carries the body of one warrior and is asked matter-of-factly by one bystander, "A friend of yours, Bill?" Cody then replies, "They were all friends of mine."

Native actors in the film included Anthony Quinn (Yellow Hand), Tatzumbia Dupea (Old Indian Woman), Chief Many Treaties (Chief Tall Bull), Margarita Martin (Indian Servant), and Chief Thundercloud (Crazy Horse). The beautiful and part–Native American actress Linda Darnell played Dawn Starlight.

The film was shot on location in Paria and Johnson Canyon, Utah.

Native Film Stars and Filmmakers

Rodolfo Acosta

Rodolfo Acosta was a popular character actor for some three decades in both films and television. He was born Rodolfo Acosta Pérez on July 29, 1920, in Chamizal, Texas.

6. Native Americans as Part of the Nation's Family (1940–1949)

Acosta's family had strong Mexican Native American roots. At the time of his birth, Chamizal was a section of El Paso, bordering the Río Grande, which often was flooded by the river. The area was a source of contention between Mexico and the United States. The dispute was settled in 1964.

During World War II, Acosta served in the U.S. Navy within the realm of intelligence. After the war, in 1945, he married Jeanine Cohen, whom he had met during his service in Casablanca in the North African theater of war. The couple had four children: Dante, Timur, Loredo, and Jeanine Acosta. His wife would later divorce him in the 1950s for allegedly having an affair with actress Ann Sheridan.

After his war service, Acosta came to the attention of Mexican film director Emilio "Indio" Fernández. At that time, Fernández was considered Mexico's greatest director. Acosta's pronounced Native American features marked him to play indigenous roles in both Mexico and the United States.

He made his film debut in the 1946 Mexican film *Yo, un Profugo* (Posa Films), starring the famed Mexican comedian Mario Moreno "Cantinflas." He would later alternate between both Mexican and U.S. films.

His films included John Ford's *The Fugitive* (1947, Argosy Pictures); *Song of the Siren* (1948, CAFISA), in which he played the lead role; *Hermoso Ideal* (1948, Ramex Films); Emilio Fernández's *Salón Mexico* (1949, Clasa Films); *Felipe de Jesus* (1949, Clasa Films); *Sueños de Prisión* (1949, Art-Mex); *Vuelve Pancho Villa* (1950, Hispano Continental); *Pancho Villa Returns* (1950, Hispano Continental), the U.S. version of the previous film; *One Way Street* (1950, Univ. Inter.); *Entre el Amor y el Cielo* (1950, Grovas); *Victims of Sin* (1950, Calderón S.A.); *Pecado* (1951, Filmex S.A.); *Bullfighter and the Lady* (1951, Republic); *Los Amantes* (1951, Calderón S.A.); *Sensualidad* (1951, Calderón S.A.); *Las Islas Marías* (1951, Rodríguez Hermanos); *Retorno al Quinto Patio* (1951, Argel Films); *El Puerto de los Siete Vicios* (1951, Isla Prods.); Emilio Fernández's *Acapulco* (1952, Intercontinental Prods.) and *El Mar y Tu* (1952, Galindo Hermanos); *El Dinero No Es la Vida* (1952, Argel Films); *Yo Soy Mexicano Nacido de Este Lado* (1952, Hispano Continental); *Yankee Buccaneer* (1952, UI); *Horizons West* (1952, UI); *Victimas del Divorcio* (1952, Calderón S.A.); *El Billetero* (1953, Cuactemoc); *San Antone* (1953, Republic); *Destination Gobi* (1953, 20th Century–Fox); *Wings of the Hawk* (1953, UI); *City of Badmen* (1953, 20th Century–Fox); *Appointment in Honduras* (1953, RKO); *Hondo* (1953, Warner Bros.); *Night People* (1954, 20th Century–Fox); *Passion* (1954, RKO); *Drum Beat* (1954, Warner Bros.); *Llévame en tus Brazos* (1954); *A Life in the Balance* (1955, Tele-Voz); *The Littlest Outlaw* (1955, Disney); *The Proud Ones* (1955, 20th Century–Fox); *Bandido!* (1956, United Artists); and *How the West Was Won* (1962, MGM), among many others. Acosta also appeared in many top-rated television shows, including *Ironside*, *Cade's County*, *The Bold Ones: The Lawyers*, *Bonanza*, *The High Chaparral*, *Mission: Impossible*, and *The Fugitive*, among others.

Rodolfo Acosta died of cancer on November 7, 1974, in Woodland Hills, California.

Chief Many Treaties

Chief Many Treaties was born William Malcom Hazlet on April 11, 1874, in Montana. He was of Blackfoot ancestry. His film credits include *Oklahoma Jim* (1931, Trem Carr Prods.); *Battling with Buffalo Bill* (1931, Universal); *The Golden West* (1932, Fox Film Corp.); *Rustlers of Red Dog* (1935, Universal); *Drums of Destiny* (1937, Crescent); *The Cowboy and the Lady* (1939, Goldwyn); *Man of Conquest* (1939, Republic); *Kit Carson*

(1940, United Artists); *Go West, Young Lady* (1941, Columbia); *My Gal Sal* (1942, 20th Century–Fox); *Jackass Mail* (1942, MGM); *Springtime in the Rockies* (1942, 20th Century–Fox); *The Deerslayer* (1943, Cardinal Pictures); *Buffalo Bill* (1944, 20th Century–Fox); *It's in the Bag* (1945, United Artists); *The Scarlet Horseman* (1946, Universal); *The Sea of Grass* (1947, MGM); *Buffalo Bill Rides Again* (1947, Shwarz Prods.); *Last of the Redmen* (1947, Columbia); *The Last Round-Up* (1947, Autry Prods.); and *Black Bart* (1948, Univ. Inter.). He died on February 29, 1948, in Los Angeles, California.

Linda Darnell

The extraordinarily beautiful and talented Linda Darnell was one of the biggest female stars of the 1940s. For most of her career she was under long-term contract to 20th Century–Fox.

This dark-haired actress with luminous dark eyes fascinated me from my childhood onward. I was sure that she was indigenous. However, I searched in vain for years through studio biographies, newspaper clippings, and numerous film history books, seeking information about her ethnicity and/or origins.

She was born Monetta Eloyse Darnell, on October 16, 1923, in Dallas, Texas. Her parents were Calvin Roy Darnell, a postal clerk, and the former Pearl Brown. As it turns out, Linda's grandfather on her mother's side, Tom Brown, was Cherokee.[29] Her mother Maggie Pearl took great pride in her Native American heritage. Ronald L. Davis wrote, "When Maggie Pearl discovered that Geronimo, the Apache chief, was a prisoner of war in Fort Sill, she made a trip to see him. She visited the nearby Caddo Reservation ... and brought home a deerskin purse that became one of her treasures."[30]

Linda Darnell became a child model at the age of 11 and made her stage debut by the age of 13. In 1937, a 20th Century–Fox talent scout invited her to Hollywood for a screen test. When he discovered that she was underage, the test was postponed. However, at the age of 15, 20th Century–Fox signed her to a film contract, and she moved to Hollywood in 1939. She kept secret the fact that she was only 15 years of age, posing instead as 17, while the studio listed her as being 19. She was cast in her first lead role in the film *Hotel for Women* (1939, 20th Century–Fox), catapulting her to film stardom.

At 20th Century–Fox, she quickly became one the most glamourous film stars of the era, along with Rita Hayworth, Betty Grable, Gene Tierney, and Carole Landis. Linda Darnell was one of the most popular pinup girls for GIs during World War II.

Her studio never publicized her indigenous ethnicity. Nevertheless, she played three Native American characters (in *The Mark of Zorro, Buffalo Bill,* and *My Darling Clementine*) with dignity and talent. She defied the system of the time, which compelled actors to portray derogatory images of indigenous people.

Darnell also played the lead in three films headlined by the studio's biggest male star, Tyrone Power: *Daytime Wife* (1939, 20th Century–Fox); *Brigham Young* (1940, 20th Century–Fox); and Lolita Quintero, the Mexican indigenous female lead in *The Mark of Zorro* (1940, 20th Century–Fox). Her other film successes of the period included *Stardust* (1940, 20th Century–Fox) and *Blood and Sand* (1941, 20th Century–Fox), again with Power.

In 1943, Darnell had a cameo as the Virgin Mary in *Song of Bernadette* (20th Century–Fox); then she appeared as Dawn Starlight, the indigenous maiden in William Wellman's *Buffalo Bill* (1944, 20th Century–Fox), and played a winning comedy role in Rene Clair's excellent fantasy film *It Happened Tomorrow* (1944, 20th Century–Fox). She also appeared as Olga in Douglas Sirk's superior film noir *Summer Storm* (1944, 20th Century–Fox). This film made Darnell a sex symbol, a change from playing pristine and innocent maidens, and she earned rave reviews.

In the film noir *Hangover Square* (1945, 20th Century–Fox), she played a seductive prostitute—another dramatic change of pace. She then played a hard-working, working-class waitress in Otto Preminger's excellent film noir *Fallen Angel* (1945, 20th Century–Fox). Darnell gave an Oscar-caliber performance that overshadowed her talented co-stars, Alice Faye and Dana Andrews. Bosley Crowther, writing in the *New York Times* (February 7, 1946), noted, "Linda Darnell is beautiful and perfectly cast as the sultry and single-minded siren."[31]

She famously played the Mexican indigenous saloon woman Chihuahua in John Ford's evocative *My Darling Clementine* (1946, 20th Century–Fox), which told the story of Wyatt Earp and Doc Holliday's gun battle at the OK Corral. Darnell gave an extraordinary performance, capturing all the hard and tender edges of a much-exploited and maligned woman and the sting of racial discrimination. Her co-stars were Victor Mature and Henry Fonda.

Darnell went on to give several more exceptional performances, including as the ambitious but poor maiden in Preminger's *Forever Amber* (1947, 20th Century–Fox); the naïve young wife in Preston Sturges' screwball comedy *Unfaithfully Yours* (1948, 20th Century–Fox); and the strongly independent minded wife in Joseph L. Mankiewicz's *A Letter to Three Wives* (1949, 20th Century–Fox). She likewise played the female lead in Mankiewicz's drama about bigotry *No Way Out* (1950, 20th Century–Fox). She was outstanding in her role and dominated the film, amid a cast that included Richard Widmark and a young Sidney Poitier.

In 1952, 20th Century–Fox cut most of its roster of film stars, and Darnell freelanced thereafter. The quality of her films declined, as did their box-office success. However, she found two other professional venues: theater and television. She was in high demand in both mediums. Darnell made her debut on television in 1954 and guest-starred in numerous popular shows, including *77 Sunset Street*, *Burke's Law*, *Cimarron City*, *Wagon Train*, *Studio 57*, *Playhouse 90*, *Climax!*, and *Schlitz Playhouse of Stars*, among others. Her other films include *Two Flags West* (1950, 20th Century–Fox); *The 13th Letter* (1951, 20th Century–Fox); *Blackbeard the Pirate* (1952, RKO); and *Second Chance* (1953, RKO), among many others. Her last film was *Black Spurs* (1965, Paramount).

Darnell was married three times, and one union produced a child. She died on April 10, 1965, in a house fire in Chicago, Illinois. She was only 41 years of age at the time of her passing.

Like all human beings, Linda Darnell had personal failings and professional ups and downs. Nevertheless, she rose to film stardom during the Golden Age of Hollywood, when women of color were confronted by a host of adversities. Her film legacy was her excellent and diverse work in cinema. She was proud of her Native American ethnicity and served as a luminous light for indigenous people in film.

Tatzumbia Dupea

Tatzumbia Dupea was born on July 26, 1849, in Lone Pine, California. She was a Piute Native American. She made only two films: *Buffalo Bill* (1944, 20th Century–Fox) and *Across the Wide Missouri* (1951, MGM).

Dupea died on February 26, 1970, in Los Angeles, California, at the amazing age of 120 years and seven months. She is buried in Forest Lawn in Glendale, California.

Emilio "Indio" Fernández

Emilio "Indio" Fernández was one of Mexico's greatest directors during its Golden Age of Cinema in the period of the 1940s and 1950s. In addition, he was a screenwriter, producer, and actor.

Fernández was born on March 26, 1904, in Sabinas, Coahuila, Mexico. His father was a Mexican mestizo general of the Mexican Revolution, and his mother was a Native American of the Kickapoo people. Fernández developed a strong sense of indigenous identity and pride, as well as pride in his country. This identity defined his later personality: strong willed and temperamental. His younger brother, Jaime Fernández, also became an actor in both Mexican and U.S. films.

Early in his adolescence, several events helped shape Fernández's fearless personality. He fled from home and enlisted as *soldado razo* (common soldier) to fight in the Mexican Revolution.[32] In 1923, he joined the revolt of Adolfo de la Huerta against the opportunistic usurper Alvaro Obregón. However, the uprising was crushed. Fernández was arrested and imprisoned, though he later made a daring escape from prison and went into exile in the United States. He lived in both Chicago and Los Angeles, and at various times he made a living as a bartender, longshoreman, press assistant, and construction worker in Hollywood movie studios. His winning personality soon earned him work as an extra and a film double.

Soon thereafter, he won bit parts in several films. Fernández made his film debut in U.S. films in the 1930 B-western *Oklahoma Cyclone* (Tiffany Prods.). Others followed: *The Land of Missing Men* (1930, Trem Carr); *Headin' North* (1930, Trem Carr); *Sunrise Trail* (1931, Trem Carr); *Svengali* (1932, Warner Bros.) with John Barrymore; *The Western Code* (1932, Columbia); *Laughing at Life* (1933, Mascot Pictures); *Flying Down to Rio* (1933, RKO) with Dolores Del Río; *La Buenaventura* (1934, First National); *Heart of a Bandit* (1934, Mexico Films); *Cruz Diablo* (1934, Mex-Art); and *Mexicana* (1935, Jorge M. Dada), a film short.

During his stay in Hollywood, Fernández was powerfully influenced by the work of Russian filmmaker Sergei Eisenstein. He was especially moved by *Que Viva Mexico!* (1932, Mosfilm), which had been shot in Mexico. Also during his stay in Hollywood, he is said to have been the nude model for what later became the Oscar or Academy Award.

In 1933, a Mexican government amnesty for revolutionaries allowed Fernández to return to Mexico. By then, he had decided to become a film director. While he broke into Mexican films, he worked in an assortment of odd jobs: boxer, taxi driver, and others. He finally earned his first Mexican film part in the 1934 film *Cruz Diablo* (Mex-Art), directed by one of the nation's key directors, Fernando de Fuentes. Fernández played his first lead role as an indigenous protagonist in *Janitzio* in 1934 (Cine. Co. Mexicana).

Mexico in the 1930s and 1940s was undergoing a cultural renaissance in the arts: literature, murals, theater, and motion pictures. The Mexican film industry was asserting its indigenous history, culture, and identity. A strong nationalist bent ran through its arts. This was the beginning of Mexico's Golden Age of Cinema, with such film stars as Tito Guízar, José Mojica, Cantinflas, Jorge Negrete, Esther Fernández, Andrea Palma, Arturo de Córdova, Pedro Infante, María Félix, and Pedro Armendáriz, as well as the

6. Native Americans as Part of the Nation's Family (1940–1949)

return of three Hollywood-based stars: Ramón Novarro, Dolores Del Río, and Lupe Vélez. This era coincided with the arrival of Fernández on the scene. Fernández made his directorial debut with *La Isla de Pasión* in 1941 (Ema Prods.) and followed it with *Soy Puro Mexicano* (1942), both headlined by the fast-rising Pedro Armendáriz.

Fernández had met and become friends with Dolores Del Río in Hollywood. Fernández approached her upon her return to Mexico in order to help her begin a second film career. He enlisted the services of Del Río, Armendáriz, and cinematographer Gabriel Figueroa for a series of films that highlighted the indigenous culture of Mexico and its landscape. The first film was *Flor Silvestre* (1942, Films Mundiales). A year later, *María Candelaria* (1943, Films Mundiales) won the Cannes Film Festival–Palm d'Or and earned Mexican cinema world acclaim. *Las Abandonadas* (1944, Films Mundiales) won Dolores Del Río the Ariel Award for Best Actress of the Year. *Bugambilia* (1944, Films Mundiales) was the fourth collaboration, all of which became revered classics in Mexican cinema.

Fernández then directed *La Perla* (1945, RKO), based on the novel *The Pearl* by John Steinbeck and headlined by Pedro Armendáriz. The film won numerous awards and honors: the Venice Film Festival Golden Lion; the Ariel Award for Best Actor (Armendáriz); Best Supporting Actor; Best Cinematography (Figueroa). It also earned the Golden Globe for Best Cinematography.

Fernández helmed *Pepita Jiménez* (1945, Águila Films), headlined by the fast-rising

Mexican director and actor Emilio Fernández, with Dolores Del Río and Lupita Tovar Kohner in the early 1940s (courtesy Lupita Tovar Kohner).

Ricardo Montalban, which was less successful. He returned to form with *Enamorada* (1946, Panamerican Films), once again collaborating with Del Río and Armendáriz. The film earned the Ariel Award for Best Actress (Del Río). Director John Ford then requested Fernández's services as producer and assistant director (uncredited) in *The Fugitive* (1947, Argosy Films), based on the novel *The Power and the Glory* by Graham Greene. It was headlined by Dolores Del Río, Pedro Armendáriz, and Henry Fonda. The film focused on the era of the *cristeros*, a period in the 1920s in which the Mexican government became anti-clerical.

In 1947, Fernández began a new collaboration with another important film star, Maria Felix (an actress of Yaqui roots from the northern state of Sonora): *Rio Escondido* (1947, Raul de Anda Prods.) and *Maclovia* (1948, Filmex S.A.). Both films co-starred Pedro Armendáriz.

As a director, Emilio was hitting his peak. His films during this era included *Pueblerina* (1949, Reforma Prods.) with Columba Dominguez (his new love); *La Malquerida* (1949, Cabrera Films) with Del Río and Armendáriz; *Salón Mexico* (1950, Clasa Films) with Marga López; *Duelo en las Montañas* (1950, Clasa Films) with Rita Macedo; and *The Torch* (1950, Eagle-Lion Films), a U.S. film (and a remake of *Enamorada*) with Armendáriz and Paulette Goddard.

However, by the early 1950s, the quality of Fernández's films, with some exceptions, began to decline, and other directors, like Julio Bracho and Roberto Galvaldón, began to win greater recognition. Fernández's directorial career continued with *Un Día de Vida* (1950, Cabrera Films); *Victimas de Pecado* (1951, Calderón S.A.); *Islas Marías* (1951, Rodríguez Prods.) with Pedro Infante; *Siempre Tuya* (1952) with Jorge Negrete; *Acapulco* (1952, Intercontinental); *Cuando Levanta la Niebla* (1952, Tele-Voz) with Arturo de Córdova; *La Red* (1953, Reforma Films) with Rossana Podestá; *Reportaje* (1953, ANDA); *El Rapto* (1953, Atlantida) with Jorge Negrete and María Félix; *La Rosa Blanca* (1955, Antillas Prods.), shot in Cuba; *La Tierra del Fuego se Apaga* (1955, Mapol Prods.); *Nosotros Dos* (1955, Diana Films) with Rossana Podestá; *Una Cita de Amor* (1958, Latino Americana S.A.) with Silvia Pinal; *El Impostor* (1960, Latino Americana Prods.); *Pueblito* (1962, Bueno Prods.) with Lilia Prado; and *Paloma Herida* (1962), shot in Guatemala and Mexico, with Columba Domínguez. Fernández then directed and acted in two films: *Un Dorado de Pancho Villa* (1967, Centauro Prods.) and *Un Crespúsculo de Un Dios* (1969, Centauro Prods.). Both films were undistinguished and not well received by the public.

After several years of decline, Fernández won wide acclaim again with *La Choca* (1974, Conacite Uno), featuring Pilar Pellicer, which earned him an Ariel Award for Best Director.

However, after this, Fernández would only direct three inconsequential films: *Zona Roja* (1976, Conacine), *México Norte* (1979, Conacite Uno), and *Erótica* (1979, Conacite Uno). He appeared adrift and unable to summon his old greatness on film. There were rumors that he drank too much and became increasingly temperamental.

Fernández began to lose his interest in directing and turned to acting. He was usually cast as indigenous characters: hard, sardonic, embittered, and often violent macho men. In Mexico, his best roles were as Villista revolutionaries in *La Cucaracha* (1959, Rodriguez Films), which reunited him for the last time with three of his key collaborators, actors Dolores Del Río, Pedro Armendáriz, and Maria Felix; and *La Bandida* (1962, Rodríguez Films) with María Félix. His last Mexican film was *Los Amantes del Señor de la Noche* in 1986 (Fenix Prods.).

In the United States, he made ten more films as an actor. He was most memorable as the decadent counter-revolutionary General Mapache in Sam Peckinpah's masterpiece *The Wild Bunch* (1969, Warner Bros.). He played smaller roles in two other lesser Peckinpah films: *Pat Garret and Billy the Kid* (1973, MGM) and *Bring Me the Head of Alfredo García* (1974, United Artists). His other films included *The Night of the Iguana* (1964, MGM); *Return of the Seven* (1966, United Artists); *The Appaloosa* (1966, Universal); *Breakout* (1975, Columbia); *Under the Volcano* (1984, Conacite Uno); *Treasure of the Amazon* (1985, Star World Prods.); *The Kidnapping of Lola* (1986, Fernando Orozco Prods.); and *Arriba Michoacán* (1987, Eco Films).

In his personal life, Fernández traveled to Cuba in 1941, where he met and married his first wife Gladys Fernández (and adopted his daughter Adela). He had a seven-year relationship with actress Columba Domínguez, which ended in a turbulent separation. His subsequent marriage to Gloria Valois Cabiedes resulted in a daughter, Xochil Fernández De Valois. He was also married to Beatriz Castaneda from 1964 to 1970.

Film historian Ephraim Katz wrote that his films "were marked by dramatic pictorial compositions, stark contrasts, and striking overall visual style. Thematically, they reflected Fernández's own background and the socio-economic conditions that prevailed in Mexico in his youth."[33]

Emilio "Indio" Fernández died on August 6, 1986, at the age of 86. After his death, Fernández's films were rediscovered by new generations and deemed national treasures in Mexican cinema. No Mexican director more proudly and powerfully documented and celebrated the indigenous history and culture of Mexico.

Jay Silverheels

One of the best-known and busiest Native American actors of the 1940s and 1950s was the Canadian-born Jay Silverheels. His signature role was that of Tonto in the very popular television series *The Lone Ranger*.

His real name was Harold J. Smith, and he was born on May 26, 1912, in the Six Nations of the Grand River First Nation, near Brantford, Ontario, Canada. His father was a Mohawk chief and military officer. As a youth, Silverheels was an outstanding athlete, especially in lacrosse and boxing. In the latter sport, he earned second place in the middleweight division of the Golden Gloves tournament in New York.

Silverheels entered films in the late 1930s and often worked as a stunt man and an extra. He was billed alternatively as Harry Smith or Harold Smith. During this time, he usually worked in serials, low-budget films, and westerns.

His big break came with the role of Coatl, an Aztec prince kidnapped by the Spanish and taken to Cuba in the lavish adventure *Captain from Castile* (1947, 20th Century–Fox) with Tyrone Power. In this role, Silverheels was able to express the plight and suffering of his native people at the hands of the Spanish conquistadores, as well as questioning the moral right of the invaders. It was a truly remarkable role, and Silverheels performed it with integrity and eloquence. At this time, native characters were generally one dimensional and limited to incomprehensible utterances.

His films included *Key Largo* (1948, Warner Bros.) with Humphrey Bogart; *Broken Arrow* (1950, 20th Century–Fox) in the role of Geronimo; *War Arrow* (1953, Univ. Inter.) with Jeff Chandler; *Drums Along the River* (1954, Univ. Inter.); *Walk the Proud Land* (1956,

Clayton Moore as the Lone Ranger and Jay Silverheels as Tonto in the popular television series *The Lone Ranger*.

Univ. Inter.), reprising the role of Geronimo; *Alias Jesse James* (1959, United Artists) with Bob Hope; and *True Grit* (1969, Paramount), among many others.

Silverheels went on to earn his greatest fame playing the role of Tonto, the friend of the Lone Ranger in the television series of the same name during 1949–1957. Both Clayton Moore (who played the Lone Ranger) and Silverheels starred in two feature films based on these characters: *The Lone Ranger* (1956, Warner Bros.) and *The Lone Ranger and the Lost City of Gold* (1958, Warner Bros.). Silverheels received criticism in some native quarters for playing the role of Tonto, who some saw a sellout or an Uncle Tom.

After the television series ended, Silverheels found it difficult for a while to finding acting assignments. He became a salesman to make ends meet and also branched out into writing poetry and founding the Indian Actors Workshop to help native actors. Gradually, however, his acting career picked up, and he was much in demand, especially on television. He appeared in several television series like *Cannon*; *Divorce, American Style*; *Cade's County*; *The Brady Bunch*; *The Virginian*; *Daniel Boone*; *Laramie*; *Rawhide*; *Wagon Train*; and *Wanted Dead or Alive*, among others.

Jay Silverheels married in 1945 and had two children. He died from complications of a stroke on March 5, 1980, in Calabasas, California, and his ashes were sent to the Six Nations Reserve, where he was born.

7

New Images and Consciousness (1950–1959)

During the 1950s, changes in Native American images and political consciousness took place. They can perhaps be attributed to the momentous events of World War II: the horrors of the battlefield, the massive destruction, and the inhumanity of the Holocaust. The world seemed to have been jolted into a higher sense of purpose and respect for others.

The U.S. films of the 1950s were impacted by the great events that were transforming the world, but Hollywood typically trivialized these events and depicted them in a contrived and condescending manner. This decade witnessed the marked decline of Hollywood as the film capital of the world. A variety of factors contributed to this shift: the ascendency of television as the primary source of entertainment; declining film audiences; the divesture of the studio-owned theaters; the assertive independence of film stars and filmmakers; the resurgence of national cinemas in Europe and the Far East; and the intimidating presence of the political climate of the House Un-American Activities Committee (HUAC). However, the greatest changes were taking place in the representation of minority characters. Several film projects were made to document the socio-historical experience of Native Americans, Mexican Americans, and African Americans.

The postwar era was strongly influenced by the Cold War, the ideological, economic, and military rivalry between the United States and the Soviet Union. Within this context, the powerful force of nationalism manifested itself throughout the Third World, especially within the decaying empires of countries such as Britain and France.

In the Americas, several nationalist movements developed, galvanizing millions of marginalized people of color, especially indigenous peoples. In 1954, the United States was compelled to remove the democratically elected President Árbenz of Guatemala. In 1959, the Cuban Revolution sparked leftist guerrilla movements in several countries in the Americas (most of them with indigenous-majority populations) such as Guatemala, Bolivia, Columbia, and Perú.

At home, the United States enjoyed unprecedented material prosperity under the resurgent Republican Party. However, the illusion of equality of opportunity was deceptive. Most people of color were consigned to a lifetime of exclusion, poverty, segregation, and limited educational opportunities. Minority communities sought redress in the courts. In 1947, in *Mendez v. Westminster*, the U.S. Supreme Court outlawed the school segregation of Mexican American children, and in the 1954 case of *Brown v. Board of Edu-*

cation, the court ruled that the school segregation of African Americans was unconstitutional. However, every minority community developed organizations, movements, and strategies to improve their lives.

NATIVE AMERICAN FILM IMAGES IN THE 1950S

Meanwhile, in Hollywood, the hysteria-induced Senator Joseph McCarthy and the HUAC made another visit during March 1951. Some 212 persons in the film, television, and theater industry were blacklisted. Others were tainted by some innocuous association of employment, marriage, or friendship and stigmatized in the unofficial "gray list." Frightened and cowed by these developments, the film industry, out of self-interest, produced a spate of melodramatic films that perpetuated the political hysteria.

The film industry fought back against television, the rise of professional sports, the blacklist, and declining film receipts in a multitude of ways. The studios launched desperate attempts to keep and/or win back their audiences through a slew of technological innovations, beginning in 1952 with *Bwana Devil* (United Artists) in "3D" and "This Is Cinerama" (Cinerama Releasing Corp.), a device that provided filmgoers with the experience of riding a rollercoaster. This development was followed by 20th Century–Fox's CinemaScope in *The Robe* (1953), Paramount's VistaVision in *White Christmas* (1954), and United Artists' 70-mm Todd-AO process in *Around the World in 80 Days* (1956). Another effort was the production of lavished biblical epics, often filmed abroad in colorful locales.

Gradually, the way of doing business changed. The film industry talent agencies became the brokers of creative talent, involving independent-minded producers and free-lancing film stars (who often demanded and got a percentage of the film earnings). Nonetheless, after 1956, film audiences declined each year.

The HUAC crippled for a generation the efforts of the film industry to address the pressing social issues and concerns, especially those of minorities and women. However, as always, maverick and progressive filmmakers bucked the entrenched system and made films that challenged the ideological status quo. The films *The Ring* (1952) and *Giant* (1956, Warner Bros.) documented the racism against Mexican Americans, and *No Way Out* (20th Century–Fox) and *The Defiant Ones* (1959, United Artists) chronicled the bigotry against African Americans. Taboo subjects like drug addiction were tackled in *The Man with the Golden Arm* (1955) and *A Hatful of Rain* (1957), and the excesses of corporate greed were explored in *Executive Suite* (1954) and *The Man in the Gray Flannel Suit* (1956, 20th Century–Fox).

For Native Americans, a significant development was the appearance of films that questioned the principles of Manifest Destiny and the U.S. government's treatment of native peoples. Several of these films were made by blacklisted (or about to be blacklisted) filmmakers. Films like *Devil's Doorway* (1950, MGM), *Broken Arrow* (1950, 20th Century–Fox), and *Apache* (1954, United Artists) presented the native point of view and three-dimensional native characters. Other films chronicled the darker sides of Manifest Destiny. John Ford's *The Searchers* (1956, Warner Bros.) and *The Last Hunt* (1956, MGM) featured leading white characters consumed by racism and revenge. Elia Kazan's *Viva Zapata!* (1952, 20th Century–Fox) focused on the Mexican indigenous leader Emiliano

Zapata during the Mexican Revolution. *Run of the Arrow* (1957, RKO) told the story of a traumatized Civil War veteran who seeks solace and peace with a Native American tribe and an interracial marriage. *Hondo* (1953, Warner Bros.) chronicled the ambiguous tale of a half-breed amid the Apache wars.

During the 1950s, westerns in particular provided a more liberal perspective about native and Euro-American relations. In *Across the Wide Missouri* (1951, MGM), a rough-hewn trapper (Clark Gable) and his fellow frontiersmen integrate their lives and loves with native tribes. *The Savage* (1952, Paramount) documents the dilemma of a white man (Charlton Heston) brought up by the Lakota and faced with the impending war of annihilation of the indigenous people of the Great Plains by the U.S. government. Delmer Daves' evocative *Drum Beat* (1954, Warner Bros.) provided an ambiguous perspective of the Modoc War in northern California in the late 1800s. Robert Aldrich's sardonic western *Vera Cruz* (1954, United Artists) was set in Mexico in the late 1860s during the French Intervention. A group of Euro-American misfit gunmen (Burt Lancaster, Ernest Borgnine, and Charles Bronson, among others) are joined by a broken-down former plantation owner named Ben Trane (Gary Cooper) to fight the predominantly Mexican indigenous resistance army. Trane is further motivated by the beautiful Nina (Sarita Montiel), a Juarista indigenous agent.

The challenge of interracial relationships was chronicled in several films. *Broken Lance* (1954, 20th Century–Fox) featured a mixed-race family headed by a white landowner (Spencer Tracy) and his native wife (Katy Jurado). *White Feather* (1955, 20th Century–Fox) documented the actual love story between a Cheyenne maiden (Debra Paget) and a white surveyor (Robert Wagner) and how their relationship fostered peace between the two communities. In *Naked in the Sun* (1957, Allied Artists), an unscrupulous slave trader in 1830s Florida captured the wife of an indigenous chief and set off a war between whites and Seminoles. *Trooper Hook* (1957, United Artists) depicted the fate of a white woman (Barbara Stanwyck) brought back to her people, only to face the stigma of having a mixed-blood son.

However, Rudolph Mate's *The Far Horizons* (1955) told the story of the famed Meriwether Lewis (played by Fred MacMurray) and William Clark (Charlton Heston) expedition of 1803 with a Manifest Destiny perspective. In the aftermath of having arranged the Louisiana Purchase with France in 1801,[1] the expansionist President Thomas Jefferson[2] sponsored the expedition in order explore and find a water route between St. Louis, Missouri, and the Pacific Ocean. The film featured a fictionalized romance between Clark and Sacajawea[3] (played by the totally miscast Donna Reed), a Shoshone woman who served the expedition as a guide and diplomat to the fifty native tribes they encountered during the 18-month trek. Contrary to the film narrative, the real Sacajawea was already married (to Canadian trapper Toussaint Charbonneau) and had a newborn child when she traveled with Lewis and Clark, and she did very little in the way of guiding. In *The Far Horizons*, as usual, the majority of indigenous roles were given to Caucasian actors. Native actors were reduced to tiny roles.

Walk the Proud Land (1956, Universal) was another film based on the true story of white Indian agent John Clum (Audie Murphy), who attempted to find peace between the Apaches and whites through mutual respect. In the film *Arrowhead* (1953, Paramount), a white scout (Charlton Heston) cannot let go of his prejudice against an Apache resistance leader (Jack Palance) who has recently been released from prison. *Navajo* (1952, Lippert Pictures) was an independent semi-documentary about a Navajo boy (Frances

7. New Images and Consciousness (1950–1959)   127

Sarita Montiel as Nina, the indigenous woman fighting French intervention in Mexico, and Gary Cooper as Ben Trane, a Euro-American mercenary, in Robert Aldrich's *Vera Cruz* (1954, United Artists).

Kee Teller) who refused to be educated in an Indian boarding school. The film, written and directed by Norman Foster, won a Golden Globe Special Award for Teller for Best Juvenile Actor. However, Teller quickly disappeared from public view and never made another film.

    Two films during this decade told the story of two respected Native Americans. *Jim Thorpe—All-American* (1952, Warner Bros.) celebrated the great athletic achievements of Jim Thorpe (played by Burt Lancaster) and provided a sympathetic biography of the Olympic athlete. A second film, *The Story of Wild Rogers* (1952, Warner Bros.), depicted the life and times of the famous Native American humorist and humanitarian Will Rogers (played by his son, Will Rogers, Jr.). Two Disney films attempted to engage the youth market in indigenous-themed films: *Tonka* (1958) revolved around a Lakota youth named Wild Bull (Sal Mineo), who proves his manhood by catching and training the young colt Tonka. However, the colt later is captured by a U.S. cavalryman and subsequently survives the Battle of Little Big Horn. By contrast, *The Light at the End of the Forest* (1958) tells the story of a young white youth (James MacArthur) who has spent his childhood with the Delaware tribe and must adjust to his former Euro-American family.

During the 1950s, native characters were portrayed more sympathetically and were more fully developed. However, the leading roles continued to be portrayed by Caucasian performers (i.e., Robert Taylor, Jeff Chandler, Burt Lancaster, Jean Peters, etc.). More often than not, native actors were consigned to supporting or featured roles, even in more liberal films. Lacking indigenous screenwriters, directors, and producers, the authentic Native American voice and experience was yet to be fully told or depicted on film.

The best-known film star of Native American roots during the 1950s was Anthony Quinn. He would win a Best Supporting Actor Academy Award for portraying Eufemio Zapata (Emiliano Zapata's brother) in the film *Viva Zapata!* (1952, 20th Century–Fox) and another for playing the painter Paul Gauguin in *Lust for Life* (1956, MGM). Another

From left: **Lloyd Bridges, Katy Jurado (a Mexican indigenous actress), Gary Cooper, and Grace Kelly in *High Noon* (1952, United Artists).**

film actor with Native American ancestry was James Garner (part Cherokee), who would go on to fame on television in the popular series *Maverick* and would later achieve film stardom at the end of the decade. Veteran actor Monte Blue played his last role (as Geronimo) in *Apache* (1954, United Artists). New male performers during the 1950s included Will Rogers, Jr., and Woody Strode.

During the decade, the busiest indigenous-origin actress was the Mexican-born Katy Jurado (1924–2002), who scored impressively in several key westerns: *High Noon* (1951, United Artists), as the strong-willed *Mexicana* and former love of Gary Cooper; *The Bullfighter and the Lady* (1951, United Artists), as the wife of the aging bullfighter (Gilbert Roland) trying to make a comeback; *Broken Lance* (1954, 20th Century–Fox), as the native wife of a rancher (Spencer Tracy); and *The Badlanders* (1958, MGM), as the Mexican native woman outcast. She became the first Mexican-born actress to be nominated for a Best Supporting Actress Academy Award for *Broken Lance*.

This decade also introduced the talented and attractive native-origin actress Jeanne Cooper (part Cherokee). She debuted in films in 1952 in *Redhead from Wyoming* and went on to co-star in some thirty films. Her best film role during the decade was in the cult classic heist film *Plunder Road* (1957). She made numerous television appearances as well before becoming a household name playing the devious matriarch in *The Young and the Restless*.

Representative Films

Devil's Doorway (1950, MGM)

Anthony Mann's *Devil's Doorway* is a key film of the 1950s in depicting the plight of Native Americans. Although it is often overshadowed by *Broken Arrow* (1950, 20th Century–Fox) and *The Searchers* (1956, Warner Bros.), *Devil's Doorway* is an uncompromising and unique film.

The narrative focuses on Broken Lance Poole (Robert Taylor), a returning Civil War veteran, who is a Shoshone native and Congressional Medal of Honor recipient. Upon his arrival home in Wyoming, joining his aged father (Fritz Leiber), he learns that the tract of land that his people have called home for generations (Sweet Meadows in the Devil's Doorway Canyon) is about to be taken over by swarms of homesteaders. As a Native American, Lance is not recognized as a U.S. citizen (native people were not recognized as such until 1924) and thus cannot hold a legal title to own land. He is assisted by a young female attorney Orrie Carmody (Paula Raymond), who herself is the object of scorn and ridicule in town.

The homesteaders are encouraged in their dispossession by corrupt land agent Verne Coolan (Louis Calhern), who spreads a rumor that there is plenty of land for the taking in Sweet Meadows and the Devil's Doorway Canyon. Caught in the middle are townspeople like Sheriff Zeke Carmondy (Edgar Buchanan), who know Lance and his family to be honorable people. However, most of them are aroused to a mob-like fever and prejudice. Lance stifles the blossoming romance between himself and Orrie due to the rampant intolerance.

Orrie appeals Lance's case but is unsuccessful. At the end of the film, Lance and the other Shoshone fight against the besieging U.S. Cavalry. Seriously wounded, Lance parleys with the commander after Orrie has manage to establish a truce. He is asked, "Where are the rest of the Shoshone?" He responds, "There isn't anymore. We're all gone." He dies with the Congressional Medal of Honor on his jacket.

The script of *Devil's Doorway* lay dormant at MGM for three years before it got the green light. Production on this film preceded that of *Broken Arrow*, which was released later that same year. However, MGM pushed back the release of *Devil's Doorway* due to the content of the film. The more conventional (with an interracial love story) *Broken Arrow* would go on to become a significant critical and box-office success. After its success, MGM went ahead and released *Devil's Doorway*, but by that time the former film had stolen its thunder and attention.

Devil's Doorway was part of a body of work in Hollywood during the late 1940s and early 1950s that began to tackle previously taboo racial and social themes. Among these films were *Pinky* (1949, 20th Century–Fox) and *Intruder in the Dust* (1949, 20th Century–Fox), about the prejudice faced by African Americans; *Gentlemen's Agreement* (1947, 20th Century–Fox) and *Crossfire* (1947, 20th Century–Fox), about anti–Semitism; *Border Incident* (1949, MGM) and *The Lawless* (1950, Paramount), about Mexican undocumented workers; and *The Ring* (1952, United Artists) and *Salt of the Earth* (1954, IUMMSW), about urban Mexican Americans and/or Chicanos.

Devil's Doorway was directed by Anthony Mann (1906–1967), a meticulous craftsman and maverick director. He had previously directed *Border Incident*, the first film to deal realistically and humanely with the plight of Mexican undocumented workers. His later body of work included several evocative and uncompromising westerns (five of them with James Stewart), peopled by characters coming to terms with their fractured consciences. In the last part of his career in the 1960s, Mann helmed two memorable epic films: *El Cid* (1961, Allied Artists) and *The Fall of the Roman Empire* (1964, Paramount Pictures).

The screenplay was written by Guy Trosper, and the impressive black-and-white cinematography was undertaken by John Alton, who often collaborated with Mann.

In *Devil's Doorway*, most of the characters have to choose between conformity and dissent. For example, Orrie and her mother make the choice to help Lance despite Orrie's already outcast status. The bartender chooses to conform with the prevailing prejudice because the new settlers will make his saloon flourish. At the expense of his previous friendship with Lance, Sheriff Zeke chooses to honor his oath to carry out the law, and he ultimately loses his life for a cause he never believed in from the beginning.

In a real way, the fictional Native American Civil War veterans shared many of the dreams of returning World War II servicemen. Although African Americans had been segregated during the war, other minorities, such as Native Americans, Mexican Americans/Chicanos, and Jews, had fought side by side with Euro-Americans. They hoped that racism and discrimination would become a relic of the past. In real life, however, racism in the United States was alive and well.

In Hollywood, the progressive bent of this and other postwar films was all but obliterated by the HUAC hearings in 1947 and 1951. The subsequent blacklist and gray list destroyed, exiled, and ended the creative talents of many of the best in Hollywood for at least a generation.

Devil's Doorway was a film ahead of its time. It met with only limited commercial success, but critical praise. In the meantime, *Broken Arrow* was a runaway success. *Devil's Doorway*'s limited commercial success was probably be attributed to the uncompromising stance of the film, the lack of a conventional love story and the offbeat casting of the romantic film star Robert Taylor.

The *New York Times* (November 10, 1950) commented, "Perhaps it is too late now to change the course of fiction which has established the American Indian as a ruthless savage, but our movie makers appear to be endeavoring to right some of the wrong they themselves have done the red man over the years."[4] The *Los Angeles Daily News* (October 21, 1950) noted that in "'Devil's Doorway' … Anthony Mann has directed Guy Trosper's literate script in exciting, visual style, constantly imparting to the happening a natural, eye-arresting quality.… Robert Taylor, with the help of effective makeup, runs in a reserved and dignified portrayal of the Indian, and acquits himself credibly in a highly difficult role."[5] *Fortnight* (October 30, 1950) commented, "'Devil's Doorway' (MGM) carries the film vogue of championing minorities back to the comparatively uncontroversial issue of the American Indian's plight.… Both [Guy] Trosper and director Anthony Mann are wise, however, for at no time does either forget melodrama for message. Camera work is excellent."[6]

More recent film critics like those in *Focus on Film* (Autumn 1972) have written about *Devil's Doorway* as follows: "Where *Broken Arrow* softens its story of discrimination against the Indian by emphasizing an idyllic love angle, and concentrate on breathtaking scenic color shots, *Devil's Doorway* is uncompromising in its statement that the Indians were maltreated after the Civil War."[7]

Broken Arrow (1950, 20th Century–Fox)

The film *Broken Arrow* marked a turning point in the portrayals of Native Americans in U.S. films. It begins with a voiceover narration from Tom Jeffords (James Stewart) and flashes back to Arizona of 1870. Jeffords, a former cavalry scout, refuses the entreaties of the commandant to scout against the Apaches. In Tucson, the citizenry is vehemently opposed to any accommodation or treaty with the Apaches. One of the leaders is Ben Slade (Will Geer), an avowed racist and native hater. Jeffords has an altercation with Slade and reminds him that natives are fighting for their land and survival. He also reminds him that it was whites who began the practice of scalping.

Jeffords informs the commandant that he will attempt to establish peace between whites and the Apaches. He enters Apache land, monitored at all times by Apache warriors, and, after several days, is allowed to meet with Cochise (Jeff Chandler), the Apache chief. Cochise permits the U.S. mail carriers to come through as a gesture of peace, and gradually a truce takes hold. In the meantime, Jeffords has fallen in love with Sonseeahray (Debra Paget), whom he ultimately marries according to Apache custom. Jeffords enlists the assistance of General Oliver Howard (Basil Ryael), and a formal treaty is signed. At this juncture, however, Geronimo (Jay Silverheels) dissents from the council and vows to continue a military resistance against whites.

Slade and some of his gold prospector friends trick Jeffords and Cochise into an ambush. They fail to kill Cochise, but Sonseeahray is mortally wounded. Overcome with grief, Jeffords attempts to dissuade Cochise from adhering to the treaty, telling him that whites do not really want peace. However, with the survival of his people at stake, Cochise maintains his commitment to the treaty.

Although *Devil's Doorway* had actually been filmed the year before, it is *Broken Arrow* that is credited with the "breakthrough" of portraying Native Americans with integrity and cultural history. This is mainly a result of two factors. First, *Devil's Doorway* is a much darker film. All the forces in that movie conspire at the end to destroy the Shoshone; they have no options for survival. Second, as a consequence of the downbeat mood of the film, it met with limited commercial success. *Broken Arrow*, in turn, presents Native Americans and whites with equal degrees of power. The latter film passionately decries the prejudice and injustice against Native Americans, but there is always a sense of hope and accommodation, as well as survival.

Broken Arrow depicts Apache customs and culture faithfully. Native characters are portrayed as integral parts of their community. Cochise, for example, tells Jeffords, "I do not betray my people, and my people do not betray me." The interdependence of leadership and community is evident throughout the film.

The character of Cochise is well developed and multidimensional. Native American leaders had previously been portrayed in U.S. films as one-dimensional villains and fanatics. Here, we see Cochise as an astute warrior and diplomat, but also as a leader, at times overburdened with the responsibilities of leadership. He is slow to trust Jeffords until he sees evidence of reciprocity. Always uppermost in his mind is the well-being of his people. Once he is assured of that guarantee, he can be compassionate toward Jeffords and General Howard.

However, *Broken Arrow* is still a flawed film. This film began the cinematic trend of using Geronimo as the adversary of any peace overtures with whites. Geronimo became a convenient villain, fanatic, and obstruction, a common enemy against whom whites and docile natives could unite. In fact, Cochise (1805–1874) died only two years after the establishment of the peace treaty with the U.S. government. However, the continued U.S. policy to subdue and force Apaches and other tribes into reservations resulted in native resistance for several more years. Geronimo (1829–1909) was twenty-four years younger than Cochise and belonged to a later generation of native leaders who faced changed conditions with whites. The scene in the film in which Geronimo defies Cochise's acceptance of the peace treaty never happened and is pure Hollywood fiction. Not only that, but a young Apache would never dare defy an Apache chief and elders once a decision had been made.

Another flaw of the film is the lack of Native Americans playing the major roles (with the exception of Jay Silverheels). Native actors in small roles included Chris Willow Bird, John War Eagle, Dolores Christine Cypert, and J.W. Cody.

Broken Arrow gained immeasurably from the ideal casting of James Stewart as the anti-heroic Tom Jeffords. His amiable, average Joe screen persona, full of human flaws and an easygoing manner, fit the role perfectly. Stewart imbued the character of Jeffords with common decency, fairness, and common sense. Additionally, *Broken Arrow* benefited powerfully and dramatically from another strong character to balance the Jeffords character.

The actor who portrayed Cochise was the prematurely gray-haired newcomer, Jeff Chandler (1918–1961), whose real name was Ira Grossel. He was of Jewish origin. So charismatic and convincing was his portrayal that he was nominated for an Academy Award for Best Supporting Actor. Chandler's excellent performance almost overshadowed Stewart's. This film would propel Chandler to major film stardom. He went on to play Cochise in two more films: *Battle of Apache Pass* (1952, Universal) and *Taza, Son of Cochise* (1954, Universal). Once again, the character of Geronimo would be used as a convenient villain to oppose the making of peace between native and whites.

The character of Geronimo was played by Jay Silverheels. As detailed in the previous chapter, he would go on to play the role of Tonto in *The Lone Ranger* television series of the 1950s.

The aforementioned factors, in addition to the interracial love story and stunning Technicolor cinematography, guaranteed *Broken Arrow* immense commercial and critical success, consigning *Devil's Doorway* to relative obscurity. *Broken Arrow* was nominated for three Academy Awards: Best Supporting Actor (Jeff Chandler); Best Screenplay Adaption (Michael Blankfort, fronting for Albert Maltz, from the novel *Blood Brother* by Elliot Arnold); and Color Cinematography (Ernest Palmer), as well as the Robert Meltzer Award from the Writers Guild of America.

Broken Arrow earned glowing reviews from critics. *Variety* (June 15, 1950) wrote, "'*Broken Arrow*' is a western a with a little different twist—the story of the attempt of whites and Apaches ... Stewart gives another engaging portrayal.... Matching him in appeal is Chandler as the feared Apache leader Cochise, investing the role with a great deal of dignity."[8] *Film Daily* (June 14, 1950) noted, "'*Broken Arrow*' is no ordinary tale about Indians and pioneers in the early day of the West. Here is an extremely dignified story brilliantly told ... Jeff Chandler is a moving, impressive impersonation of the brilliant Indian leader Cochise."[9] The *Hollywood Reporter* (June 12, 1950) called it "a warm and sensitive script which accomplishes the miracle of portraying the American Indian as a person much more than the stereotypes rug peddler or vicious savage.... Jeff Chandler's dignified and intelligent characterization of Cochise, the chief, is perfectly splendid. Chandler makes the Indian a real human being."[10]

Delmer Daves was both the director and the screenwriter. In his youth, Daves had spent time among the Hopi and Navajo. According to Ephraim Katz, "Although variable in thematic quality, his films were always interesting to watch and were imbued with humanity and sympathetic understanding for characters in conflict with their environment."[11] Daves' other native-themed films included *Drum Beat* (1954, Warner Bros.) and *The Last Wagon* (1956, Warner Bros.).

Much of the sensitivity and progressive bent of the film must be attributed to the screenplay by blacklisted writer Albert Maltz (1908–1985), whose work was not acknowledged by the Screen Writers' Guild until 1990. Instead, the screenplay was attributed to Michael Blankfort (1908–1982). Maltz was a novelist and playwright. He worked as one of the film crew in the Academy Award–winning documentary *Moscow Strikes Back* (1942, Republic) and had penned such notable films as *This Gun for Hire* (1942, Paramount), *Pride of the Marines* (1945, Warner Bros.), and *The Naked City* (1948, Universal).

In October 1947, Maltz became one of the Hollywood Ten, convicted of contempt of Congress for refusing to cooperate with the House Un-American Activities (HUAC) while investigating the alleged Communist influence in Hollywood. He spent ten months in prison and was subsequently blacklisted. After leaving prison, Maltz lived for eleven years in Mexico and did not see *Broken Arrow* until his return to the United States in 1962. It took eight more years before he worked again using his own name in *Two Mules for Sister Sara* (1970, Universal) and *Scalawag* (1973, Paramount). As it happened, the man who fronted for Maltz on *Broken Arrow*, Blankfort, testified in 1952 before the HUAC as a "friendly witness." With this act, the friendship between Maltz and Blankfort ended forever.

Broken Arrow was shot on location in northern Arizona (near Flagstaff and the Fort Apache Reservation) and used Apache extras.

The Savage (1952, Paramount)

The Savage was directed by the veteran George Marshall (1871–1975), who helmed every type of film genre for six decades. It was written by Sydney Boehm and based on the novel *The Renegade* (1949). The impressive cinematography was done by the noted John F. Seitz (1892–1979). Most of the film was shot on location in the Black Hills of South Dakota.

The film's narrative concerns Jim Aherne, Jr. (played as an adult by Charlton Heston), who, as a child, is the only survivor of a Crow attack on a wagon train. He is subsequently rescued by a Lakota chief. Jim is renamed Warbonnet and mentored by Chief Yellow Eagle (Ian MacDonald). When gold is discovered in the Black Hills, white prospectors rush in to acquire the land, despite the Treaty of Fort Laramie. Warbonnet is torn between his white ancestry and his adopted Lakota identity. The remainder of the narrative focuses on his dilemma.

Newcomer Charlton Heston was cast as the adult Warbonnet. Caucasian actors played the key native roles: Joan Taylor as Luta; Don Porter as Running Dog; Ted de Corsia as Iron Breast; and Angela Clarke as Pehang. Native American actors were cast in minor roles, which included Chief American Horse and Ben Black Elk, Sr.

The film received some mixed reviews. The *New York Times* (January 2, 1953) noted, "Best of all Mr. Heston, the focal point of the entire proceedings, is a strapping young man who can act. Principally due to his spunky, laconic emoting as the loyalty-torn adopted white member of a Sioux tribe who engineers peace."[12]

The film content apparently had a noted effect on the film's star Charlton Heston (who was later active politically on Hollywood's left, and then on the right). In his youth, Heston spoke passionately about the injustices perpetrated against Native Americans: "Now that I've worked with the Sioux [as advisors on the film]. I think that there should be a movie made about the modern-day Sioux and people should talk to them. Maybe somebody should get up from their hind legs and scream about them ... here are people really worth waving a flag for."[13]

According to Heston's biographer Marc Elliot, Paramount executives were less than thrilled about the actor's comments, which may have resulted in the studio selling his contract back to independent producer Hal Wallis. In reference to this incident, Elliot noted, "If Heston was aware of the negative reaction to his remarks at the studio, he never showed it and didn't give an indication that he cared at all what the execs thought or did with his contract."[14]

Jim Thorpe—All-American (1953, Warner Bros.)

The film *Jim Thorpe—All-American* focused on the life of James Francis Thorpe (1887–1953), Sac and Fox (Sauk), one of the nation's greatest athletes. It was directed by the great director, Hungarian-born Michael Curtiz (1886–1962), who had directed such notable films as *Adventures of Robin Hood* (1938, Warner Bros.) and *Casablanca* (1942, Warner Bros.), for which he won an Academy Award for Best Director. The screenplay was written by Everett Freeman and Douglas Morrow; Frank Davis (additional dialogue); Vincent X. Flaherty and Douglas Morrow (story); and Russell Birdwell and Jim Thorpe (biography).

The lead role was played by former acrobat Burt Lancaster (1913–1994), an Academy

Award winner for Best Actor in *Elmer Gantry* (1960, United Artists). Although he was thirty-eight years old at the time, Lancaster possessed sufficient athletic ability to be convincing in the sporting scenes. Phyllis Thaxter was cast as Thorpe's girlfriend and later wife Margaret Miller; Charles Bickford as Pop Warner, Thorpe's coach at Carlisle; and Steve Cochran as Thorpe's athletic and romantic rival Peter Allendine. Native American actors included Sonny Chorre as Wally Denny and several others in bit parts. Some of the film was shot at the Indian Bowl and Bacone College (doubling for the Carlisle Indian Industrial School) in Muskogee, Oklahoma.

The narrative focuses on the life of Jim Thorpe (see the entry in Chapter 5 for a fuller biography of Jim Thorpe): his dreams as a youth; the bloom of his athletic prowess at the Carlisle Indian Industrial School; and his relationship with the young lady he came to love and ultimately marry. The highlight of the film included Thorpe's unprecedented achievement at the 1912 Olympics and the Olympic Committee's removal of his medals because he had received a small payment for playing baseball during one summer. The film also documents his career in professional football, his fall into alcoholism, and his later recognition as the greatest athlete of the first half of the 20th century. Missing from the film was Thorpe's lifelong struggle to improve the lives of native people, such as organizing native actors for better opportunities in the film industry.

Burt Lancaster is convincing in his fluid athletic ability and reenactment of some of Thorpe's greatest sports achievements. Lancaster was a highly respected progressive in the film industry who was very involved in advancing equal rights for minorities and women. His demeanor as a humble and sincere Native American young man is comes through and is very evocative. However, one cannot help but wonder what a Native American actor could have done with this role. Lancaster would go on to portray Massai, the legendary Apache warrior, in the film *Apache* (1954, United Artists) and to debunk some of the mythology of white settler life in *Unforgiven* (1961, United Artists). Lancaster would also play a burned-out and disillusioned army scout involved in futile action against a Native American warrior in *Ulzana's Raid* (1972, Universal).

Jim Thorpe—All-American received generally positive reviews and went on to become a commercial success (grossing $188 million when adjusted for inflation).[15]

The Last Hunt (1956, MGM)

The film *The Last Hunt* featured one of the most hateful and psychotic Euro-American characters of the 1950s, though it has been long overshadowed by John Ford's *The Searchers*. Richard Brooks directed and wrote the film (based on novel of the same name by Milton Lott). It was produced by Dore Schary, and the impressive cinematography was done by Russell Harlan.

Some 80 percent of the film was shot on location at the Custer State Park and the Badlands National Park in South Dakota, home to the Lakota people. The film used actual footage of buffalo being killed by U.S. government marksmen during the "thinning of the buffalo herd." This footage served to depict the historic slaughter of Euro-Americans in their march westward.

The film is set in 1883 and begins with a narration explaining that at one time there were more than sixty million buffalo roaming the Great Plains, but thirty years later only half of that number still existed. The narrative involves the partnerships of two veteran buffalo hunters, Scott McKenzie (Stewart Granger) and Charles Gibson (Robert Taylor).

McKenzie eventually becomes sickened by the slaughter of the bison. However, Gibson becomes obsessed with the killing and develops a psychotic hatred of all Native Americans and their way of life. He pursues a native raiding party, kills them, and abducts a native girl (Debra Paget). Her presence, combined with his racism, takes him over a mental abyss.

The character of Gibson has parallels to the character of Ethan in *The Searchers*. Although Gibson is located on the Great Plains and Ethan roams through the arid Southwest, both share a psychotic affinity. Both hate Native Americans and want to exterminate them. Ethan kills the natives he encounters and/or maliciously demeans others. In turn, Gibson despises Jimmy (Russ Tamblyn), who is a half-breed, and attempts to rape the native girl he has taken hostage. Ethan demeans the relatives he thinks have been tainted by native blood and sets out to search for his niece Debbie and eradicate her native captors. Both are frightening characters rooted in the ethos of Manifest Destiny and the mythology of winning the west.

Robert Taylor was cast in the role of Gibson, again playing against his usual typecasting as a romantic lead. His performance in this film is arguably the best of his entire career. He had previously played the Shoshone Medal of Honor winner in the harrowing *Devil's Doorway* (1950, MGM). The popular British-born Stewart Granger was cast as hardbitten McKenzie, who is repulsed by the slaughter of the buffalo and the increasing paranoia of his partner. Caucasian actress Debra Paget was cast as the indigenous girl. She had played indigenous maidens in *Broken Arrow* (1950, Universal) and again in *White Feather* (1954, 20th Century–Fox). Unfortunately, *The Last Hunt* did not feature a single speaking role for Native American actors.

The film received generally positive reviews. Bosley Crowther, in the *New York Times* (March 1, 1956), wrote, "*The Last Hunt* is aimed to display the low and demeaning influence of a lust for slaughter upon the nature of man ... [Gibson], played by Robert Taylor, is a bestial and brutal type who hate Indians and likes to kill them almost as much as he likes to kill buffaloes."[16]

Sitting Bull (1954, United Artists)

Hollywood executives cashed in on Native American–themed films in the aftermath of the box-office success of *Broken Arrow*. One of these was the film *Sitting Bull*, directed by Sidney Salkow, who specialized in "B" action films; the screenplay was written by Salkow and Jack DeWitt. The film was shot in Mexico for budgetary considerations. However, the rocky arid terrain chosen for filming is completely different from the rolling Great Plains where the story is set.

Irish American actor J. Carrol Naish was cast in the role of Sitting Bull. Naish was an excellent character actor who often specialized in a variety of ethnic and villainous roles. However, here he is totally miscast and unconvincing. His acting and demeanor are inconsistent with the native persona. Iron Eyes Cody (Italian actor Espera Óscar de Corti) was cast in the role of "loose cannon" Crazy Horse, in addition to serving as the technical advisor. Douglas Kennedy played George Armstrong Custer. The two nominal romantic leads were Dale Robertson and Mary Murphy (best known for her performance with Marlon Brando in the biker film *The Wild One*).

The threadbare script revolves around the efforts of Major Robert Parrish (Dale Robrtson), who served during the Civil War and presently is under the command of the glory-seeking Custer. Parrish is court-martialed after voicing anger over the mistreatment of the Lakota people. He travels to Washington, D.C., to convince President Ulysses S. Grant to meet with Sitting Bull to prevent war in the Great Plains; instead, Grant downgrades him to the rank of captain.

The other native leader, Crazy Horse, is portrayed as eager for conflict and war, similar to Custer himself. Eventually, as Euro-Americans stream into Lakota lands, war erupts. It climaxes with the Battle of the Little Big Horn, where Custer and his troops are defeated.

In the meantime, Parrish is court-martialed once more, this time for helping Sitting Bull elude the U.S. Cavalry. Just as Parrish is being brought out to be executed by a firing squad, Sitting Bull arrives and successfully pleads with President Grant for Parrish's life. The film proposes a proverbial happy ending, contrary to history.

The weak script, poor acting (especially by the white actors portraying the native leaders), and glaring historical inaccuracies doomed the film. First, Grant and Sitting Bull never met each other, nor was there a peaceful coexistence after Custer's defeat between the U.S. government and native tribes—in fact, just the opposite occurred. Second, Crazy Horse was not a "loose cannon" but a highly respected leader.

The real Sitting Bull was born in 1831 and was a Hunkpapa Lakota "holy man." He was an important leader in the native resistance against the U.S. government. After Custer's defeat in 1876, Sitting Bull sought refuge in Canada. However, the harsh conditions his people endured there compelled him to return to the United States in 1881 and surrender. He was murdered by Indian agency police in the Standing Rock Indian Reservation in 1890. Sitting Bull continues to be much revered and venerated by Native Americans.

The reviews of *Sitting Bull* were overwhelmingly negative, especially regarding the misguided casting of white actors in native roles and the numerous distortions of history. Bosley Crowther, writing in the *New York Times* (November 26, 1954), dismissed "J. Carrol Naish hissing through his choppers and his war paint as a patient, peace-loving Sitting Bull and with Douglas Kennedy acting Colonel Custer as though he were high-school Horatio at the bridge, this ... picture should barley serve to entertain the horse-happy kids."[17]

Chief Crazy Horse (1955, Universal)

The film *Chief Crazy Horse* was a western that attempted to document the life of an important Native American leader. However, the continued practice of casting white actors in all native roles severely undermined its credibility and sincerity.

Chief Crazy Horse was helmed by veteran director George Sherman. The screenplay and the story were written by Gerald Drayson Adams and Franklin Coen, and the story was by Adams. The cinematography was undertaken by Harold Lipstein.

The real Crazy Horse is one of the most legendary and iconic Native American leaders in history. He is said to have been born during 1840–1845 somewhere in the northern Great Plains. His father was Oglala and his mother a Miniconjou of the Lakota people. Crazy Horse was a great horseman and warrior. Contrary to the film's title, Crazy Horse was never a chief. However, he fought in numerous battles against the invading U.S. Cavalry with great distinction and daring. He was one of the important native leaders who defeated Custer at the Battle of Little Big Horn in 1876.

In the aftermath of the Custer defeat, the U.S. government launched a devastating war against the tribes of the Great Plains. In order to protect his people from further punitive actions, Crazy Horse surrendered on May 5, 1877, in Fort Robinson, Nebraska. He was murdered on September 5, 1877, by the military guards and buried by his people in an undisclosed location. His image was never captured in sketches or photos. A huge monument to Crazy Horse has been in the process of being built since 1948, on the other side of the Mount Rushmore National Memorial, in the Black Hills, South Dakota. To native peoples throughout the Americas, Crazy Horse remains a respected and venerated hero.

The lead role of Crazy Horse was played by Victor Mature (1913–1999), who had been hugely popular and successful in such biblical epics such as *Samson and Delilah* (1949, Paramount); *The Robe* (1953, 20th Century–Fox); *Demetrius and the Gladiators* (1954, 20th Century–Fox); and *The Egyptian* (1954, 20th Century–Fox). Mature brought a unique spirituality (one that was powerfully effective in his biblical roles) to the character. However, a weak script and poor direction, as well as an all-white cast, burdened the film. The well-intentioned spirituality became the object of scorn by critics. The few Native American actors included Pat Hogan as Dull Knife.

The film received mostly negative reviews. Bosley Crowther, in the *New York Times* (April 28, 1955), wrote, "*Chief Crazy Horse*, the Indian hero ... isn't exactly crazy, but neither is he too bright ... this fine-feathered, war-painted chieftain, played by Victor Mature, is going around snorting defiance and listening to the voice of a heavenly choir."[18]

Hondo (1953, Warner Bros/Wayne-Fellows Prods.)

The film *Hondo* is the best-known western based on a book or story by written by western writer Louis Amour. It was also one of several westerns made during the 1950s that documented more realistically the relations between white settlers and native peoples.

The film was directed by Australian-born John Farrow (1904–1963), who would go to win an Academy Award for Best Writing/Best Screenplay for the film *Around the World in 80 Days* (1956, United Artists). The last scenes were helmed by an uncredited John Ford when Farrow was compelled to leave the production due to contractual obligations. The film was co-produced by Wayne-Fellows Productions with Warner Brothers. The screenplay was written by James Edward Grant and based on the July 5, 1952, *Collier's* short story "The Gift of Cochise" by Louis L'Amour (real name Louis Dearborn LaMoore). The evocative cinematography was undertaken by Archie J. Stout, Louis Clyde Stoumen, and Robert Burks. The film was shot in 3D (at the height of this technical innovation).

The title role of Hondo was played by John Wayne, and the female lead was former theater actress Geraldine Page, who was nominated for an Academy Award for Best Supporting Actress. The film featured such John Ford stock company regulars such as Ward Bond, Leo Gordon, James Arness, and Paul Fix.

The film is set in 1874 in New Mexico. The narrative involves the mixed-blood Hondo (John Wayne), who arrives at a ranch where Mrs. Angie Lowe (Geraldine Page) and her son Johnny (Lee Aaker) live. Both Angie and Johnny have been deserted by Angie's useless husband (Leo Gordon). They are visited by Vittorio (Michael Pate) and several Apache warriors, many of whom Hondo has known for a long time. Vittorio makes it known that he is not at war with them. Vittorio adopts the boy and respects Hondo's relationship with Angie.

Later in the film, Hondo kills Mr. Lowe (Leo Gordon) in self-defense in a bar. However, Angie informs Hondo that her late husband was a gambler and an opportunist who married her for her inheritance. Once again, war erupts between the white settlers and the Apache. In the end, Hondo asks Angie and her son to leave with him in a wagon train that will pass by his farm. He and Angie hope to marry and care for Johnny together.

Hondo garnered overall positive reviews and over the years has earned more praise as a film that captured the rough edges of frontier life. The character of Hondo reflects a more progressive attitude toward Native Americans. Hondo is said to be part Apache and has lived among the natives. His late wife was also Apache. His relationship with the Apache warrior Vittorio is cordial and respectful, and there is a sense of mutual admiration for the code of masculine conflict and violence. There is actual dialogue and interaction between Hondo and the Apaches, although (with the exception of Vittorio) they are reduced to faceless visitors. The cinematography captures the spiritual beauty and ethos of the arid Southwest. However, the ending of the film reverts to the conventional conclusion of most westerns: the proverbial rescue of settlers by the U.S. Cavalry.

The only Native American actor who had a significant role was Rodolfo Acosta, who played Silva. Other native actors played bit roles. The role of Vittorio, the Chiricahua Apache chief, was played by the Australian actor Michael Pate, who was often cast in native roles.

Hondo made $231.90 million in world gross when adjusted for inflation.[19]

The Searchers (1956, Warner Bros.)

One of the most disturbing films ever made about the U.S. wars against Native Americans was John Ford's *The Searchers*. This film, along with *Devil's Doorway* and *Broken Arrow*, was one of the key films of the 1950s in terms of the portrayal of Native Americans.

The narrative begins when the darkness is broken by the door of a cabin being opened to the arid landscape that lies outside and the coming of a lone rider, Ethan Edwards. Ethan has returned three years after the end of the Civil War (having fought on the side of the Confederacy). He is embittered, haggard, and an Indian hater. He scorns his adopted nephew Martin Paley (Jeffrey Hunter) because he is one-eighth Cherokee, treating him as a boarder and not part of the family.

Later, there is a Native American raid upon Ethan's brother's home, led by Chief Scar (Hendry Bandon). Most of the family is killed in the raid. As a result, Ethan's pathological hatred of Native Americans increases. A posse is organized by the Rev.-Captain Samuel Clayton (Ward Bond), a leader of the Texas Rangers. Ethan and Martin join the group. After a skirmish, Clayton attempts to stop Ethan, who does not let the native warriors recover their dead. The realization of Ethan's pathological obsession eventually leads to the posse's disintegration. A breaking point is reached when Ethan shoots out the eyes of a dead Comanche, so that he will never find a resting place in the afterlife.

Ethan and Martin continue their search for years until they get information from Emilio (Antonio Moreno) regarding the exact whereabouts of Chief Scar. Along the way, they find the remnants of a native village massacred by the U.S. Cavalry, which distresses Martin, but not the revenge-filled Ethan. With the assistance of Clayton and his rangers, they lead a raid against Scar's band and search for Ethan's lost niece Debbie (Natalie Wood). When Scar is killed in the skirmish, Ethan proceeds to take Scar's scalp. He had also vowed to kill Debbie because she has slept with an "Indian buck." However, when he finally finds her, his bigotry subsides, and they return home: Debbie to the extended Jorgensen family (John Qualen, Olive Carey), and Martin to his girlfriend (Vera Miles). However, in the last scene, Ethan is alienated from everyone in the family reunion. He stands alone, holding his left elbow with his right hand; then he breaks the stand, turns around and returns to the outdoors. The cabin door closes, and there is complete darkness.

The Searchers is a complex film. At various times, the story is told from one of three perspectives: Ethan, Martin, and Clayton. Ethan Edwards is perhaps the most complicated character ever to appear in a John Ford film. Jay Robert Nash and Stanley Ralph Ross wrote, "Both Indians and whites are shown capable of committing acts of compassion and savagery. There are no easy answers here, nothing is simple as good and evil. Ford does not want us to judge his West, but merely to understand it and ourselves."[20]

When the film was first released, it received positive reviews. *Variety* (March 13, 1956) noted, "The John Ford directorial stamp is unmistakable. It concentrates on the character and established a definite mood. Winston C. Hoch's Vista Vision lensing and other technical aspects are topnotch quality, particularly Max Steiner's music."[21] The *Los Angeles Times* (March 13, 1956) wrote, "While Ford has often probed the West for his dramas and his rare scenic panoramas, he seems in '*The Searchers*' to have penetrated more deeply than usual into life on the frontier."[22] The *Hollywood Reporter* (March 13, 1956) likewise commented, "The preachments that make so many Westerns sound phony are totally absent from this one. Yet, by letting events speak for themselves, it manages to be both accurate and fair. The sight of the Indians trying to save their children from the avenging white men tugs at the heart."[23]

More recent critics have reassessed *The Searchers* and given it a more exhaustive deconstruction. *Rolling Stone* (July 10, 1993) wrote, "*The Searchers* is the best and most emotionally devastating western ever crafted.... Wayne gives a towering performance that seems to grow in bruising power with the years. Ethan's obsession with racial, sexual and cultural purity is ingrained, part of the American mind-set that has lasted for generations."[24] *Reader* (June 25, 1993) commented, "John Wayne, in a performance that exposes all the negative aspects of the heroic character he portrayed for Ford and others over the years, is Ethan Edwards, a man so coarsened by the struggle of survival that he is forever exiled from the civilized world of home and family."[25]

Run of the Arrow (1957, Universal-RKO)

The film *Run of the Arrow* is an unconventional western written, produced and helmed by maverick director Samuel Fuller (1912–1997), a novelist, screenwriter, producer, and director. His stories often featured solitary men in the midst of a crisis that is a turning point in their lives. His films were made outside of the studio system and often tackled unconventional or controversial topics.

Run of the Arrow was financed by RKO Pictures. However, when the studio went bankrupt before the film was released, Universal bought the film and released it. The cinematography was done by the notable Joseph Biroc (1912–1996), who would win an Academy Award for Best Cinematography (along with Fred J. Koenekamp) for *The Towering Inferno* (1974, 20th Century–Fox/Warner Bros.).

The role of O'Meara was played by the unconventional leading man Rod Steiger

(1925–2002), who would win an Academy Award for Best Actor in 1968 for *In the Heat of the Night* (United Artists). The leading U.S. Army officers were played by Brian Keith and Ralph Meeker.

The legendary Spanish film actress and singer Sarita Montiel (1928–2013), whose speech was dubbed by newcomer Angie Dickinson, played Yellow Moccasin. Montiel was an actress of stunning beauty and versatile talent. She became a star in her native Spain in the early 1950s, followed by stardom in Mexican cinema. In her brief Hollywood career, she was cast as a Mexican señorita in *Vera Cruz* (1954, United Artists) and *Serenade* (1956, Warner Bros.).

The narrative is set at the end of the Civil War in 1865. A Confederate soldier named O'Meara (Rod Steiger) is embittered and angry over the defeat of the South. He refuses to acknowledge the end of the war with the surrender of General Robert E. Lee at Appomattox. O'Meara travels to the West, where he becomes friendly with the Lakota, who accept him despite his many shortcomings. He becomes an honorary member of the tribe and lives with them. There he finds a home and escape from the trauma of the Civil War.

O'Meara falls in love and marries a Lakota woman named Yellow Moccasin (Sarita Montiel) and hopes for a peaceful live. However, soon thereafter, the U.S. Army builds a fort in Lakota land. The westward expansion of white settlers leads to conflict and then war. At a certain point, O'Meara must look to his conscience and examine his own allegiance to either the Lakota or the United States.

The film received mixed reviews, but since its release it has developed a cult following. *Run of the Arrow* broke new ground in that it depicted a white character who, traumatized by war, seeks and finds a home in Native American culture. Unlike the literary character of Hawkeye (in *Last of the Mohicans*), who chose to appropriate native culture and live in the middle of the Euro-American and native worlds, O'Meara chooses to become an exile from his own culture. The film humanizes native society, not as a perfect society, but one in which there is a cohesive sense of communal life. It is also one in which outsiders like O'Meara are allowed to join and become part of the community without the prejudice and stigmatization found in the white culture. Many years later, the film *Dances with Wolves* (1990, Orion) would follow a similar narrative.

As was usual during this era, the key Native American roles were portrayed by Caucasian actors: Charles Bronson as Blue Buffalo; Jay C. Flippen as Walking Cayote; and H.M. Wynant as Crazy Wolf, among others. Real Native Americans were reduced to bit parts and extras. The film was shot on location in St. George, Utah.

The Battle for Apache Pass (1952, Univ. Inter.)

In the aftermath of the commercial and critical success of *Broken Arrow* (1950, 20th Century–Fox) and Jeff Chandler's charismatic performance of Cochise, Universal International produced *The Battle of Apache Pass*. In this film, Chandler played once again Cochise. It was directed by veteran George Sherman and based on a screenplay by Gerald Drayson Adams.

The highly fictionalized narrative is set during 1861–1862. It depicts two important events: the Bascom Affair (1861) and the Battle of Apache Pass (1862). In the film, Major Jim Colton (John Lund) of the U.S. Cavalry has a strong and respectful relationship with Cochise (Jeff Chandler), chief of the Apache. However, an unscrupulous and ambitious

Indian agent named Neil Baylor (Bruce Cowling) invents a false Apache attack and the kidnapping of a farmer's son. Baylor then convinces the gullible and inexperienced Lieutenant George Bascom (John Hudson) that the false events actually occurred. (Major Colson is otherwise occupied and unaware of the false reports.) Bascom also spreads the rumor that Cochise is to blame. In fact, Baylor has secretly paid some of the disgruntled Apaches (including Geronimo) to initiate attacks on the U.S. Cavalry.

As a result of the deception, Bascom leads a punitive expedition against the Apaches. His objective is to apprehend Cochise and his entire family. The effort results in a tragedy, as the hostages on both sides are killed. Soon thereafter, the Apaches and the U.S. Cavalry confront each other at the Battle of Apache Pass, which is said to be the first time Apache warriors faced artillery.

The film received mixed reviews. Howard H. Thompson, in the *New York Times* (May 10, 1952), wrote, "A glum, episodic recounting of the bristling conflict between redskins and the U.S. Cavalry, fanned by some white treachery ... and an incisive repeat performance by Jeff Chandler as Cochise, the Apache chief of '*Broken Arrow*.'"[26]

Although both the Bascom Affair and the Battle of Apache Pass are historical events, the narrative of the film is greatly fictionalized. The most glaring misrepresentation is that the film has Geronimo being paid off to attack the U.S. Cavalry! As in *Broken Arrow*, the character of Geronimo is used as a convenient means of dividing the Apache tribe and also as a scapegoat to blame for the lack of peace. This was a common device in many native-themed films. They would depict "sensible native leaders," who complied with white wishes, while condemning authentic and unpliable leaders of Native American resistance.

Jeff Chandler once again lends dignity to the role of Cochise, and Susan Cabot portrays his wife Nona. This film featured many young and soon to be famous actors, including Richard Egan and Hugh O'Brien, as well as veterans like Bill Williams, John Lund, and Regis Tooney. Native American actors in the film included Jay Silverheels as Geronimo (reprising his role from *Broken Arrow*). As was the custom, most native actors were reduced to bit parts and extras.

The Battle at Apache Pass was shot on location in some impressively scenic locations, such as Arches National Park, in Utah. Made on a budget of $681,000, the film was a significant commercial success, grossing $2 million in its initial release.

Taza, Son of Cochise (1954, Univ. Inter.)

Taza, Son of Cochise built on the successes of two previous films *Broken Arrow* and *The Battle of Apache Pass*. The studio was convinced that it had a presold audience.

The film was directed by the very capable Douglas Sirk (1897–1987), who usually helmed elegant and romantic melodramas. It was produced by the notable Ross Hunter, who produced many of Sirk's film soap operas.

The impressive cinematography was undertaken by the legendary Russell Metty (1906–1978), who won an Academy Award for Best Cinematography for *Spartacus* (1960, Universal). The screenplay was written by George Zuckerman, and the story was by Gerard Drayson Adams.

The highly fictionalized narrative is set in the aftermath of the death of Cochise (Jeff Chandler) and the Apache Wars. Cochise's oldest son Taza (Rock Hudson) lives in peace with the Euro-American settlers. However, his brother Naiche (Bart Roberts) has an irrational desire for vengeance and war against the whites. He also desires Oona (Barbara Rush), who is Taza's betrothed.

Naiche begins a war with the help of a "renegade" Apache Geronimo, fighting against the white settlers. The ensuing conflict is compounded by the racist and war-mongering Captain Burnett (Gregg Palmer). At the end of the film, the Chiricahua Apache are confined in an Indian reservation. Also in confinement are Geronimo and some of his warriors.

This film builds on the revisionist history previously depicted in both *Broken Arrow* and *The Battle of Apache Pass*. Once again, the film perpetuates the idea that Native Americans have a propensity for violence and mayhem. Here, Naiche is depicted as irrationally going to war. The film does not provide any context for why he might be embittered or upset about the condition of the Apache Nation.

As in previous films, Geronimo (here played by Ian MacDonald) is portrayed as a renegade and violent warrior on the fringes of Apache society. The film's premise is that indigenous people who are meek and humble are acceptable, but those who fight against injustice and the robbery of their land are renegades. The film's poster exclaimed, "He [Taza] Led the Apache Nation Against Geronimo's Pillaging Hordes!"

The real Taza (born 1843), son of Cochise, was chief for only two years (1874–1876). The Chiricahua Reservation was actually established in 1874 (two years after Cochise died) by General Oliver Howard. In 1876, the Chiricahua were then moved to the San Carlos Indian Reservation, one of the most unhospitable places in Arizona. In the same year, Taza was part of an Apache delegation to visit Washington, D.C. There he caught pneumonia and died on September 26, 1876. He was buried in the Congressional Cemetery in Washington, D.C. (most likely against the wishes of the Apache people). His mother, Dos-the-she; his half-sisters, Dash-den-zhoos and Naithlotonz (Naiche-dos); and his brother, Naiche, would go on to live in captivity at Mescalero.

For the third and last time, Jeff Chandler portrayed Cochise at the beginning of the film in a cameo. Rock Hudson, at this point in his career, was nearing film stardom. He gives a sincere performance but is completely miscast, as is Barbara Rush as his bride-to-be. As usual, Native American actors were reduced to bit parts. These included Seth Bigman and others.

Taza, Son of Cochise received lukewarm reviews and became only a moderate commercial success ($85.5 million when adjusted for inflation).[27] Despite its faults, the film included some spectacular locales, such as Sands Falt, Castle Valley, Devil's Garden, Professor Valley, and Arches National Park in Utah.

The Seven Cities of Gold (1955, 20th Century–Fox)

The Seven Cities of Gold is the only U.S. film ever made about the colonization of California by the Spanish and the imposition of their culture on Native Americans.

The film was directed by veteran Richard D. Webb (1903–1990), who helmed many westerns and won an Academy Award for Best Assistant Director for *In Old Chicago* (1938, 20th Century–Fox), now a defunct category. In 1955, he also directed *White Feather* (20th Century–Fox), another Native American–themed film.

The Seven Cities of Gold was written by Richard L. Breen, based on the 1951 novel *The Nine Days of Father Serra* by Isabelle Gibson Ziegler. The striking cinematography was done by the noted Lucien Ballard.

The narrative is set in 1768 and depicts the arrival of the Spanish in California. The expedition is led by Captain Gaspar de Portola (Anthony Quinn) and his lieutenant José Mendoza (Richard Egan). Father Junípero Serra (Michael Rennie) has also been assigned to the expedition. Upon their arrival in what today is the San Diego area, the Spaniards meet an unspecified Native American tribe led by Matuwir (Jeffrey Hunter).

Father Serra brokers an uneasy peace between the two groups. However, at a certain point, Mendoza seduces a native maiden named Ula (Rita Moreno), who later commits suicide. The Spanish colonizers are then faced with annihilation. In the end, Mendoza gives himself up as the culprit. Frustrated with their failed attempt to win over the native population, the Spaniards begin to depart from the area when they suddenly see a Spanish ship.

One of the major weaknesses of the film is that all the major native roles are played by non-native performers. The popular Jeffrey Hunter was cast as the lead native role of Matuwir, and he is totally miscast and unconvincing. Puerto Rican actress Rita Moreno is more convincing as Ula. Actual native actors play only bit roles. The film also does not identify the specific California tribe, and it depicts so-called native rituals that are clearly the inventions of the white filmmakers. *The Seven Cities of Gold* is interesting because it focuses on the colonization of California, but the depiction of the contact is heavily fictionalized and revisionist.[28]

The depiction of Father Junípero Serra, who founded the 21 California Catholic missions, is romanticized and fictionalized. He was born Junípero Serra y Ferrer (1713–1784) in Catalan, Spain. He was beatified by Pope John Paul II on September 25, 1988, much to the dismay of Native Americans. The Spanish missions were self-sufficient economic units in which native people served in peonage: growing crops, raising livestock, and producing numerous products, to say nothing of building the missions themselves. The average life span of a Native American in the missions was only five years. Natives were wards of the missions, compelled to work without pay and often punished for their presumed transgressions. Professor Deborah A. Miranda has written, "Serra did not just bring us Christianity. He imposed it, giving us no choice in the matter. He did incalculable damage to a whole culture."[29]

The reviews of the film were mixed. Bosley Crowther, in the *New York Times* (October 8, 1955), wrote, "Father Serra, according to this picture, was a man of gentle ways and boundless faith.... Anthony Quinn gives a reasonable performance as the rugged leader of the expedition, but Jeffrey Hunter as the young Indian chieftain and Rita Moreno as the maiden are quite absurd."[30]

The film grossed $43.5 million when adjusted for inflation.[31]

Ambush (1950, MGM)

The western *Ambush* was an example of the traditional and proverbial Hollywood film focusing on the U.S. Cavalry fighting Native Americans in the Southwest without any historical context or different points of view. However, behind the scenes, the key collaborators of the film were caught in the vicious politics of the Cold War and the HUAC crusade to root out Communist influence in the motion picture industry. Clearly, politics reflected art and art reflected politics during this tumultuous era.

Ambush was the last feature directed by Sam Wood (1884–1949). During his career, he had directed such notable films as *A Night at the Opera* (1935, MGM); *Goodbye Mr.*

Chips (1939, MGM); *Gone with the Wind* (1939, MGM), temporarily replacing director Victor Fleming for twenty-four days; *Kitty Foyle* (1941, RKO); *Pride of the Yankees* (1942, RKO); and *For Whom the Bell Tolls* (1943, Paramount). He had been a liberal voice early in his career but gradually turned to the right by the mid–1940s. In 1944, he both founded and served as president of the Motion Picture Alliance for the Preservation of American Ideals, which persuaded the House Un-American Activities Committee to investigate Communism in the film industry. Wood is said to have carried a notebook in order to write down the names of those in the industry whom he thought were Communists. According to his daughter, Jean Wood, her father's crusade "transformed Dad into a snarling, unreasoning brute."[32] In his will, Wood indicated that none of his children would inherit anything until they filed an affidavit that they had never been Communists. Wood died of a heart attack shortly after he finished directing *Ambush*.

The film was written by Marguerite Roberts (1905–1989), one of the best-known woman screenwriters the era. Her screenplay was based on a serial story titled *Ambush*, published in 1948 by Luke Short. In 1933, her contract with MGM paid her $2,500 per week (one of the highest salaries for a writer in Hollywood). However, in 1951, she and her husband refused to testify before HUAC, and she was blacklisted for nine years (finally writing the film *Diamond Head* in 1962). Ironically, her best later screenplay (and perhaps her best overall) was for *True Grit* (1969, Paramount), which won John Wayne (a longtime conservative) his only Academy Award.

Ambush focuses on the efforts of Ward Kinsman (Robert Taylor), a broken-down scout and prospector. He is hired by the U.S. Cavalry to find Mary Carlyle (Marta Mitovich), the daughter of a general, who has been kidnapped by Apaches. Along the way, Ward finds Ann Duverall (Arlene Dahl), Mary's sister, who informs him that her sister has been taken by an Apache leader called Diablito (Charles Stevens). Ward and the soldiers eventually rescue Mary and return her to the fort. In the meantime, he has fallen in love with her sister Ann.

The film was headlined by the popular Robert Taylor (who himself was a friendly witness to the House Un-American Activities Committee).[33] Taylor's role in this film was in stark contrast to his sympathetic Native American role in *Devil's Doorway* (released that same year). The film co-starred Arlene Dahl and John Hodiak. A positive aspect of this film was that Native American actors portrayed the key native roles: Charles Stevens as Diablito, Chief Thundercloud as Tana, and other bit parts.

Bosley Crowther, in the *New York Times* (January 19, 1950), wrote, "Mr. Taylor is left at the fadeout with a halo of glory and the girl. Dozens of stalwart fellows—United States Cavalrymen—and countless Apache Indians are mowed down in the final ambuscade. Even the sly Apache chieftain is swiftly and beautifully dispatched when lying among the fallen Indians."[34]

Apache (1954, United Artists)

In the wake of *Devil's Doorway* and *Broken Arrow*, other films in the 1950s improved the Native American film image. One of most commercially successful of this body of work was *Apache*, directed by the maverick director Robert Aldrich.

The film begins with the surrender of Geronimo (Monte Blue) in the 1880s. One young warrior, Massai (Burt Lancaster), refuses to lay down his arms but is subdued and shackled with Geronimo and the other Apache warriors and scouts, who are then shipped to Florida by way of St. Louis. During the trip, Massai makes a daring escape and embarks on an arduous trek back to Apache territory. There he seeks out Nalinle (Jean Peters) but is betrayed by her alcoholic father Santos (Paul Guilfoyle). Again escaping, Massai wages a one-man guerrilla war against white settlers. Nalinle eventually follows him, even though Hondo (Charles Bronson), an Apache scout for the U.S. Cavalry, desires her.

Hondo and the clever Indian tracker Al Sieber (John McIntire) become obsessed with capturing Massai. When Nalinle becomes pregnant, Massai is compelled to plant a cornfield to survive. In the film's conclusion, Sieber, Hondo, and their men finally locate Massai. In the cornfield, Massai defeats Sieber but lets him live when he hears that Nalinle has given birth to his son.

Apache was produced by the powerful independent production company of film star Burt Lancaster and Harold Hecht (Hecht & Lancaster). They would go on to produce such important films such as *Vera Cruz* (1954, United Artists), *Marty* (1955), and *Sweet Smell of Success* (1957, United Artists). The film was based on the novel *Bronco Apache* by Paul Wellman, which told the true story of Massai, an Apache warrior who was one of Geronimo's band who, in the late 1880s, fought a one-man war against Euro-American settlers and the U.S. Cavalry. Veteran screenwriter James B. Webb, who had penned many westerns since 1941, was assigned the task of adapting the story for the screen. Webb would later win an Academy Award for his screenplay for *How the West Was Won* (1963, MGM).

Cast as Massai was the film's producer and superstar Burt Lancaster (1913–1984), a new type of versatile and independent-minded film star and producer that evolved in post–World War II Hollywood. Beyond his acrobatic physique and box-office draw, Lancaster was also one of the film industry's more politically progressive members. He had previously portrayed one of the best-known Native Americans in modern history, Jim Thorpe, in the film *Jim Thorpe—All-American* (1951, Warner Bros.).

What gives *Apache* its unique place in film history is Massai's indestructible passion for his resistance. His defiance of the European settlers never wanes. Though in the end he, too, must lay down his arms to protect his wife and son, he never psychologically capitulates. He might be compelled to become a farmer in order to survive, but even then he wages a different type of guerrilla warfare: endurance to live to fight another day. His mistrust of white men is permanent. He is not broken by the U.S. military might or softened by opportunistic olive branch overtures. He remains resolute. He knows that his spirit will never be broken.

Apache represents the apex of the post–*Devil's Doorway* films. Critics had begun to protest that the film industry was going to extremes in apologizing to Native Americans and being overkind. Thereafter, films focusing on Native Americans would be seen through either the eyes of dissident whites (i.e., *Soldier Blue*) or those of pathological white settlers (i.e., *The Searchers*). There would be no more films seen from the native perspective until the advent of Native American cinema in the 2000s.

Lancaster brought his unique brand of athleticism and intensity to the role Massai. Jean Peters, who had portrayed the Native American wife of Mexican revolutionary Emiliano Zapata in *Viva Zapata!* (1952, United Artists), was also convincing. The role of the aged Geronimo was played by the part-Cherokee movie veteran Monte Blue, who had been a big star in the 1920s, though the arrival of sound and impending middle age had reduced Blue's career to bit parts thereafter. His role as Geronimo would be the last of his film career. As was true for most films of this era, Native Americans were cast only in minor roles.

The location shooting was an asset to the film, most of which was shot on location in around Sonora, California, and Sedona, Arizona.

Lancaster and director Robert Aldrich would go on to collaborate in one other film: *Ulzana's Raid* (1972), about a doomed regiment attempting to capture another Apache warrior. *Apache* opened one month after the historic *Brown v. Board of Education* decision (1954). Lancaster saw this ruling as a sign that the nation was ready for a true story of resistance by Native Americans.

As always, the Hollywood film industry cashed on the Apaches' legendary reputation as warriors by using the name in scores of westerns. The connotations conjured up the notion that "Apache" was synonymous with "terror." Such films included *The Apache Kid* (1941, Republic); *Apache Trail* (1942, MGM); *Apache Rose* (1947, Republic); *Apache Chief* (1949, Lippert); *Apache Drums* (1951, Universal); *Apache War Smoke* (1952, MGM); *Apache Woman* (1955, Golden); *Apache Ambush* (1956, Columbia); *Apache Warrior* (1957, 20th Century–Fox); *Apache Territory* (1958); *Apache Rifles* (1964, 20th Century–Fox); *Apache Gold* (1965, Columbia); and *Apache Uprising* (1966, Paramount), among others.

Reviews of *Apache* were generally positive. The *Los Angeles Times* (July 22, 1954) commented, "Burt Lancaster plays one mixed-up kid in 'Apache' ... We know Massai is fighting to right the injustices visited upon his conquered people, but his methods of attack and reprisal too often seem plain loco."[35] *Variety* (June 30, 1954) said, "Lancaster, as Massai, the warrior Apache, and Jean Peters, as Nalinia, his squaw, play the Indian roles with understanding that avoids the usual stereotypes. As these stars handle the characters they are seen as humans."[36]

Viva Zapata! (1952, 20th Century–Fox)

The film *Viva Zapata!* was made during the height of the HUAC visit and investigation of Communist activity in the Hollywood film industry. Even more, the film's director Elia Kazan (a former member of New York's Group Theatre and leftist) became one of the most notorious "friendly witnesses" for the House Un-American Activities Committee.

The ambivalent ideological leanings of both Kazan and novelist-turned-screenwriter John Steinbeck grossly distorted and falsified the image of Mexican Native American leader Emiliano Zapata and the Mexican Revolution. Kazan would write later in his autobiography about the film, "I started taking notes on a film about Emiliano Zapata in 1944. It's the first film I made from an idea that attracted me—a revolutionary fights a bloody war, gains power, and then walks away—one I started and saw through the end."[37]

Kazan's view of Zapata walking away from power is pure distortion of history. Emiliano Zapata (1879–1919) was a small Native American landowner from the southwestern state of Morelos, who, in an alliance with Francisco "Pancho" Villa (1877–1923), represented the aspirations of the native and mestizo peasantry and marginalized social classes for social change during the Mexican Revolution (1910–1920). Zapata was assassinated on April 10, 1919, on the orders of Venustiano Carranza, the corrupt leader of the counter-revolution. At the time of his death, Zapata was still actively involved in the revolutionary movement.

Kazan's and Steinbeck's cooperation with the HUAC brought political contradictions and ambiguities to the film. Initially it was going to be shot in Mexico. However, the Mexican technicians objected to the historical distortions and the casting. Kazan attributed this protest to a Communist conspiracy: "We knew that Communists in Mexico would

Marlon Brando as Emiliano Zapata and Jean Peters as his wife in *Viva Zapata!* (1952, 20th Century-Fox).

try to capitalize on the peoples' reverence for Zapata by working his figure into their propaganda."[38] As a consequence, the film's location shooting was moved to the semi-arid southern Texas (which was completely different from the semitropical state of Morelos).

Not surprisingly, the political right attacked Kazan's stance as well, accusing him of glorifying a Communist rebel. In order to appease the critics on the right, Kazan and Steinbeck created a fictional character named Fernando, who, according to Kazan, presented the "Communist mentality." Fernando "typified the men who use just grievances of the people for their own ends, who shift and twist their course, betray any friend or principle to get power and keep it."[39]

Aside from the self-serving polemics of Kazan and Steinbeck, the film has numerous distortions and omissions. In one scene, two Zapatistas are depicted as ideological disciples who look to their northern neighbor for ideological mentorship and guidance: "In the United States, the government governs, but with the consent of the people.... Here we have a President, but no consent." In another scene, one that recalls the worst of the Native American and Mexican stereotypes, Zapata and Villa are sleeping under a tree in typical Hollywood fashion. A guard comments, "They're deciding the fate of Mexico." During their sleepy conversation, Villa asks Zapata whether he can read. Zapata nods in the affirmative (although the beginning of the film shows Zapata as an illiterate, which is a definite distortion). Villa then tells him, "Then you're the president. There is nobody else. Do I look like a president? There isn't anybody else." This pathetic and simplistic scene reveals Kazan and Steinbeck's abysmal understanding of the Mexican Revolution.

Anthony Quinn found it difficult

working with Kazan: "I wondered how I ever worked with him. And this was a man who truly was a card-carrying communist. I did not begrudge him his politics, but his cowardice was tough to ignore. Jesus, the man was Red and yellow!"[40]

The film's moments of dramatic power must be attributed to the charisma and skill of the performers, who managed to imbue the characters with dramatic passion: Marlon Brando as Zapata and Anthony Quinn as his brother Eufemio Zapata. Quinn would win the Best Supporting Actor Academy Award for this role (the first Mexican to do so). The film was populated by only a few native and/or Mexican performers: Margo as the *soldadera* and Movita (Castaneda) as one peasant's unfaithful wife. The rest of the cast were mostly New York actors, with heavy brown makeup, method-acting posturing, and mismatched ethnicities. Ironically, the leading lady of the film, Jean Peters (who played Zapata's wife), who had no formal training in acting, is much more convincing than her "trained" New York peers.

Viva Zapata! received excellent reviews. *Time* (February 11, 1952) noted, for example, "Viva Zapata! makes the Tiger out to be a pretty tame cat. According to history, Zapata was not only a great folk hero and agrarian emancipator, but also a cruel, cunning Guerrero Indian whose notorious Death Legion made human trenches of the enemy and staked living men to anthills."[41]

Many years later, Tony Thomas, reviewing Marlon Brando's films, wrote, "Certainly it is an idealized concept of Emiliano Zapata, whom historians claim was far more self-seeking and bloodier than depicted by Zanuck, Steinbeck, and Kazan."[42]

Native Film Stars and Filmmakers

Jeanne Cooper

Jeanne Cooper was one of the outstanding actresses of the 1950s through the 2000s. She won praise and fame in both films and television. Although she is best remembered for her role as the strong matriarch in *The Young and the Restless*, she also left behind an impressive number of film roles.

She was born on October 25, 1928, in the little town of Taft, California. Her father, Albert Troy Cooper, was Cherokee and English. Her mother, Sildeth Evelyn Moore, was Cherokee and Irish. Cooper's parents met in Oklahoma, where both of the families lived in the oil fields.

Like most children of Native American roots, Jeanne Cooper experienced prejudice. She recalled in her autobiography, "Tragically, in Oklahoma in the early 1900s, full-blooded Native Americans, many of whom worked side by side with my father and grandfather, were targets of cruel discrimination and the shameful epithet 'red niggers,' by too many bigots and bullies."[43]

Cooper made her film debut in *The Redhead from Wyoming* in 1953 (Univ. Inter.) and went on to appear in more than thirty films. Her best roles were in the heist thriller *Plunder Road* (1957, Regal Films); the prison drama *House of Women* (1962, Warner Bros.); the drama *The Intruder* (1962, Pathé-America); and the crime drama *Black Zoo* (1963). Her film credits included *The Man from the Alamo* (1953, Univ. Inter.); *The Houston Story* (1955, Columbia); *Let No Man Write My Epitaph* (1960, Columbia); *13th West St.* (1962,

Columbia); *The Glory Guys* (1965, United Artists); *Tony Rome* (1967, 20th Century–Fox); *The Boston Strangler* (1968, 20th Century–Fox); *There Was a Crooked Man* (1970, Warner Bros.); *Kansas City Bomber* (1972, MGM); *The All-American* (1973, Warner Bros.); *The Tomorrow Man* (2002, Bedford); and *Dead Air* (2009, Team Cherokee Prods.).

Cooper guest-starred in many of the top television shows of the era, including *Maverick, Surfside Six, The Untouchables, Cheyenne, The Man from U.N.C.L.E., Perry Mason, The Twilight Zone, Dr. Kildare, Death Valley Days, Wanted Dead or Alive, Bonanza, Wagon Train, Rawhide, Hawaiian Eye, 77 Sunset Strip, Ironsides,* and *The Big Valley,* among many others. She also appeared as a regular in the television series *Bracken's World* during 1969–1970. However, she gained legendary television fame as the matriarch in daytime television series *The Young and the Restless* from 1973 to 2013. She won the Daytime Emmy Award for Outstanding Lead Actress in a Drama Series in 2008. She had been nominated for this award nine other times.

Jeanne Cooper passed away on March 26, 2013, after catching an infection.

James Garner

James Garner earned fame in theater, film, and television. He was born James Scott Bumgarner on April 7, 1928, in Norman, Oklahoma. He recollected in his autobiography, "Charlie Meek, my mother's father, was Native American. My maternal great-grandparents disowned Abbie [Garner's grandmother] when she married him.... I don't know anything else about Grandpa Charlie because everybody pretended he didn't exist." As a child, his education about Native Americans was limited. He recalled, "Growing up I knew I was one-quarter Cherokee, but I have to admit I was a little afraid of Indians.... The schoolbooks didn't help. They gave the impression that Indians were 'savages' who attacked without provocation. And our teachers didn't tell us that when Europeans came to North America, it was a disaster for the previous tenants."[44]

Garner's family moved to Los Angeles, California, where he attended Hollywood High School and Norman High School. He served in the National Guard for seven months and then served in the U.S. Army for fourteen months during the Korean War. He was wounded twice and won a Purple Heart.

Upon his return from the service, Garner drifted into acting. In 1954, he had a role in the Broadway production of *The Caine Mutiny* opposite Henry Fonda and John Hodiak. He made his film debut in *Toward the Unknown* in 1956 (Warner Bros.) and made a strong impression in *Sayonara* in 1957 (Warner Bros.) opposite Marlon Brando. This film led to his being cast as the title character in *Maverick*, a television series produced by Warner Brothers from 1957 to 1960. Garner became immersed in a contract dispute with Jack Warner, sued, and won out of his contract.

He was one of the few television stars to make the transition into major film stardom with such films such as *Darby's Rangers* (1958, Warner Bros.); *The Children's Hour* (1961, United Artists); *The Great Escape* (1963, United Artists); *The Thrill of It All* (1963, Univ. Inter.); *The Americanization of Emily* (1964, MGM); *Grand Prix* (1966, MGM); *Hour of the Gun* (1967, United Artists–MGM); *Marlowe* (1969, MGM); *Support Your Local Sheriff* (1969, United Artists); *Skin Game* (1971, Warner Bros.); *Victor Victoria* (1982, MGM); *Murphy's Romance* (1985, Columbia), for which he received his only Academy Award nomination for Best Actor; *Maverick* (1994, Warner Bros.); *Space Cowboys* (2000, Warner Bros.); and *The Ultimate Gift* (2007, New Line Cinema).

In 1969, Garner founded Cherokee Productions, which produced some highly successful films.

From 1974 to 1980, he starred in the highly successful television series *The Rockford Files*, in which he played a private detective. Garner won an Emmy Award for this role. In 1983, he sued Universal Studios in relation to earnings from *The Rockford Files*. The suit was eventually settled out of court in 1989.

In 2006, Garner co-narrated the highly acclaimed documentary *The Trail of Tears: Cherokee Legacy* (Rich-Heape Films). The American Indian Film Festival gave the film its Best Feature Documentary award. *Trail of Tears* was directed by Chip Richie.

Over the course of his long career in both film and television, Garner won numerous awards. These included the 1958 Golden Globe Award for Best Promising Newcomer (Male); the 1977 Primetime Emmy Award for Outstanding Lead Actor in a Drama Series, for *The Rockford Files*; the 1987 Primetime Emmy Award for Outstanding Comedy/Drama Special, for *Promise*; the 1990 Golden Globe Award for an Actor in a Mini-Series or Motion Picture Made for TV, for *Decoration Day*; the 1993 Golden Globe Award for an Actor in a Mini-Series or Motion Picture Made for TV, for *Barbarians at the Gate*; and the 2004 Screen Actors Guild Lifetime Achievement Award, among many others.

James Garner died of a heart attack on July 19, 2014.

Margo

Margo was born Maria Marguerite Guadalupe Teresa Bolano Castillo y O'Donnell, on May 10, 1917, in Mexico City. Her father was a Spanish medical doctor; and her mother was a Mexican citizen.

As a child, she was coached by Eduardo Cansino, the father of Rita Cansino (later Rita Hayworth) and by the age of nine she was dancing professionally. At a later age she worked with her uncle Xavier Cugat and his orchestra in Mexican nightclubs and later toured with them to New York City, where they helped popularize the rumba. She was attractive and had a pleasing personality, which caught the attention of audiences.

By the early thirties she had become a well-known dramatic actress on Broadway. Margo was spotted by a talent agent and she was contracted to make films. She was cast opposite Claude Rains in the impressive Ben-Hecht–Charles MacArthur written and produced *Crime Without Passion* (1934, Paramount). The dark melodrama was about an attorney (Rains) who knows the intricacies of the law; and who in a fit of jealousy kills his mistress (Margo), or thinks he has done so. Margo earned widespread acclaim for her portrayal. In this film and thereafter she was billed simply as "Margo." Later, she would often be cast as a doomed and suffering victim.

She was cast in support of Carole Lombard and George Raft in the very popular *Rumba* (1935, Paramount). She was once again impressive in as Joaquin Murrieta's ill-fated girlfriend in William A. Wellman's superior *The Robin Hood of El Dorado* (1936, MGM) opposite Warner Baxter. Margo repeated her Broadway role in the film adaptation of Maxwell Anderson's *Winterset* (1936, RKO). The piece was a thinly disguised examination of the Sacco and Vanzetti case of the 1920s. Although critically acclaimed, it was not a commercial success. Perhaps her most famous role was as the young lady who suddenly ages and dies when she leaves Shangri-La in Frank Capra's classic *Lost Horizon* (1937, Columbia) based on the James Hilton novel and starring Ronald Colman.

One of Margo's close friends was actress Lupita Tovar, who recalled, "Margo I knew since she was probably the age of 13, when she used to take dancing lessons from Eduardo Cansino. Later, she married Francis Lederer. Francis Lederer was a close friend of my husband (Paul Kohner). Then she divorced him. That was not a very good match. When she married Eddie Albert, we became very close friends."[45]

Thereafter, her film appearances were infrequent and less prominent. The reason for this was the fact that in 1950, her name and that of her husband Eddie Albert appeared in *Red Channels*, an anti–Communist pamphlet that branded persons as Communists. This was despite the fact that Albert had joined the Navy during World War II and had fought with distinction in the South Pacific. The pamphlet justified their actions because she had supported the Hollywood Ten, supported aid to refugees, and advocated peace. Both Margo and Albert suffered significant career damage. Although, both would eventually recover with the passing of that turbulent era, they never reached their full potential in the Hollywood industry. She had one more good role, that of the *soldadera* in Elia Kazan's *Viva Zapata!* (1952, 20th Century–Fox).

Margo was very involved in civic and cultural activities in Los Angeles. She was the co-founder of the most important Mexican American cultural center in Los Angeles, Plaza de la Raza. In 1974, she was appointed Commissioner of Social Services for the City of Los Angeles. She passed away of cancer on July 17, 1985.

Her films include: *Miracle on Main Street* (1939, Arcadia Pictures); *The Leopard Man* (1943, RKO); *Behind the Rising Sun* (1943, RKO); *Gangway for Tomorrow* (1943, RKO); *I'll Cry Tomorrow* (1955, MGM); *From Hell to Texas* (1958, 20th Century-Fox); and *Who's Got the Action?* (1962, Paramount). She made extensive appearances on television during the 1950s and 1960s.

Margo was married to Czech actor Frances Lederer from 1937 to 1941, and to Eddie Albert (1945 until her death). They had a son, Edward Albert, who was also an actor. Her husband Eddie Albert found fame again in several popular television series in his later career. He died at the age of 99 of pneumonia on May 26, 2005. Their only son, Edward Albert died of lung cancer on September 22, 2006.

Movita

Movita was born Movita Luisa Castañeda, on April 12, 1916, in Nogales, Arizona, on a train travelling from Mexico to Nogales. She was of Mexican ancestry, and undoubtedly had indigenous roots. She grew up to be a very beautiful young lady. She had dark features and dark hair, and as a result she was often cast as Mexican or native maidens, and exotic roles, especially as South Seas maidens.

She made her film debut in *Dios del Mar* (1930, Paramount), a Hollywood Spanish-language film. Her films included *Flying Down to Rio* (RKO) in 1933, and her best known role was as the Tahitian girl who falls in love with Fletcher Christian (Clark Gable) in Frank Lloyd's *Mutiny on the Bounty* (1935, MGM), which won the Best Picture Academy Award for that year.

Thereafter, she was mostly cast in small roles in B films into the 1950s, with some exceptions. Director John Ford cast her in three of his films: *The Hurricane* (1937, Goldwyn) as Arai, a South Seas maiden; *Fort Apache* (1948, Argosy Pictures) as Guadalupe, an Apache maiden; and *Wagon Master* (1950, Argosy Pictures) as a Navajo woman.

Her small role in *Viva Zapata!* (1952, 20th Century-Fox) was uncredited, and she also worked on television. She and Marlon Brando were already romantically linked, and she became his second wife (1960–1962), although she was eight years older than him. She had two children with Brando, Miko C. Brando and Rebecca Brando. She lived to the age of 98, passing away on February 12, 2015.

Her films include: *Captain Calamity* (1937, Talisman Studios); *Tower of Terror* (1941, ABPC); *Lady Without a Passport* (1950, MGM); *The Furies* (1950, Paramount); *Kim* (1950, MGM); *Ride, Vaquero* (1953, MGM); *Dream Wife* (1953, MGM); and *Apache Ambush* (1955, Columbia), among others.

Will Rogers, Jr.

Will Rogers, Jr., had a moderately successful film and television career in the 1950s and 1960s. He was born William Vann Rogers on October 20, 1911, in New York City. He earned a Bachelor of Arts degree from Stanford University in 1935. As he grew up, he was noted for his remarkable resemblance to his famous father.

Rogers was commissioned a second lieutenant in the Reserve Officer Training Corps. During World War II, he enlisted as a private and was commissioned in field artillery. He served in the 893rd Tank Destroyer Battalion. During his military service, Rogers was elected to the House of Representatives (California) and sworn into office on January 3, 1943 (78th Congress). However, he did not complete his term, as he returned to active duty in the U.S. Army. As a result, he resigned from Congress on May 23, 1944.

During the war, Rogers served in General Patton's Third U.S. Army and was wounded in action. He received the Bronze Star and was relieved of active duty on March 1, 1946.

Rogers won the Democratic nomination for U.S. senator for California in 1946 but lost the election. Thereafter, he was a delegate to the Democratic conventions in 1948, 1952, and 1956. However, his apparent desire to gain higher officer never came to fruition.

Rogers had actually made his film debut in 1921's *The Jack Rider* (Seeling Prods.) as a child. His follow-up film was *The Vengeance Trail* (1921, Seeling Prods.). In 1949, he played his father in a cameo role in *Look for the Silver Lining* (Warner Bros.).

Like his father, Rogers became skilled with the rodeo rope and had an infectious sense of humor that made him charismatic. Seeing his potential as a film star, Warner Brothers cast him to play his father in *The Story of Will Rogers* (1952) opposite Jane Wyman. The film was directed by the notable Michael Curtiz. The film was a moderate hit, and Rogers continued his film career with projects such as *The Eddie Cantor Story* (1953, Warner Bros.), in another cameo role playing his father; *The Boy from Oklahoma* (1954, Warner Bros.); *Wild Heritage* (1958, Univ. Inter.); and *Swiss Family Robinson: Lost in the Jungle* (2000, Trans-World Artists).

His television credits included *Burke's Law*, *Schlitz Playhouse*, *Matinee Theater*, and *The American Adventure*.

Will Rogers, Jr., retired to a ranch in Tubac, Arizona. He died on July 9, 1993, of a self-inflicted gunshot wound after suffering failing health due to several strokes, hip replacements, and a heart condition. He was 81 years of age.

Woody Strode

Woody Strode was a football player (both college and professional), wrestler, and actor. He was born on July 25, 1914, in Los Angeles, California. His father's ancestry was a mixture of Blackfoot-Creek and African American bricklayer, and his mother, who worked as a seamstress, was a mixture of African American and Cherokee. It is unknown whether Strode's native ancestry was several generations removed.

Although by his own admission he was short and fat as a child, Strode grew up to be 6 feet, 4 inches, and a great athlete. He attended Jefferson High School. His football prowess gained him a scholarship to UCLA.

Strode and his friend Kenny Washington (another legendary football player from southern California) gained employment at the Warner Brothers lot and quickly made an impression on the film stars and producers. Strode played football with the Hollywood Bears Football team. During World War II, he joined the U.S. Force and served in the Pacific theater. After the war, he and Washington became the first African Americans to be signed with the Los Angeles Rams football team. However, racism and his marriage to a Hawaiian royal, Princess Luukialuana Kalaeloa (better known as Luana), resulted in Strode being cut from the Rams. Thereafter, he played with the Canadian Calgary Stampeders, and he later became a wrestler.

Strode made his film debut in John Ford's *Stagecoach* (1939, United Artists). During the 1940s, his films included *Sundown* (1941, United Artists), *Star-Spangled Rhythm* (1942, Paramount), and a series of B-adventure films.

In the 1950s, his roles became more prominent in A-list films: *Caribbean* (1952, Paramount); *Androcles and the Lion* (1952, RKO); and *Demetrius and the Gladiators* (1954, 20th Century–Fox), among others. In 1956, Cecil B. DeMille cast Strode in his epic *The Ten Commandments* (Paramount). He played two roles: the king of Ethiopia and then one of Bita's bearers, who enters Moses' house during the Passover scene. More big-budget films followed: *The Buccaneer* (1958, Paramount); *Pork Chop Hill* (1959, 20th Century–Fox); and *The Last Voyage* (1960, MGM).

In 1960, director John Ford cast Strode in the title role of *Sergeant Rutledge* (Warner Bros.), a Buffalo Soldier unfairly court-martialed for the rape and murder of a white woman. His performance earned rave reviews from critics. Strode would later comment, "Mr. Ford told me. 'You know, Woody, it's pretty rough to make a star out of you, but I'm going to make you a character actor and you'll make some money.'"[46]

His next role became his best known. Strode played the role of the gladiator Draba in Stanley Kubrick's *Spartacus* (1960, Universal). In the movie, Draba is chosen to fight Spartacus (Kirk Douglas) to the death. During the shooting of the gladiatorial combat scene, Laurence Oliver (who played Marcus Crassus) told Strode that he had been a fan when he had played football. Strode then told Oliver, "I don't know what I am doing here in your business." The British actor responded, "What you're about to do, I could never do."[47]

By this time, Strode had earned considerable respect for his acting talent and sense of integrity. He was cast by John Ford in three more films: *Two Rode Together* (1961, Columbia), for the first time playing a Native American role; *The Man Who Shot Liberty Valance* (1962, Paramount); and *Seven Women* (1966, MGM), Ford's final film. Strode also played a ferocious villain in *Tarzan's Three Challenges* (1963, MGM), starring Jock Mahoney, the legendary former stuntman. He was then cast in three excellent and successful westerns: Richard Brooks' *The Professionals* (1966, Columbia); *Shalako* (1968, Cinerama Releasing), in another Native American role; and Sergio Leone's classic spaghetti western *Once Upon a Time in the West* (1968, Paramount). The latter film made him a star of spaghetti westerns in Europe, and Strode began to earn significant money.

Strode's later films included *Boot Hill* (1969, Euro Int.); *Che!* (1969, 20th Century–Fox); *The Revengers* (1972, National General Pictures); and his final film, *The Quick and the Dead* (1995), among others. He wrote his autobiography, titled *Gold Dust*, in 1990.

Woody Strode died of lung cancer on December 31, 1994, in Glendora, California. He was 80 years of age. He was buried at the Riverside National Cemetery in Riverside, California. His only son, Kalai, died in 2014 of the same disease that took his father's life.

8

The Winds of Change (1960–1969)

During the 1960s, the winds of change were propelled by a new and idealistic generation, too young or unwilling to accept the status quo. However, this shift was slow to impact most Native Americans' quality of life. During this decade, indigenous people appeared consigned to oblivion and invisibility in both films and the media. However, within indigenous communities, the seeds of change were quietly beginning to grow.

The 1960s will forever be remembered as the decade in which the foundations of authority throughout the world were rocked to their core. Worldwide youth, anti-war, civil rights, and women's movements changed the face of government, culture, and politics. In the United States, communities of color and women, who had been silenced, marginalized, and shunned for centuries, rose to make their voices heard on the subjects of justice, equality, civil rights, and human dignity.

At his inauguration, President John F. Kennedy stated, "Those who possess wealth and power in poor nations must accept their own responsibility. They must fight for those basic reforms which alone can preserve the fabric of their society. Those who make peaceful revolution impossible make revolution inevitable."[1] However, the ideological limits of the Cold War and the self-interest of both camps made self-determination in the Third World impossible and conflict inevitable.

Throughout the Third World, nationalist liberation movements developed, challenging the moribund empires of Britain, France, and Portugal in Africa and Asia, as well as newer hegemonies such as the United States in Latin America. In the Americas, the United States attempted to undermine the Cuban Revolution through invasion in 1961 and an economic blockade thereafter. (The subsequent U.S. military intervention in the Dominican Republic in 1965 was euphemistically rationalized as "preventing another Cuba.") In 1962, the Cuban Missile Crisis brought the world to the brink of nuclear war. Gradually, the idealism of Kennedy's Alliance for Progress gave way to Green Berets and military advisors as the Cold War was replicated throughout the Americas between the status quo military regimes and insurgent guerrilla movements and civil reform movements.

At home, the assassination of President Kennedy in 1963 foreshadowed the social tensions and political division that would soon grip the country. The impetus of President Johnson's "War on Poverty" lost ground as the U.S. escalation in the Vietnam War depleted funds for the social agenda. Racial integration met with increasingly violent resistance, and the anti–Vietnam War movement evolved into a mass movement that challenged the ideological tenets of the Cold War. Hundreds of ghettos broke into rioting, and in 1968 two more assassinations (those of Martin Luther King, Jr., and Robert F. Kennedy) tore the national social fabric. The FBI escalated a number of illegal activities, including the harassment of dissidents, wiretaps, and the suppression of the Black Panthers. By the end of the decade, a "law and order" presidential candidate, Richard M. Nixon, made an unlikely but spectacular political comeback after having been written off following his defeat in the 1960 presidential election and the 1964 California gubernatorial election. In 1968, Nixon was elected president.

NATIVE AMERICAN FILM IMAGES IN THE 1960s

In the 1960s, Native American film images underwent a slight change of representation. Hollywood films reflected the winds of change gradually. Native American actors remained few in number. Their roles in film and television, inevitably, were small and insignificant. Native American narratives were almost nonexistent. Native people were invisible not only in film and television but also in real life. The nation appeared to have totally forgotten them.

In the early part of the decade, films depicted native people in the Manifest Destiny mode. The film *A Thunder of Drums* (1961, MGM) rehashed the proverbial theme of Native Americans as the main impediment to the settling of the west. John Ford's *Two Rode Together* (1961, Columbia) depicted the efforts to recover several white captives taken by Comanches. The offbeat and independent film *The Exiles* (1961, MacKenzie) showed, in a semi-documentary manner, the impoverished lives of a Native American community in the Bunker Hill area of Los Angeles. The story of Ira Hayes (the Pima soldier who helped raise the U.S. flag at Iwo Jima) was depicted in *The Outsider* (1961, United Artists).

How the West Was Won (1962, MGM), an epic western, chronicled the westward march of several generations of Euro-American settlers through ethnocentric eyes, with only a moment's passing reference to the native peoples who originally inhabited the land. Arnold Laven's *Geronimo* (1962, United Artists) cast the blond, blue-eyed actor Chuck Connors (then the star of the popular television series *The Rifleman*) as Geronimo. Native Americans were portrayed sympathetically in this film, but the narrative plays loosely with the hard facts. According to the film, when Geronimo and his men surrendered, they were treated fairly by the U.S. government, which is a direct contradiction of what actually happened. *Requiem for a Heavyweight* (1962, Columbia) told the heartbreaking story of a Native American heavyweight boxer (played by Anthony Quinn) at the very end of his career and how he is compelled to become a wrestler and exploit his native culture. *Kings of the Sun* (1963, United Artists) depicted the pre–Columbian world of the Mayan people.

As the decade progressed, a few changes took place. For example, in Raoul Walsh's *A Distant Trumpet* (1964, Warner Bros.), an idealistic young West Point officer, Lieutenant Matthew Hazard (Troy Donahue), comes into conflict with his commanding officer, Major General Quaint (James Gregory), when the latter insists that a surrendering Chiricahua chief be sent to prison in Florida. At the end of the film, Hazard travels to Washington, D.C., to request that the chief be sent instead to his Arizona reservation. The request is subsequently granted.

Anthony Quinn as Mountain Rivera, an over-the-hill heavyweight boxing contender, and Julie Harris as Grace Miller, the compassionate social worker, in *Requiem for a Heavyweight* (1962, Columbia).

John Ford's *Cheyenne Autumn* (1964, Warner Bros.) documented the true story of the epic and heroic efforts of the Cheyenne people to return to their homeland. This film depicts the conflicts of Major Brandon (George O'Brien, of *The Iron Horse* fame), an ambitious martinet, and Captain Archer (Richard Widmark), a disillusioned officer who despises U.S. government policy.

Island of Blue the Dolphins (1964, Universal) told the true story of a young indigenous maiden (Celia Kaye) who survived alone for 18 years in the Channel Islands off the California coast in the early 1800s, after her tribe was forced to leave by the Spanish. Later, after she was rescued, she died of dysentery and was buried in the Santa Bárbara Mission cemetery. The film was based on the Newberry Award–winning novel of the same name by Scott O'Dell. Another youth-oriented film, *Indian Paint* (1965, Crown Inter.), focused on the rites of passage of a native youth (Johnny Crawford) and his efforts to tame a painted pony.

The western comedy *Cat Ballou* (1965, Columbia) told the story of a drunken gunfighter (Lee Marvin, in an Oscar-winning performance) hired to protect a young woman (Jane Fonda) from the railroad's attempt to rob her ranch. He is assisted by his friend Jackson Two-Bears (Tom Nardini), an indigenous gunman. Burt Reynolds played the lead character in the spaghetti western *Navajo Joe* (1966, United Artists), seeking revenge against a group of outlaws who massacred his tribe. Ralph Nelson's *Duel at Diablo* (1966, United Artists) involved a group of disparate characters amid the escape of Apaches from a reservation. In turn, *Johnny Tiger* (1966, Universal) focused on the efforts of a jaded but well-meaning teacher (Robert Taylor) to win over a Seminole youth (Chad Everett) caught between traditional and nontraditional culture.

The film *Shalako* (1968, Cinerama Releasing) focused on the efforts of a hardened tracker (Sean Connery) who takes a group of wealthy Europeans on a trek out west. *The Scalphunters* (1968, United Artists) featured an old and grizzled trapper (Burt Lancaster) who gets a sympathetic helping hand from the Kiowas in his battle of wits against a roving group of scalphunters. Raquel Welch played a fearless Yaqui woman leading her people against a forced tribal movement in *100 Rifles* (1969, 20th Century–Fox) under the counter-revolutionary government of Victoriano Huerta in Mexico. Last but not least, *Tell Them Willie Boy Is Here* (1969, Universal) depicts the true story of a wrongly accused Paiute man (Robert Blake) in 1909 California and the massive manhunt that ensues to capture him.

The advent of the spaghetti western brought more stereotypical images of Native Americans and Mexicans. Native people and Mexicans were portrayed as people unable to control their innate violence and sexual appetites. Native and Mexican women were depicted as scheming *cantineras* (saloon women), prostitutes, and thieves. These roles were all played by European performers, and badly so. The spaghetti westerns were characterized by extreme close-ups, gory and blood-soaked shootouts, and acts of violence. This genre featured operatic-like music and disorienting music scores, as well as hordes of vicious outlaws, revenge-filled desperados, and traumatized gunfighters. Most were filmed in Italy, with multiethnic casts, and directed by Italian filmmakers. Later, the genre expanded to films being shot on location in Spain, Germany, and other European locales, though most were set in the arid U.S. Southwest, northern Mexico, and/or during the Mexican Revolution (1910–1920). More than six hundred spaghetti westerns were made between 1960 and 1978.[2]

The invisibility of Native Americans in film and television only mirrored their economic and social despair. Poverty, alcoholism, unemployment, and harsh discrimination savaged the lives of another generation of native people. Lacking political power, they were completely forgotten by the federal, state, and local governments. These conditions would give rise to Native American activism and renaissance in the 1970s.

Representative Films

Cheyenne Autumn (1964, Warner Bros.)

It has often been said that John Ford's *Cheyenne Autumn* was his attempt to make up for the glorification of Manifest Destiny and the genocide against Native Americans that he himself presented in his films. The film has a factual basis, and it focuses on the forced removal of the Cheyenne people from their homeland and their valiant efforts to return.

The narrative is set during 1878–1879. The film begins with the long-expected visit of a congressional committee, to which the malnourished and emaciated Cheyenne tribe members hope to make their grievances known. They wait patiently all day long in the hot sun, only to learn that the committee altered its itinerary due to traveling discomforts.

Fed up with more of the same governmental disdain and arrogance, the Cheyenne decide to leave the unhospitable reservation in Oklahoma and make the long 1,500-mile trek back to their homeland in Yellowstone (in Wyoming). They are led by Chief Little Wolf (Ricardo Montalban) and Dull Knife (Gilbert Roland). Dull Knife complains, "We are asked to forget much; the white man remembers nothing."

The military is ordered to bring the Cheyenne back to Oklahoma. The commanding officer, Major Braden (George O'Brien), is an ambitious and vainglorious man concerned more with his self-advancement than the plight of the natives. Captain Archer (Richard Widmark) is a well-intentioned officer in love with the Quaker schoolteacher Deborah Wright (Carroll Baker). Her beliefs seal her commitment to the natives, and Archer's empathy for them grows in proportion to his love for her.

Dull Knife and Little Wolf, older and world-weary, contrast with the young and cocky firebrand Red Shirt (Sal Mineo), the son of Spanish Woman (Dolores Del Río). Red Shirt attempts throughout the journey to seduce one of Dull Knife's wives.

At this point in the campaign, Archer takes a few days of personal leave and travels to Washington, D.C., to plead the Cheyenne's case. He meets with Secretary of the Interior Carl Schulz (Edward G. Robinson), a veteran of the Battle of Gettysburg and sympathetic to the native cause.

At different intervals of the narrative, information is introduced about the nation's reaction to the Cheyenne plight, especially in the West regarding the native flight. Scenes depict the hysteria fueled by the press. There is a short comic sequence in Dodge City with Wyatt Earp (James Stewart) and Doc Halliday (Arthur Kennedy), where both are too preoccupied with their poker game to give credence to the rampant hysteria. Earp asks an overwrought barroom customer, "Have you ever read anything true in that paper?" This scene dramatized the white settlers' unfounded prejudice and fears. It was Ford's attempt to depict the difference between the false concept of the West and the harsh truth.

Midway through their journey, the Cheyenne seek temporary shelter at Fort Robinson, where a tyrannical Captain Oscar Wessels (Karl Malden) has them imprisoned. The natives break out again to avoid starvation. In the meantime, Schulz, who has been kept informed of the Cheyenne plight, travels to the frontier with Archer. There he helps negotiate with the Cheyenne and guarantees their relocation to a new reservation.

John Ford was more closely associated with the western film genre than any other filmmaker. However, though it was the western genre that catapulted him to film prominence and the pantheon of great directors, in fact, only a small percentage of Ford's film output was westerns. In the 1920s, Ford constructed Native American images that perpetuated the ethnocentric stereotypes and the lore of Manifest Destiny. These images continued in his sound films, such as *Stagecoach* (1939) and *Drum Along the Mohawk* (1939). In the 1940s, in the aftermath of the horror of World War II, his image of natives became more subdued and humane in films such as his famous U.S. cavalry trilogy: *Fort Apache* (1948, Republic); *She Wore a Yellow Ribbon* (1949, Republic); and *Río Grande* (1950, Republic). In *Fort Apache*, for example, two officers (John Wayne, Pedro Armendáriz) seek a reconciliation with Cochise despite the arrogant martinet commanding officer (Henry Fonda), who is bent on destroying the natives. In *Wagonmaster* (1950, Republic), Native Americans are compared to the Mormons as society's outcasts.

In one of his later films, *The Man Who Shot Liberty Valance* (1962, Paramount), Ford offered an analogy that could be applicable for his westerns and the Hollywood film industry: "When the legend becomes fact, print the legend."

Cheyenne Autumn was an attempt by Ford to make up for his past transgressions. In an interview with *Esquire Magazine* (1964) with then reporter and future film director Peter Bogdanovich, Ford stated, "There are two sides to every story, but I wanted to show their [the Indians'] point of view for a change. Let's face it, we've treated them very badly—it's a blot in our shield; we've cheated and robbed, killed, murdered, massacred and everything else, but they kill one white man and, God, out come our troops."[3]

The film was based on the book *Cheyenne Autumn* (1953) by Mari Sandoz, which itself had been based on the actual events of 1878–1879, when 286 Cheyenne (the remnants of several thousand who had been forcibly moved to a barren reservation) broke out from their reservation and began a 1,500-mile journey back to their homeland.

Although Ford attempted to portray the Indian "point of view," the film is primarily depicted through Captain Archer's eyes. In fact, *Apache* (1954) was the last film seen from a native's point of view for many years.

Cheyenne Autumn is a flawed film, but it is also a genuine and effective effort to rectify almost half a century of revisionism by one of Hollywood's most important directors. While the story is seen through the eyes of Archer, the Cheyenne are portrayed with dignity and integrity. Throughout the film, they are depicted through close-ups and low-angle shots that exemplify their deeper sense of humanity than white characters.

The *Motion Picture Herald* (November 11, 1964) wrote, "[A]dding commendable portrayals are … Dolores Del Río.… Exterior scenes were beautifully filmed in parts of Arizona, Utah and Colorado under the expert direction of William Clothier. The picture was skillfully directed by Ford."[4] *The Los Angeles Times* (December 20, 1964) likewise commented, "Ostensibly, the theme is the plight in which so many Indian tribes found themselves during the westward march of the white man … only the dignity which Ricardo Montalbán, Gilbert Roland, Victor Jory, Dolores Del Río and few other impart their portrayals that rekindle our own sympathy for them all."[5]

Kings of the Sun (1963, United Artists)

The film *Kings of the Sun* depicted the pre–Columbian cultures of the Mayans and the people of the Gulf coast. Although well meaning in its intent, it was not entirely successful, though this film marked one of the rare times when Hollywood depicted the Mayan people.

The creative talent behind this film was truly impressive. It was directed by J. Lee Thompson (1914–2002), a British-born filmmaker who specialized in big-budget films. He is best remembered for *The Guns of Navarone* (1961, Columbia) and *Taras Bulba* (1962, United Artists). The screenplay was penned by James R. Webb (1909–1974), who won an Academy Award for Best Writing, Story and Screenplay (Written Directly for the Screen) for *How the West Was Won* (1963, MGM). The impressive cinematography was done by one of the few Mexican American cinematographers in U.S. films, Joseph Patrick "Joe" MacDonald (1906–1968). His credits included such notable films as *Pinky* (1940, 20th Century–Fox) and *The Sand Pebbles* (1966, 20th Century–Fox), for which he received an Academy Award nomination for Best Cinematography.

The narrative is set in Meso America centuries before the coming of Europeans. In the Yucatan area, King Balam (George Chakiris) assumes the throne after his father has been killed by tribes who use metal blades, led by Hunac Ceel (Leo Gordon). Balam is advised by his priests to leave the Yucatan peninsula and go north to the Gulf of Mexico area. There (in what is today Texas) he marries the Ixchel (Shirley Anne Field), the daughter of the local chief, in order to make an alliance.

The Mayans clash with the native tribe led by Black Eagle (Yul Brynner), whom they take prisoner. During his captivity, Black Eagle falls in love with Ixchel. Eventually, both indigenous tribes learn to coexist, and they unite to defeat Hunac Ceel and his invading warriors.

The film was only a moderate commercial success. Producer Walter Mirisch would later state, "Kings of the Sun was not successful, either critically or commercially. It wasn't made for the right reasons, and that is most often an insuperable handicap. Our creative team lacked the passion for what we were doing and its commercial values could not overcome that."[6]

Kings of the Sun received mixed reviews. Bosley Crowther, in the *New York Times* (December 26, 1963), wrote, "Miss Field seems a pallid specimen among the redskins, but she fares better than poor Richard Basehart. As the high priest of the Mayans, swathed in dirty dresses and adorned with a mountainous gray wig, he looks exactly like the late Maria Ouspenskaya."[7]

The most important shortcoming of the film was the casting of the lead actors, who were all non–Native American. The charismatic and Russian-born actor Yul Brynner was then still at the height of his career. Due to his inherent exoticism and persona, he was physically passable as Black Eagle. However, the British-born Shirley Anne Field as Ixchel; the Greek American George Chakiris as Balam; Richard Basehart as Ah Min; Brad Dexter as Ah Haleb; and Leo Gordon as Hunac Ceel were completely miscast and unconvincing in their respective roles.

Much more convincing are the Mexican native actors: Armando Silvestre as Isatai, and others in bit roles.

Shalako (1968, Cinerama Releasing)

The film *Shalako* was a British western headlined by an international cast. Although not considered a "spaghetti western," it was filmed in Spain.

The film was helmed by veteran Edward Dmytryk (1908–1999), a Canadian-born (son of Polish-Ukrainian immigrants) director.[8] It was based on a book by Louis L'Amour, and the screenplay was written by James Griffith and Hal Hopper. The film was shot on location in Almeria, Spain. *Shalako* boasted a strong international cast headed by Sean Connery (in his only western role), Brigitte Bardot, Stephen Boyd, Honor Blackman, and Jack Hawkins.

The basic narrative involves the adventures of tracker and hunter named Shalako (Sean Connery) in New Mexico in the 1880s. A frontiersman named Bosky Fulton (Stephen Boyd) and a group of his men have been employed to take a group of European aristocrats on a hunting trip into Apache territory. One day, the French countess Irina Lazaar (Brigitte Bardot) goes out on her own and is attacked by Apache warriors. She is rescued by Shalako (Sean Connery), an ex–U.S. Cavalry officer dedicated to keeping whites out of Native American land. Both Shalako and Irina promise Chato (Woody Strode), the Apache chief, to keep their compatriots out of native land. However, the arrogance and defiance of the white visitors lead to a violent confrontation with the Apaches.

Shalako has many elements of conventional U.S. westerns. However, it was heavily influenced by the spaghetti westerns that developed in Italy in the 1960s. The film depicts jaded characters, marked by duplicity and amorality, and revenge. The character of Shalako is sympathetic to the plight of Native Americans. He fought against them in the U.S. Cavalry but also witnessed the U.S. government's punitive and destructive policy against the natives. Shalako is a deeply disillusioned character who has seen the horrible things human beings can do to one other. However, he has a hard time controlling the ingrained superiority and prejudice of the European aristocrats, who demean and denigrate native people.

Woody Strode was cast as Chato, the Apache chief. Strode had African-Creek-Blackfoot blood from his father and African-Cherokee ancestry from his mother. Strode had previously played a Native American role in John Ford's *Two Rode Together* (1961, Columbia).

The most distracting aspect of the film is the fact that the Spanish geography is not convincing as the U.S. Southwest. In light of the fact that *Shalako* was shot overseas, it had only a few Native American actors, including Chief Tug Smith as Loco and Rodd Redwing (although some sources question his native ethnicity) as Chato's father.

Two Rode Together (1961, Columbia)

John Ford's *Two Rode Together* is a film that tackled prejudice against Native Americans and Mexicans in the U.S. Southwest in the 1800s.

By the mid–1950s, Ford had begun to deconstruct his own mythology of the Old West, which he had created in his westerns from the 1920s to the 1950s. The hard truths about Manifest Destiny and Native American genocide became pronounced in *The Searchers* (1956, Warner Bros.). The film *Two Rode Together* belongs to the autumn years of Ford's directorial career. It was based on the book *Comanche Captives* (1960) by Will Cook. Former *New York Times* film critic Frank Nugent (who had written *The Searchers* and nine other Ford films) wrote the screenplay.

The narrative is set in in the 1880s, in Tascosa, Texas. Marshall Guthrie McCabe (James Stewart) is a grizzled gunman who is not above getting 10 percent of the earnings of the dubious activities that go on in the saloon owned by Belle Aragon (Annelle Hayes). He is approached by his friend, First Lieutenant Jim Gary (Richard Widmark), to accompany him in bringing back some white settlers captured years ago by the Comanche. In exchange, McCabe is promised some of the ransom money.

McCabe goes along with the plan reluctantly, as he knows that the white relatives pressuring the army to proceed with the rescue will be ultimately disappointed by the futile effort. Upon reaching the Comanche camp, he bargains with Chief Quanah Parker (Henry Brandon) for the release of four white captives. Of the four, two refuse to go back (a younger woman who is married with children and an older woman). In the end, McCabe and Gary return with two former captives. One of them, Running Wolf, articulates his hatred for white people, but he is forced to live with his alleged white mother. He ends up killing the woman and is subsequently lynched by an outraged white mob.

The second rescued captive is Elena de la Madriaga (Linda Cristal), a Mexican señorita (herself of indigenous heritage). Upon her return to the town, she is ostracized by the white community for having been the wife of Stone Calf (Woody Strode), thus falling into degradation. She is told that she should commit suicide to hide the shame of consorting with Native Americans. McCabe comes to her defense and gradually falls in love with her. However, after another humiliation, she opts to leave the town and move to California. McCabe leaves with her.

Two Rode Together makes a stinging social statement about the hypocrisy of the white community toward Native Americans and Mexicans in 1880s Texas. The film stresses the whites' sense of superiority over native people and Mexicans. The 1836 Texas Constitution, written after the Euro-American rebellion, denied voting rights to Mexicans and Native Americans and perpetuated the institution of slavery for African Americans. All three communities would endure decades of de jure and de facto segregation.

In the film, the well-meaning efforts of McCabe and Gary, both decent men, prove illusory. Two of the white captives refuse to return at all. A third, Running Wolf, has been traumatized by the punitive campaigns of violence and terror against the Comanches. The fourth, Elena, has endured her ordeal but realizes upon returning to the town that she is despised by the very people who sought the captives' release.

McCabe and Gary are far from the pristine white western heroes created by dime novels and Ford films. They are cynical, sardonic, tough, and wise to the blatant racism and genocidal campaigns against native peoples. They can do little (perhaps only in solitary gestures) to keep their humanity alive. *Two Rode Together* is a disturbing film about the aftermath and consequences of the mythology created by Manifest Destiny.

The film received mixed reviews, with some exceptions. Eugene Archer, in the *New York Times* (July 27, 1961), wrote, "Credit for this realistic approach to frontier life must go in large measure to the no-nonsense direction of Mr. Ford ... Linda Cristal has moments of pathos as a Mexican señorita who survives captivity as a chieftain's squaw, only to be ostracized by her would-be-saviors for her failure to commit suicide her religion forbids."[9]

Linda Cristal (b. 1934) was cast in the role of Elena de la Madriaga. Cristal was born to an Italian mother and a French father in Argentina. She first gained stardom in Mexican films during 1952–1956, when she made eight films. In 1956, she made her U.S. debut in *Comanche* (United Artists), playing another Mexican lady. Today, she is perhaps best remembered as the Mexican American ranch matriarch Victoria Montoya in the television series *High Chaparral* (1967–1971).

Despite the progressive content of *Two Rode Together*, the casting of white actors in Native American roles is both a disappointment and counterproductive. Ford cast white actor Henry Brandon in the most important native role: Chief Quanah Parker. Brandon had been previously cast by Ford in another key native role, that of Scar in *The Searchers* (1956, Warner Bros.). Woody Strode was cast as Stone Calf, his second role as a Native American. Navajos were cast as extras in the film.

How the West Was Won (1962, MGM)

How the West Was Won was a big-budget, epic western chronicling the lives of three generations of Euro-American immigrants and settlers in the west. The film ads boasted thirteen major stars. However, only eight of these were proven box-office draws and bona fide stars (John Wayne, James Stewart, Henry Fonda, Gregory Peck, Carroll Baker, Richard Widmark, Robert Preston, and Debbie Reynolds). The movie was narrated by Spencer Tracy. It employed three important directors: John Ford, Henry Hathaway, and George Marshall, as well as Richard Thorpe (who was uncredited and directed the transitional scenes).

The film was based on a screenplay by James R. Webb. It was filmed in three-strip

Cinerama. Budgeted at $15 million, it went to become a huge box-office success, grossing some $431.7 million when adjusted for inflation.[10]

How the West Was Won garnered three Academy Awards: Best Writing, Story and Screenplay (James R. Webb); Best Film Editing; and Best Sound (Franklin Milton). The breathtaking cinematography was done by four of the best in the film industry: Charles Lang, Jr., Milton Krasner, William Daniels, and Joseph LaShelle. The film was 180 minutes in length.

The film featured six segments: "The Rivers" (1839); "The Plains" (1851); "The Civil War" (1861–1865); "The Railroad" (1868); "The Outlaws" (1889); and an epilogue. The narrative tells the story of the Prescott family (Karl Malden and Agnes Moorehead, along with their two daughters, Carroll Baker and Debbie Reynolds). They begin their journey in 1839 in the Ohio Valley. Four generations live through the white settlement of the Southwest in the aftermath of the Mexican-American War (1846–1848); the Euro-American expansion in the Great Plains in the 1850s; the Civil War of 1861–1865; and the coming of the railroad in 1868.

How the West Was Won was highly praised by the majority of critics. Unbelievably, these critics never noticed that the film had a minuscule number of Native American characters, and not one truly developed indigenous character. The first two segments ("The Rivers" and "The Plains") featured faceless native people, but then they disappear completely until the segment of "The Railroad." *How the West Was Won* is an ethnocentric film that avoids the subject of Native American genocide, the reservation system, and five hundred broken treaties with native tribes. The film is a feel-good exercise in entertainment (charismatic film stars, adventure, romance), but absent of the hard truths.

The few Native American performers in *How the West Was Won* included Beulah Archuletta (Arapaho Woman), Ben Black Elk, Sr. (Arapaho Chief), and Buddy Red Bow (Arapaho Man). The film also featured hundreds of Native American extras.

A Thunder of Drums (1961, MGM)

This film depicts the clash between a young commander from the East (George Hamilton) and the disgraced commander of a fort out west (Richard Boone). *A Thunder of Drums* features the traditional battles between the U.S. Cavalry and Native Americans. Here, the Comanches are blamed for the depredations of white settlers carried out by Apaches. The film was representative of the narratives during the early 1960s before the counterculture era of the late 1960s.

This unremarkable film was directed by veteran Joseph M. Newman (1909–2006). The screenplay was written by the prolific James Warner Bellah (1899–1976), who had co-written two John Ford films: *Sergeant Rutledge* (1960) and *The Man Who Shot Liberty Valance* (1962, Paramount).

The Outsider (1961, Univ. Inter.)

The Outsider was the first film to tell the story of Ira Hayes (1923–1955), a Pima, and one of the servicemen who raised the U.S. flag at Iwo Jima. The film was directed by Delbert Mann (1920–2007), a prolific television and film director who won the Academy Award for Best Director for *Marty* (1955, United Artists). *The Outsider* was written by Stewart Stern (1922–2015), better known for his script of *Rebel without a Cause* (1955, Warner Bros.).

As told in the film, Ira Hayes was born in the Pima Indian Reservation in Arizona. At the time of his enlistment in the U.S. Marine Corps, he has never been outside the confines of the reservation. In the service he is treated like a pariah and called "Chief!" Despite enduring harsh discrimination, he possesses a quiet courage and reserves of tenacity.

Hayes took part in the famous Battle of Iwo Jima (February 19–March 26, 1945) in the South Pacific. He was one of the six U.S. servicemen who raised the flag on Mount Suribachi. In the film, the iconic photo wins Ira and his fellow Marines widespread fame. However, Ira falls into a severe depression due to the horrors that he has witnessed during the war. His condition worsens after he is recruited to sell war bonds, and he soon leaves the U.S. Marines.

Ira returns to the reservation and further withdraws into deep depression. However, he manages to pull himself together to attend the Iwo Jima Memorial at Arlington Cemetery in Washington, D.C., on November 10, 1954. After this event, he returns to the reservation, where he dies of exposure and alcoholism at the age of 32.

The role of Ira Hayes was played by the popular film star Tony Curtis, who at this time in his career was transitioning from a romantic matinee idol into a dramatic actor. Curtis was nominated for a Laurel Award for Best Actor for his performance. However, although Curtis tries his best in the part, he is miscast. The most telling and irritating aspect of the role is the heavy brown grease that was put on white performers who were playing most of the Native Americans, adding to the lack of authenticity.

There were a few Native American actors in this film. The legendary Charles Stevens played Ira's grandfather. It was his last film role. Native actors also included Vince St. Cyr as Leonard Hayes. In real life, St. Cyr was a highly decorated World War II and Korean War veteran. In addition, John War Eagle played Mr. Goode.

The film was shot on location at the Gila River Indian Reservation, Soldier Field in Chicago, and Camp Pendleton in California.

The Outsider was not a commercial success, and it is now a forgotten film. The life of Ira Hayes was later depicted in Clint Eastwood's *Flags of Our Fathers* (2006, Warner Bros.), in which Hayes was played by a Native American actor, Adam Beach.

Duel at Diablo (1966, United Artists)

Duel at Diablo was one of the increasingly gritty and violent westerns made in the late 1960s. These films were heavily influenced by the spaghetti westerns in their amoral and cynical depiction of the Old West.

The film was directed by Ralph Nelson (1916–1987), who had helmed *Lilies of the Field* (1963, United Artists) and *Soldier Blue* (1970, Avco Embassy). The screenplay was written by Marvin H. Albert and Michael M. Grilikhes. Their script was based on the novel *Apache Uprising* (1957). The film was co-produced by James Garner, who also played the main character.

The film's narrative focuses on a group of disparate characters in southern Utah in the late 1880s. Jess Remsberg (James Garner), an army scout, is looking for the murderer of his Native American wife. Along the way, he rescues Ellen Grange (Bibi Anderson), the wife of the Apache warrior Chata (John Hoyt), and takes her to a fort. There Toller (Sidney Poitier), a former Buffalo Soldier and horse wrangler, plans to join an army detail on a dangerous mission. Lieutenant McCallister (Bill Travers), an ambitious officer, is planning to lead a group of twenty-five inexperienced soldiers to Fort Conchos with the assistance of Jess and Toller. The group is ambushed by party of Apaches who have broken out of the reservation, led by Chata. Predictably, at the end of the film the Apaches are defeated and sent back to the reservation.

Duel at Diablo received mixed reviews. Robert Alden, in the *New York Times* (January 16, 1966), wrote, "James Garner, a man of experience at this Western trade, is a plainsman whose blood is red and who bleeds when he is beaten, who suffers agonies when his Indian wife is killed, whose tiredness with the pointless struggle is evident in every line of his weather-beaten face."[11]

Duel at Diablo raises some serious questions about prejudice and racism in the Old West. For example, Ellen is condemned for choosing not to kill herself, instead becoming the wife of a native warrior and having a mixed-blood child (similar to what happens in *Two Rode Together*). In the end, she is so tormented by the white community that she flees back to Chata. In turn, Jess Remsberg is a man broken with sorrow after his native wife is murdered by a white man who carries her scalp as a trophy. As a result, Jess becomes obsessed with revenge.

The film shows empathy for the plight of the Native American warriors who have broken out of the reservation and their heartfelt desire to be free. However, the natives' point of view is submerged in the conventional narrative of "whites versus Indians." The film raises questions about prejudice against Native Americans and the hypocrisy of white settlers. However, in the final scenes the film collapses into pattern of the typical hard-edged westerns made in the late 1960s. The narrative's full potential is never realized.

As usual, the key Native American roles were played by white actors (an example is John Hoyt in the important role of Chata). Native American actor Eddie Little Sky played Alchise, and Dawn Little Sky was Chata's wife.

Johnny Tiger (1966, Universal Pictures)

Johnny Tiger displays the decade's evolution in terms of the depiction of native people and native life. It is a contemporary story, shot in the city of Longwood in northern Florida, as well as in Sanlando Springs.

This film was directed by Paul Wendkos and written by Philip Wylie, Paul Crabtree, and Thomas Blackburn. It was based on "Tiger on the Inside" by R. John Hugh. The film tells the story of George Dean (Robert Taylor), a widower, who has been fired from his professorship. He takes his three children to a Seminole reservation to teach and begin life anew. There Chief Sam Tiger (Fred Rainey) is old and dying, but he has hopes that his nephew, Johnny Tiger (Chad Everett), will become educated and serve as the chief of his people. Johnny, however, is undisciplined and cynical.

Dean, recognizing the young man's intelligence and leadership qualities, tries to win Johnny over so that other Seminoles will go to school. Dean is also shocked and angered by the poverty and squalor of the reservation and complains to the health official (Geraldine Brooks). She informs him that the government cares little for the reservation.

Dean's daughter Barbara (Brenda Scott) and Johnny fall in love. She finally convinces Johnny to attend the school, but his grandfather sees that as assimilation. In the end, Barbara and Johnny run away, feeling that they could never reconcile with their parents, who espouse different social views.

Film star Robert Taylor is said to have had high hopes for this thoughtful and serious film. Lawrence J. Quirk noted, "His disappointment—indeed chagrin—was great when the commerce-minded overlords at Universal decided that this just wasn't what audiences really wanted in 1966 and ran it as the second half of a double-bill with *Munsters Go Home*."[12] The film received poor publicity and bookings. As a result, it quickly disappeared from public view. *Johnny Tiger* later received only a few screenings on television, and it has never been available on video or DVD.

Most reviewers of the film universally praised the film and its message. The *New York Times* (June 16, 1966) noted, "'*Johnny Tiger*,' a drama of the conflict between traditional and Americanized Seminoles spurred by the impact of a dedicated white teacher on their ways of life, was filmed in Florida's Everglades country and has indications of honesty and purpose."[13]

The film benefited from the on-location shooting in Seminole country, the native culture ambience, and native performers. It made a genuine effort to provide an accurate perspective on life in a Native American reservation, the condition of the native peoples' lives, and the long-standing concerns and issues.

Native Film Stars and Filmmakers

Celia Kaye

Celia Kaye came to prominence in the early 1960s in both film and television roles. She was born Celia Kaye Burkholder on February 24, 1942, in Carthage, Missouri. She is of Cherokee and German descent.

Kaye made her acting debut in 1962 in the television series *Tales of Wells Fargo*. She also played the daughter of Loretta Young in the television series *The New Loretta Young Show* between 1962 and 1963.

In 1964, she played her most famous role, that of Juana Maria, the young Native American girl who survived for 18 years in one of the Channel Islands off the coast of California, in the film *Island of the Blue Dolphins* (1964, Universal). She was one of three young actresses honored with the Golden Globe Award for Most Promising Newcomer—Female and garnered positive reviews for the film.

Kaye went on to a long and successful career in film and television. Her films include *Wild Seed* (1965, Universal); *Fluffy* (1965, Universal); *The Final Comedown* (1972, New World Pictures); *Big Wednesday* (1978, Warner Bros.); and *Conan the Barbarian* (1982, De Laurentiis). Her numerous television credits include *Wagon Train*, *The Green Hornet*, *The Adventures of Ozzie and Harriet*, *The Iron Horse*, *The Young Lawyers*, and *Little House on the Prairie*.

Celia Kaye was married and divorced from screenwriter and director John Milius, and the union produced one daughter, Amanda.

Linda Redfearn

Linda Redfearn graced the screen for a few years in both television and motion pictures. She was born Linda Moon Redfearn on December 2, 1939, in Dallas Texas. Her ancestry was Cherokee and English. She was the youngest of three siblings.

At the age of 26, she moved to California in search of an acting career. A tall (5 feet, 9 inches) and attractive lady, she was able to quickly make an impression and acquired roles in both television and films.

Redfearn made her film debut in the cult science-fiction film *The Omega Man* (1971, Walter Seltzer Prods.) as one of the nocturnal characters that have survived a nuclear blast. She played the leading female native role of Toma in *I Will Fight No More Forever* (1975, David Wolper Prods.) about the life of Chief Joseph. Her television appearances include the mini-series *How the West Was Won* (1976–1979, MGM) and television shows such as *Hawaii Five-0*, *The Quest, and Born to the Wind*. Her films include *Larry* (1974, Tomorrow), a TV film, and *The White Buffalo* (1977, United Artists). However, she retired from films soon after these appearances.

Redfearn went on to live in McKinney, Texas, with her husband, former NFL football player Guy Reese. They were married for twenty years. Reed passed away in 2010.

Ned Romero

Ned Romero was a man of many talents, including opera singer and actor in films and television. He was born on December 4, 1926, in Franklin, Louisiana. He was of Citimacha native ancestry (a tribe from Louisiana), as well as Spanish and French heritage. He graduated from Louisiana State University, where he majored in music.

After completing his education, Romero began his career as an opera singer in 1943. He went on to headline with the San Francisco Opera and later performed in Los Angeles. He appeared in such musicals as *Oklahoma!*, *Kismet*, and *Kiss Me Kate* on the stage.

He made his television debut in the television series *The Many Loves of Dobie Gillis* in 1963. Other television experiences included *Police Woman, The Six Million Dollar Man, Ironside, Death Valley Days, The Incredible Hulk, Adam-12, Emergency!, Kung Fu, Land of the Lost, Star Trek: Voyager, Custer, Santa Barbara,* and *Star Trek: The Next Generation*. He played Sergeant Rivera in the series *Dan August* during 1970–1971 with Burt Reynolds.

Perhaps his most important role was that of the revered Chief Joseph in the television film *I Will Fight No More Forever* (1975, David Wolper Prods.). His film credits include *Hang 'Em High* (1968, United Artists); *Tell Them Willie Boy Is Here* (1969, Universal); and *Expiration Date* (2006, Roadkill Prods.). He made his film debut in *The Violent Ones* in 1967 (Feature Film Corp.).

Ned Romero died on November 4, 2017, in Palm Desert, California, at the age of 90 years.

Vince St. Cyr

One of the most visible Native American actors of the 1960s was Vince St. Cyr. He was born June 30, 1930, in the Winnebago Indian Reservation in Nebraska.

In 1950, St. Cyr enlisted in the U.S. Marines and served with distinction in the Korean War. For his service, he was awarded the Bronze Star, the Korean Service Medal, the United Nations Ribbon and additional honors. He left the service in 1952 with the rank of sergeant. Upon his return to the Winnebago Indian Reservation, he co-founded the Nebraska Platoon with other Nebraska veterans.

Upon his return from active duty, St. Cyr married his longtime sweetheart, Ida Mae

Saunsoci from Macy, Nebraska. After their marriage, the couple moved to Inglewood, California, where he worked in the Northrop Aircraft Corporation in the area of design. The marriage produced three children (one of whom died before St. Cyr's own passing).

St. Cyr made his film debut in 1958 in *Light in the Forest* (Disney). His films included *Wild and Innocent* (1959, Univ. Inter.); *Yellowstone Kelly* (1959, Warner Bros.); *The FBI Story* (1959, Warner Bros.); *Comanche Station* (1960, Columbia Pictures); *The Outsider* (1960, Univ. Inter.); *Lonely Are the Brave* (1962, Univ. Inter.); *The Plainsman* (1966, Universal); *The Fastest Guitar Alive* (1967, MGM); *True Grit* (1969, Paramount); *A Man Called Horse* (1970, Cinema Center Films); *There Was a Crooked Man* (1970, Warner Bros.); *The Bounty Man* (1972, ABC Films), a TV film; *Billy Two Hats* (1974, Algonquin); *I Will Fight No More Forever* (1975, David Wolper Prods.), a TV film; *Against a Crooked Sky* (1975, Feature Films for Families); and *The Macahans* (1976, MGM). He also appeared in numerous television series, including *Emergency, The High Chaparral, Star Trek, Daniel Boone, The Beverly Hillbillies, Laredo, The Virginian, Empire,* and *The Tall Men.*

In 1978, St. Cyr returned to the Winnebago Indian Reservation and worked as an emergency medical technician and community health professional from 1980 to 1982. He continued to be active in the acting field, in addition to branching out in children's educational programs in nearby Omaha, Nebraska.

Vince St. Cyr passed on March 16, 1997, in Sioux City, Iowa, after a long illness. He was buried at the Native American Church Cemetery in Winnebago, Nebraska, with full military honors.

9

The American Indian Movement and the Reel Invisibility (1970–1979)

The 1970s witnessed the rise and militancy of the American indigenous movement. This movement called into question the U.S. government's policy toward First Nations, including the hundreds of broken treaties, mismanagement of indigenous lands and resources, and continued disregard and neglect. Unfortunately, the decade continued the invisibility of indigenous people in films and other media.

On the world stage, the decade was one of continuing ideological hostility between the East and West. In Latin America, insurgents and civil organizations continued to press against predatory military juntas and cliques financed and bolstered by U.S. dollars and military advisors. The United States finally withdrew from Vietnam during March 1972, and President Richard Nixon was forced to resign in August 1974 after a series of illegal activities.

Expectations were high for the signing of the Strategic Arms Treaty, but it was forestalled by the Soviet invasion of Afghanistan in 1978. In the meantime, the Organization of Petroleum Exporting Counties raised oil prices, pushing the industrialized world into an economic and energy crisis. During 1979, the Shah of Iran, a western ally, was overthrown.

In the Americas, the status quo was in flux. In 1973, the democratically elected president of Chile, Salvador Allende, was overthrown by a U.S.–sponsored military coup led by General Pinochet. In Nicaragua, in July 1979, the Sandinistas toppled the forty-year-old Somoza dynasty/dictatorship, which had been supported by the United States. The push-and-pull forces of capital and labor attracted millions of Mexican undocumented workers into low-paying jobs in the United States, while the media accused them of "stealing jobs."

In the late 1970s, President Jimmy Carter's focus on "human rights" represented a shift in U.S. foreign policy. The *Bakke* case, decided in 1978, undermined the federal government's commitment to affirmative action in order to make up for the past discrimination of minorities and women. Nevertheless, by the end of the decade, people of color and women had made some gains, including an increase in university enrollment, ethnic and women studies, and bilingual education.

For Native Americans, the 1970s gave rise to a wave of change after decades of being dubbed the "Vanishing Americans." Several Native American organizations were founded in the wake of rising native consciousness and concerns about shrinking reservation land and pressing social issues. The best known group was the American Indian Movement (AIM), which was dedicated to holding the U.S. government accountable for the five hundred broken treaties, the dumping of toxic waste into reservations and continued efforts to pillage the reservations' natural resources, the endemic poverty and squalor natives were forced to endure, and the continued marginalization of and racism against native peoples.

Numerous activities were undertaken to remind the nation of the plight of Native Americans. On November 20, 1969, eighty-nine Native Americans, who called themselves Indians of All Tribes (IOAT), occupied Alcatraz Island in San Francisco Bay. The federal prison of Alcatraz had been closed on March 21, 1963; the takeover was a symbolic act of the reclamation of native land and the unjust policy toward native people. The occupation lasted from November 20, 1969, to June 11, 1971. The occupation became a media event, and thousands rallied in the activists' support.

In the autumn of 1972, Native American activists crisscrossed the country in what became known as the Trail of Broken Treaties, or the Pan American Native Quest for Justice, to dramatize the history of the government breach of some five hundred treaties signed with native tribes. The caravan arrived in Washington, D.C., in the first week of November. It marked the largest gathering of native people at the nation's capital with the intent of negotiating a new relationship with the U.S. government.

Initially, the Nixon administration refused to meet with the AIM representatives or accept the Twenty-Point position paper. As a result, the activists proceeded to take over the Department of the Interior building, where the Bureau of Indian Affairs (BIA) was housed. The federal government promised to negotiate treaty rights and other issues, but it was evident that they were stalling for time. The occupation caught President Nixon (who was basking in his electoral victory) by surprise. Ironically, Nixon had opposed the termination policy since the 1950s.

On November 8, after AIM had left the BIA offices, the administration agreed to discuss the Twenty-Point position paper, except amnesty, which it intended to address separately. Later, on December 22, 1973, Nixon would sign the Menominee Restoration Act, which restored the Menominee federal recognition, as well as land taken previously. However, by then, Nixon's days in office were numbered, as he had been crippled by the Watergate scandal and the subsequent investigation.

The Native American movement's high point came during the Wounded Knee siege, which began on February 17, 1973, in the Pine Ridge Reservation, South Dakota. It was the site of the infamous massacre in 1890 of defenseless women, children, and elderly native people by the U.S. 7th Cavalry (General Custer's former regiment). Members of the Pine Reservation and AIM took over the tiny hamlet to make a strong political statement about the dire conditions at the reservation (and in the nation at large) for Native Americans. Of the 350 occupiers, there were fewer than 100 men; the vast majority were women.[1]

The reservation was quickly surrounded by the U.S. Army, the FBI, federal marksmen, tanks, and heavy armor. Russell Means, one of the leaders of AIM, articulated the purpose of the takeover: "Most of our demands were for action that the U.S. government had already agreed to in 1868—to enforce the provisions of the Fort Laramie Treaty by returning our sacred Black Hills and reestablishing an independent Oglala Nation.... We called for Senator J. William Fulbright's Foreign Affairs Committee to investigate U.S. compliance with 371 treaties it had signed with Indian nations."[2]

Efforts to negotiate an end to the conflict failed to materialize. During the siege, two Native Americans and one African American within the occupied area were killed and/or disappeared. In the end, these deaths contributed to the decision to end the occupation. The federal siege ended on May 8, 1973, after seventy-one days.

The Wounded Knee siege made headlines throughout the world and earned unprecedented coverage of the plight of Native Americans in the United States. Native Americans throughout the nation and the rest of the Americas were galvanized by what was happening at Wounded Knee. Churches, organizations, activists, and celebrities expressed their support for the efforts of Native Americans and their campaign for justice.

In 1975, the Pine Ridge Reservation again became the focus of conflict.[3] It continues to be the poorest county in the United States.[4]

NATIVE AMERICAN FILM IMAGES IN THE 1970S

During the 1970s, despite the news coverage documenting Native American concerns and issues, the film industry for the most part was slow and/or unwilling to depict indigenous life or concerns. The opportunities for indigenous actors and filmmakers were limited, and the tradition of casting non-native actors in the tiny number of native roles continued. Even well-meaning films perpetuated this enduring practice.

Relatively few films were made that featured indigenous characters or indigenous actors. Native American roles continued to be incidental to film narratives. The western *The McMasters* (1970, Distrifilm) focuses on a black Civil War veteran from the Union Army (Brock Peters) who becomes part-owner of a ranch in the new South and, in the process, becomes the owner of indigenous women. His new status arouses the wrath of ex–Confederate veterans, who seek his downfall. Despite the fact that this film was shot in New Mexico, the two indigenous roles (Robin, the native woman, and White Feather) were played by non-indigenous actors.

The movie *Flap* (1970, Warner Bros.) was the only film during this decade in which the lead role of Flapping Eagle was played by a Native American actor—namely, Anthony Quinn. The film was based on the novel *Nobody Loves a Drunken Indian* (1967) by Cliff Huffaker and told the story of older groups of embittered and alcoholic indigenous men in a reservation in the Southwest. *Flap* was shot on location in the Santa Clara Pueblo in New Mexico. During the making of the film, an alliance of different native tribes took over the former penitentiary Alcatraz; the occupation would last almost two years. The studio publicized the film with the tagline "The Indians have already claimed Alcatraz…. City Hall may be next!"

Flap ultimately failed to enunciate the dire social conditions faced by indigenous people and their call for change and accountability of the hundreds of broken treaties. The highly respected director Carol Reed, who helmed the film,[5] was totally out of his element. All the key roles other than the leads were played by non-native actors, which undermined the film's good intentions. Native actors Rodolfo Acosta and John War Eagle were relegated to two tiny roles. The film generally received negative reviews, though some critics praised Quinn's performance. Howard Thompson, in the *New York Times* (January 1, 1971), wrote, "Finally, at long last, there comes a movie about the bleak plight of today's American Indian that is funny as it is moving. That's '*Flap*' for Flapping Eagle, which also provides Anthony Quinn with his best role in years, as the dim-witted tribal revolutionary and con man and the pride and problem of the home reservation."[6]

The western *Buck and the Preacher* (1971, Columbia) features an ex–Union sergeant (Sidney Poitier) and a former slave (Harry Belafonte) who travel west in search of a better life and to help freed slaves. However, former slave owners hire outlaws to bring back their former slave labor. Hard pressed to elude their pursuers, the black pioneers are helped by Native American warriors. *Chato's Land* (1972, United Artists) focuses on one lone Apache warrior, the titular Chato (Charles Bronson), in New Mexico in the 1870s, who methodically wipes out an entire white posse. (This film was actually shot in Spain.) Sidney Pollack's *Jeremiah Johnson* (1972, Warner Bros.), set in the Rocky Mountains, depicts the rather romanticized story of the real-life white mountain man (Robert Redford) in the aftermath of the Mexican-American War. In the film, Johnson engages in an uneasy battle of wits and diplomacy with the Crow tribe. However, the real John Jeremiah Johnston (1824–1900) was no peace-loving recluse; in fact, his nickname was John "Liver-Eating" Johnson.

Several films attempted to address the social conditions of Native Americans. *When the Legends Die* (1972, 20th Century–Fox) was based on the highly respected novel by Hal Bortland. The film depicts the life of a young Ute youth (Frederic Forrest) who works in the rodeo circuit and his friendship with a world-weary white mentor (Richard Widmark). As usual, a non-indigenous actor was cast as the native youth. Tom Gries' *Journey through Rosebud* (1972, GSF) was shot on location in the Rosebud Indian Reservation in South Dakota. The film focuses on the dissipated life of a Lakota named Frank (Robert Forester) and his Lakota girlfriend Shirley (Victoria Racino). A white youth named Danny (Kristofer Tobari), who is evading the military draft, joins the Lakota at the Wounded Knee siege. *Journey through Rosebud* was never released theatrically; as with so many other movies, its main weakness was the casting of non-native actors in the two lead roles.

The House Made of Dawn (1972, Morse) was based on the novel by N. Scott Momaday (b. 1934), with received the Pulitzer Prize (awarded in 1969 for fiction). Momaday, who has mixed Cherokee, Irish, English, and French ancestry, is a groundbreaking novelist, essayist, and poet. *House Made of Dawn* focuses on a traumatized World War II veteran Abel (Larry Littlefeather) who returns to his reservation in New Mexico. The film received lukewarm reviews and limited distribution. Today, it is considered a Native American cult film.

The White Dawn (1974, Paramount) depicts the coming of Europeans to the Northern Canada Artic in 1896 and their desire to exploit the native Inuit. However, the most highly acclaimed performance by a Native American actor came in *One Flew Over the Cuckoo's Nest* (1975, United Artists), in which Will Sampson played the tall and silent Native American Chief Bromden, thought to be deaf and mute. Although it was a supporting role, Sampson won rave reviews, but no Oscar nomination.

The film *Billy Jack* (1971, Warner Bros.), produced by maverick actor, producer, and director Tom Laughlin, introduced a mixed-blood, martial arts expert and Vietnam War veteran to audiences. This film and its sequels proved hugely popular with general audiences, especially Native American moviegoers. Two underappreciated films chronicled the dying of the Old West.

The White Buffalo (1977, United Artists) tells the story of a fateful meeting of the celebrated gunfighter Wild Bill Hickok and legendary Lakota warrior Crazy Horse during a buffalo hunt. *A Man Called Horse* (1970, Cinema Center Films) focuses on the trials and tribulations of a white man captured by the Lakota. In turn, *Ulzana's Raid* (1972, Universal) documents one of the last military actions of the so-called Indian Wars. *The Master Gunfighter* (1975, Warner Bros.) is an offbeat California western about the plight of the California indigenous people, while Ralph Nelson's *Soldier Blue* (1970, Avco Embassy) debunks the mythology of how the West was won. Robert Altman's *Buffalo Bill and the Indians, or Sitting Bull's History Lesson* (1976, United Artists) features Buffalo Bill (Paul Newman) living out the mythology created about him by Ned Buntine (Burt Lancaster).

The 1970s introduced several talented Native American actors, including Sacheen Littlefeather, Will Sampson, Chief Dan George, Stella Garcia, Dawn Little Sky, Eddie Little Sky, A Martinez, and Richard Romancito, among others.

Representative Films

The White Buffalo (1977, United Artists)

The film *The White Buffalo* is set in the Dakotas. The protagonists are Wild Bill Hickok and Crazy Horse, two legendary individuals of the Old West. Both become involved in the hunt for a white buffalo, which symbolizes death. The film was directed by J. Lee Thompson, and the screenplay was written by Richard Sale. The script was based on the novel *The White Buffalo*, also penned by Sale.

The narrative is set in 1874. Former marshal and gunfighter Will Bill Hickok (Charles Bronson) is tormented by nightmares of his own death and the rampage of an albino buffalo. He also beset by relatives of men he has previously killed, like Whistling Jack Kilian (Clint Walker) and his men.

Hickok meets up with an old flame, Mrs. Poker Jenny Schermerhorn (Kim Novak), who tries desperately to rekindle their past love—to no avail. In addition, Hickok now needs to wear dark glasses due to the onset of glaucoma (possibly as a result of syphilis). He enlists the help of old friend Charlie Zane (Jack Warden), a former frontiersman and rabid native hater, in order to hunt down the white buffalo.

In the meantime, the legendary Crazy Horse (Will Sampson), of the Lakota people, has lost a child to the white buffalo. He, too, sets out to hunt the animal. In the course of the hunt, Crazy Horse and Hickok meet. At one point, Hickok saves the life of Crazy Horse. Subsequently, when Kilian and his men ambush Hickok, Crazy Horse rescues him. Both Crazy Horse and Hickok respect each other and develop a temporary friendship of cooperation to destroy the rampaging beast.

Once both men complete their mission, however, the partnership unravels. Crazy Horse tells Hickok that because he had killed a revered medicine man years earlier, they cannot continue to be friends, and if they ever meet in battle, he must kill him. Hickok understands and respects this statement, and they bid each other farewell.

The White Buffalo is an evocative film about the end of the frontier. In one scene, when Hickok gets off a train, he is awed by the thousands of buffalo bones piled up along the tracks. The town is muddy, filthy, and populated by failed prospectors, burned-out harlots, broken-down alcoholics, and seedy gunmen.

Will Sampson gives an impressive performance as the enigmatic Crazy Horse and captures the nobility and charisma of the historical man. He is depicted as a grieving father, the protector of his people, and a reflection of the spirituality of his culture. He is dignified with Hickok and respectful of their uneasy alliance while hunting the white buffalo. But Crazy Horse has the integrity to communicate to Hickok that the latter's previous acts of violence against his people will deter them from ever meeting again in friendship.

Bronson himself, a greatly underestimated actor, is also very good as Wild Bill Hickok, a man whose time is running out. He is also a flawed man haunted by his numerous killings. In fact, both Hickock and Crazy Horse would be murdered only eleven months apart. Crazy Horse was killed by U.S. Cavalry guards on September 5, 1877, while imprisoned in Fort Robinson, Nebraska. Hickok, in turn, would be murdered on August 2, 1876, by one Jack McCall (a drunk) in Deadwood, South Dakota. There is an implication throughout the film that both men will die soon.

Aside from Will Sampson, Native American actors in this film included Linda Redfearn (Black Shawl), Chief Tug Smith (Old Worm), and dozens of Native Americans cast in small roles and as extras.

The White Buffalo was shot in several locations in Arizona, New Mexico, and Colorado. This greatly underappreciated and much maligned western has over the years become a cult film.

The *Billy Jack* Films (1968–1977)

During the years 1968–1977, four films were released, written, produced, and directed by and starring independent filmmaker Tom Laughlin. The films developed cult followings and were huge commercial successes, especially given their low budgets. The lead character was named Billy Jack, who was of mixed Navajo-white ethnicity.

When Tom Laughlin died on December 12, 2013, the *Indian Country Media Network* website (December 17, 2013) wrote the following obituary: "Tom Laughlin, who died on Thursday at the age of 82, wasn't Navajo—and didn't claim to be. But as the writer, director, and star of Billy Jack, he portrayed a 'half-breed' white–Navajo hero who served in Vietnam and was a master of *hapkido*, a character who strongly resonated with a good deal of the Native moviegoing public. Both *Billy Jack* (1971) and *The Trial of Billy Jack* (1974) were box-office successes, and a contemporary Native American action hero was an appealing idea to Indians who'd grown weary of seeing their people in loin cloths and speaking pidgin ('him heap big chief') on the silver screen."[7] These comments reflected the genuine sentiment felt for Laughlin's memory in the Native American community.

Tom Laughlin was born in Milwaukee, Wisconsin, to Euro-American parents in 1931. He took up acting in college and went on to perform on the stage, on television, and in a few films before coming to prominence. During the 1960s, he branched out into writing, directing, and producing. He met Delores Taylor in college, and soon thereafter they were married. They would become filmmakers together.

The seed for the character of Billy Jack was planted on a visit that both Laughlin and Taylor made to the town in Winner, South Dakota. According to the official Tom Laughlin website, Laughlin had visited the small town of Winner, at the very heart of the Rosebud and Pine Ridge Reservation, and witnessed the devastating poverty of its indigenous inhabitants. Laughlin saw "a collection of Indians that huddled in the sweltering heat of summer and deadly freeze of winters hoping for odd jobs or help from locals. Tom couldn't believe what he was seeing. He'd never imagined that human beings could be treated this way. And he vowed then and there to make a difference."[8]

The Born Losers (1968, American International)

Born Losers was directed by T. C. Frank (a pseudonym for actor Tom Laughlin), and the screenplay was penned by Elizabeth James. The film was produced by Laughlin, Delores Taylor, and Don Henderson.

The simple narrative involves Billy Jack, of mixed Navajo and white heritage, an ex–Green Beret veteran of the Vietnam War. He becomes involved in battling a violent motorcycle gang that is terrorizing a coastal community in California. Billy is victimized because he is part Native American, but he effectively battles both the bigoted police and the motorcycle gang using his extensive martial arts skills. In the process, he meets and is attracted to Vicky Barrington (Elizabeth James, the screenwriter, here cast as the bikini-clad girl harassed by the motorcycle gang). At the end of the film, Billy is mistaken for a biker and wounded by a policeman, but he recovers.

The reviews for *The Born Losers* were mostly negative. Bosley Crowther, writing in the *New York Times* (August 19, 1967), called it "a sickening little motorcycle melodrama … Tom Laughlin stoically plays a war veteran recluse who almost singe-handedly squelches the gang…. A battered-looking Jane Russell makes a brief, growly appearance as one of the parents."[9]

Born Losers was shot in only three weeks with a minuscule budget. The filmmaking is at times amateurish and clichéd, and not all of the characters are well developed. However, there is a raw energy that characterizes the film, emanating especially from first-time director Laughlin. Even more, the novelty of a part Native American modern action hero in a Hollywood film was something totally new at the time. The film was anti-establishment and caught the passion of the counterculture youth movement of the time. The violent motorcycle gang is a metaphor for the U.S. Army in Vietnam. The film is set in a white, middle-class community. Billy Jack is an outsider, fighting both injustice directed at innocent people and the prejudice against Native Americans.

Born Losers had no "name" film stars. The only well-known actor was Jane Russell, who plays the mother of a raped girl. There are no Native American actors in the film, despite the title character being part Native American.

American International released the film, and it did only fair business. However, it was subsequently re-released in 1974, after the release of the follow-up film *Billy Jack*, and made even more money than in the original release. *Born Losers* had a budget of $360,000 and went on to gross some $26,535,973 (in 1968 dollars).

Billy Jack (1971, Warner Bros.)

The film *Billy Jack* was directed by Tom Laughlin (using once again the name of T.C. Frank) and produced by Mary Rose Solti (also Laughlin); it starred Laughlin himself in the second cinematic appearance of the character of Billy Jack. The screenplay was penned by Frank Christina (Laughlin again) and Theresa Christina (Laughlin's wife, Delores Taylor).

In this film, Billy Jack (Tom Laughlin) becomes aware of an alternative Freedom School, whose student body is generally made up of counterculture youth. The school is administered by Jean Roberts (Delores Taylor). However, the multiethnic school is victimized by the gang of Bernard Posner (David Roya), the son of the corrupt and racist political boss (Bert Freed).

The violence against the Freedom School worsens when a Native American student is killed and Jean is raped. Billy eventually confronts Posner and his gang, ultimately killing him. Billy is subsequently besieged by the police and compelled to surrender to them. As he is taken away, hundreds of supporters manifest their support for him by raising their fists and cheering his efforts.

Billy Jack is a much better film than *Born Losers*. The second film had a bigger budget and a better script. The characters are also more fully developed. The Billy Jack character is given depth, dimension, and a Native American center. He has a specific purpose and mission—namely, to defend the Freedom School and the children. In addition, he is now grounded through his relationship with Jean. The moral centerpiece of the narrative is the right to an education with critical thinking, respect for diversity, and dissent from ethnocentrism.

Billy Jack received mixed reviews. Howard Thompson, in the *New York Times* (July 29, 1971), wrote, "For a film that preaches pacifism, '*Billy Jack*' seems fascinated by violence, of which it is full. The title hero is this well-aimed but misguided drama is a muscular young Indian, an ex–Green Beret, who periodically appears to save a 'freedom school.'"[10]

This film featured a few Native American actors. These included Susan Sosa as Sunshine and a few others.

Upon its initial release, *Billy Jack* failed at the box office. However, Laughlin subsequently booked the film himself with theaters. Bolstered by improved distribution and promotion, it proved a great commercial success. The film had a budget of $800,000 and went on to gross some $98 million (in 1971 dollars).

The Trial of Billy Jack (1974, Taylor-Laughlin Prods.)

The Trial of Billy Jack was directed, co-produced (along with Joe Cramer), and co-written (with Delores Taylor) by Tom Laughlin, who also starred in the third entry of the Billy Jack films. The music score was undertaken by the legendary Elmer Bernstein.

The film opens with Billy Jack's trial on the charges of involuntary manslaughter (based on the events of the previous film). He is found guilty by the court and sentenced to prison.

In the meantime, the students of the Freedom School, an alternative school made up of runaways and Native American youth from the Navajo Nation reservation, dedicate themselves to rebuilding their school. They raise funds to get a new building and eventually establish their own television station and a newspaper. They also conduct investigative reporting and expose the corruption of elected officials.

Billy Jack is eventually released, and he makes concerted effort to rebuild his life. In the process, he undergoes a series of Native American vision quests. He also becomes involved with a militant Native American group that opposes an effort by the federal government to remove recognition of the Native American tribe and open the land up to developers. Subsequently, a Native American is arrested for poaching on what was reservation land, and the case goes to court.

The Freedom School assists the accused poacher, in addition to holding a hearing on Native American rights and child abuse. Eventually, the FBI becomes involved and taps the school's phones. The National Guard is mobilized around the school and, in one confrontation, kills four of the students and wounds hundreds more. The film draws an analogy between the student killings and the My Lai massacre in Vietnam in 1968. After coming to the defense of the embattled students, Billy Jack once more goes to court. There he indicates that he witnessed another massacre during his military service in Vietnam.

As with its predecessor, *Billy Jack*, this film received mixed reviews. Vincent Canby, in the *New York Times* (November 14, 1974), wrote, "Its part pageant, part kung in action film, part Western, par earnest civics lesson, part *Show Boat* melodrama, part recollection of the various horrors of the Tate nineteen-sixties and early nineteen-seventies updated (sometimes desperately) to make contact with today."[11]

The Trial of Billy Jack is perhaps the best and most ambitious of the five Billy Jack films. In this third installment of the series, Billy Jack finally returns to the reservation. The film greatly benefits from having been shot in the Indian Country, especially the iconic Monument Valley, the Canyon de Chilly, and Window Rock (the capital of the Navajo Nation). The film captures life in the reservation, including the poverty and despair of inhabitants. The militant indigenous organization that Billy Jack joins is obviously modeled after the American Indian Movement (AIM).

The Trial of Billy Jack covers the passionate issues of the era: the Native American movement, the Vietnam War, corporate greed, government corruption, poverty, and racism. However, the film was criticized by some as being too long, at almost three hours.

There were numerous Native American actors in the film, including Sacheen Littlefeather (Patsy Littlejohn), Gus Greymountain (Blue Elk), Rolling Thunder (Thunder Mountain), Sandra Ego (Indian Maiden), Trinidad Hopkins (Vision Maiden), Buffalo Horse (Little Bear), Jean Newburn (Militant Indian Lawyer), George Aguilar (Elk's Shadow), Susan Sosa (Sunshine), and several others in bit parts.

The film was shot in Monument Valley in the Four Corners (Arizona, New Mexico, Colorado, and Utah). It had a budget of $2.5 million and went on to gross some $89 million (in 1974 dollars).

Billy Jack Goes to Washington (1977, Billy Jack Enterprises)

Billy Jack Goes to Washington was the fourth film focusing on the character of Billy Jack. The film was directed by Tom Laughlin and produced by Frank Capra, Jr. (son of director Frank Capra, who had directed *Mr. Smith Goes to Washington*). The screenplay was written by Laughlin and his wife and co-star, Delores Taylor. Once again, Elmer Bernstein wrote the music score.

The narrative focuses on the selection of the next U.S. senator after one of the state senators suddenly dies. Billy Jack is appointed to serve out the remainder of the term. The senior senator of the state, Joseph Paine (E.G. Marshall), attempts stop Billy's efforts to defeat a nuclear power plant proposal (which will curb nuclear power). Billy wishes instead to build a national youth camp in the site suggested for the power plant.

Paine succeeds in preventing Billy from being in the Senate on the day of the vote. In the meantime, other powerful men from his state promise to destroy him politically. Billy is approached by several men who intend to bribe and manipulate him. However, Billy rebuffs their offers.

Billy finally becomes aware of his predicament and the attempts to remove him from the Senate. On the Senate floor, he is prevented from speaking against the building of the nuclear plant. Paine then attempts to expel him from the Senate. Billy's assistant quits his position after a lobbyist is murdered for taking the wrong side. At the last moment, Billy is able to conduct a filibuster. He exposes Paine and all the efforts of political chicanery and corruption. He collapses at the end, but not before Paine finally admits the whole rotten campaign to destroy Billy and build the nuclear plant.

This film is almost a scene-by-scene remake of Frank Capra's *Mr. Smith Goes to Washington* (1939, Columbia). Although the time frame is updated, the film has moments of good drama and convincing passion. Laughlin had originally asked James Stewart to play his famous role once again, but he declined. Astutely, Laughlin surrounded himself with a group of seasoned and accomplished actors, including Pat O'Brien, E.G. Marshall, and Sam Wanamaker. Delores Taylor returned in the role of Jean. Newcomer Lucie Arnaz played the role of Saunders, Billy's senatorial secretary (the original role had been played by Jean Arthur), and Suzanne Somers appeared as the character named Sue.

Billy Jack Goes to Washington did not have a wide release and was shown only in limited screenings. Laughlin blamed poor distribution, as well as people in the federal government. In an interview that Laughlin gave on CNN's *Showbiz Tonight* (1995), he stated, "At a private screening, Senator Vance Hartke got up because it was how the Senate was bought out by the nuclear industry. He got up and charged at me.... And he said, 'You'll never get this released. This house you have, everything you have will be destroyed.'"[12] Senator Vance Hartke (1919–1977) was a Democratic U.S. senator from 1959 to 1977 from the state of Indiana.[13]

Although the first three Billy Jack films had been hugely successful, *Billy Jack Goes to Washington* was a commercial failure.

The Return of Billy Jack (1986)

This film was produced and written by Tom Laughlin; he planned to appear in the film alongside his wife, Delores Taylor. It was shot in New York City and Toronto, Canada. The narrative involved Billy Jack leading a campaign against child pornographers in New York City. However, the film was not completed.

During the making of *The Return of Billy Jack* in Toronto, Tom Laughlin experienced a head injury from a defective breakaway bottle. By the time Laughlin had recovered from his injury, the funds for the film had been exhausted. As a consequence, filming never resumed. Laughlin sought to sell the project to a major studio but was unsuccessful. It is said that only one hour of actual film was completed when the shooting abruptly ended.

Laughlin tried for years to complete the project. However, his efforts never came to fruition. Another failed effort was to the idea of making Billy Jack into a television series. In one interview in 2005, Tom Laughlin stated bitterly, but resolutely, "We the people have no representation of any kind.... It's now the multinationals. They've taken over. It's no different than the 70's, but it's gotten worse. And if you use words like 'impeachment' or 'fascist' you're a nut on a soapbox."[14]

The commercial failure of the fourth film and the inability to complete the fifth installment brought an end to the Billy Jack films. Sometimes a film's success is due to the fact that it is in sync with audiences. *The Return of Billy Jack* was started nine years after 1977's *The Trial of Billy Jack*. By this time, film audiences had moved on. Laughlin's initial audience had been teenagers and college students. By 1986, this audience had become adults (now mostly married with children and careers), and their tastes had changed.

The failure of the Billy Jack franchise may also be due to the fact that the decade of 1970s had ushered in a different type of film. In addition, while Tom Laughlin's fierce independence had brought him success as a filmmaker, he had also alienated powerful individuals in the film industry, as well as many of the money men who financed the major studios. His left-leaning politics also played a role in his outcast status. The history of Hollywood is littered with the tattered careers of visionary filmmakers whose politics and/or independence led to their destruction and downfall.

However, for the purpose of this book, the Billy Jack films depicted the first Hollywood Native American film hero (albeit one of mixed blood) in the modern era. Authentic native heroes like Geronimo, Cochise, Sitting Bull, and others had been stereotyped or denigrated by Hollywood. The Billy Jack films came in the midst of the Native American movement of the 1970s, which brought a renaissance of native pride, activism, and militancy. For Native American film audiences, the character of Billy Jack resonated with a sense of agency in an art form that had denigrated their history and culture for almost one hundred years.

Ulzana's Raid (1972, Universal)

Robert Aldrich's *Ulzana's Raid* has been seen by some as a metaphor for the Vietnam War. However, for this writer, the film condenses the history of the numerous Indian Wars that were waged by the United States against indigenous peoples.

Ulzana's Raid was directed by Robert Aldrich, a maverick and fiercely independent filmmaker. It was his third collaboration with film star Burt Lancaster. Aldrich had previously directed Lancaster in *Vera Cruz* (1954, United Artists) and *Apache* (1955, United Artists), in which Lancaster had played Massai, the legendary Apache warrior. The screenplay was written by Alan Sharp, based on a real raid led by the enigmatic warrior Ulzana, a Chiricahua Apache.

The narrative is set in Arizona in the 1880s at the end of the Indian Wars. After years of U.S. punitive expeditions, the Apaches endure a forced relocation to the unhospitable San Carlos Indian Reservation. Ulzana and a group of native warriors break out and proceed to raid Euro-American settlers for more than one thousand miles. The eastern-educated and inexperienced Lieutenant Garnett DeBuin (Bruce Davison) is ordered to locate and either kill or apprehend Ulzana and his men. He is accompanied by an aging and burned-out army scout named Macintosh (Burt Lancaster), who cautions DeBuin about his gross assumptions about the Apaches and the terrain. Macintosh, in turn, is assisted by an Apache scout Ke-Ni-Tay (Jorge Luke), who is scorned for scouting against his own people.

The miscalculations and blunders of DeBuin result in the near annihilation of his men, including Ke-Ni-Tay. Macintosh is also mortally wounded, but not before DeBuin finally understands the hard-won wisdom the older scout imparted about fighting the Apaches.

In the film, Ulzana is surrounded and commits a warrior's suicide. However, the end of the real Ulzana remains unknown. Some say that he died in battle, while others think that he and some of his warriors escaped to the rugged Sierra Madre Mountains in Mexico.

Ulzana's Raid demolishes all the ethnocentric mythology of the winning of the West by Euro-Americans. This narrative harshly documents the poverty and oppression of the Apaches at the infamous San Carlos Reservation, as well as the brutality of both the U.S. Army punitive expedition and the tenacious Apache resistance. It is a war without quarter. There is no romanticism—just the U.S. military strategies and countermoves by the Apaches.

The character of Ulzana, as portrayed in the film, has the moral high ground, which is to resist and fight the occupiers of his native land. Ke-Ni-Tay represents the native scouts who decide (whether by choice or coercion) to serve with the U.S. Army against their own people. He struggles with his conscience and endures the insults of his white comrades-in-arms. However, he understands that his predicament can never change.

Both director Robert Aldrich and screenwriter Alan Sharp intended this film to serve as a metaphor for the Vietnam War. That it may well be. However, the undeniable fact is that all U.S. wars against people of color in the Third World had their genesis in the "Indian Wars" that began in the colonial era.

Mexican Native American actor Jorge Luke (1942–2012) was cast as Ke-Ni-Tay, and Joaquín Martínez played Ulzana. George Águilar, Marvin Fragua (b. 1952, in the Jemez Pueblo, New Mexico), Larry Colelay, Henry Camargo, Gil Escandón, Frank González, and Wallace Sinyella were cast as native braves. Chinese American actress Aimee Eccles was cast as Macintosh's native woman.

Ulzana's Raid uses the Apache language in the scenes featuring the Apache characters. The film was shot on location in the Coronado National Forest, Nogales, Sonoita, Huachuca Mountains, Whetstone Mountains, Harshaw, and Tucson in Arizona, as well as Las Vegas and Valley of Fire State Park in Nevada.

The film received enthusiastic reviews. Ben Sachs, in a retrospective review that appeared in the *Chicago Reader* (August 1, 2013), wrote, "As the *Raid* unfolds, the cavalry's mission seems increasingly futile. It becomes clear that the military leaders have no practical solution to the Apache problem other than killing as many of them as possible—and that their course of action has triggered a seemingly endless cycle of violence."[15]

Many critics ranked *Ulzana's Raid* as one of the top ten films of 1972. However, this film (unlike Aldrich's first two films with Lancaster) was not a commercial success. It made only $10.1 million in adjusted domestic gross.[16]

A Man Called Horse (1970, Cinema Center Films)

A Man Called Horse was one of several films in the 1970s that attempted to depict Native American culture in a more sympathetic light. This film ushered in two others with the same character: *The Return of a Man Called Horse* (1976, United Artists) and *Triumphs of a Man Called Horse* (1983). The first film was directed by Eliot Silverstein and written by Jack DeWitt. The screenplay was based on the novel *A Man Called Horse* by Dorothy M. Johnson.

The narrative is set in the early 1880s in the Dakotas. It involves the adventures of English Lord John Morgan (Richard Harris), who is part of a hunting expedition. He is captured by the Lakota people, and his assistants are killed. However, Morgan is saved by Yellow Hand (Manu Tupou) and taken to a Lakota village. There he undergoes mockery and ridicule by the villagers.

After this ordeal, Morgan wins the respect of the Lakota for his endurance. He meets and falls in love with Running Deer (Corrina Tsopei). He also meets Batise (Jean Gascon), who is half Lakota and half French. Batise becomes his interpreter and friend. Eventually, Morgan becomes a leader within the tribe.

The film received mixed reviews. The *New York Times* (April 30, 1970) wrote, "The film ... places great stress on authenticity of ritual and language ('80 per cent of the dialogue,' says my production notes, 'is Sioux, and in old Sioux at that!').... The Indian princess who wins Lord John's hand is played by Corrina Tsopei, a Miss Greece who went on to oblivion as Miss Universe of 1964. In details, '*A Man Called Horse*' is conventionally absurd."[17]

The filmmakers strove for authenticity in their depiction of the native rituals, and the film had a Native American consultant. However, the ritual depicted in the film called the Sun Vow Initiation does not exist in the Lakota culture: it was an invention of the screenwriter. In this scene, actor Richard Harris was doubled by the legendary stuntman Yakima Canutt (whose name came from the town in which he was born in the state of Washington). The scene was purposely exploitive and made to create controversy.

In the Lakota culture, there is a ritual known as the Sun Dance. It is often misunderstood by white culture. In biblical times, the Hebrew people would make an offering of a goat or sheep to God, which reflected the believer's gratitude. In Lakota culture, however, a person would offer his own blood to the Great Creator. In his autobiography, Russell Means wrote about his Sun Dance experience as follows: "On the fourth day, we pierced.... It was painful, but as mothers say when describing childbirth, it was a pure and holy moment, more spiritually fulfilling than agonizing. It helped me feel what all men owe women, the hallowed relationship between female and male."[18]

Another major critique of *A Man Called Horse* is that the filmmakers continued the old practice of casting non-native people in the key native roles. The highly respected Australian actress Judith Anderson was cast in the role of Buffalo Cow Head; Corrine Tsopei (Miss Greece and Miss Universe of 1964) played Running Deer; Manu Tupou (who was actually from Fiji) played Yellow Hand; Michael Baseleon (a Euro-American) played Longfoot; Tamara Garina (Russian) played Elk Woman; and Iron Eyes Cody, of Sicilian ancestry, played the medicine man. This casting undermined the efforts to achieve authenticity and the intent of the film.

Native American actors in *A Man Called Horse* included Eddie Little Sky (Black Eagle), Mexican Native American Lina Marin (Thorn Rose), Jackson Tail (Medicine Man), and Manuel Padilla, Jr. (Leaping Buck). Other native actors cast in the film were Samuel White Horse, Justin Thin Elk, Frank Rabbit, Jr., Vince St. Cyr, Sonny Skyhawk, and Edward Eagle, among others. Clyde Dollar was listed as the film's historian and technical advisor.

The film was shot in Arizona and South Dakota, as well as Sonora and Chihuahua in Mexico.

The Return of a Man Called Horse (1976, United Artists)

The sequel to *A Man Called Horse* was released six years after the original feature film. *The Return of a Man Called Horse* was directed by Irvin Kershner and written by Dorothy Johnson and Jack DeWitt.

The threadbare narrative is set in the 1840s and focuses on the forced removal of the Lakota people by unscrupulous trappers (with U.S. government connivance). When John Morgan (Richard Harris), who now lives in England as the 8th Earl of Kildare, is informed of these events, he leaves both his fiancée and his landed estate and returns to help his Lakota friends. Morgan proposes a plan for them to overpower the thieves and return the land to the Lakota. Once again, the narrative features the condescending theme of a white hero teaching the Lakota how to fight and leading them to victory.

The Return of a Man Called Horse was well-meaning film, but it is merely ordinary in quality. This film repeats the Sun Vow Initiation, resulting in exploitive and unnecessary scenes. And as before, the casting of white actors in the key native roles undermines any attempt to bring authenticity to the film. Gale Sondergaard was cast as the ancient Elk Woman and is completely unconvincing. Mexican and U.S. Native American actors were cast in several roles: Jorge Luke (Running Bear), Enrique Lucero (Raven), Regina Herrera (Lame Wolf), and Eugenia Dolores (Brown Dove), among others.

The reviews for the film were generally negative. Roger Ebert, writing in the *Chicago Sun-Times* (August 19, 1976), noted, "There are four main movements in the plot: Return, Reconciliation, Revenge and Rebirth. If this seems a little thin for a two-hour movie, believe me, it is, even with all the portentous music trying to make it seem momentous."[19]

The film was shot on location in England and in South Dakota.

Triumphs of a Man Called Horse (1983, Jensen Farley Pictures)

Seven years after the release of *The Return of a Man Called Horse*, the third installment, *Triumphs of a Man Called Horse*, was released. Richard Harris appeared in a cameo as the title character. However, it was clear that the makers of the third film had nothing to add to the narrative, and the result was mediocre at best.

This film received mostly negative reviews. *TV Guide* wrote, "This rip-off sequel to *A Man Called Horse* (1970) and *The Return of a Man Called Horse* (1976) cashes in on the popularity of its predecessors. Richard Harris appears briefly as the 'Man Called Horse,' an aging Englishman who has headed a Sioux tribe for 30 years while raising his son, Koda.... The film is anything but a triumph."[20]

The Master Gunfighter (1975, Warner Bros.)

The Master Gunfighter is a western that focuses on the annihilation of the Chumash Native Americans of California. It was directed by Frank Laughlin, the son of Tom Laughlin and Delores Taylor, and co-written by Tom Laughlin and Harold Lapland. (Laughlin was then riding high with the success of the Billy Jack films.) The story and screenplay were based on the Japanese film *Goyokin* (1969), which had been written by Kei Tasaka and Hideo Gosha. The film was produced by Phillip L. Parslow and narrated by Burgess Meredith.

The narrative is set in 1856, near Santa Bárbara, California, in the aftermath of the Mexican-American War (1848–1848). After the U.S. takeover of the Southwest, thousands of Euro-American settlers rushed into California to seize control of the land. A group of wealthy Mexican landowners led by Paulo Santiago (Ron O'Neil) decides to detour a shipment of U.S.-acquired gold that was found in the California Gold Rush. The Mexican landowners, suffering from the theft of their land and high taxation, intend to plunder the gold. In order to deceive the authorities, they decide to blame and massacre Chumash Native Americans.

Finley (Tom Laughlin), Paulo's estranged brother-in-law, who was adopted by a Mexican family, becomes aware of the plot and attempts to save his own family and the Chumash. Finley is a master gunfighter and master swordsman. However, he fails in his

9. The American Indian Movement and the Reel Invisibility (1970–1979)

efforts and goes into exile to Mexico. Finley returns three years later in order to prevent another massacre of the Chumash. In the process of carrying out his work, he falls in love with the beautiful señorita Eula (Bárbara Carrera).

The Master Gunfighter received mixed reviews. *Variety* (October 8, 1975) wrote, "A curious blend of amateurish plotting and slick production values, Tom Laughlin's *The Master Gunfighter* also presents an ambiguous moral attitude toward the old West. The oater, attractively lensed in northern California locations, alternates sermonizing with gunfights and sword fights."[21]

The film was strikingly shot (by cinematographer Jack A. Marta) in northern California. It includes elements from the spaghetti westerns, such as their amoral characters (as well as their penchant for gratuitous violence), and from the Asian martial arts films of the early 1970s. The film also featured elements of Marlon Brando's *One-Eyed Jacks* (1961, Columbia), a cult western that was shot on the northern California coast and also depicted the duplicity and betrayal of friendship.

The Master Gunfighter focused on the rarely documented aftermath of the Mexican-American War and its harsh treatment of Mexicans and Native Americans. In the DVD extra features, Tom Laughlin commented that one of the unique aspects about *The Master Gunfighter* was that it covered the three layers of political conquest and its aftereffects in California: the Spanish mistreatment of native peoples; the plight of the mestizo Mexican/native peoples during 1821–1848; and the U.S. appropriation of the Southwest and its policy of prejudice against Mexican/native peoples.[22]

The Island of Dr. Moreau (1977, American International Pictures), featuring Bárbara Carrera (a Nicaraguan indigenous actress) as Maria, the human hybrid. Carrera had earlier played a prominent role in 1975's *The Master Gunfighter*.

Native American actors in the film included the Nicaraguan-born Bárbara Carrera. She was the daughter of a European father and a mother who was half Native American (probably descended from the Miskito native people). Carrera won a Golden Globe Award for Best Acting Debut in a Motion Picture—Female. Other Native Americans included Carmen Cristina Moreno, Geo Anne Sosa, and others in bit parts and as extras. The film also featured an authentic Chumash drum ritual, never documented previously on film.

The Master Gunfighter was not the great success that the Billy Jack films had been. However, it was a moderate success.

Despite mostly being savaged by critics upon its release, *The Mas-*

ter *Gunfighter* is an evocative, complex, and intriguing western. At the heart of the narrative is Laughlin's passion for the plight of Native Americans. The film was shot in Monterey, Carmel, Big Sur, and La Purisima Mission State Historic Park, Lompoc, in northern California.

Soldier Blue (1970, Avco Embassy Pictures)

One of the most significant films about Native Americans was *Soldier Blue*, which sought to address the long pattern of genocide against native peoples. This film focused on the infamous Sand Creek Massacre that took place on the Eastern Colorado Plains in 1864. There the Colorado militia, led by Colonel John M. Chivington, massacred hundreds of Cheyenne and Arapahos.

The film begins as a U.S. Cavalry detail is accompanying a paymaster. The group includes Cresta Lee (Candice Bergen), who has been recently rescued from the Cheyenne after having been held captive for several years. The military escort is attacked and decimated by a Cheyenne war party. Only Cresta and Private Honus Grant (Peter Strauss) survive; the latter is a naïve and idealistic soldier who refuses to believe Cresta's stories about U.S. Cavalry atrocities like scalping and rape of Native American women. As they make their way back to safety, Cresta attempts to make Grant understand that indigenous people have a legitimate right to defend "their land."

The two travelers encounter Isaac Q. Cumber (Donald Pleasance), who provides them with food. However, Grant discovers that Cumber is running guns to the Cheyenne. Grant burns his wagon and flees with Cresta. As their odyssey progresses, they become intimately involved, but they are unable to reconcile their differences about the Cheyenne. Cresta leaves Grant and returns to Spotted Wolf (Jorge Rivero), to whom she was previously married. However, she finds him with a new wife (Aurora Clavel).

In the meantime, Grant reaches a U.S. Cavalry unit, which is on its way to Sand Creek (where the soldiers plan to slaughter the Cheyenne led by Spotted Wolf). The group is led by the psychotic Colonel Iverson (John Anderson). Spotted Wolf attempts to negotiate a peace with Iverson, carrying a white flag as he approaches. However, his effort to parlay is disregarded, and the army attacks. Spotted Wolf has an opportunity to kill Grant, but hesitates when he sees the collar he had previously given Cresta. Finally, the massacre comes to an end. When Grant finds Cresta cradling a dead native child, she asks him, "You have a prayer? Do you have a poem, soldier blue? Say something pretty."

Iverson makes a speech after the massacre to his troops: "You have made another part of America a decent place for people to live. We have given the Indian a lesson they will never forget." Afterward, Grant and a few other soldiers are dragged off in chains for refusing to partake in atrocities and Cresta departs with the native survivors. The narrator states that on November 29, 1864, at Sand Creek, a unit of the Colorado Cavalry numbering in excess of 700 men massacred more than 500 Native Americans, more than half of whom were women and children. More than 100 scalps were taken, and many bodies were dismembered. There were also numerous reports of native women having been raped.

In an interview with *Films and Filming* (March 1970), director Ralph Nelson stated, "I became attracted to *Soldier Blue* really out of my children's homework. I was going through the history book.... I thought, such a distorted picture of what really happened at that time: we won the West by pure, simple conquest, and that was not indicated at all."²³

Nelson's two previous films—*Requiem for a Heavyweight* (1962, Columbia) and *Lilies of the Field* (1963)—had garnered warm reviews. However, *Soldier Blue* received mixed reviews. *Time* (February 2, 1970) commented, "The greatest violence of *Soldier Blue* is done off-screen—to Director Nelson's image. Five years ago, a righteous Hollywood organization entitled Operation Moral Upgrade awarded him a halo-shaped pin for his work on Lilies of the Field.... However, after the release of Soldier Blue, Nelson received another letter from the group. 'Apparently,' Nelson says, 'Mrs. Van new Kirk, the head of the group, recently saw an article about the film. I got a horrible letter drumming out of the corps. I am no longer an angel. I consider it an honor.'"²⁴

Playboy (November 1970) wrote, "Director Ralph Nelson (*Lilies of the Field*) plainly intends to set America's pioneer history straight while simultaneously noting the atrocities committed by U.S. troops in Vietnam follow a long-established military tradition."²⁵ In a similar vein, *Variety* (August 17, 1970) commented, "It would appear obvious that Nelson is trying to correlate this allegedly historical incident with more current events, as a production footnote quotes him saying the massacre, which occurred in 1864, 'caused a shock comparable to that which has recently followed reports of a massacre by American soldiers at My Lai.'"²⁶

The *Hollywood Reporter* (August 12, 1970) noted, "It is merely the reverse stereotype of a bad Indian–good man mythology, a reversal that other films have accomplished with far less gore and ponderous ironies."²⁷ The *New York Times* (September 20, 1970) likewise wrote, "For an American to see '*Soldier Blue*' is to experience, I imagine, something comparable to what a German, a 'good German' of decent sensitivity, experienced when he witnessed the extermination camps opened after World War II."²⁸

The screenplay of *Soldier Blue* was written by John Gray, based on the novel *Arrow in the Sand* by Theodore V. Olsen. And, contrary to the comments of one reviewer, the song sung by Buffy Sainte-Marie (a Canadian Native American) became a hit single. In fact, *Soldier Blue* was a huge success outside the United States. In England, it was the third-most successful film of the year.

Native Film Stars and Filmmakers

Chief Dan George

Chief Dan George burst into the limelight with a masterful performance in *Little Big Man* and went on to win wide acclaim. He was born Geswanouth Slahoot on July 24, 1899, in Tsleil-Waututh, North Vancouver, British Columbia, Canada. His English name was Dan Slaholt. When he entered a residential school, his name was changed to George.

In his youth and later in his adult life, George worked in a variety of jobs: construction worker, longshoreman, school bus driver, and band chief of the Tsleil-Waututh Nation during the period of 1951–1963 (when they were known as the Burrard Indian Band). He broke into acting at the age of 60 in 1960 in the television series *Cariboo County*, playing the character of Ol Antoine (pronounce "Antwine"). Thereafter, he made his film debut in *Smith!* (1969, Disney).

George came to prominence in his role as the aged chief in the film *Little Big Man* (1970, Cinema Center Films) opposite Dustin Hoffman and Faye Dunaway. For his extraordinary performance, he was nominated for the Academy Award for Best Supporting Actor. He won the New York Film Critics Award, the National Society of Film Critics, and Laurel Award for Best Supporting Actor.

George played prominent supporting roles as a native elder in several more films: *Cancel My Reservation* (1972, Naho Prods.); *Alien Thunder* (1974, Onyx Films); *The Bears and I* (1974, Disney); *Harry and Tonto* (1974, 20th Century–Fox); *The Outlaw Josey Wells* (1976, Warner Bros.); *Shadow of the Hawk* (1976, Columbia); *Americathon* (1979, Lorimar Films); *Spirit of the Wind* (1979, Raven Pictures); and *Nothing Personal* (1980, Famous Players). He also appeared in several television series: *The Beachcombers*; *The Incredible Hunk*; *What Really Happened to the Class of 65?*; *McCloud*; *Kung Fu*; *Marcus Welby, M.D.*; and *Cade's Country*. He co-starred in the television mini-series *Centennial* in 1978 (Universal).

George was active in the Native American community as a spokesman and lecturer about First Nations and non-native people, seeking to foster understanding and respect between the two groups. He was also an accomplished musician and poet. His album *Chief Dan George & Fireweed-In Circle* was released in 1974.

He was made an Officer of Canada in 1971, and a postage stamp of him was issued by the Canada Post Office in 2008 honoring "Canadians in Hollywood."

Chief Dan George died on September 23, 1981, in Vancouver, British Columbia, Canada, at the age of 82.

Shadow of the Hawk (1976, Columbia), with Chief Dan George as the shaman Old Man Hawk.

Stella García

Stella García was a Mexican Native American–origin actress who had a long career in theater, television, and film. She was one of the most promising actresses at the beginning of the 1970s.

She was born Stella Martha Macías on July 6, 1942, in Los Angeles, California. She made her film debut in *The Private Lives of Adam and Eve* in 1960 (Universal). Her subsequent film appearances included *Fun in Acapulco* (1963, Paramount), *Hook, Line, and Sinker* (1969, Columbia), and *Change of Habit* (1969, Universal).

García was then cast by Dennis Hopper, fresh from his triumph in *Easy Rider* (1969), to play María, a Peruvian prostitute, in his directorial debut *The Last Movie* (1971, Universal). Shot in the remote Andes of Perú, *The Last Movie* chronicled the adventure of a

9. The American Indian Movement and the Reel Invisibility (1970–1979) 189

movie stuntman named Kausa (Hopper), who stays on in a film location site after the movie company has moved on and traces the impact of the event upon the nearby Indian village. Among the numerous cameos were Julie Adams, Peter Fonda, Sylvia Miles, Kris Kristofferson, Rod Cameron, Dean Stockwell and directors Samuel Fuller and Henry Jaglom.

The Last Movie would go on to win an award at the Venice Film Festival. In the United States, however, it received mixed reviews and was a commercial failure, though Stella García's performance was uniformly praised. *Variety* (September 7, 1971) wrote, "[The] film suffers from a multiplicity of themes, ideas, and a fragmented style with flash-forwards and intertwined and only suggested plot structure.... Stella García is effective as the native girl. She is not moved by the dead she does not know, while Hopper has an American innocence tempered with violent rage when things go beyond his ken. Their lovemaking scenes are lucid, emotional and sexy."[29]

Impressed with her performance, Universal Studios signed García for a second film. She was cast as the female lead of Helen Sánchez, a Mexican American activist involved in the struggle over dispossessed land in New Mexico during the early 1900s in John Sturges' *Joe Kidd* (1972, Universal). The film starred Clint Eastwood and Robert Duvall. A film of mixed quality and less historical truth, it nevertheless was a commercial hit.

Stella García (center, others unidentified) in *The Last Movie* (1971, Universal).

Reviewers once again noted García's performance. The *Los Angeles Times* (July 19, 1972) remarked, "Stella García stands out as Chama's spirited aide."[30]

In 1996, García had a featured role in John Schlesinger's *Eye for an Eye* with Sally Field and Ed Harris; a year later, she played a businesswoman in *Playing God* (1997). Her television appearances included *Lawmen, Surfside Six, The Great Adventure, The Virginian, Kraft Suspense Theatre, Run for Your Life, Laredo, The Fugitive, The F.B.I., I Spy, The Outsider, Name of the Game, Mod Squad, The Bold Ones: The Lawyers, The Bill Cosby Show, Gunsmoke, The Rookies,* and *Live Shot*.

Stella García died on October 25, 2006, in Los Angeles, California. She was 64 years old.

Michael Horse

Michael Horse is a Native American actor, ledger painter and jeweler. He was born Michael James Heinrich on December 21, 1949, in Los Angeles, California. His mother was Nacie Belle Posten (according to her marriage certificate to George Heinrich, dated July 10, 1953). Horse's father was born in Florida to Austrian parents. Miss Posten was born in 1931; her father, Wilber Posten, hailed from West Virginia, and her mother, Violet Howell, was from Idaho (of Swedish descent). However, Horse insists on his website that he is of Native American descent (Yaqui).

Horse made his film debut in the role of Tonto in *The Legend of the Lone Ranger* in 1981 (Universal). This film failed both at the box office and with critics. However, over time Horse has displayed his versatility in both film and television.

His films include *The Avenging* (1983, First National); *Love at Stake* (1987, Medale); *Buckeye and Blue* (1988); *Deadly Weapon* (1989, Empire Pictures); *House of Cards* (1993, A&M Films); *Lakota Woman: Siege at Wounded Knee* (1994, Turner), a television movie in which he played Russell Means; *500 Nations* (1995, Tig Prods.), voice only; *Navajo Blues* (1996, Just Ducky Prods.); *In the Birdseye* (2002, Alberta Filmworks); *Blue Ground* (1999, AKA Birdseye Prods.); *Skinwalker Ranch* (2013, Deepstudios); and *I Filmed Your Death* (2017, Azbest Films). He has also made numerous television appearances, including *Twin Peaks*; *Sons of Tucson*; *JAG*; *Malcolm in the Middle*; *Roswell*; *Walker, Texas Ranger*; and *North of 60*, among others.

Michael Horse married Sandra Dee Dombrowski in 1993.

Sacheen Littlefeather

Sacheen Littlefeather is best remembered for one solitary act of courage at the Academy Awards ceremony in 1973. It happened while Native Americans were besieged after the Wounded Knee takeover at the Pine Ridge Reservation in South Dakota.

Littlefeather was born Marie Louise Cruz in Salinas, California. On her father's side she was Yaqui, Pueblo, and Apache. On her mother's side she was Dutch, French, and German. Her father was from the White Mountain Apache, as well as the Yaqui tribe of Arizona.

During her study at California State University, Hayward, Littlefeather developed a strong consciousness as a Native American. In 1969, as part of the Indians of All Tribes (IOAT), she took part in the occupation of Alcatraz Island.

Actor Marlon Brando had been a longtime supporter of Native Americans. In his autobiography he wrote, "I don't think anything equals the hypocrisy the United States has exhibited toward Native Americans. Our leaders have called for their annihilation in the name of democracy; in the name of Christianity; in the advancement of civilization; in the name of all the principles we have fought wars to uphold."[31]

On March 27, 1973, the 45th Academy Awards, held at the Dorothy Chandler Pavilion in Los Angeles, was the site of a pivotal moment in awakening the conscience of the nation to the plight of Native Americans. Brando had been nominated for Best Actor for his performance in *The Godfather* (1972, Paramount). He wrote later, "Celebrating an industry that had systematically misrepresented and maligned American Indians for six decades, while at that moment two hundred Indians were under siege at Wounded Knee, was ludicrous ... if I did win an Oscar, I realized it could provide the first opportunity in history for an American Indian."[32]

Brando asked his friend, native actress Sacheen Littlefeather, to go to the ceremony and refuse his Oscar if he won. He also asked her to express his disappointment regarding the portrayal of Native Americans in U.S. films and to acknowledge his support for the activists at Wounded Knee.

When actors Roger Moore and Liv Ullmann read the names of the Best Actor nominees, it was announced that Brando had won the coveted award. Littlefeather then took to the stage dressed in traditional native regalia and politely refused the Oscar on Brando's behalf. It was an epiphany for the nation. Tens of millions watched on television and held their breath as they saw a lone Native American woman on the stage withstand boos from the audience.

Littlefeather was given only sixty seconds to speak—not enough time to read Brando's fifteen-page speech. So, instead, she introduced herself as the president of the National Native American Affirmative Image Committee. Despite being threatened with physical removal, she proceeded to explain the reason for Brando's refusal of the Oscar, especially in light of the "recent happenings at Wounded Knee." After the Academy Awards, she read the entire speech at a press conference. To its credit, the *New York Times* published the full text the next day.

After this incident, Littlefeather was effectively blacklisted in the film industry. Some blamed Marlon Brando for not refusing the Oscar himself, while others simply resented being reminded of the nation's long history of abuse toward native people. Littlefeather received numerous threats, and her friends were visited by the FBI. A vicious rumor also circulated that she was not a real Native American. However, many other people came to her defense. Both César Chávez and Coretta Scott King (Dr. Martin Luther King's widow) expressed their sincere support. To Native Americans, especially to those surrounded at Wounded Knee, it brought inspiration.

Littlefeather continued her acting career, though with limited success. In the Native American community, however, she has been seen as a role model and is highly respected. She has lived in San Francisco for many years and been active as a head woman dancer in many powwows, as well as a health-care educator. In the 1980s, she worked with Mother Teresa in caring for AIDS patients in hospice care. Inspired by her work, she became a founding board member of the American Indian AIDS Institute, based in San Francisco.

Littlefeather has helped produce numerous Native American films, and in 1984 she shared an Emmy for her work on PBS's *Dance in America: A Song for Dead Warriors*. She is a co-coordinator of the Kateri Prayer Circle of San Francisco.

Her films include *The Laughing Policeman* (1973, 20th Century–Fox), uncredited;

Counselor at Crime (1973, Star Films, S.A.); *Freebie and the Bean* (1974, Warner Bros.), uncredited; *The Trial of Billy Jack* (1974, Taylor-Laughlin Prods.); *Winterhawk* (1975, Pierce Film Prods.); *Johnny Firecloud* (1975, 20th Century–Fox); *Shoot the Sun Down* (1981, Leeds Prods.); *Brando* (2008, Grief Co.); *Reel Injun* (2009, NFB), a documentary; and *Sacheen* (2018, One Bowl Prods.).

Sacheen Littlefeather is now an elder in the Native American community. Though she is presently battling cancer, she remains committed to the betterment of her people.

Dawn Little Sky

Dawn Little Sky was a Native American actress in the 1970s. She was born Dawn Gates on April 17, 1930, at the Standing Rock Reservation in North Dakota. She later married native actor Eddie Little Sky, and they had five children.

She made her film debut in *Ten Who Dared* in 1960 (Disney). Her films include *Cimarron* (1960, MGM); *Gypsy* (1962, Warner Bros.); *Duel at Diablo* (1966, United Artists); *Journey through Rosebud* (1972, GSF); *Billy Two Hats* (1974); *The Apple Dumpling Gang* (1975); *Lakota Woman: Siege at Wounded Knee* (1994), a television film; and *Neither Wolf Nor Dog* (2016, Roaring Fire Films). Her television credits include *Gunsmoke*; *Have Gun, Will Travel*; *Rawhide*; and *Daniel Boone*, among others.

Eddie Little Sky

One of the most visible Native American performers in the 1970s was Eddie Little Sky. He was born Edsel Wallace on August 15, 1926, in the Pine Ridge Indian Reservation, South Dakota. His parents, Wallace Little, Sr., and Wileminna Colhoff, were both Oglala Lakota. He was educated at the Holy Rosary Indian Mission School.

During World War II, Little Sky served in the U.S. Navy in the Pacific theater. After his war service, he worked as a bareback and rodeo rider. He also married Dawn Gates, a Native American actress. Their union produced five children.

Little Sky made his film debut in *Revolt at Fort Laramie* in 1956 (United Artists), playing Red Cloud. He was encouraged by Audie Murphy, the World War II decorated hero-turned-actor, to pursue a career in films. Thereafter, his films included *Westward Ho the Wagons!* (1957, Disney); *Big-Foot Wallace* (1957, Four Star Prods.), an early television film; *Tomahawk Trail* (1957, United Artists); *Apache Warrior* (1957, 20th Century–Fox); *Gun Fever* (1958, United Artists); *Missouri Traveler* (1958, Buena Vista); *The Light in the Forest* (1958, Disney); *Tonka* (1958, Disney); *Escort West* (1959, United Artists); *The FBI Story* (1959, Warner Bros.); *Heller in Pink Tights* (1960, Paramount); *Hell for Leather* (1960, United Artists) with Audie Murphy; *Buffalo Gun* (1961, Globe Pictures); *Sergeants Three* (1962, United Artists); *Seven Faces of Dr. Lao* (1964, MGM); *The Hallelujah Trail* (1965, United Artists); *Duel at Diablo* (1966, United Artists); *The Professionals* (1966, Columbia); *The Last Challenge* (1967, MGM); *Paint Your Wagon* (1969, Paramount); *Soldier Blue* (1970, Embassy Pictures); *Breakheart Pass* (1975, United Artists); and *The Car* (1977, Universal). He earned wide acclaim for playing Black Eagle in *A Man Called Horse* in 1970 (Cinema Center Films).

Little Sky made numerous appearances in many television shows, including *Broken Arrow*; *Sugarfoot*; *Bronco*; *The Rifleman*; *Bat Masterson*; *The Rebel*; *Maverick*; *Have Gun,*

Will Travel; *Cheyenne*; *Mr. Ed*; *Wagon Train*; *My Favorite Martian*; *Daniel Boone*; *The High Chaparral*; and *The Wild, Wild West*, among others.

He retired from acting in the late 1970s and later worked as the director of the Oglala Tribal Parks Recreation Authority.

Eddie Little Sky died of lung cancer on September 5, 1997, in Pennington, South Dakota. He was buried at the Little Flat Family cemetery at Oglala, South Dakota. He was 71 years of age.

A Martínez

A Martínez is a Mexican Native American–origin actor who has had a long, versatile and highly respected career in theater, television, and film. He was born Adolpho Laurue Martínez, III, on September 27, 1948, in Glendale, California, to parents of Mexican descent. Martínez is also one-eighth Cherokee. He was the oldest of six children.

Martínez attended Verdugo Hills High School in Tujunga and then studied acting at UCLA. He did Equity Theatre and was a member of various rock and roll bands. While at UCLA, he played rhythm guitar and sang for a band called Tujunga.

He was discovered by Fred Roos in a UCLA drama class. Roos was casting American International Pictures' *The Young Animals* (1968) and gave Martínez a featured role. Ironically, the film depicted a Mexican American student strike in which most of the leads were non–Latino. Martínez scored thereafter in an episode of *Ironsides*, playing a militant Brown Beret sympathetically. He was typecast in several roles as an assassin, pimp and pusher. He would recall about these television roles, "I was the young Chicano street guy who was in the wrong place at the wrong time, and seemed to be guilty of a crime.... But somehow the hero of the show could sense that I had a good heart, then prove that it was circumstantial evidence and I was innocent. Occasionally I played the friend of the important guy."[33]

Martínez also appeared in two television mini-series: first was the role of the peasant Tranquilino in NBC's popular mini-series *Centennial* (1979, Universal), opposite Bárbara Carrera, Richard Chamberlain, and Silvana Gallardo, and then a featured role in *Roughnecks* (1980, Rattlesnake Prod.). Martínez would later remark, "I have a different kind of attitude than many Chicano actors. I don't reject the image. I'd like to play other parts. But this is how I got started and I'm certainly not ashamed to play these roles."[34]

His best role was that of Juan Seguín, a Mexican leader in San Antonio, Texas, who became embroiled on both sides of the Texas revolt of 1836 in Jesus Treviño's excellent *Seguín* (1981, PBS). Martínez later commented, "It was a watershed event for me. I got to actually demonstrate my heart for the first time. And it also was a chance to come together with the community of Chicano actors who normally don't get to work together."[35] It was a time fondly remembered by the actor: "I could not complain in those days, because I was working and I felt that my ethnicity was a benefit to me. I came on the scene with some training at the right time."[36]

In 1972, he played Cimarron, a substantial role in Mark Rydell's *The Cowboys* (Warner Bros.), starring John Wayne, a western telling how a group of green youths complete a cattle drive after the cattle boss (Wayne) is killed. Martinez referred to this film as "the linchpin of my career as an actor.... All of a sudden, I had a profile and I started to get offers for work. It really gave me momentum for the first time."[37] However, after this important role, Martínez's film career stagnated in rather undistinguished films. He had a featured role in the crime-drama *The Take* (1974, Columbia) with Eddie Albert and Billy Dee Williams; played Aquino in the film adaptation of Graham Greene's *The Honorable Consul*, retitled as the film *Beyond the Limit* (1983, Paramount) with Michael Caine, Richard Gere and newcomer Elipidia Carrillo; and played a supporting role in the routine *Walking the Edge* (1985, Cinema Overseas) with Nancy Kwan and Robert Forster. He also played the Native American lead Buddy Red Bow in the evocative *Powwow Highway* (1989, Handmade Films), a film that has since acquired deserved cult status among Native Americans. Martínez likewise played the supporting role of Garcia in the misfire *She-Devil* (1989, Orion) with Meryl Streep and Silvia Miles.

He has co-starred in numerous television films: *Hunters Are for Killing*; *Mallory: Circumstantial Evidence*; *Probe*; *The Abduction of Saint Anne*; *Death Among Friends*; and *Exo-Man*, among others. He also played the lead as a cop tracking down the Hillside Strangler in NBC's *Search for the Night Stalker* (1989). Martínez commented, "There just aren't enough Latin roles to go around. You never get the chance to do the lead, and each one becomes so important. I've never been frustrated with the roles I've played, but like every other actor in town, you'd like to be doing great roles in film."[38]

Martínez established himself in the role of agent-turned-detective Cruz Castillo, one of a handful of Latino roles in daytime soap operas, in NBC's *Santa Bárbara* in 1984. The show lasted eight seasons and then went into syndication in more than forty countries. For this role, Martínez won the IMAGEN award and an Emmy in 1990 after being nominated several times, the first Latino to do so. About the role, he commented, "If you're going to do something like this, it's wonderful to play someone that you can respect."[39]

In 1992, he left *Santa Bárbara* to play a regular on *L.A. Law* for two seasons. In relation to Latino roles, he remarked, "I've played peasants and professionals. Occasionally you hear someone say that it is considered hot to be Hispanic now. I think that's a relative judgment, but it's certainly better now than it's ever been."[40]

During 1994, Martínez played the lead role of Tiburcio Vásquez in Luis Valdez's *Bandido* at the Los Angeles Mark Taper Forum. Martínez commented about the legendary character, "Tiburcio continues to be a heroic figure in the Mexican community.... When I was younger; I thought that he was like Robin Hood; he was robber at a time when his culture was being trashed, and you could sort of understand it. And having it now, it becomes apparent to me that he was caught in a situation from which there was no graceful escape."[41] Director Valdez had nothing but praise for Martínez's performance: "I was very happy he accepted the role and equally happy to see he was a good an actor onstage as in film and TV, which isn't always the case. Some actors can't make the leap. But he trained in theater. It is a natural return for him."[42] Unfortunately, the play did not meet with either the critical or the commercial success expected.

Martínez has continued to star in television films, among them *She Led Two Lives* (1994, NBC) with Connie Selleca and *Deconstructing Sarah* (1994, USA Network) with Rachel Ticotin. He played the lead in the excellent HBO film about the plight of contemporary Native Americans titled *Grand Avenue* (1996) and co-starred in the sci-fi film *The Terminators* (2009).

He has been married since 1982 to Leslie Bryans. The union has produced two children. About marriage, he stated, "Having a family brings out a more efficient side of you."[43]

Martínez has had a long and successful career on television. He played Agent Nick

"Coop" Cooper in *Profiler* (1996–1997); Ray DiLucca in *General Hospital* (2001–2001); Michael Olivas in *For the People* (2002–2003); Assemblyman Danilo Zamesca in *CSI: Crime Scene Investigation* (2005–2007); Ray Montez in *One Life to Live* (2008–2009); Ramon Montgomery in *The Bold and the Beautiful* (2011–2012); Jacob Nighthorse in *Longmire* (2012–2017); and Eduardo Hernandez in *Days of Our Lives* (2015–2017).

His most recent films include *California Solo* (2012, Cherry Sky Films); *California Winter* (2012, Intrinsic Value Films); *Jimmy P.* (2013, Orange Studio); *Curse of Chucky* (2013, Universal); *The Embryo* (2016, Enembryo); *Symphoria* (2017); *Second Sunrise* (2017); and *On Painted Wings* (2017, Rudderpost Films).

Richard Romancito

Richard Romancito was a film actor for a brief time in the 1970s and then transitioned into writing. He was born in Albuquerque, New Mexico, on September 26, 1953. He is of Taos and Zuni Pueblo ancestry.

He made his film debut in *Showdown* (1973, Universal) opposite Dean Martin and Rock Hudson, playing a Native American tracker. He had a significant role in the film *Rooster Cogburn* in (1975, Universal) opposite John Wayne and Katherine Hepburn, in which he played the native youth Wolf (Lobo) who accompanies the pair in hunting down the outlaws who murdered several people in the Christian mission.

In 1977, Romancito had a leading role in the "ABC Weekend Special" series segment *Tales of the Nunundaga,* in which he played Black Eagle. His last film role was in *Nightwing* (1979, Polyc International).

Soon thereafter, Romancito left the acting field and transitioned into writing and screenwriting. He moved to the Taos Pueblo and became employed by the *Taos News*. In that capacity, he received several awards for both photojournalism and writing. In 2006, he won the Governor's Cup Short Screenplay Award for his adaptation of *Benito's Gift*, based on his own short story. He subsequently directed a short film based on his screenplay.

He presently is the editor of the *Taos News* entertainment and arts section magazine titled *Tempo*. He also works for the newspaper's website.

Will Sampson

Along with Chief Dan George, Sampson become one of the best-known Native American performers of the 1970s. His acting skill and quiet dignity in *One Flew Over the Cuckoo's Nest* brought him overnight fame and acclaim.

He was born Will (Sonny) Sampson on September 27, 1933, in Okmulgee, Oklahoma. He was a full-blooded Muscogee (Creek). His parents were William "Will" Sampson and Mabel Sampson.

Sampson made a living in rodeos (often bronco busting) for some twenty years. While making his rounds in the rodeo circuit, actor-producer Michael Douglas and producer Saul Zaentz spotted the imposing 6'7" figure when they were casting the native role of Chief Bromden for *One Flew Over the Cuckoo's Nest*. After an interview, Sampson was given the role of lifetime, though he had never acted in his life before.

Sampson's quiet dignity and reserve in *One Flew Over the Cuckoo's Nest* in 1975 (United Artists) opposite Jack Nicholson earned wide praise. Other notable roles followed:

One Flew Over the Cuckoo's Nest (1975, United Artists), with Jack Nicholson as Randel McMurphy and Will Sampson as "Chief" Bromden.

Ten Bears in *The Outlaw Josey Wales* (1976, Warner Bros.) with Clint Eastwood and Crazy Horse in *The White Buffalo* (1977, United Artists) with Charles Bronson. His other films included *Crazy Mama* (1975, New World Pictures); *Buffalo Bill and the Indians, or Sitting Bull's History Lesson* (1976, United Artists); *Orca* (1977, Paramount); *Cowboysan* (1978, AFI), a short film; *Fish Hawk* (1979, CFDC); *Insignificance* (1985, Palace Pictures); *Poltergeist II: The Other Side* (1985, MGM); and *Firewater* (1986, Cannon).

His television appearances included *Vegas$*; *Born to the Wind*; *The Yellow Rose*; *Wildside*; and *Tall Tales & Legends*. His television movies included *Relentless* (1977, CBS); *The Hunted Lady* (1977, NBC); *Standing Tall* (1978, NBC); *Alcatraz: The Whole Shocking Story* (1980, NBC); and *The Gunfighters* (1987, Columbia Tri-Star), which was his last film role. He also appeared in two mini-series: *The Mystic Warrior* (1984) and *Roanoak* (1986).

In addition to his work in film and television, Sampson did theater and was an accomplished painter. His work has been exhibited in the Philbrook Museum of Art and the Gilcrease Museum. During 1983, he both founded and served on the board of directors of the American Indian Registry for the Performing Arts.

Sampson was plagued by the chronic degenerative condition known as scleroderma, which affected his skin, heart, and lungs. After undergoing a lung and heart transplant at the Houston Methodist Hospital in Texas, he passed away on June 3, 1987, of kidney failure. He was 53 years of age.

The Will Sampson Road (east of Highway 75 near Preston, Oklahoma, was named in his memory. It is located in Okmulgee County, where he was born.

10

Dashed Expectations (1980–1989)

The decade of the 1980s was characterized by the disappointed expectations of indigenous people in terms of improved socio-economic status. However, there was an improvement in their depiction in films and the media, though opportunities did not increase as much as had been hoped.

On the world stage, the 1980s began with a series of U.S. interventions in Latin America and the Middle East under the Reagan administration. However, it ended with a historic thaw of United States–Soviet Union relations.

The U.S.–orchestrated boycott of the Moscow Olympics in 1980 sent a message of dissatisfaction with the continued presence of Soviet troops in Afghanistan. After Ronald Reagan became president in 1981, his administration waged an intense (albeit covert) eight-year war against Nicaragua and a counterinsurgency in El Salvador. Reagan capped his gunboat diplomacy with the invasion of tiny Grenada. His policies culminated in the Iran-Contra Scandal, in which arms were sold to Iran in exchange for guns sent to counterrevolutionaries (Contras) fighting the Sandinistas in Nicaragua. In the Middle East, the Palestinian question remained unresolved. At this time, Europe began the process of creating a unified economy, and Japan became the world's third most industrialized power. At the end of the decade, a new Soviet leader, Mikhail Gorbachev, initiated political and economic policies that contributed to fundamental changes in East-West relations.

In the meantime, the United States played host to hundreds of thousands of Central American refugees fleeing civil wars in their homelands, as well as Mexican workers responding to the U.S. economy's insatiable appetite for cheap labor. A pervasive jingoism and xenophobia began to assert itself. In California in 1986, an "English is the Official Language" proposal was passed. It was the beginning of several measures that would be instituted across the nation, aimed primarily against immigrants from Mexico and Central America.

NATIVE AMERICAN FILM IMAGES IN THE 1980s

After the peak of Native American activism in the 1970s, the 1980s became a time of dashed expectations in films and television. The goodwill of the public did not concretely translate into fixed improvement in the lives of indigenous people, whether in real life or *reel* life.

During the 1980s, relatively few Native American appeared in films. The western genre remained the main venue for indigenous performers in both theatrical motion pictures and television films.

Only a few films had a narrative involving Native Americans as a focal point; of these, six were westerns. For example, *The Mountain Men* (1980, Columbia) told the story of two mountain men (Charlton Heston, Brian Keith) and their way of life. The film was effective in capturing the time period of the mid–1800s amid the stunning Wyoming scenery. However, the fact that white performers were cast in the native roles (i.e., Victoria Racina, Stephen Macht, Victor Jory) undermined its authenticity.

Windwalker (1981, Pacific International) had a mostly Native American cast and told an evocative tale of survival in the early 1800s in Utah before the coming of Europeans. *The Legend of Walks Far Woman* (1982, EMI Television) was a television film set in Montana. It focuses on an extraordinary Blackfoot woman (Raquel Welch, née Tejeda) who lives through decades of the U.S. expansion into the Great Plains.

The film *The Border* (1982, Universal) focuses on a burned-out U.S. Border Patrol agent named Charlie Smith (Jack Nicholson), who is tempted to succumb to corruption. Smith develops a romantic relationship with a young Mexican indigenous woman named Maria (Elipidia Carrillo).[1] Vincent Canby, in the *New York Times* (January 29, 1982), wrote, "At night, the Rio Grande, which forms the U.S.–Mexican border at El Paso, teems with poor, desperate, illiterate Mexicans seeking entrance into the land of milk, honey, bigotry, and exploitation."[2]

Running Brave (1983, Buena Vista) chronicled the life of Billy Mills, a Lakota long-distance runner, who unexpectedly won the 10,000-meter gold medal at the 1964 Tokyo Olympics. By contrast, John Boorman's *The Emerald Forrest* (1985, Embassy Pictures) focuses on the disappearance of the son of a Euro-American engineer (Powers Boothe) in the Amazon rainforest and the ramifications of this incident many years later. Gregory Nava's evocative *El Norte* (1984, Cinecom/Island Alive) focuses on the turbulent lives of two Mayan siblings (David Villapando and Zuide Slva Gutierrez) who flee their native Guatemala during the civil war. They travel through Mexico and then enter the United States (as undocumented persons), only to find despair and dislocation.[3]

The documentary *Broken Rainbow* (1985, Earthworks Prods.) was co-directed and co-produced by Maria Florio and Victoria Mudd. It chronicled the federal government's forced relocation of 10,000 Navajos from Black Mesa in Arizona to a desolate desert in the Navajo Reservation in the Four Corners region of Utah, Colorado, Arizona, and New Mexico. This event occurred in the aftermath of the controversial Navajo-Hopi Land Settlement Act of 1974. Most critics of the relocation argued that it was arranged by corporations in order to pillage and plunder the uranium, oil, and other natural resources from the reservation. The documentary depicted the long and heartbreaking history of land grabs, genocide, reservations, and endemic poverty of indigenous people. The film won the Academy Award for Best Feature Documentary for 1985.

It was narrated by actor Martin Sheen; the title song was written by Laura Nyro and the music composed by Paul Apodca, with other music by Fred Myrow and Rick Krizman.

Oliver Stone's *Salvador* (1986, Helmdale) chronicles the civil war in El Salvador and the plight of the native and mestizo-majority victims of the brutal conflict. *Loyalties* (1986, CBC) is set in the isolated Alberta region of Canada and focuses on the reconciliation between a Native American housekeeper (Tantoo Cardinal) and her upper-crust woman employer over a long-ago misunderstanding.

10. Dashed Expectations (1980–1989) 199

The Border (1982, Universal), starring Elipidia Carrillo as Maria, a Mexican indigenous woman, and Jack Nicholson as Charlie Smith, a disillusioned border patrolman.

The western *Young Guns* (1988, 20th Century–Fox) is about the legendary William "Billy the Kid" Bonney and his *pistoleros* during the Lincoln County War during 1877–1878 in New Mexico. It includes one Native American gunman Jose Chavez y Chavez (played by Lou Diamond Phillips). *War Party* (1988, Hemdale) is set in contemporary Montana during a reenactment of the 100th anniversary of a battle between the Blackfoot tribe and the U.S. Cavalry. However, continued racial hatred leads to real violence and bloodshed.

The Mission (1986, Warner Bros.) documents the true story of the Guarani people of South America and the intrusion of the Spanish and Portuguese.

Representative Films

Running Brave (1983, Buena Vista)

Running Brave chronicles the unexpected victory of Native American long-distance runner Billy Mills in the 10,000-meter event at the 1964 Tokyo Olympics. The film was directed by Canadian filmmaker D.S. Everett (Donald Shebib) and written by Shirl Hendryx and Henry Bean, based on the life of Billy Mills.

The narrative focuses on the life of Billy Mills, a member of the Oglala Lakota tribe. He was born Makata Taka Hela ("Love your country") on June 30, 1938, in the Pine Ridge Reservation, South Dakota. He became an orphan at the age of 12. He was a runner and boxer in his adolescence, but he gave up boxing in order to concentrate on running.

Mills attended the University of Kansas on an athletic scholarship. At the university, he became a three-time NCAA All-American cross-country runner, and in 1960, he won the Big Eight cross-country championship. He also competed in track and field; he and his team won the 1959 and 1960 outdoor national championships. Contrary to what some have said, Billy Mills was not an unknown at the 1964 Olympics. Rather, he had a long and impressive history in world-class cross-country and track and field competition.

After graduating with a physical education degree, Mills enlisted in the U.S. Marine Corps. He rose to the rank of first lieutenant in the Marine Corps Reserve at the time of his participation in the 1964 Tokyo Olympics.

At the Olympics, Mills qualified for the 10,000 meters and the marathon. Ten thousand meters equals 6.2137 miles and involves running 25 laps on an Olympic-sized track. The favorite to win the 1964 Olympic race was the legendary Australian Ron Clarke. This event also featured the cream of the world's long-distance runners in what was considered a Golden Age of Distance Runners: Pyotr Bolonikov (Russia), the defending champion; Murray Haldberg (New Zealand), who had won the 5,000-meter event at the 1960 Rome Olympics; Mohammed Gammoudi (Tunisia); Mamo Wolde (Ethiopia); and Kokichi Tsuburaya (Japan). In one of the greatest upsets in Olympic history, Billy Mills passed Clarke and Gammoudi in the last ten yards to win the race. His time was a blistering 28:24.4, some 50 seconds faster than he had ever run, and a new Olympic record. Nobody from the United States had ever won this event before (and none have done so since).

In the marathon, Mills came in 14th (with a time of 2:22:55.4); Clarke took 9th place, while the winner was Abbe Bikila (Ethiopia) with a time of 2:12:11. However, it should be borne in mind that, although there is a general marathon world record (and in direct contrast to the 10,000-meter event), every marathon course is different, with varying inclines and downhills.

Mills later founded the Running Strong for American Indian Youth program, which is dedicated to helping native youth with life's basic needs of food, water, and shelter, in addition to developing self-esteem and self-sufficiency. Mills continues to serve as a spokesman and role model and travels across the nation speaking and inspiring new generations of Native American youth. Mills has been the recipient of many honors and awards, including the Presidential Citizen's Medal, given to him by President Barack Obama.

The film *Running Brave* highlights Mills' performance in the 1964 Tokyo Olympics. He was portrayed on screen by the then very popular Robby Benson (a non-native actor). Mills' coach, Bill Easton, was played by Pat Hingle. The film cast numerous native actors: Graham Greene (Eddie), August Schellenberg (Billy's father), Denis Lacroix (Frank Mills), Tantoo Cardinal (Caroline), and Barbara Blackhorse (Young Catherine), among others. Much of the film was shot on location in the Pine Ridge Reservation.

Running Brave is an inspiring film about a young native man who could have easily been destroyed and overwhelmed by the many adversities that confronted him from a young age. Robby Benson, who plays Billy Mills (apparently chosen for his box-office appeal) brings a genuine sincerity and innocence to his role that is convincing and moving. However, he is even better in meeting the incredible physical demands of the role. He underwent a grueling training regimen to approximate a world-class distance runner, and he captures Mills' unique style of running. The 1964 Tokyo Olympics, the climax of the film, is a truly exciting and breath-taking sequence.

Running Brave is only the second Hollywood film to chronicle the glory of great Native American athletes. Before this film, *Jim Thorpe—All-American* (1952, Warner Bros.) had celebrated Jim Thorpe's Olympic achievements.

The film generally earned positive reviews. Roger Ebert, in the *Chicago Sun-Times* (November 11, 1983), wrote, "A poor kid with a lot of disadvantages sets his sights on the stars, has some important preliminary victories, has a setback, loses heart, almost quits.... Mills is played in the movie by Robby Benson, a sound but sort of unexciting actor who seems to specialize in these sincere roles."[4]

Unfortunately, poor marketing and distribution resulted in *Running Brave* grossing only some $3 million in United States, on an estimated budget of $8 million. However, the film has proven very popular in K–12 schools.

The Mission (1986, Warner Bros.)

The Mission tells the story of the religious intrigues of the Catholic Church and the development of the missions in South America during the 1700s. The film was British production. It was directed by Roland Joffe, an English-French filmmaker who had directed *The Killing Fields* (1984, Warner Bros.) about the Khmer Rouge atrocities in Cambodia in the 1970s. The screenplay was written by English playwright and screenwriter Robert Bolt, who had won two previous Academy Awards for Best Adapted Screenplay for *Doctor Zhivago* (1965, MGM) and *A Man for All Seasons* (1966, Columbia).

The film's narrative focuses on the efforts of Jesuit priest Gabriel (Jeremy Irons) to convert the Guaraní native people living along the Paraguayan and Argentine border. Due to his humility and goodwill, he is able to win them over and build a mission. However, Rodrigo Mendoza, a slaver and mercenary (Robert De Niro), invades the mission area and takes hundreds of native prisoners. Soon thereafter, he learns that his fiancée

Carlota (Cherie Lunghi) is in love with his younger brother Felipe (Aiden Quinn). Angered, he kills his brother in a duel. Mendoza is arrested and charged with murder but is acquitted.

At this point, Mendoza experiences an epiphany and sincerely attempts to make amends for his previous crimes. He seeks out Father Gabriel, who helps him change his violent life. Eventually, Mendoza becomes a Jesuit himself and vows to defend the mission from other slavers. Unfortunately, under the 1750 Treaty of Madrid, the pope transfers the mission land to the Portuguese Crown, which does not protect mission land or the Native Americans. Father Gabriel and Mendoza oppose the ruling and seek to protect the native population. Eventually, a combined force of Spanish and Portuguese soldiers attacks the mission and captures its inhabitants, despite a brave resistance by the indigenous people.

The true events revolved around the implementation of the Treaty of Madrid in 1750 and the resistance by the Guaraní during the Guaraní War (1754–1756). The character of Father Gabriel is based on the Jesuit Roque Gonzalez de Santa Cruz, who is considered a Paraguayan saint. The screenplay was based on the book *The Lost Cities of Paraguay* by Father C.J. McNaspy, S.J., who also served as a consultant during the making of the film.

The stunning cinematography by Chris Menges captured the Guaraní's evocative way of life. The film was shot on location in Brazil, Columbia, Paraguay, and Argentina.

Native American actors and non-actors played the native roles and brought a powerful authenticity to the film. These included Bercelio Moya (Indian Boy), Sigifredo Ismare (Witch Doctor), and Asunción Ontiveros (Indian Chief), among others. The real-life Jesuit Daniel Berrigan (1921–2016) played the role of Father Sebastian. Berrigan was an anti–Vietnam War activist, poet, educator, and lecturer. He became one of the famous Catonsville Nine (Catholic activists who burned draft board files to protest the Vietnam War). Berrigan subsequently spent time in prison for the offense but became an icon to those who championed social justice.

The Mission is a heartbreaking film of hope and expectation, but also one that chronicles the many intrigues of the colonial Catholic Church and European-dominated nation-states of the 1700s in the Americas. It documents the treacherous policies enacted against the native people of the continent. However, it also celebrates the courage of dissident clergy who sided with the native people in their struggle against these intrigues.

The Mission received positive reviews. Sheila Benson, writing in the *Los Angeles Times* (November 14, 1986), stated that "'*The Mission*' is a haunting spectacle, it is serious and in many ways successful."[5] Rita Kampley, in the *Washington Post* (November 14, 1986), noted, "'The Mission' effectively dramatizes yet another chapter in the ruthless European conquest of the Americas. It'll make you hate the whole of western civilization with every fiber of your being."[6] The film won an Academy Award for Best Cinematography for Chris Menges. It also won the Golden Globes for Best Screenplay (Robert Bolt) and Best Original Score (Ennio Morricone). However, the film, which cost an estimated $25.4 million to produce, only made some $17.2 million in gross earnings.

Windwalker (1981, Pacific International Enterprises)

The film *Windwalker* focuses on the Crow and Cheyenne people. It was directed by Keith Merrill and written by Ray Goldrup, based on a novel by Blaine M. Yorgason. This film features the Cheyenne and Crow languages, with subtitles in English.

The film's narrative is set in the late 1790s in Utah. Windwalker (Trevor Howard) is an elder in the Cheyenne tribe. During his youth, his wife Tashina was killed and two of his sons abducted by a Crow hunting party. After years of searching, he dies without finding his missing sons. Following his funeral, Windwalker's remaining son, Smiling Wolf (Nick Ramos), takes his family to rejoin their tribe. On the way, they are attacked by Crow warriors, and Smiling Wolf is severely wounded. The Supreme Being calls upon the spirit of Windwalker and touches him with life again. Windwalker rejoins his family and, using Cheyenne medicine, heals the wounds of his son. Then he leads them to a sacred Cheyenne cave.

Later, Smiling Wolf and his two sons ambush a Crow raiding party, capturing their leader. The captured leader is revealed to be one of Windwalker's abducted sons, who then rejoins the Cheyenne tribe.

At the end of the film, Windwalker approaches his old Crow leader and rival, intending to make peace. However, the latter refuses Windwalker's overtures, resulting in an armed battle. Windwalker's returned son takes the place of his aged father and defeats the old rival. After Windwalker sees that his family is reunited and at peace, he returns to the afterlife, where he is reunited with his wife Tashina.

At the beginning of the film's production, Chief Dan George was initially cast as Windwalker. When George became unavailable, English actor Trevor Howard replaced him. Despite being a great actor, Howard is not completely convincing as the aged Windwalker. However, Nick Ramos is outstanding as Smiling Wolf, as is the late Silvana Gallardo as Little Feather. Non-native actors were cast in two important roles: Serene Hedin played Tashina, and James Remar was the younger version of Windwalker.

This film captures much of the way of life before Europeans came upon the land. It is evocative and beautifully acted, and the narrative is excitingly told. In a refreshing change, there are no white characters.

Windwalker generally received positive reviews. Janet Malsin, in the *New York Times* (March 13, 1981), wrote:

> "*Windwalker*" comes from Pacific International Enterprises, the outfit behind the Wilderness Family movies, which have been wholesome, cheerful, moderately interesting and (for anyone who can tolerate those qualities) not half bad. "*Windwalker*" is more of the same, but it's also a feather in the company's cap, so to speak. It is performed by a mostly Indian cast in the Cheyenne and Crow languages, and takes care not to represent its Indian characters in the ways Hollywood traditionally has…. "*Windwalker*" … is nicely played by Nick Ramos, as the two brothers; James Remar as the young Windwalker, and Trevor Howard as the man in maturity. Mr. Ramos, like most of the cast, is of Indian descent, but why the film makers found it necessary to import Mr. Howard for this project is worthwhile question.[7]

Native American actors in this film included Silvana Gallardo (Little Feather); Nick Ramos (Smiling Wolf); Dusty McCrea (born Ardythe M. Ironwing) (Dancing Moon); Ivan Naranjo (Crooked Leg); and Chief Tug Smith (Tashina's father). The film was shot in Utah.

Native Fxilmmakers and Film Stars

Dusty McCrea

Dusty McCrea was a Native American actress who enjoyed a short film career in the 1980s and 1990s. She made her acting debut in the television series *The Virginian* in

1968, in the episode titled "The Heritage." She also had a supporting role in the film *Windwalker* in 1981.

She was born Ardythe M. Ironwing on July 4, 1940, in South Dakota. She married Jody McCrea (son of the legendary film star Joel McCrea) in 1976, and they remained together until her death.

McCrea died of diabetes on March 31, 1996, in Hondo, New Mexico.

Ivan Naranjo

Ivan Naranjo was a Native American actor of Blackfoot and Southern Ute ancestry. He was born on January 24, 1937, in Colorado.

He worked as a horseback rider in Buffalo Bill's Wild West Show in the Disney Paris theme park in France. He was married twice: first to Kasumi (1958–1972), in a union that produced three children, and then to Kareen (1997–2004).

Naranjo made his acting debut in the television series *Then Came Bronson* in 1970s. Other television appearances included *The High Chaparral*, *Adam-12*, *The Bold Ones: The Lawyers*, *Mission Impossible*, *The Partridge Family*, *Colombo*, *Gunsmoke*, *Kung Fu*, *Cannon*, *Eight Is Enough*, and *Malcolm in the Middle*, among others.

His film credits included *Windwalker* (1981, Pacific Int. Enterp.), *The Man Who Wasn't There* (1983, Paramount), and *Easy Wheels* (1989, New Star Enter.). He also had roles in several television films and mini-series, including *Centennial* (1978–1979, Universal) and *The Trial of Standing Bear* (1988, NETV), among others. He provided the voice for the character of Tonto in the animated television series *The Tarzan/Lone Ranger/Zorro Adventure Hour* in 1980.

Ivan Naranjo died on October 24, 2013, in Thousand Oaks, California.

Nick Ramos

One of the more visible Native American performers of the 1980s was Nick Ramos. He was born Nickolas George Ramus on September 9, 1929, in Seattle, Washington. He belonged to the Blackfoot Native American tribe and grew up in Spokane, Washington.

Ramos became a professional actor with his debut in the television series *The Wide World of Mystery* in 1973. Thereafter, he appeared in numerous other television shows: *Gunsmoke*; *The Chisholms* (mini-series); a recurring role in *Falcon Crest*; *Stingray*; *Northern Exposure*; *MacGyver*; *Walker, Texas Ranger*; *Little House in the Prairie*; and *Dr. Quinn, Medicine Woman*, among others.

He played leading roles in several television films: *I Will Fight No More Forever* (1975, David Wolper Prods.); *Kit Carson and the Mountain Men* (1977, Disney); *Centennial* (1978–1979, Universal), TV mini-series; *Son of Morning Star* (1991, Republic TV), TV mini-series; *The Legend of Walks Far Woman* (1982, EMI); *The Mystic Warrior* (1984, Warner Bros.); *Geronimo* (1993, Turner); and *The Treasure of Painted Forest* (2006, Painted Forest Films). He also appeared in several theatrical films: *Star Trek IV: The Voyage Home* (1986, Paramount); *Windwalker* (1981, Pacific Int. Enterp.); *Invasion U.S.A.* (1985, Cannon Films); and *3 Ninjas Knuckle Up* (1995, TriStar).

He was married to Mary Harriet Howard (1948–1955), and the union produced three children.

Nick Ramos died on May 30, 2007, in Benson, Arizona, at the age of 77.

11

A Quincentennial of Misappropriation (1990–1999)

The year 1992 marked the 500th anniversary of Columbus' fateful voyage, which in its wake brought genocide upon the native peoples of the Americas through disease, slavery, murder, and the appropriation of two continents by the European powers. When the long-anticipated First Continental Meeting of Indigenous Peoples took place in Quito, Ecuador, during the summer of 1990, one Guatemalan Native American delegate noted, "These 500 years have meant nothing but misery and oppression for our people. What have we to celebrate?" The *Los Angeles Times*, reviewing Kirkpatrick Sale's book *The Conquest of Paradise*, wrote, "Columbus's landing and subsequent behavior [served] as the model for later explorers who plundered the New World for gold and set in place a civilization that committed genocide and 'ecocide' against the natives and their environment."[1]

The 1990s brought profound changes to the world at large, politically, economically, and culturally. Beyond the 500th anniversary of the European incursion and the beginning of Native American genocide, this decade marked two other important historical events: the end of the Cold War and the advent of the millennium.

In 1993, a Mexican Native American movement called the Ejercito Zapatista de Liberación Nacional (EZLN), or Zapatista Army of National Liberation, rose up against the Mexican government on January 1, 1994, in the southern state of Chiapas (which had a majority-indigenous population and was one of the poorest regions in the nation). On the date of the uprising, the North American Free Trade Agreement (NAFTA) was supposed to take effect. The rebellion brought worldwide focus on the five centuries of poverty, disease, and marginalization endured by Native Americans. Once again, native issues and faces reminded the world that there were more than 100 million native people in the Americas, and they would not be consigned to oblivion.

After decades of ideological and economic rivalry and the threat of nuclear annihilation, the Cold War came abruptly to an end. The immediate impact of this pivotal event was the demilitarization and improvement of relations between the United States and the former Soviet Union. This development was followed by the collapse of the governments of Eastern Europe and the Soviet-backed Warsaw Pact. The end of the Cold War and nuclear war tension was cause for genuine celebration around the world. However, despite the advent of the globalization of the world economy and the era of post-nation-states, the vast majority of people in the Third World remained trapped in a marginalized and impoverished existence.

In Latin America, the market economy's failure was glaringly obvious from Haiti to Mexico to Brazil. Poverty, illiteracy, malnutrition, unemployment, inflation, and recession ravaged all Latin American nations. The 1990s brought an end to the insurgencies in Nicaragua, El Salvador, and Guatemala (all with Native American–majority populations). Some of the most murderous and predatory military regimes in the Americas, those in Argentina and Chile, were compelled by mass civic resistance and economic downturns to move toward political reconciliation and a democratic process.

Much of the latter part of the decade was focused on the pressing issue of "ethnic cleansing," especially in the former Yugoslavia. However, a form of ethnic cleansing on an even greater scale remained ignored until long after the genocide had taken place. Such was the case in Guatemala, where an armed conflict had been taking place for some thirty-six years. The Truth Commission established under the Guatemala peace accords presented a 3,500-page report on human rights violations documenting that some 200,000 people had been killed. The report determined that 83 percent of the victims had been Mayans. It went on to state that the violence was "fundamentally directed by the state against the excluded, the poor, and above all, the Mayan people, as well against those who fought for justice and greater social equity." According to the *Boston Globe*, "In presenting the report, Christina Tomuschar, the commission's coordinator, delivered a withering critique of the role played by the United States, particularly the CIA and the military, in contributing to the human rights violations detailed in the report."[2]

NATIVE AMERICAN FILM IMAGES IN THE 1990S

The decade of the 1990s marked the quincentennial of the Europeans' appropriation of the Americas. For Native Americans everywhere, it was a time of reflection, mourning, and prayer, as well as a reaffirmation of self-determination.

During the 1990s, the Native American film image was in its most diverse state since the 1910s. Some of the films produced during this period were set in pre–Columbian times, the colonial era and/or the 1800s; several also tackled the issue of modern-day indigenous survival in both the United States and Mexico.

The breakthrough film of this decade was Kevin Costner's *Dances with Wolves* (1990, Orion), which focused on the adventures of a disillusioned Civil War soldier and his contact with the Lakota people of the northern plains. This film was followed by a body of work that pushed the film image of native people in significant new directions. *The Black Robe* (1991, Goldwyn) was set in 1834 New France and depicted the determined efforts by Jesuit priests a to Christianize indigenous people at all costs. *The Dark Wind* (1991, Seven Arts) was a mystery drama based on a novel by Tony Hillerman and set in the Navajo Nation. It focused on two tribal police, Jim Chee (Lou Diamond Phillips) and Fred Ward (Joe Leaperman). This film was directed by documentary filmmaker Errol Morris and produced by Robert Redford. However, it was never released. According to Susan King in the *Los Angeles Times* (April 28, 2015), "The film, said Robert Redford wasn't any good and wasn't released.... 'It was miscast. It was ill-conceived and I didn't think it was the right beginning for the series. It wasn't distributed.'"[3]

The documentary *Incident at Oglala* (1992) was a powerful chronicle of the shootout at Wounded Knee between the FBI and the Lakota, as well as the trial of Leonard Peltier.

Squanto: A Warrior's Tale (1994, Disney) told the story of Squanto (played by Adam Beach), a Patuxete who was kidnapped by the English in the 1700s and taken to England. He managed to escape and return to his people many years later, only to find most of his tribesmen dead and the land devastated. *The Indian in the Cupboard* (1995, Paramount) was a family fantasy in which a little Indian figure comes to life after being locked in a magical cupboard.

The most controversial Native American–themed movie of the decade was the animated feature *Pocahontas* (1995, Disney/Buena Vista), which focused on the famous indigenous maiden of the Powhatan people. According to the romanticized Euro-American story, she fell in love with Englishman Captain John Smith, inspiring her to save him from being killed by her father. However, the real Pocahontas was born Matoaka in 1596. She was kidnapped in 1613 by the English. She was then Christianized and given the name of Rebecca. In 1614, at the age of 17, she married the tobacco planter John Rolfe and bore him a son. She was thereafter taken to England, where she was introduced to high society as "the civilized savage." She died in 1617, at the age of 20 or 21, as a result of one of the diseases brought by Europeans to the Americas (possibly smallpox).

In 1907, Pocahontas became the first Native American ever to be honored by a postage stamp. There have been numerous films, plays, documentaries, books, and songs about her. However, Pocahontas stands as the most famous Native American female victim in U.S. history, exploited for her gender and ethnicity.

The stereotype and mythology about Pocahontas persist in the Euro-American world, regardless of the historical facts. Chief Roy Crazy Horse of the Powhatan Renape Nation stated that the animated film *Pocahontas* "distorts history beyond recognition" and "perpetuates a dishonest and self-serving myth at the expense of the Powhatan Nation."[4] Angela Aleiss, in the *Los Angeles Times* (June 24, 1995), wrote, "Trapped within a patriarchal definition, Hollywood's Indian women are rarely shown as having anything more important in life than their male relationships."[5]

Richard Attenborough's *Grey Owl* (1999) depicted the life of "Grey Owl" Archibald Belaney (1888–1938), an English trapper and later a noted conservationist. In the process, he also appropriated a Native American identity.

Men with Guns (1997, Clear Blue Sky) was set in Mexico (allegedly "somewhere in Latin America") and focused on a dying doctor's search for his medical students in Southern Mexico. There he comes into contact with the harsh realities facing native peoples and their culture. By contrast, *Thunderheart* (1992) featured a mixed-blood FBI agent (Val Kilmer) searching for a native fugitive in the Pine Ridge Reservation in South Dakota and his growing consciousness of the plight of his own people. The film *Maverick* (1994, Warner Bros.), based on the popular television series of the 1950s and 1960s, had a well-developed Native American hero (Grahame Greene) who matches wits with two card-playing gamblers (James Garner, Mel Gibson).

New Native American performers came to prominence in the 1990s and went on to have long and successful careers in film and television. Graham Greene and Wes Studi had significant roles in *Dances with Wolves*, and both earned critical acclaim. Noted Native American activist John Trudell had an important role as a native fugitive in *Thunderheart*. Mexican native Damián Delgado was a standout as the army deserter in *Men with Guns*. The most prominent native female performer was Sheila Tousey, who played the female lead in *Thunderheart*.

Native actors who were active during the 1990s included Evan Adams, Nathanial

Maverick (1994, Warner Bros.), featuring Graham Greene as Chief Joseph (with feathers), a humanized indigenous person with a sense of humor, and Mel Gibson as Bret Maverick, a legendary gambler and womanizer.

Arcand, Rodrigo Puebla, and Carlos Palomino, among others. This decade also introduced the highly acclaimed indigenous director Chris Eyre and poet-turned-screenwriter Sherman Alexie.

Representative Films

Dances with Wolves (1990, Orion)

The modern Native American film image begins with *Dances with Wolves*. The native portrayals in this film were the culmination of more than a century of films and thousands of images that went back and forth regarding whether natives were shown as sympathetic or villains.

The narrative focuses on John Dunbar (Kevin Costner), a Union officer in the Civil War who is asked to choose his own post after an act of heroism and/or madness. He decides to go to the farthest reaches of the frontier because he "wants to see it before it disappears." He is transferred from the Civil War killing fields to the Dakota plains.

Dunbar arrives at a remote outpost that has been assigned to him by an almost insane Major Fambrough (Maury Chaykin) but finds it deserted. However, despite the entreaties of the wagon master Timmons (Robert Pastorelli), he decides to stay at his new post.

In his solitude, Dunbar begins to dance around his fire during the lonely nights, accompanied by a semi-domesticated wolf. The neighboring Lakota observe him and name him "Dances with Wolves." Over time, he gradually earns their trust, and vice versa. Dunbar also meets an emotionally traumatized white woman, Stands with a Fist (Mary McDonald), who becomes his interpreter and subsequently lover. He develops a close friendship with one of the leaders of the native village, Kicking Bird (Graham Greene).

When the U.S. Army returns to the area, Dunbar is mistaken for a deserter. He is rescued from his imprisonment by his Lakota friends and goes to live with them. The prejudice of the whites results once more in war between the Lakota and the U.S. Army, but Dunbar remains loyal to the Lakota. The U.S. policy of forced removals and ethnic cleansing compels the Lakota to move north to Canada. As the group nears the Canadian border, Dunbar realizes that he must break away from his friends, because the army will use his presence to justify its hunt against the Lakota. Dunbar departs from the Lakota into the surrounding forest, leaving deep friendships with the people who sheltered him.

Dances with Wolves marked the directorial debut of Kevin Costner (b. 1955), who was then enjoying enormous popularity after a series of extremely successful films like *The Untouchables* (1987, Paramount), *No Way Out* (1987, Orion), *Bull Durham* (1988, Orion), and *Field of Dreams* (1989, Universal). To his credit, Costner bucked the studio and the money people to make a breakthrough film. In this movie, the native actors speak in the Lakota language, the customs and traditions were depicted faithfully, and native actors were able to finally bring to life fully developed roles that celebrated their humanity, dignity, and culture. The film was shot on location in South Dakota and Wyoming (over some seventeen weeks) and employed thousands of native people both in front of and behind the camera.

Dances with Wolves proved to be an enormous success, both critically and commercially. The film went a long way toward creating a renaissance in Native American culture, traditions, history, and respect. It earned rave reviews. *Variety* (November 1, 1990) commented:

> In his directorial debut, Kevin Costner brings a rare degree of grace and feeling to this elegiac tale of a hero's adventures among the Sioux ... it makes effective drama, and, if interpreted metaphorically, the scene conveys the spirit of rape and plunder that had vanquished the Sioux culture within a mere 13 years of this story's unfolding, according to the screen epilogue.... Its bold use of subtitled Lakota language (the Sioux language) for at least a third of the dialogue, it's clear the filmmakers were proceeding without regard for the rules.... Native American actor Graham Greene (as a holy man Kicking Bear) and Rodney Grant (as the warrior Wind In His Hair) give vivid, transfixing performances, bringing much spirit and skill.[6]

Newsweek (November 19, 1990) remarked on "the movie's ... genuine respect for a culture we destroyed without a second thought.... The large Native American cast—Graham Greene as the wise Kicking Bear, Dunbar's first ally; Rodney A. Grant as ... Wind In His Hair; and Floyd Red Crow Westernman as the old chief ... create noble ... human characters."[7] The *Chicago Sun-Times* (November 9, 1990) likewise noted, "The movie makes amends, of a sort, for hundreds of racist and small-minded Westerns that went before it. By allowing the Sioux to speak their own tongue, by entering their villages and observing their ways, it sees them as people, not as whooping savages in the sights of Army rifle."[8]

Many praised *Dances with Wolves* for its cultural accuracy, the use of the Lakota language, and the Native American cast; however, it is still a film about natives told from

Dances with Wolves (1990, Orion), with Rodney Grant (Wind in His Hair) left, and Graham Greene, (Kicking Bear) right.

one white man's point of view. Its flaws include the portrayal of the Kiowa as savages without context or history. In addition, native languages had been used before. For example, the Náhuatl language had been used in *Captain from Castile* (1947, 20th Century-Fox) and Cheyenne and Crow were used in *Windwalker* (1981).

Some Native American leaders harshly criticized the film, most notably Russell Means. Means would write in his autobiography, "I thought of it as a Lawrence of the Plains, an overblown saga that merely substituted a new cliché for the old, the reverse side of the same racist coin. Most of its Indians were good guys, but they remained simple savages who needed a 'civilized' white messiah."[9]

Dances with Wolves was nominated for twelve Academy Awards, of which it won seven: Best Picture; Best Director (Kevin Costner); Best Writing, Adapted Screenplay (Michael Blake); Best Cinematography (Dean Sempler); Best Film Editing (Neil Travis); Best Music, Original Score (John Barry); and Best Editing (John Williams II, Bill W. Benton, Gregory H. Watkins, Jeffrey Perkins). Graham Greene was nominated for Best Supporting Actor, and Mary McDonnell for Best Supporting Actress. The film won the American Indian Festival Best Picture award and numerous international awards. It grossed $393.2 million in domestic earnings and $901.3 million in world earnings when adjusted for inflation.[10]

In sum, despite its weak points, *Dances with Wolves* is an important film, and it marked a turning point in the evolution of a more positive image of Native Americans in U.S. cinema.

Retorno a Aztlán/Return to Aztlan (1991, Coop. Jose Revueltas)

Retorno a Aztlán is a Mexican film set in the Aztec world just before the arrival the Spaniards in 1516. It was directed and written by Juan Mora Caltett.

Like the earlier *Captain from Castile* (1947, 20th Century–Fox), this film uses the Náhuatl language and was shot on location in Mexico (principally in the state of Hidalgo). In addition, the cast was made up of Mexican Native American actors: Rodrigo Puebla as Moctezuma; Amado Sumaya as Tlacaelel; Rafael Cortes as Ollin; Damián Delgado as Dirty Lad; and Socorro Avelar as Coatlicue I, among many others.

In the film, the Aztec world is plagued by severe droughts. As a consequence, internal strife between warriors and priests breaks out. Emperor Moctezuma (Rodrigo Puebla) orders a group of priests to go to Aztlán (which means "a place in the North" in the Náhuatl language). Aztlán (somewhere in the present U.S. Southwest) was the original homeland of the Mexicas, who later changed their name to Aztecs upon their arrival in central Mexico. Moctezuma hopes that in Aztlán the prayers and offerings to the goddess Cotlicue will bring an end to the droughts and strife.

Retorno a Aztlán was a commercial and critical success. The film's small budget was the object of some critiques because at times the final product had the look of a documentary. However, the film especially resonated with Mexican audiences and their Native American past and present. In 2006, director Juan Mora indicated that producer-director-actor Mel Gibson had copied scenes from *Retorno a Aztlán* in his movie *Apocalypto*.[11]

Retorno a Aztlán is a deeply evocative film about pre–Columbian Mexico, reproducing in exact detail the language, culture, wardrobe, and religion. For a Native American, it is especially moving and powerful, for this film presents the human challenges and predicaments of a people attempting to overcome the challenges of nature. It compels the viewer to wonder and reflect on how the Americas would have been different had the Europeans not invaded.

Retorno a Aztlán was part of the *nuevo cine mexicano*, which began in the 1990s. This period was considered a "rebirth of Mexican cinema" after decades of exploitive and violent *sexicomedias*, *luchador* movies, and simple-minded drug-revenge films (which often went directly to video).[12] The *nuevo cine mexicano* sought to reverse the trend of trashy and mediocre quality in Mexican films. This new cinema focused on the Native American and mestizo national identity, as well as the social issues of poverty, corruption, gender equality, and the rise of the drug cartels. This movement produced movies such as *Like Water for Chocolate* (1992, Miramax), *Y Tu Mamá También* (2001, 20th Century–Fox), *Amores Perros* (2000, Zeta-Alta Vista), and others. It also gave rise to new directors like Alfonso Cuarón and Guillermo Del Toro, who later crossed over into Hollywood films.

Incident at Oglala (1992, Miramax Films)

Incident at Oglala is a documentary that chronicles the well-known events at the Pine Ridge Reservation in 1975. It starts by reviewing the history of unresolved homicides at the Pine Ridge Reservation in South Dakota, primarily stemming from the conflicts between traditional (typically full-blooded native peoples) and nontraditional (often mixed-blood natives) factions in the early 1970s. Due to these conditions, the traditional faction decided to invite the American Indian Movement (AIM) to come to Pine Ridge to help in their struggle.

In 1975, two FBI agents were investigating the theft of a pair of boots allegedly taken by Jimmy Eagle, an AIM supporter. According to the historical record, the agents followed a vehicle into the Jumping Bull entry point in the Pine Ridge Reservation. A shootout subsequently ensued in which the two agents and one Native American were killed.

The film then documents the subsequent trial of Darrell (Dino) Butler and Robert Robideau through both the prosecution and the defense perspectives. Both men were acquitted of the charges. In the aftermath of this trial, Leonard Peltier was extradited from Canada and tried for the deaths of both FBI agents. Peltier was found guilty in a controversial trial in 1977 and given two concurrent life sentences.

This film was directed by Michael Apted, who would later make a theatrical film loosely based on the same events titled *Thunderheart* in 1992 (TriStar). *Incident at Oglala* was narrated by actor-director Robert Redford.

Incident at Oglala was highly praised and proved to be an important record of contemporary Native American history. The *Washington Post* (May 22, 1992) wrote, "It is hard to leave '*Incident at Oglala*' without concluding that Leonard Peltier is innocent of his murder charges. Only willfully partisan will disagree his trial was anything but a government-cooked travesty ... shows the unscrupulous lengths government prosecutors and the FBI went to in order to get their man."[13] Janet Maslin of the *New York Times* (February 15, 2005) likewise wrote, "*Incident at Oglala* achieves what it set out to do, not only in Mr. Peltier's behalf but also in that of his people."[14] Years later, Kenneth Turan, writing in the *Los Angeles Times* (September 6, 2014), called *Incident at Oglala* "an even-handed cry of outrage, a coolly passionate documentary that focuses a piercing ray of light on an American scandal."[15]

The Last of the Mohicans (1992, 20th Century–Fox)

The Last of the Mohicans was based on James Fenimore Cooper's famous novel *The Last of the Mohicans: A Narrative of 1757*. The 1992 film was also based on the 1936 screenplay written by Philip Dunne (see the 1936 version entry for the narrative). The latter film was directed by Michael Mann and produced by Mann and Hunt Lowry, with the rewritten screenplay co-written by Mann and Christopher Crowe. The film was shot on location in the lush Blue Ridge Mountains around Asheville in North Carolina.

The 1992 film received mostly glowing reviews. Rita Kempley, in the *Washington Post* (September 25, 1992), wrote, "'*The Last of the Mohicans*,' a rapturous revision of the schoolroom classic, follows the trail blazed by '*Dances with Wolves*,' and more recently '*Unforgiven*.' ... Credited with the concept of the noble savage, Cooper would scarcely recognize Chingachgook, wonderfully played by American Indian Movement activist leader Russell Means."[16] Roger Ebert, in the *Chicago Sun-Times* (September 25, 1992), noted, "'*The Last of the Mohicans*' is not as authentic and uncompromised as it claims to be—more of a matinee fantasy than it wants to admit—but it is probably more entertaining as a result."[17]

The casting of indigenous actors made a positive difference in the native roles. They included the noted activist Russell Means (Chingachgook), Eric Schweig (Uncas), Wes Studi (Magua), and another noted native activist, Dennis Banks (Ongewasgone). Numerous other native actors were cast in bit roles and as extras. In addition, authentic native languages were used throughout the film.

Despite the film's good intentions, patterns of real-life prejudice against native people continued. In his autobiography, Russell Means noted, "Despite Michael's [Mann] enlightened attitudes, I nevertheless experienced Hollywood bigotry during the production. Some crew people and even actors casually called me and other Indians 'chief' and 'redskins' to our faces! When the weather turned wet, I was laughingly accused of having

The Last of the Mohicans (1992, 20th Century–Fox), starring (from left; Russell Means (Chingachgook), Eric Schweig (Uncas), and Daniel Day-Lewis (Hawkeye; others unidentified).

done a 'rain dance'—a joke."[18] Means also wrote about how acting had changed his life: "The movies offered me something else, too—a better way to get messages about my people to the world. Ours is a celebrity-driven society. If Marlon Brando has something to say, he can always get on television—not because he's smarter than everyone else, but because he's famous."[19]

The Last of the Mohicans was both a critical and a commercial success, grossing $162.2 million domestically when adjusted for inflation.[20] It also won an Academy Award for Best Sound (Mark Smith, Chris Jenkins, Simon Kaye, and Doug Hemphill).

Men with Guns (1998, Clear Blue Sky)

John Sayles' *Men with Guns* is a rare and unique film, one that focuses on the contemporary and continuing marginalization of the indigenous people in Latin America. It tells the story of Humberto Fuentes (Federico Luppi), a wealthy doctor in Mexico City who caters to an upscale clientele. He is a widower whose grown children offer him little empathy. He decides to embark on a journey in order to discover what happened to the young doctors he trained as part of an international health program.

In the impoverished outskirts of the city, Fuentes finds Bravo (Roberto Sosa), who had been his best student and now operates a black market of medicine. He then makes his way to the poorest state of the republic, Chiapas, in search of his other students. Along the way, Fuentes meets Conejo (Dan Rivera González), a young boy who was the product of his mother's rape and who has now been abandoned. It is through Conejo that the doctor becomes aware of the army's murderous campaign of intimidation, torture and murder against the indigenous peoples.

Fuentes and Conejo then run across Domingo (Damián Delgado), an embittered indigenous young man and army deserter who further confirms the army's atrocities. As the three continue their journey, they meet Portillo (Damián Alcazar), a former priest traumatized by his inability to practice what he preached. They are detained by an army barricade and Portillo is taken away, perhaps to be "disappeared." In the camp, they find hundreds of indigenous people who have been forced out of their villages, and Fuentes puts some of his medical skills to use. Leaving the camp, the travelers encounter a young Indian woman named Graciela (Tania Cruz) and make their way to Cerca Del Cielo, a haven for landless indigenous people, high in the mountains, where they hope to find one of Fuentes' former students.

When they arrive at the summit, Fuentes discovers that his student has been killed by the army. Heartbroken and disillusioned from his previous ignorance and his loss of innocence, he states, "It's my legacy." Fuentes' subsequent death makes Domingo finally withdraw from his cynical apathy, and he commits himself to working with the refugees.

John Sayles, an independent director with impeccable progressive credentials from such films as *Matewan* (1987, Cinecom) and *Lone Star* (1996, Columbia), commented about why he made this film, "One of the things the movie is about is about the responsibility to know.... What is your police force doing? What is your government doing? What is your company doing? And not to pretend that you can't know. And there is that point between ignorance and willful ignorance."[21] The film was shot on location in the Mexican states of Vera Cruz, Chiapas and Mexico City; except for a few scenes in English, it was almost entirely in Spanish or in the Mayan dialects of Náhuatl, Tzotzil and Kung. Cast in a small role was David Villapando, who had played the Mayan youth so memorably in Gregory Nava's *El Norte* (1983, Amer. Playhouse).

Men with Guns is a remarkable film in many ways. Using the metaphor of a quest for the meaning of a life lived, the film places the protagonist in a nether world of unexpected challenges and conflicts that adds powerfully to the narrative. The characters are complex, compelling and convincing, and they propel the narrative forward. Lastly, the film presents an evocative look at the contemporary plight of indigenous peoples with sensitivity and depth.

Men with Guns received enthusiastic reviews, although commercially it was restricted to art houses. The *Hollywood Reporter* (September 15, 1997) commented, "This film title refers to the native population's classification of all foreign invaders—from Hernando Cortes's to the current military brigands—as 'men with guns.' They are to be feared and avoided.... The players are well-chosen, especially Luppi as the regal doctor and Damián Delgado as the brutal-and-brutalized soldier."[22] The *New York Times* (March 6, 1998) noted that "this is an allegory about war and responsibility, confronting the burden of history as hauntingly as this director's films so often have.... It is rendered with great vividness by varied and evocative settings, by meticulous attention to detail, and by a large cast of indigenous nonprofessional actors."[23]

The film won the Donostia-San Sebastián International Film Festival for "expressing with sensitivity and efficiency one of the essential problems of our time." It also received the International Catholic Film Association (OCIC) Grand Prix Award, as well as the Solidarity Award for director John Sayles. Other awards for which *Men with Guns* was nominated include the Golden Globe for Best Foreign Language Film and the British Independent Film Awards' Best Foreign Independent Film for 1998.

The unique motion picture soundtrack, with its mix of pre–Columbian indigenous music, hip-hop, and Columbian dance music, won wide praise and was released by Rykodisc during February 24, 1998.

Smoke Signals (1998, Shadow Catcher)

The most celebrated film about Native Americans of the 1990s (aside from *Dances with Wolves*) was *Smoke Signals*. This was the first U.S. film in history to be directed, written, produced, and acted by Native Americans. As such, it provided an insightful Native American perspective about native lives, culture, and issues.

The narrative takes place in the Coeur d'Alene Indian Reservation in Idaho. It focuses on Victor Joseph (Adam Beach), whose parents Arnold (Gary Farmer) and Arlene (Tantoo Cardinal) are lifelong alcoholics. His parents' addiction leads to domestic violence and parental neglect until, eventually, Arnold leaves his family to go live in Arizona.

Victor is befriended by Thomas Builds-the-Fire (Evan Adams), a masterful storyteller, though at times obnoxious. As a child, Thomas was rescued from a house fire by Arnold, although his parents perished in the blaze. Thomas has come to understand and recognize the goodness in Arnold, despite his addiction and poor parenting.

One day Arlene receives a phone call informing her that Arnold has died. Victor and Thomas travel to Arizona to recover his remains. There they meet Arnold's neighbor Suzy Song (Irene Bedard), who came to respect and understand Arnold in a way that his son did not. Victor comes to understand that his father cared for him deeply but was never able to express his love, perhaps due to his frustration with his alcoholism. After Victor and Thomas return home with Arnold's ashes, Victor scatters the ashes into the Spokane River, mourning the father he never truly knew. In that moment he is able to forgive his father and come to terms with his new understanding of his life.

The screenplay was written by Native American Sherman Alexie. The script was based on his book *The Lone Ranger and Tonto Fistfight in Heaven*. This film also marked the directorial debut of Chris Eyre. It featured an almost entirely Native American cast and introduced a trio of young performers: Adam Beach, Evan Adams, and Irene Bedard. The supporting cast was made up of veteran native actors, including Gary Farmer, Tantoo Cardinal, Monica Mojica, Leonard George, and noted activist John Trudell. The film was shot on location at the Coeur d'Alene Indian Reservation.

Director Chris Eyre (left) and writer Sherman Alexie on location for *Smoke Signals* **(1998, Shadow Catcher).**

Irene Bedard and Adam Beach in *Smoke Signals* (1998, Shadow Catcher).

What made *Smoke Signals* unique, in addition to the native cast, screenplay, and director, was the novelty of the story being told from a Native American perspective and within the context of native history and culture. The film presents ordinary native people in the reservation with the typical human concerns of family, friends, social appearances, and worrying about the future. We see the domestic challenges of parents, the yearnings and inquiry of children, and the social fabric of community in a native reservation. Missing are the stereotypes and one-dimensional characters of more than a century of U.S. films. There are no white missionaries, BIA bureaucrats, caricature shamans, or white heroes.

Native American scholar Amanda J. Cobb noted of the film, "Humor is key to *Smoke Signals'* depiction of a uniquely Indian context, and to Eyre and Alexie's effort to break down stereotypes for non-Native audiences.... For Native viewers, Eyre and Alexie use humor the way many Native Americans do—as a way to 'bear witness,' as a survival tool, as show of support."[24]

Smoke Signals was hailed widely for its refreshing take on contemporary native life and characters, as well as using reflection and humor as catharsis. The film received the National Board of Film's "Special Recognition for Excellence in Filmmaking," the American Indian Film Festival's Best Film award, and the Sundance Film Festival's Filmmakers Trophy (Chris Eyre), among many other accolades. As usual, however, the Academy Awards failed to recognize the significant achievement or historic importance of this Native American film.

Film critics generally praised *Smoke Signals*. James Sterngold, writing in the *New York Times* (June 21, 1998), noted, "He [Sherman Alexie] said in an interview recently that one of his primary goals was to take away from so-called white experts the responsibility for describing contemporary Indian culture. His aim, he said, is not to avoid criticism of Indian society but to make sure that it is Indians doing the criticizing and interpreting."[25] Both Alexie and Chris Eyre gave credit to the American Indian Movement and the native activists of the 1970s, who made movies like *Smoke Signals* possible.

Geronimo (1993, Columbia)

The film *Geronimo* focused on the legendary Apache warrior and resistance fighter. There have been numerous Hollywood films about Geronimo, all of which were blatant distortions of the actual events. This contemporary rendition benefited from Native American casting and authentic on-location shooting, but once again history was seen from a white perspective.

Geronimo: An American Legend (1993, Columbia), with Wes Studi (left) as Geronimo and Victor Aaron as Ulzana.

The film was directed by Walter Hill, best known for action films. He wrote the script for Sam Peckinpah's *The Getaway* (1972, First Artists); directed and wrote *Hard Times* (1976, Columbia); and produced *Alien* (1978, 20th Century–Fox). *Geronimo* was written by John Milius and Larry Gross, based on a story by Milius. Milius also specialized on directing and writing action films, having done both for *The Wind and the Lion* (1975, MGM/Columbia).

The film's narrative is a fictionalized account as seen through the eyes of a young second lieutenant named Britton Davis (Matt Damon), who accompanies the U.S. Cavalry during the war against the Apache in the Southwest. After Geronimo (Wes Studi) first decides to settle in the infamous San Carlos Reservation, he undergoes and witnesses the many deprivations against himself and his people: racism, beatings, insufficient food, and constant humiliations. He and other warriors subsequently break out and launch their last campaign against the invading Euro-Americans, both civilian and military.

Another military unit is sent against Geronimo and his men. The new army is led by General Crook (Gene Hackman). He is assisted by Lieutenant Charles B. Gatewood (Jason Patric) and Chief of Scouts Al Sieber (Robert Duvall). At the end of the film, in the fictional rendering of history, Gatewood convinces Geronimo to surrender.

The film, although well meaning, fails to capture even the rudiments of who Geronimo really was or why he fought so fiercely in defense of his people and land. Co-screenwriter John Milius stated, "I like Geronimo just as he was, a human predator.... I love the Apaches and Geronimo was the ultimate Apache. But Geronimo was more than an Apache[;] he was the essence of a misfit rebel and he would never give up. He was a troublemaker and I understand that. Even among his own people he was a trouble maker."[26]

Not surprisingly, *Geronimo*, which was made for an estimated $35 million budget, only made $18 million. The film received mixed critical reviews. Roger Ebert, in the *Chicago Sun-Times* (December 10, 1993), wrote, "But [Euro-]Americans are not quick to describe our treatment of the Indians as genocide, and even a somewhat revisionist film like '*Geronimo*' is careful to describe the conflicts between the U.S. government and Indians 'hostiles' as a war. ...Even this film sees him primarily as an outsider, and takes a white point of view, showing us white men who are better or worse only in relation to their contemporaries."[27] Desson Howe, in the *New York Times* (December 10, 1993), noted, "But '*Geronimo*' still feels like a whitewash—the American equivalent of watching the story of South African warrior Shaka, as told by Boer filmmakers and featuring the willing participation of modern-day Zulus."[28]

Native American actors cast in the film included Wes Studi (Geronimo); Carlos Palomino, the former welterweight boxing champion (Sergeant Turkey); Victor Aaron (Ulzana); Pato Hoffman (Dreamer); Steve Reevis (Chato); Rino Thunder (Old Nana); Stuart Proud Eagle (Sergeant Dutchy); and Jackie Old Cayote (Apache Vision Woman), among others. The film was shot on location in Arizona, Utah, and California.

Thunderheart (1992, TriStar)

The film *Thunderheart* is loosely based on the events leading up to the Wounded Knee incident that took place in 1975. It was directed by Michael Apted, who had recently directed the documentary *Incident at Oglala*, which reviewed the events leading to the death of two FBI agents and a Native American in 1975 at the Pine Ridge Reservation in

South Dakota. *Thunderheart* was co-produced by Robert DeNiro, John Fusco (who wrote the screenplay), and Jane Rosenthal. The film was made using both the Lakota and the English language.

The narrative is set in the 1970s and involves FBI agent Ray Levoi (Val Kilmer), a mixed blood assigned to the Bear Creek Reservation in South Dakota. In the film, there have been numerous unresolved homicides in a struggle between traditional and non-traditional factions, in which the latter holds the power and influence. The Aboriginal Rights Movement (ARM) is now involved in assisting the traditional faction. Levoi is under the command of the legendary FBI agent named Frank "Cooch" Coutelle (Sam Shepard), an arrogant and bigoted man. Coutelle works closely with the traditional faction and its vigilante force headed by Jack Milton (Fred Ward).

Levoi's consciousness is gradually raised as he becomes aware of the deep-rooted racism by whites and the poverty confronting native people. Walter Crow Horse (Graham Greene), a reservation policeman, helps educate Levoi about the powerful economic and political forces that covet the uranium deposits in the reservation. Two other native persons serve to enlighten Levoi: Maggie Eagle Bear (Sheila Tousey), a single mother and native activist, and Grandpa Sam Reaches (Chief Ted Thin Elk), a venerated elder, deeply affect Levoi's misguided mission of counterinsurgency.

The film's locale contributed much to the authenticity of the narrative. *Thunderheart* was shot on location in South Dakota, which included the historic Pine Ridge Reservation, where Wounded Knee (the site of the infamous 1890 massacre) is located. In the film, Pine Ridge is called the Bear Creek Reservation. Another strength of the film was the casting of real Native Americans, many of whom were involved in the Native American civil rights movement. John Trudell, an important leader of this movement, was cast in the role of Jimmy Looks Twice, a fugitive activist. Dennis Banks, a co-founder of the American Indian Movement (AIM), is seen in a bit part during powwow scenes. Chief Ted Thin Elk, a real Lakota elder, played the highly respected Grandpa Sam Reaches.

Reviews were generally positive, and the film was an unexpected commercial success. Janet Maslin, of the *New York Times* (April 3, 1992), noted that the film had a "documentary attentiveness to detail" and highlighted the fact that the "film's outstanding performance comes from Graham Greene, an Oscar nominee for *Dances with Wolves*.... Mr. Greene proves himself a naturally magnetic actor who deserves to be seen in other, varied roles."[29]

NATIVE AMERICAN FILM STARS AND FILMMAKERS

Evan Adams

Evan Adams earned wide acclaim for his portrayal of the young Native American whose incessant storytelling occasionally upsets his friend Victor in *Smoke Signals*. He was born Evan Tiesla Adams on November 15, 1966. He is a Coast Salish from the Sliammon First Nation, near the Powell River, in British Columbia, Canada.

Adams is an accomplished playwright and actor; presently he is also a medical doctor. His plays include *Snapshots*, *Janice's Christmas*, *Dreams of Sheep*, and *Dirty Dog River*. His plays have been produced primarily in Canada, but also abroad. On stage he has had roles in such productions such as *Dry Lips Oughta Move to Kapuskasing* and *Lear*. He appeared in the documentary *Just Watch Me: Trudeau and the 70s Generation*, sharing his experiences as a gay man. He has also appeared extensively on Canadian television in such shows as *Neon River, These Arms of Mine, The L Word, Beachcomers, Da Vinci's City Hall, Beachcombers,* and *Wolf Canyon.*

Adams made his film debut in Michael J.F. Scott's *Lost in the Barrens* in 1990 (Atlantis Films). However, it was his second film that brought him to prominence and wide acclaim. In Chris Eyre's groundbreaking film *Smoke Signals* (1998, Shadow Catcher), he played Thomas Builds-the-Fire, the nonstop storyteller who befriends Victor (Adam Beach). Adams won the Independent Spirit Award for Best Debut Performance for this role. He later starred as a gay Native American in Eyre's *The Business of Fancydancing* (2002, Falls Apart Prods.), for which he won the Los Angeles Outfest award.

Adams, however, had always wanted to be a doctor. He had worked with great dedication with many First Nations health programs in Canada. He was appointed the first Aboriginal health physician advisor of British Columbia on April 2007. Adams commented, "It has been my lifelong dream to work directly with First nations and Aboriginal peoples on our wellness and prosperity at this level. I'm grateful to the Office of the Provincial Health Officer for the past seven and a half years. I feel I'm coming home."[30]

More recently, Adams has returned to acting in supporting roles in several Canadian films, such as *Indian Horse* (2017, Devonshire) and *Kayak to Klemtu* (2018, Goldenberg). He has also appeared in several television shows, including *Artic Air, Raven Tales,* and *The L Word.*

Sherman Alexie

Sherman Alexie is perhaps the best-known and honored contemporary Native American writer. He has written novels, short stories, and poetry. In 1998, he also became a screenwriter with the film *Smoke Signals.*

He was born Sherman Joseph Alexie, Jr., on October 7, 1966, in Spokane, Washington. As a child, he lived in the Spokane Indian Reservation. His father, Sherman Joseph Alexie's, ancestry was from the Coeur d'Alene tribe, while his mother, Lillian Agnes Cox, was of Spokane, Choctaw, Colville, and European ancestry.

Sherman was born with hydrocephalus, a condition manifested through an abnormally large amount of cerebral fluid located in the cranial cavity. At the age of six, he underwent surgery; afterward, doctors warned that he was still in danger of an early death and/or mental disabilities. However, the surgery proved successful, and Sherman did not sustain mental damage, although he did experience side effects from the operation.

He was the victim of much teasing in grammar school due to his abnormally large head. As a result, he did not undergo many of the rites of passage of native male youth. He attended high school outside the reservation, where he excelled academically and in basketball.

Sherman obtained a scholarship in 1985 to Gonzaga University, a Catholic institution, in Spokane, Oregon. However, Sherman began drinking heavily and dropped out of college. Later, he attended Washington State University. There Alex Kuo, a noted Chinese American poet, became his mentor. His support changed Sherman's life for the better. Sherman discovered literature, especially the works of poetry by Native Americans.

In 1992, he published his first collection of poetry: *The Story of Fancydancing: Stories and Poems*. However, it is beyond the scope of this book to provide an in-depth analysis of Sherman's literary works. His collections of poetry include *First Indian on the Moon* (1993), *Water Flowing Home* (1996), and *Face* (2009), among others. His short story collections include *The Lone Ranger and Tonto Fistfight in Heaven* (1993), *Ten Little Indians* (2004), and *War Dances* (2009), among others. His novels include *Reservation Blues* (1995), *Indian Killer* (1996), *The Absolutely True Story of a Part-Time Indian* (2007), *and Flight* (2007), among others.

In 1998, Sherman wrote his first screenplay for the film *Smoke Signals*. He based the story and characters on several of his works. His other screenplays include *The Business of Fancydancing* (2002, Outrider Pictures), which he also directed, and *49?* (2003, Sherman Alexie), a documentary. He was a presenter in the film *The Exiles* (2008) and a participant in *Sonicsgate* (2009, 2R Prods.), a documentary about the departure of the NBA Supersonics from Seattle, Washington.

Sherman has won numerous awards and honors for his writing: the National Endowment for the Arts Poetry Fellowship in 1992; the PEN/Hemingway Award for Best Book of Fiction for the short story collection *The Lone Ranger and Tonto Fistfight in Heaven* in 1993; and the Lila Wallace–*Reader's Digest* Writer Award in 1994, among many others.

In 2005, Sherman became a founding member of the organization Longhouse Media, which promotes native youth cultural expression and social change through filmmaking. He remains actively involved in the Native American and other communities' struggle for social change and social justice. In 2012, Arizona HB 2281 prohibited the teaching of Mexican American and/or Chicano studies in the K–12 school curriculum, as well as the reading of Sherman's own works. In response, he stated, "Let's get one thing out of the way: Mexican immigration is an oxymoron. Mexicans are indigenous. So, in a strange way, I'm pleased that the racist folks of Arizona have officially declared, in banning me alongside Urrea, Baca, and Castillo, that their anti-immigration laws are also anti–Indian."[31]

Sherman is married to Diane Tomhave, a Native American, and they have two children. The couple lives in Seattle, Washington.

Nathaniel Arcand

Nathanial Arcand is a Native American actor best known for the series *North of 60* and also for several films. He was born on November 13, 1971, in Edington, Alberta, Canada. His native ancestry is Nehilawe (Plains Cree) from the Alexander First Nation Reserve.

Arcand made his film debut in *Savage Land* in 1994 (Savage Land Prods.). His films include *Crazy Horse* (1996, Turner), a TV film; *The Legend of Two-Path* (1998, Roanoke); *Chasing Indigo* (1999, Rollerloon); *The Doe Boy* (2000, Vozza Prods.); *Grey Owl* (1999, CPTC); *Skins* (2002, Starz!); *Ginger Snaps Back* (2001, Lions Gate); *Black Cloud* (2004, Old Post Films); *The Unknown* (2005, Diversa Films); *Pathfinder* (2006, 20th Century–Fox); *Two Indians Talking* (2010, Moving Images); *Indian Road Trip* (2017, Whistler Film); *Dead Again in Tombstone* (2017, Universal); and *Hard Powder* (2018, Studio Canal).

His television credits include a co-starring role in the television film *Johnny Tootall* in 2005 and the role of William MacNial in the series *North of 60* (1994–1997). Other television appearances include *Due South, Before We Ruled the Earth, The Lone Ranger, Da Vinci's Inquest, Heartland* (2007–), *Montana Sky, Murdoch Mysteries, Longmire,* and *Artic Air*.

Arcand has branched out into directing and has helmed four projects: *TSTGO Teaser* (2017), a television film; *Coyote's Crazy Smart Science Show* (2017), a television series segment; *Tail Gate Cooking* (2017), a film short; and *Sister, Daughter* (2017), another film short.

He has been honored with several awards for his acting roles, including the American Indian Film Festival Best Supporting Actor award in 2005 for *Johnny Tootall* and the Aboriginal Role Model of Alberta Performing Arts award in 2006, among others.

He is married to Jolene Arcand, and they have two sons, Griffen and Jaden.

Dennis Banks

Dennis Banks was a legendary leader in the Native American community. Over the past decades, he also became a lecturer, writer, and actor.

He was born on April 12, 1937, in the Leech Lake Indian Reservation in Minnesota. He is of the Chippewa tribe. He is also known as Cuning (Naawakamig in the Dounle Vowel System). In the Ojibwe language, this name means "In the center of the universe."

Like many Native Americans, Dennis Banks suffered the hard sting of racial discrimination at an early age, as well as the marginalization of his native culture. He was taken from his parents and educated in an Indian boarding school. As a young adult, he served in the U.S. Air Force and was stationed in Japan.

In 1968, Banks co-founded the American Indian Movement in Minneapolis, Minnesota. Thereafter, he was an active participant in most of the key events of the Native American civil rights movement for the next several decades. He was involved in the occupation of Alcatraz Island (1969–1971), the Trail of Broken Tears march (1972), and the occupation of Wounded Knee at the Pine Ridge Reservation, South Dakota (1973), among many others. He was put on trial numerous times and served time in prison in connection with his political activism.

He made his film debut as Dead Crow Chief in *War Party* (1988, Hemdale). Other film credits include *Thunderheart* (1992, Tristar); Ongewasgone in *The Last of the Mohicans* (1992); *Older than America* (2008, MPI); and *California Indian* (2011, Against the Wind), as himself. He also appeared in *We Shall Remain: Part V, Wounded Knee* (2009, PBS) and was the subject of a documentary titled *A Good Day to Die* (2010, Timecode), in addition to his appearances in numerous other documentaries related to native history.

Banks was married three times and had eleven children, several stepchildren, and one grandchild.

He wrote his autobiography (with Richard Erdos) titled *Ojibwa Warrior: Dennis Banks and the Rise of the American Indian Movement* in 2004. The book was widely praised for its passion, detail, and candor. In the book, Banks wrote about what his generation had achieved: "We were the prophets, the messengers, the first-starters.... Out of AIM came a new breed of writers, poets, artists, actors, and filmmakers.... We have only made a dent in solving our many problems. We leave much to do for the new generations coming up."[32]

For the rest of his life, he continued to be involved in the many issues facing the

Native American community. Dennis Banks died on October 29, 2017, in Rochester, Minnesota, from complications related to pneumonia.

Adam Beach

Adam Beach has been perhaps the most visible Native American male actor in the last two decades. His success must be attributed to his talent and hard work, rather than the Hollywood film industry's level playing field.

He was born on November 11, 1972, in Ashern, Manitoba, Canada. His roots are mostly Saulteaux, with some additional Icelandic ancestry on his great-grandmother's side. During his childhood, he lived with his parents and two siblings on the Lake Manitoba Dog Creek First Nation Reserve by Lake Manitoba. At the age of eight, his mother was killed by a drunk driver; soon thereafter, his father drowned nearby. It was never determined whether his death was a suicide or an accident.

Beach and his two brothers went to live with their grandmother during the ages of eight to twelve; and later, with an aunt and paternal uncle in the Winnipeg area. During his studies at Gordon Bell High School, Beach took a drama class; soon thereafter, he dropped out of school to play the lead role at the Manitoba Theatre for Young People. He went on to perform in local theater. At the age of eighteen, he played a small role in the television series *Lost in the Barrens* and appeared in several television shows, including *Touched by an Angel* and *Walker, Texas Ranger*. These roles led to being cast as a regular in two television shows: *North of 60* and *The Rez*.

In 1995, Adam played the lead in the film *Dance Me Outside* (Cineplex). His big break came in 1998, as one of the two leads in the groundbreaking film *Smoke Signals* (Shadow Catcher).

Since then, he has played several memorable film roles, such as Private Ben Yazzie in *Windtalkers* (2002, MGM) and Ira Hayes in *Flags of Our Fathers* (2006, Warner Bros.). His performance in the latter film earned him wide acclaim. He commented regarding playing the role of Hayes, "Ira Hayes has been played before as this raging alcoholic who is angry at the world.... This isn't a one-dimensional only-Indians-drink-alcohol portrayal. He was a person fighting a battle. Here, we got to see his full range of human qualities. This film gave him his spirit back."[33]

Another important role Beach has played was that of Charles Eastman in *Bury My Heart at Wounded Knee* (2007, HBO). He has also played Officer Jim Chee in three PBS films based on Tony Hillerman novels: *Skinwalkers* (2002), *Coyote Waits* (2003), and *A Thief of Time* (2004).

Beach's body of work includes *Coyote Summer* (1996, Leucadia Film); *Song of Hiawatha* (1997, Hallmark); *Joe Dirt* (2001, Columbia); *Cowboys and Indians: The J.J. Harper Story* (2003, CBS), a Canadian television film; *Johnny Tootall* (2005, Brightlight), a Canadian television film; *Comanche Moon* (2008, CBS), a television mini-series; *Big Love* (2010, California Pictures); *The Stepson* (2010); *Cowboys and Aliens* (2011, Universal); *A Warrior's Heart* (2011); *Ice Soldiers* (2013, Hideaway Pictures); *Suicide Squad* (2016, Atlas Entertainment); *Hostiles* (2017, Grisbi Prods.); *Terra Firma* (2018, Greenwomb); *Hit Man* (2018, Futurist Ape Prods.); *Juanita* (2018, Homegrown Pictures); and *Coyote Howls* (2018, Light Dancing Prods.), among others. His many television appearances include *JAG*; *Law & Order: SVU*; *Hawaii Five-O*; *Arctic Air*; *Revolution*; *Combat Hospital*; *Big Love*; *Moose TV*; *Third Watch*; *Everwood*; *The Dead Zone*; *Higher Ground*; *First Wave*;

Madison; *Touched by an Angel*; *The Rez*; *Walker, Texas Ranger*; *Lonesome Dove*; and *Backstrom*.

He has won several important awards: the 1995 American Indian Festival Best Actor award for *Dance Me Outside*; the 1995 First Americans in the Arts Award for Best Actor for *My Indian Summer*; and the 1998 San Diego World Film Festival Best Actor award for *Smoke Signals*, among others. When asked in an interview what he represented to Native Americans, Beach stated, "I do acknowledge my status as a role model for Native American people. I carry it on my sleeve. I do want a young generation to look at me and say, 'Wow, what did he do to achieve such status in Hollywood?' I want Native children to have success within their hopes and dreams."[34]

He has been married three times and has fathered three children.

Irene Bedard

Irene Bedard is one of many talented Native American actresses who have had several prominent roles. She was born on July 22, 1967, in Anchorage, Alaska. She is of Yupik, Cree, Inupiat, and Metis descent.

Bedard made her film debut in the role of Mary Crow Dog in the television film *Lakota Woman: Siege of Wounded Knee* in 1994 (Turner). She was nominated for a Golden Globe for Best Performance by an Actress in a Mini-Series or Motion Picture Made for Television.

Her films include *Squanto: A Warrior's Tale* (1994, Disney); *Pocahontas* (1995, Disney), as the voice of the title character; *Grand Avenue* (1996, HBO), a TV film; *Crazy Horse* (1996, Turner), a TV film; *Navajo Blues* (1996, Just Ducky Prods.); *True Women* (1997, Hallmark), a TV film; *Song of Hiawatha* (1997, Hallmark); *Naturally Native* (1998, Red-Horse Native Prods.); *Smoke Signals* (1998, Shadow Catcher); *Two for Texas* (1998, TNT), a TV film; *Wildflowers* (1999, Filmsmith Prods.); *Greasewood Flat* (2003, Indican Pictures); *Planting Melvin* (2005, Junebug Films); *Miracle of Sage Creek* (2005, Talmarc); *The New World* (2005, New Line Cinema), as the mother of Pocahontas; *Tortilla Heaven* (2007, Anchor Bay); *Cosmic Radio* (2007, Cosmic Prods.); *The Tree of Life* (2011, Cottonwood Prods.); *Vertical* (2013, Baylor Films); and *The Wind of Heaven* (2018, IM3 Global), among others. Her television credits include *The Marshal*; *The Real Adventures of Jonny Quest*; *Profiler*; *Adventures from the Book of Virtues*; *Roughnecks: The Starship Troopers Chronicles*; *The Outer Limits*; *The Agency*; *Into the West* (mini-series); *The Spectacular Spider-Man*; *Longmire*; and *The Mist*, among others.

In 2004, Bedard won the American Indian L.A. Film and TV Award for Best Lead Actress in a Feature Role for her role in *Greasewood Flat*, and in 2006 she won the NAMIC Vision Award for Best Dramatic Performance for her role in *Into the West* (Dream Works).

Tantoo Cardinal

Tantoo Cardinal began her film career in the 1980s and, through sheer talent and skill, has built a prolific career in film and television. She was born in Anzac, Fort McMurray, Alberta, Canada, on July 20, 1950. Her mother, Julia Cardinal, was of mixed Cree-French origins. She was raised by her maternal grandmother in Anzac, Canada.

Cardinal married Fred Martin right after high school. However, her political activism interfered with their relationship, and they divorced in 1976. They had a son named

Cheyenne. She later married John Lawlor, and the union produced one daughter and a son.

Cardinal came to acting through her political involvement in the early 1970s, the height of the modern era of Native American activism. She made her film debut in 1975 in a film short titled *He Comes without Calling* (NFB). Her films include *Death Hunt* (1981, Golden Harvest); *Running Brave* (1983, Disney); *Dances with Wolves* (1990, Orion); *Black Robe* (1991, Alliance Co.); *Spirit River* (1993, Credo); *Before Columbus* (1993, NFB), narrator; *Legends of the Fall* (1994, TriStar); *500 Nations* (1995, Tig Prods.), voice only; *Smoke Signals* (1998, Shadow Catcher); *In Jest* (1999, Kingdom); *The Lost Child* (2000, Hallmark); *The Thief of Time* (2004, PBS); *Older Than America* (2008, MPI); *Tales of an Urban Indian* (2009, Soapbox Prods.); *Fathers & Sons* (2010, Raven West); *Maina* (2013, Equinoxe); *On the Farm* (2016, Full Flood Prods.); *ARQ* (2016, XYZ Films); and *Ghostkiller* (2018, Stretches Plenty Prods.), among many others. Her television appearances include *Street Legal*; *By Way of the Stars*; *Dr. Quinn, Medicine Woman*; *North of 60*; *Canada: A People's History*; *Myth Quest*; *Tom Stone*; *Windy Acres*; *H20*; *Indian Summer: The Oka Crisis* (mini-series); *Moccasin Flats*; *The Guard*; *The Englishman's Boy*; *Shattered*; *The Killing*; *Blackstone*; and *Frontier*, among others.

Tantoo Cardinal in *Smoke Signals* (1998, Shadow Catcher).

Tantoo Cardinal has been honored with many awards for her acting roles. She was the recipient of the Theatrical Sterling Award for Best Actress for the play *All My Relations* in 1990; an honorary degree from the University of Rochester in 1993; the Order of Canada in 2009 (for her numerous efforts and contribution to the development of Aboriginal performing arts in Canada); and the 2015 ACTRA Award of Excellence. She remains one of the most accomplished Native American actresses of her generation.

Damian Delgado

Damian Delgado was born in Oaxaca, Mexico, of Native American ancestry. He obtained a degree in dramatic literature and theater at Theater University Center in Mexico. In addition to acting, Delgado is a dancer of both ballet and modern dance.

He made his film debut in the notable Mexican film *Retorno a Aztlán/Return to Aztlán* (Jose Revueltas Coop.), which is set in pre–Columbian Mexico. His subsequent films included *Lenta Mirada en torno a la busqueda de seres firmes* (1992, Morelos Cinema.), a film short; *Desiertos mares* (1995, Desiertos Films); and *Corner of Paradise* (1997, Nordisk Films).

In 1997, he played Domingo, the angry Native American army deserter in John Sayles' *Men with Guns* (Clear Blue Sky) and won wide acclaim. He also co-starred in *These Unions Don't Make Me Cry* (1997) and *Un embrujo* (1998, FFCC). In 1998, he played the dual roles of Topilzin and Tomás in *La otra conquista* (Carrasco & Domingo), a film focusing on the Spanish psychological conquest, specifically through the Catholic religion.

Delgado's other films include *La vida loca* (1999, OXXO); *Ravenous* (1999, ETIC Films); *Barrio 13 al desnudo* (2000, Filmoimagen); *Green Stones* (2001, Conaculta); *El camino de las ceibas* (2001, Laceiba Films), a film short; *Alien 51* (2004); *English as a Second Language* (2005, Cima Prods.); *Baja Beach Bums* (2009, Petri Dish Prods.); *Somewhere* (2010, Focus Features); and *Like a Roiling Stone* (2016). His U.S. television credits include *The Shield*, *Medium*, *Law & Order: LA*, *Eagleheart*, and *The Bridge*.

Chris Eyre

Chris Eyre is the best-known Native American film director working in the United States. He was born in 1968 in Portland, Oregon, and is a member of the Arapaho and Cheyenne tribes.

In 1998, Eyre both directed and produced the groundbreaking film *Smoke Signals* (Shadow Catcher). This widely praised film was honored with the Sundance Film Festival Filmmakers Trophy, as well as the Audience Award. In the same year, the American Indian Film Festival gave *Smoke Signals* its Best Film award.

Eyre's next film was *The Doe Boy* in 2001 (Vozza Prods.), in which he only served as producer. That same year, he directed the film short *Things We Do*. His second feature film, *Skins* (2002, Starz!), was set in and shot at the Pine Ridge Reservation in South Dakota. This film focused on the lifelong conflict between two brothers. He also directed *Skinwalkers* (2003, PBS), which was based on a Tony Hillerman novel. The film was set in the Navajo Nation and chronicled the work of two native tribal policemen (Adam Beach and Wes Studi).

In 2003, Eyre directed and produced the film *Edge of America* (Showtime). It told the true story of an African American teacher who was hired at the Three Rivers Reservation, Utah, to teach high school English and went on to coach the girls' basketball team. In 2004, he directed *A Thief of Time* (PBS), another film based on a Tony Hillerman novel and also set in the Navajo Nation. *A Thief of Time* was the 2004 Sundance Film Festival opening night film. In 2006, Eyre was honored with the Directors Guild of America award for Outstanding Directorial Achievement in Children's Program for the film.

In 2005, he directed *A Thousand Roads* for the Smithsonian's National Museum of the American Indian, based in Washington, D.C. This film focused on four Native Americans who live in different places (Perú, New Mexico, Alaska, and New York) and how they struggle to survive in society.

Eyre's other films include *Imprint* (2017, Linn Prods.), producer only; *We Shall Remain* (2008, PBS), director; *Hide Away* (2011, MMC Joule Films), director; and *Dead River* (2018, Badlands Features). His television credits as a director include *Friday Night Lights*, *Native Century*, *Freedom Riders*, and *Law & Order: SVU*.

Recently, Eyre was appointed as the chairperson of the film department at the Santa Fe University of Art and Design. He continues to write scripts and plan film projects.

Gary Farmer

Gary Farmer has been one of the most recognizable native actors in the last thirty years. He has excelled in both drama and comedy. He was born Gary Dale Farmer on June 12, 1953, in Ohsweken, Ontario, into the Cayuga Nation and Wolf Clan of the Haudenosaunee/Iroquois Confederacy. He obtained his education at Syracuse University and Ryerson Polytechnic University. There he majored in film production and photography.

Farmer made his film debut in *Police Academy* (1984, Warner Bros.). His film credits include *The Big Town* (1987, Columbia); *The Believers* (1987, Orion); *Powwow Highway* (1989, Handmade Films); *The Dark Wind* (1991, Corolco Pictures); *Dead Man* (1995); *Smoke Signals* (1998, Shadow Catcher); *Stolen Heart* (1998, Backroad Film); *Touched* (1999, Ranfilm Prods.); *The Score* (2001, Paramount); *Skins* (2002, Starz!); *The Big Empty* (2003, Aura Entertainment); *Coyote Waits* (2003, PBS); *A Thief of Time* (2004, PBS); *One Night with You* (2006, Kite Hill Pictures); *Swing Vote* (2008, Touchstone); *The Timekeeper* (2009, Telefilm Canada); *California Indian* (2011, Against the Wind Prods.); *Path of Souls* (2012, High Definition Pictures); *Winter in the Blood* (2013, Ranchwater Films); *Peter and John* (2015, Kingdom); and *Blood Quantum* (2018, Prospector Films), among others.

On television, Farmer was one of the voices in the groundbreaking Native American documentary *500 Nations* in 1995. He has made many other television appearances: *Miami Vice, China Beach, Street Legal, Forever Knight, The Rez, Promised Land, The Pretender, The West Wing, Dice, Screen Owls, Lord Have Mercy, Mutant X, Indian Summer, Moose, The Border, Easy Money, Blackstone, Longmire, The Red Road, Zoo,* and *Guilt Free Zone,* among others.

In addition, he has a blues band called Gary Farmer and the Troublemakers and has released two CDs: *Love Songs and Other Issues* in 2007 and *Lovesick Blues* in 2009. He has also recorded an audiobook of Louise Erdrich's novel *The Round House.*

Farmer remains active in a host of activities in the Native American communities. He is a highly respected person in his community for his long career and his many accomplishments.

Annie Gallipeau

Annie Gallipeau is a Native American actress who came to prominence in the 1990s. She was born in 1979, in Maniwaki, Quebec, Canada.

Gallipeau is best known as the female lead in *Map of the Human Heart* (1992, AFFC); other appearances include *Grey Owl* (1999, CPTC) and *Maina* (2013, Equinoxe). She also starred in the television series *Shehaweh* during 1992.

Graham Greene

One of the most recognizable and busiest Native American actors since the 1990s has been Graham Greene. He remains versatile, playing both dramatic and comedic roles in film and television.

Greene was born on June 22, 1951, in the Six Nations Reserve, in Ontario, Canada. He is of the Oneida tribe. As a young adult, he lived in Hamilton, Ontario.

Greene had his first taste of show business as an audio technician for a rock band. He would attend and graduate from the Indigenous Theatre's Native Theatre School program in 1974. Thereafter, he performed in professional theater in Toronto, Canada, and later in England.

Greene made his television debut in *The Great Detective* in 1979. His film debut came in *Running Brave* in 1983 (Disney). Subsequent films included *Revolution* (1985, Goldcrest Films) and the native cult film *Powwow Highway* (1989, Handmade Films) with A Martinez and Gary Farmer. He also appeared in the television series *Spirit Bay*. However, it was the role of Kicking Bear in Kevin Costner's *Dances with Wolves* (1990, Orion) that brought Greene widespread acclaim. He was nominated for an Academy Award for Best Supporting Actor for this performance.

Greene followed up with roles in *Where the Spirit Lives* (1989, Amazing Spirit); *Thunderheart* (1992, TriStar); *Benefit of a Doubt* (1993, Benefit Prods.); *Rain Without Thunder* (1992, Taz Pictures); *The Last of His Tribe* (1992, HBO); *Medicine River* (1993, CBS); *Spirit Rider* (1993, Credo), a TV film; *Cooperstown* (1993, Amblin), a TV film; *The Broken Chain* (1993); *Maverick* (1994, Warner Bros.); *Savage Land* (1994, Turner), a TV film; *Die Hard with a Vengeance* (1995, 20th Century–Fox); *The Education of Little Tree* (1997, Allied Films); *Song of Hiawatha* (1997, Telegenic); *Grey Owl* (1999, CPTC); *The Green Mile* (1999, Castle Rock); *Skins* (2002, Starz!); *Into the West* (1995, DreamWorks), a TV film; *Twilight Saga: New Moon* (2009, Temple Hill); and *Tales of an Urban Indian* (2009, Soapbox Prods.), a TV film.

In 1995, Greene was one of the character voices in the groundbreaking documentary produced by Kevin Costner titled *500 Nations* (Tig Prods.). He also played the recurring role of Slick Nikai in *Coyote Waits* (2003) and *The Thief of Time* (2004). Both PBS films were based on the novels of Tony Hillerman.

Graham Greene began his fourth decade in film with such features as *Chasing Shakespeare* (2013); *Atlantic Rim* (2013); *Maina* (2010, Equinoxe); *Winter's Tale* (2014, Village Roadshow); *Wind River* (2017, Acadia); *The Shock* (2017, Summit); *Molly's Game* (2017, STX Prods.); and *Astronaut* (2018, BUCK).

On television, Greene has remained busy in such shows as *Northern Exposure* and *The Red Greene Show*. He also played Mr. Crabby Tree in *The Adventures of Dudley the Dragon*, a show for children; he won the Gemini Award for this role. Greene has made appearances in many other series: *Murder, She Wrote*; *Lonesome Dove*; *HBO First Look*; *The Outer Limits*; *Exhibit A: Secrets of Forensic Science*; *Numb3rs*; and *Longmire*, among others.

Graham Greene has been named a Member of the Order of Canada in 2015. He is highly respected in the Native American community as a role model, artist, and elder. He has been a pioneer for the improvement of native film images, as well as for opportunities within the industry.

Karina Lombard

One of the new native actresses of the 1990s was the former model Karina Lombard. She came to prominence as the wife of Brad Pitt in the popular film *Legends of the Fall* (1994).

Lombard was born on January 21, 1969, in Tahiti, French Polynesia, the youngest of five siblings. Her mother, Nupuree Lightfoot, is a Lakota medicine woman. Her father, Henri Lombard, is of Italian and Swiss-Russian descent. As a child, she lived throughout Europe and attended several boarding schools. She speaks multiple languages: French, German, Spanish, and Italian. At the age of eighteen, she moved to New York City, where she became a model and, later, an actress.

A Calvin Klein photo shoot that featured a Native American theme brought Lombard to prominence. Her photos were featured in *Elle* and *Vogue* magazines. In New York, she did theater at the New York City Gallery, the Lee Strasberg Theatre Institute, the Neighborhood Playhouse, and the Actors Studio.

She made her film debut in *The Island* (1991). She also had small role in *The Doors* (1991) as a Warhol actress. Other films followed, including *Wide Sargosso Sea* (1993) and *The Firm* (1993). Her most important role was the native daughter Isabel Two in the critically and commercially successful film *Legends of the Fall* (1994) opposite Brad Pitt and Anthony Hopkins.

Lombard's other films include *Last Man Standing* (1996); *Kull the Conqueror* (1997); *Expose* (1998); *Guardian* (2001); *Deception* (2003); *Big Kiss* (2004); and *Jo's Boy* (2011). She has also performed on television in *The L Word* and *The 4400*. She had a recurring role on FX's *Rescue Me*, and in 2016 she played the Shawnee chief Nonhelema in the NBC series *Timeless*.

Russell Means

One of the most unlikely Native American film stars of the 1990s was Russell Means, one of the true giants in the struggle for Native American justice, sovereignty, and the return of native land. He was born on November 10, 1939, in Porcupine, on the Pine Ridge Reservation, in South Dakota. His father was Oglala Lakota, and his mother, Yankton Dakota, was from Greenwood, South Dakota. His native name was Wanbli Ohitika, which means "Brave Eagle" in the Lakota language. In 1942, Means' family moved to the San Francisco area, seeking a better life away from the poverty in the reservation.

Means had a turbulent childhood and adolescence. His father was an alcoholic, and Russell himself fell into a spiral of truancy and drugs. He graduated from San Leandro High School and afterward attended four colleges. Later, he lived in several reservations.

In Cleveland, Ohio, Means became politically active with Native American leaders. In 1968, he joined the American Indian Movement (AIM) and became perhaps its best-known leader. In 1970, he became the first AIM national director.

He was an active participant of every key political event involving Native American activism from the 1960s to the present, including the occupation of Alcatraz Island, the Caravan of Broken Treaties, the siege of Wounded Knee, and the takeover of the Bureau of Indian Affairs (BIA) in Washington, D.C., among others. He was subsequently involved numerous political trials.

Means was married five times, four of which ended in divorce. He was married to his fifth wife, Pearl Means, until his death. He had seven children and three adopted children.

In 1992, he made his film debut in the role of Chingachgook in *The Last of the Mohicans* (20th Century–Fox). Many other films followed: *Natural Born Killers* (1994, Warner Bros.); *Wagons East* (1994, Crolco); *Windrunner* (1994, Leuicadia); *Pocahontas* (1995, Disney), voice only; *Buffalo Girls* (1995, CBS); *The Pathfinder* (1996, 20th Century–Fox), a TV film; *Song of Hiawatha* (1996, Hallmark); *Pocahontas II* (1998, Disney), voice only; *Black Cat Run* (1998, Citadel); *Thomas and the Magic Railroad* (2000, Hit Entertainment), voice only; *Wind River* (2001, Mad Dog Prods.); *Cowboy Up* (2001, Code Entertainment); *29 Palms* (2002, Davis Entertainment); *Black Cloud* (2004, High Maintenance); *Unearthed* (2007, Cold Iron Pictures); *Intervention* (2007, Scion Pictures); *Pathfinder* (2007, 20th Century–Fox); *Rez Bomb* (2008, Roaring Fire Films); *Tiger Eyes* (2012, Tashmoo Prods.);

and *Days and Nights* (2014, Arte Cine Prods.). In addition, Means was featured in several documentaries, including *Images of Indians: How Hollywood Stereotyped the Native American* (2003), a television project; *Wounded Heart: Pine Ridge and the Sioux* (2006), narrator; *Questions for Crazy Horse* (2010); and *Conspiracy to Be Free* (2014), made by filmmaker Colter Johnson.

Means made numerous television appearances on shows such as *Walker, Texas Ranger*; *The West*; *Touched by an Angel*; *Remember WENN*; *Duckman*; *The Profiler*; *Nash Bridges*; *Black Cat Run*; *Family Law*; *Curb Your Enthusiasm*; and *Banshee*. He also co-starred in two television mini-series: *We Shall Remain* (2009, PBS) and *Into the West* (2005, DreamWorks).

Russell Means died of esophageal cancer on October 22, 2012. His ashes were scattered in the Black Hills of South Dakota. He was eulogized by the *New York Times*, which said that Means "became as well-known a Native American as Sitting Bull and Geronimo."[35] ABC News commented that Means "spent a lifetime as a modern American Indian warrior … call[ing] national attention to the plight of impoverished tribes and often lamented the waning of Indian culture."[36]

In 1995, Means had written (with Marvin J. Wolf) a highly acclaimed autobiography titled *Where White Men Fear to Tread*. In the book, he wrote, "I hope to be remembered as a fighter and as a patriot who never feared controversy—and not just for Indians. When I fight for my people's rights, when I stand up for our treaties, when I protest government lies and illegal seizures and unlawful acts, I defend Americans, even the bigoted and misguided."[37]

Carlos Palomino

Carlos Palomino was a welterweight boxing champion and currently works as an actor. He was born on August 10, 1949, in San Luis Rio Colorado, Sonora, Mexico, of Yaqui ancestry. He moved to Los Angeles, California, at the age of ten.

Palomino began boxing at an early age. He was an All-U.S. Army boxing champion in 1971 and 1972. He also won the 1972 National AAU Light Welterweight Champion at 137 pounds, where he defeated the future Olympic gold medalist Ray Seales.

When he left the army, Palomino attended Orange Coast College and California State University, Long Beach. He worked as a professional boxer between 1972 and 1979. He became the World Boxing Council welterweight champion between 1976 and 1979. He made a boxing comeback during 1997–1998. His total boxing record stands at 31 wins, 4 losses, and 3 draws. Of these, he won 19 by knockout. In 2004, Palomino was inducted into the International Boxing Hall of Fame.

He began his acting career with an appearance in the television show *Taxi* in 1978. In 1980, Miller Light signed him as a spokesman, and he did numerous television commercials. His other television credits include *NYPD Blue*, *Legmen*, *Highway to Heaven*, *Knight Rider*, *Hill St. Blues*, *Jake and the Fatman*, *Reba*, *Star Trek: Voyager*, and *Diagnosis Murder*, among others.

Palomino made his film debut in *Dance of the Dwarfs* (1983, Panache Inc.). His other film credits include *Stanger's Kiss* (1983, Kill Prods.); *Rampage* (1987, De Laurentiis); *Legal Tender* (1991, Prism Films); *Geronimo: An American Legend* (1993, Columbia); *Price of Glory* (2002, New Line Cinema); *Turn of Faith* (2002, CAOH Prods.); and *Callejero* (2015, Suspect Filmworks).

At present, Palomino divides his time between acting and Tony Baltazar's charity organization which help kids with a strange blood disease.[38]

Eric Schweig

Eric Schweig is perhaps best known for having played Uncas, the son of Chingachgook, in the most recent film version of *The Last of the Mohicans* (1992). Schweig was born on June 19, 1967, in Inuvik, Northeast Territories, Canada. He is of mixed heritage: Chippewa-Inuvialuk-Dene and Portuguese-German.

Schweig was the oldest of seven children, all of whom were forcefully removed and then adopted out of their native culture as part of Canada's attempt to assimilate native peoples. His mother died of alcoholism in 1989, as a consequence of losing her children. Schweig was adopted by a French-German family who spoke English. He lived in Inuvik until the age of six. Thereafter, he lived in Bermuda, and then the family returned to Canada.

Schweig ran away from his adopted family at the age of sixteen and settled in Toronto, Ontario. He made his acting debut in 1985 in the play *The Cradle Will Fall*, produced by the Theatre of Change at the Actors Lab. In 1987, he made his film debut in *The Shaman's Source* (Braves Prods.), which garnered many other film offers.

His most important film role of Uncas came in *The Last of the Mohicans* (1992, 20th Century–Fox). Schweig's other films include *By the Way of the Stars*-mini-series (1992, Iduna Prods.); *The Broken Chain* (1993, Turner); *Squanto: A Warrior's Tale* (1994, Disney); *The Scarlet Letter* (1995, Allied Stars Ltd.); *Tom and Huck* (1995, Disney); *Dead Man's Walk* (1996); *Big Eden* (2000); *Skins* (2002, Starz!); *Cowboys and Indians: The John Joseph Harper Story* (2003); *Missing* (2003); *Into the West* (1995, DreamWorks); *One Dead Indian* (2006, Sienna Films); *Indian Summer: Bury My Heart at Wounded Knee* (2007, HBO); *A Flesh Offering* (2010, High Definition); *Maina* (2013, Equinoxe); and *Poignant* (2016, J&J Prods.), among others.

His television appearances include *Cashing In*, *Blackstone*, *Elementary*, *Supernatural*, and *Longmire*. He also provided his voice for the epic television documentary *500 Nations* (1995, Tig Prods.).

Schweig received the 2000 Grand Jury Award L.A. Outfest for Outstanding Actor for the film *Big Eden*. In 2011, he was nominated for a Leo Award for Best Lead Performance by a Male in a Dramatic Series for his role of Chief Andy Fraser in the television series *Blackstone*.

He has made numerous speaking engagements in Canada and the United States about his struggles with alcohol, drugs, adoption, and the foster care system.

Michael Spears

Michael Spears is a Native American actor who was born on December 28, 1977, in Chamberlain, South Dakota. His parents belong to the Kul Wicasa Oyate Lakota, Lower Brule Tribe of South Dakota. He has six siblings (his younger brother Eddie is also an actor).

Spears made his film debut as the child "Otter" in Kevin Costner's *Dances with Wolves* (1990, Orion). His film credits include *Skins* (2002, Starz!); *Imprint* (2007, Linn Prods.); *Seeing: Homecoming* (2002, Video Verite); *The Legend of Hell's Gate: An American*

Conspiracy (2011, 4Go West Prods.); *Winter in the Blood* (2013, Ranchwater Films); *The Activist* (2014, Media in Sync); and *The Red Man's View* (2019, Biograph Studios).

In addition, Spears has co-starred in several television films and mini-series, including *The Broken Cord* (1992, Universal), a TV film; *The Broken Chain* (1993, TNT), a TV film; and *Into the West* (2005, DreamWorks), a TV mini-series. He has also appeared on the television show *Longmire*.

Wes Studi

Wes Studi has long been one of the most recognizable and respected native actors in the film industry. He has portrayed both villains and heroes in scores of westerns, as well as in contemporary films.

He was born Wesley Study on December 17, 1947, in Nofire Hollow, Oklahoma, a rural area in Tahlequah, which was named after his mother's family. His family was Cherokee. He spoke only Cherokee until elementary school; he attended Chilocco Indian Agricultural School (high school) and graduated in 1964. He majored in dry cleaning. Thereafter, he taught the Cherokee language and co-founded a Cherokee-language newspaper. He also tried ranching after his first marriage ended.

In 1967, Studi was drafted into the U.S. Army and went on to serve some eighteen months in the Vietnam War. This experience politicized him, and he became actively involved in the Native American civil rights movement. In 1973, he was an active participant in the Wounded Knee siege at Pine Ridge, South Dakota.

After his military service, Studi studied acting, after a friend told him that it was a good way to meet women. He made his film debut in *The Trial of Standing Bear* in 1988 (PBS), which he followed up with a small role in the Native American cult film *Powwow Highway* in 1989 (HandMade Films). In 1990, his role as a Pawnee leader in *Dances with Wolves* (Orion) won him wide recognition. His appearance as Magua in *The Last of the Mohicans* (1992, 20th Century–Fox) cemented his standing as charismatic native actor. As of the present, he has some 92 film and television credits.

Studi played the title role in *Geronimo: An American Legend* in 1993 (Columbia) and garnered wide acclaim. Among his more important roles are those of Seth in *Broken Chain* (1993, TNT); Red Cloud in *Crazy Horse* (1997, Turner), a TV film; Wovoka in *Bury My Heart at Wounded Knee* (2007, HBO); and Major Ridge in *Trail of Tears* (2008, PBS). He also played Lieutenant Joe Leaphorn in three PBS films based on the novels of Tony Hillerman: *Skinwalkers* (2002), *Coyote Waits* (2003), and *A Thief of Time* (2004). Other films include *Streets of Laredo* (1995 TV film, De Passe); *Undisputed* (2002, A Band Apart Films); *Into the West* (2005, DreamWorks), a TV mini-series; *The New World* (2005, New Line Cinema); *Comanche Moon* (2008, CBS Paramount); *Older Than America* (2008, MPI); *Avatar* (2008, 20th Century–Fox); *The Only Good Indian* (2009, TLC Films), producer; *Road to Paloma* (2013, Boss Media); *A Million Ways to Die in the West* (2014, Bluegrass Films); and *Hostiles* (2017, Grisbi Prods.), among others.

Studi has also appeared on television in several shows, including *The Flash*; *The Way West* (voice); *Penny Dreadful*; *Adventures from the Book of Virtues*; *Promised Land*; and *The Directors* (as himself). In addition, he was one of the narrators in the epic documentary about Native Americans titled *500 Nations* in 1995.

He received many awards, including the Western Heritage Award (shared with cast and crew) for *Geronimo: An American Legend* in 1994; the Dreamspeakers Film and Festival Career Achievement Award in 1998; and the First American in the Arts Artist of the Decade Award in 2000, among others.

Studi currently lives on a farm near Santa Fe, New Mexico, with his wife Maura Dhu. He has two sons (one from his first marriage) and one daughter. Studi has served as an honorary chair in national endowment campaign of the Indigenous Language Institute. He and his wife also perform in a band called Firecat of Discord.

Michelle Thrush

Michelle Thrush is a Native American actress who was born on February 6, 1967, in Calgary, Alberta, Canada. She made her film debut in *Isaac Littlefeathers* (1984, Lauron Inter.), a Canadian feature. Her other films include *Showdown at Williams Creek* (1991, British Columbia); *Dead Man* (1995, Pandora Film); *Skins* (2002, Starz!); *Jimmy P* (2013, Why Not Prods.); and *The Northlanders* (2016, Manifold Pictures), among others. Her television credits include *This Blows*, *Tin Star*, *Blackstone*, *Hell on Wheels*, *Artic Air*, *Mixed Blessings*, *Moccasin Flats*, and *North of 60*, among others.

Gordon Tootoosis

Gordon Tootoosis began his film career in 1974. His breakout role was that of One Stab, a Cree shaman and loyal friend of Colonel William Ludlow in *Legends of the Fall* (1994, 20th Century-Fox). The film was a huge commercial and critical success. The One Stab character was the omniscient narrator of the lives of Ludlow and his three sons, their trials and tribulations, loves and hates. Tootoosis' role brought an evocative and insightful rendition of them as an indigenous observer, and his quiet dignity and spirituality were the heart and soul of the film.

Upon his death, Tantoo Cardinal, the highly respected actress who was a friend and co-star of Tootoosis, told CBC News of Canada that he "had great respect for his traditions, great respect, and he carried them with him. You know, some people have a sense of soul and spirit as a kind of being separate, but Gordon he breathed these things." "Actor Gordon Tootoosis dies Family." CBC News, July 5, 2011.

He was born on October 25, 1941, in the Pound Maker Reserve, in Saskatchewan, Canada. He was of Stoney and Cree ancestry. He had thirteen siblings and was reared in the Plains Cree tradition until he was taken from his parents and placed in a Catholic residential school as part of Canada's federal policy of assimilating Native Americans.

Tootoosis was a founding member of the board of directors of the Saskatchewan Native Theatre Company. In his life, he served as an activist, social worker, and band chief. He received the Order of Canada in 2004 for his indelible roles in both Canada and the United States and for being an inspiring role model for Aboriginal youth.

He made his film debut in *Alien Thunder* in 1974 (Onyx Films) opposite Chief Dan George. His many films include *Black Robe* (1991, Alliance); *Leaving Normal* (1992, Mirage); *Hawkeye* (1994); *Legends of the Fall* (1994, 20th Century-Fox); *Pocahontas* (1995, Disney), voice only; *Pocahontas: The Legend* (1995, Alliance); *Lone Star* (1996, Columbia); *Crazy Horse* (1996, Turner); *Open Season* (2006, Columbia), voice only; *Bury My Heart at Wounded Knee* (2007, HBO); *Doomsday Prophecy* (2011, Cinetel Prods.); and *Guns, Girls, and Gambling* (2011, Freefall Films). His television appearances include *Red Serge*; *MacGyver*; *Friday the 13th: The Series*; *North of 60*; *Hawkeye*; *The Magnificent Seven*; *Dead Man's Gun*; *Blackstone*; *Wapos Bay: The Series*; and *By Way of the Stars*, among others.

Gary Tootoosis died after being hospitalized for pneumonia in Saskatoon, Canada, on July 15, 2011.

Sheila Tousey

If native roles for men are rare in U.S. films, leading roles for native actresses are even rarer. One of the better-known native leading ladies over the past decades has been Sheila Tousey. She was born June 4, 1960, in Keshena, Wisconsin. She is of Munsee-Stockbridge and Menominee ancestry and grew up in both reservations.

Tousey began dancing at powwows as a small child and then on stage during her time at the University of New Mexico, Albuquerque. She had initially intended to study law but switched to English. From there, she was drawn to theater arts courses and acting. After graduating, she completed the graduate acting program at the Tisch School of the Arts at New York University. Thereafter, she performed both on and off Broadway. In 1994, she directed her first play, *An Evening at the Warbonnet*, at the University of New Mexico.

Tousey made her film debut in Michael Apted's *Thunderheart* (1992, TriStar) opposite Val Kilmer, Sam Shepard, and Graham Greene. Since then, her films have included *Medicine River* (1993, CBC); *Slaughter of the Innocents* (1993, Belbo Films); Sam Shepard's *Silent Tongue* (1994, Belbo Films), a TV film (voiceover narration); and *Lord of Illusions* (1995, Shapiro-Glikenhaus). In 1994, she had one of her best roles as Molly, a native woman with two children who lives in the inner city and tries to hold on to her native culture in the HBO film *Grand Avenue*. Tousey garnered rave reviews for this performance.

Her later films include *Son of Hiawatha* (1997, Telegenic); *Sparkler* (1997, Cliffjack); *Ravenous* (1999, ETIC Films); *Wildflowers* (1999, Filmsmith Prods.); *Backroads* (2000, Off Line); *The Other Side* (2000, Koncept Films), a short film; *Two Grey Hills* (2001, Banana Boat Films); *Christmas in the Clouds* (2001, Random Ventures); and *Johnny Tootall* (2005, Brightlight).

In 2000, she performed in the play *The Late Henry Moss* with renowned playwright and director Sam Shepard. She was the only female actress in the distinguished cast, which included Nick Nolte, Sean Penn, and Woody Harrelson. Shepard commented, "She's a great actress and has a lot of guts. She will hold her own with the guys."[39]

In 2002, Tousey was cast as Emma Leaphorn, the wife of Lieutenant Leaphorn (Wes Studi) in the film *Skinwalkers* (PBS), based on the novel by Tony Hillerman. She reprised this role in two more films based on the writer's novels: *Coyote Waits* (2003, PBS) and *A Thief of Time* (2004, PBS).

Tousey also co-starred in the television two mini-series *Dreamkeeper* (2003) and *Into the West* (2005). Her television appearances include *Law & Order*, *Law & Order: SVU*, *The X-Files*, and *The Jury*.

John Trudell

John Trudell was one of best-known leaders of the cotemporary Native American civil rights movement. In addition to his political activism, he was a poet, writer, musician, and actor. He was born on February 15, 1946, in Omaha, Nebraska. His father was Santee, and his mother's ancestry was Mexican Native American.

Trudell's early life was spent on the Santee Reservation, located in in northern

Nebraska. His childhood normalcy ended when her mother died, when he was six years old. During this time, he developed a lifelong passion for rock and roll, an art form that would become a powerful influence later in his life. He ultimately dropped out of high school and joined the U.S. Navy in 1963, serving until 1967.

In 1968, Trudell married Fenicia "Lou" Ordonez in California. He also attended college for a short period of time, majoring in radio and broadcasting. However, powerful historical events soon overtook his life and that of others in his generation. Trudell joined the Alcatraz Island takeover from November 20, 1969, to June 11, 1970. This action inspired a wave of Native American activism, including the founding of the American Indian Movement. Trudell would go on to participate in most of the pivotal events of the Native American movement for the next several decades; he also served as the chairperson of the American Indian Movement, based in Minneapolis, Minnesota, for most of the 1970s. In the documentary *Trudell* (2005, Appaloosa Pictures), there is a quote from an FBI memo about Trudell: "He is extremely eloquent, therefore extremely dangerous."[40]

Trudell suffered one of his most devastating moments of his life when, on February 12, 1979, his second wife, Tina Manning, along with their three children and his mother-in-law, died under mysterious circumstances in a house fire at the Duck Valley Indian Reservation, Nevada. Trudell always maintained that the tragedy was the result of arson and politically motivated, while others argued that it was an accident.

Trudell published his first book of poetry, *Living in Reality: Songs Called Poems*, in 1982. In the same year, Trudell began recording his poetry. In 1983, he released his debut album, titled *Tribal Voices*, on his very own Peace Company label. It featured both drums and vocals of traditional Native American music. Well-known artists like Jackson Browne, Kris Kristofferson, Indigo Girls, John Fogerty, Willie Nelson, Bonnie Raitt, and Bob Dylan rushed to support his work. Kiowa guitarist Jesse Ed Davis joined Trudell in producing three albums: *AKA Graffiti Man* (1986), *But This Isn't El Salvador* (1987), and *Heart's Jump Bouquet* (1987). Trudell's prolific album output also included *Fables and Other Realities* (1991), *A.K.A. Graffiti Man* (1992), and *Johnny Damas & Me* (1994).

In 1999, Trudell founded a band called Bad Dog and went on tour. The group produced the album *Blue Indians* in 1999. His other albums included *Stickman Poems Lyrics* (1999); *Bona Davis* (2001); *Madness and the Moremes* (2001); *Crazier Than Hell* (2010); *JT-DNA (Descendants Now Ancestor)* (2001), which includes his best-known speeches; *Through the Dust* (2014); and *John Trudell & Bad Dog—Live à Fip* (2005).

A true renaissance man, Trudell also branched out into the acting field. In 1989, he had a small role in *Powwow Highway* (Handmade Films). In 1992, he appeared as indigenous activist in Michael Apted's *Incident at Oglala* (Miramax Films), produced and narrated by Robert Redford, focusing on the 1975 events at Wounded Knee. That same year, Trudell appeared as Jimmy Looks Twice, a Native American activist very much like himself, in Michael Apted's *Thunderheart* (TriStar Pictures), a feature film based loosely on the Wounded Knee events. He also had a small role in the Chris Eyre's groundbreaking *Smoke Signals* (1998, Shadow Catcher), as well as significant roles in *On Deadly Ground* (1995, Warner Bros.) with Steven Seagal and *Dreamkeeper* (Hallmark TV film) as Coyote; he likewise served as narrator for *A Thousand Roads* (2005, NMAI). Filmmaker Heather Rae produced a documentary on John Trudell titled *Trudell* (Appaloosa Films) in 2005.

Trudell had considerable success with his book *Lines from a Mined Mine: The Words of John Trudell* (2008, Appaloosa Pictures), which features some twenty-five years of lyrics, essays, and poems.

Trudell was married twice. He had three children: two girls and one son. He maintained a long-term relationship with Marcheline Bertrand (actress Angelina Jolie's mother), who died of cancer in 2007.

He was profoundly concerned about the increasingly polluted planet. Trudell remarked in the documentary that was made about him, "One earth, one mother, one does not sell the earth the people walk upon. We are the land, how do we sell our mother? How do you sell a star? How do we sell the air?"[41]

John Trudell died of cancer on December 8, 2015. Before passing away, he reportedly said, "My ride has shown up. Celebrate love. Celebrate life."

John Trudell as Jimmy Looks Twice in *Thunderheart* (1992, TriStar).

12

Native Voices and Native Images (2000–2010)

The 2000s witnessed the agency of indigenous people throughout the Americas in organizing to bring about social justice, to protect and recover their land and resources, and to elect left-of-center governments (where they were the majority population) that empowered their communities. U.S. film images in this time period provided a diverse number of Native American–themed narratives and forms of creative control.

The decade of the millennium arrived with the global fear of some type of technological meltdown and chaos, but it did not happen. The Cold War receded into history, but the specter of terrorism and narcoterrorism dramatically changed the national security and civil liberties of millions around the world. A worldwide recession (the worst economic meltdown since the Great Depression) also damaged the foundations of most nation-states in the First World. These twin calamities fueled xenophobia and the demonization of the darker peoples of the world. The popular media became the major venue for demagoguery, intolerance, and stereotypes.

The United States had begun the decade enjoying its longest era of economic expansion and prosperity in history, inaugurated under President Bill Clinton. A federal budgetary surplus and implementation of the North American Free Trade Association (NAFTA) further bolstered the hopes of many. However, on September 11, 2001, the tranquility and security of the nation were shattered forever by the terrorist attacks on the Twin Towers and the Pentagon. There had been acts of terror abroad for decades, but never on such magnitude within the continental United States or in the rest of the world. The shock and trauma of the attack was incalculable psychologically, politically, and economically. The direct effect on the United States was the militarization and heightened security of all government institutions, ports, and airports. Congress also passed the USA Patriot Act, which essentially made it legal for the government to deny and restrict constitutional rights for purpose of national security.

President George W. Bush and his administration quickly capitalized on the nation's trauma by becoming involved in two foreign military invasions, which provided a catharsis for some. The first was the invasion of Afghanistan, which had harbored the perpetrators of the 9/11 attacks, and the second was the invasion of Iraq (which had the world's second-largest reserve of oil!) under the excuse that the Iraqis had "weapons of mass destruction." The latter assertion proved to be completely false, but the millions of dead, maimed, and refugees was entirely real.

Midway through the second Bush term, a deep-rooted recession took place during December 2007–June 2009. The economic downturn began in the housing market and quickly spread to other sectors of the national economy, bringing economic ruin, unemployment, homelessness, and suffering not seen since the Great Depression. The recession, which began in the United States, quickly spread throughout the rest of the world. The interdependent nature of the world's economies (as a result of globalization) brought the First World to its proverbial knees. The Third World, which lived under a permanent depression, felt the consequences as well.

In the United States, federal, state, and local legislation was proposed or passed that reflected the growing xenophobia, racism, and intolerance for "otherness" and difference. These efforts included English-Only laws, racial profiling (as in Arizona's SB 1070),[1] and proposals to deny citizenship to U.S.–born children of undocumented workers. In 2012, the state of Arizona also outlawed the Tucson Unified School District's Chicano (or Mexican American) studies program based on an obscure 2000 law that took effect in 2011. This law prohibited any program that "promotes resentment toward a race or that promotes 'the overthrow of the U.S.' or that encourages 'ethnic solidarity instead of pupils as individuals.'"[2]

The economic crises further fueled a movement toward privatizing public education supported by corporations and opportunistic politicians. Many saw it as a blatant effort to destroy the last public service unions (national labor unions' membership was down to only 8 percent from the high of 36 percent in 1945). A proliferation of corporate and billionaire benefactors flooded the media, demonizing teachers and pledging to help minority students. Diane Ravitch wrote, "In Hollywood films and television documentaries, the battle lines are clearly drawn. Traditional public schools are bad; their supporters are apologists for the unions. Those who advocate for charter schools, virtual schools, and 'school choice' are reformers; their supporters insist they are championing the rights of minorities."[3]

The 2010 U.S. Census revealed a very different ethnic makeup from that reflected in the media, especially in film and television. The nation's population had increased to 308,745,538. Latinos remained the country's largest ethnic minority, with 50,477,594 (16.3 percent of the total population). This was an increase from 35.3 million in the 2000 U.S. Census. The census also revealed that, contrary to the rampant xenophobic claims about dangerous foreigners, 62 percent of Latinos were born in the United States, while 38 percent had been born outside the nation.[4]

The states with the largest number of Latinos were California, Nevada, Texas, New Mexico, Florida, and Colorado. States registering a significant growth of Latino residents included North Carolina, Virginia, Oregon, Idaho, Illinois, Pennsylvania, New York, Connecticut, Rhode Island, and Massachusetts. According to the 2010 U.S. Census, minorities made up 35 percent of the nation's population. The breakdown for the different Latino communities was as follows: Mexicans, 29.3 million; Puerto Ricans, 4.1 million; Cubans, 1.5 million; Salvadorians, 1.5 million; and Dominicans, 1.2 million. Latinos from Central America added up to 3.6 million; those from South America totaled 2.5 million. Minorities were projected to be the majority by the year 2050.[5]

The 2010 U.S. Census results listed by race and/or ethnicity were as follows: White, 196,817,552 (63.7 percent); Black or African American, 37,685,848 (12.2 percent); American Indian and Alaska Native, 2,247,098 (0.7 percent); Asian, 14,465,124 (4.7 percent); Native Hawaiian and other Pacific Islander, 481,576 (0.15 percent); two or more races,

5,966,481 (1.9 percent); some other race, 604,265 (0.2 percent).[6] However, both the population numbers and the percentage of Native Americans can be called into question. Mexicans, Salvadorians, and Guatemalans are clearly Native American–majority peoples. Because respondents often answer this question by naming their country of origin, the Native American origin is frequently lost.

This writer would argue that there are more than twenty million Native American–origin people in the United States based on the census data. These numbers do not even include the estimated 10–12 million undocumented workers from beyond the southern border (the majority of whom are Mexican and, to a lesser degree, Central American).

Sadly, the ethnic composition of the nation is not reflected in film and television. According to the *Screen Actors Guild Report 2009* (on the year 2008), Latinos made up only 6.4 percent of roles in films and television (the majority in incidental roles); blacks, 13.3 percent; Asian-Pacific Islanders, 3.8 percent; and Native Americans, 3.8 percent.[7]

NATIVE AMERICAN FILM IMAGES IN THE 2000S

During the first decade of the new millennium, 2000–2009, Native American film images built on the progress made in the previous decade. Native American images began in the 1990s to improve, although wider opportunities for native talent remained limited. The massive box-office and critical success of *Dances with Wolves* jump-started a native renaissance, as well as a wider interest in all things Native American. As a result, more native performers were in demand for more native roles.

This decade introduced a new group of Native American actors. Those who had garnered recognition in the 1990s continued to be prominent in the 2000s. The best known of these were Adam Beach, Graham Greene and Wes Studi, all of whom continued to enjoy successful careers in film and television. An unexpected event was the continued film and television presence of activist-turned-actor Russell Means, who had made a powerful debut in *Last of the Mohicans*.

Several feature films as well as television films were released with Native American themes. One of the earliest of these was *The Other Conquest/La Otra Conquista* (2000, Arenas Entertainment), which depicted the Spanish conquest of the Aztecs' hearts and minds through religion of the Aztec peoples.

Atanarijuat: The Fast Runner (2001 Odeon Films), a Canadian film, directed by Inuit director Zacharias Kunuk, became the first film to be directed, written, and acted in the Inuit language. It was set in the Inuit past and carried on in the oral tradition. This film tells the story of Atanarijuat, whose marriage to his two wives has repercussions of life and death. The film won wide critical acclaim and numerous awards, including the 2002 American Indian Film Festival for Best Director, Best Actor (Natar Ungalaaq), and Best Actress (Lucy Tulugarjuk).

Chris Eyre's *Skins* (2002, Starz!) depicted the love/hate relationship between two indigenous brothers. It was set in an impoverished reservation in South Dakota. The film *Windtalkers* (2002, MGM), by contrast, focused on the Navajo code talkers during World War II in the Pacific theater of war. The film was directed and produced by John Woo. The main weakness of this film is its focus on Sergeant Joe Enders (Nicolas Cage), who is in charge of protecting the Navajo code talkers, who are reduced to supporting roles (Adam Beach, Charlie Whitehorse, Vincent Whipple). The fascinating story of the Navajo code talkers and their personal stories were apparently not deemed interesting enough to receive more attention. Film critic Roger Ebert, writing in the *Chicago Sun Times* (June 14, 2002), commented, "The filmmakers have buried [the Native American story] beneath battlefield clichés, while centering the story on a white character played by Nicolas Cage."[8]

Black Cloud (2004, High Maintenance) focuses on the hopes and dreams of a young Navajo boxer in the amateur ranks. *Hidalgo* (2004, Touchstone) is about Frank Hopkins (1865–1851), a legendary part-Lakota, part-white rider who claimed to have won some 400 horse races. In the film, he leaves his job in a wild west show to compete against Bedouins in a horse race in 1891 Arabia. Hopkins was played by Danish American actor Viggo Mortensen (who bore no remote resemblance to being half Native American).

Chris Eyre's *A Thousand Roads* (2005, NMAI) depicts the everyday lives of four different Native Americans. *Trudell* (2005) is a passionate documentary about the life of John Trudell (see biography entry for Trudell in the previous chapter), co-founder of the American Indian Movement (AIM), poet, writer, musician, and activist. Erin Meister, writing in the *Boston Globe* (March 10, 2006), noted, "The film is a thought-provoking and graceful portrait of a tenacious peace warrior whose frankness is his greatest weapon."[9]

Clint Eastwood's *Flags of Our Fathers* (2006, Warner Bros.) depicted the war heroism and trauma of Ira Hayes during World War II in the Pacific theater. *Imprint* (2007, Linn Prods.) was supernatural thriller set in the context of Lakota culture. *Bury My Heart at Wounded Knee* (2007, HBO Film) was a cable television film based on the best-selling book of the same name by Dee Brown. The film covers the period of the 1860s and 1970s in the lives of Native Americans as the United States launches the last of the Indian Wars. The Native American cast included Adam Beach as Dr. Eastman, August Schellenberg as Sitting Bull, and Gordon Tootoosis as Red Cloud, among others. This film won six Emmy Awards, including Outstanding Made for Television Movie. Virginia Heffernan of the *New York Times* (May 25, 2007) wrote, "This project was doomed to overreach and to sermonize. To begin with, it's about American Indians, who ever since Sacheen Littlefeather declined Marlon Brando's Oscar in 1973 have scared the chutzpah out of Hollywood."[10]

Pathfinder (2007, 20th Century–Fox) tells the story of a group of Vikings who arrive in North America well before 1492. This film featured indigenous activist Russell Means as the aged character Pathfinder. The theatrical feature film *Older Than America* (2008, MPI) is a supernatural Native American–themed story about the infamous Indian boarding schools and the traumas that they inflicted on native communities. It was written, directed, and produced by Georgina Lighting, the first Native American woman to complete all these multiple tasks (she also starred in the film). The cast included Adam Beach, Wes Studi, Tantoo Cardinal, and Dennis Banks, among others. *Older Than America* won the 2008 American Film Festival awards for Best Director (Georgina Lighting) and Best Supporting Actor (Wes Studi).

Comanche Moon (2008, CBS mini-series) was based on the novel of the same name by Larry McMurtry. It is a prequel to the *Lonesome Dove* mini-series and a sequel to *Dead Man's Walk*. The narrative is set in Texas in the 1850s. Native actors included Wes Studi, Adam Beach, David Midthunder, and Floyd "Red Crow" Westerman, among others. Despite earning several Emmy nominations, this mini-series generally met with negative reviews. Some reviews especially criticized the stereotypical Mexican portrayals, as well as the representation of frontier women.

Representative Films

Apocalypto (2006, Icon)

The film *Apocalypto* focuses on the Mayan people of southern Mexico and Guatemala, depicting their lives just before the arrival of the Europeans in 1492. It was directed and produced by Mel Gibson (with Bruce Davey). The screenplay was written by Gibson and Farhad Safinia (an Iranian-born film director).

When asked about why he had chosen the Mayan civilization as a backdrop to the film, Gibson told the *Global Heritage Fund* (November 2, 2007), "It's really the characteristics that brought about their downfall, which were present in the collapse of other civilizations, which I thought would serve as a really interesting and heretofore unexplored backdrop for the story. It is mysterious, and I suppose that appealed to me."[11] Both Gibson and Safinia wanted to make a film about either the Aztecs or the Mayans before the coming of the Europeans. Safinia told the *Washington Post* (December 15, 2006), "The Mayans were far more interesting to us.... You can choose a civilization that is bloodthirsty, or you can show the Mayan civilization that was so sophisticated with an immense knowledge of medicine, science, archeology and engineering."[12]

The narrative is set in the early 1490s. A small village in the Yucatán Peninsula is attacked by Mayan warriors, who are in search of slaves and sacrificial victims. Jaguar Paw (Rudy Youngblood), the son of the village chief, escape with his wife and child and eludes the intruders for a time. However, Jaguar Paw is eventually caught and taken to a large city (full of both pestilence and violence), where he is supposed to be sacrificed. However, during a solar eclipse, he once again escapes. Jaguar Paw then returns to rescue his family. As they flee to the coast, they see several Spanish ships landing on the beaches.

Apocalypto has elements of gritty realism, fascinating characters, lush cinematography, and evocative moments of the pre–Columbian Mayan experience. However, an obsession with unrelenting violence can be observed throughout its narrative. Little mention is made of the Mayans' considerable achievements in medicine, agriculture, astronomy, mathematics (they invented the concept of zero, for example), and engineering. Certainly pre–Columbian societies were not perfect or idyllic. Nonetheless, they maintained an ecological balance between the needs of their societies and a reverence for the fruits of nature. There were no mass witch burnings, bubonic plagues, religious persecutions, or genocides.

One of the assets of *Apocalypto* is its authentic native casting and the attention given to cultural details in language, clothing, and motifs. The film captivates the viewer and takes him/her on a journey of discovery in the Mayan world. However, its major shortcoming remains the redundant violence, reminiscent of the old Hollywood stereotypes of native people as savages.

Apocalypto received generally positive reviews. A.O. Scott, in the *New York Times* (December 8, 2006), wrote, "The brutality in 'Apocalypto' is so relentless and extreme that it sometimes moves beyond horror into a kind of grotesque comedy, but to dismiss it as excessive and gratuitous would be to underestimate Mr. Gibson's seriousness."[13] However, others criticized *Apocalypto* for its many historical inaccuracies. For instance, there is no recorded evidence of a system of mass slavery in the Mayan civilization. In addition, the depiction of mass human sacrifices was pointed out as another historical inaccuracy. Mayan human sacrifice was carried out on a small scale and often involved the sacrifice of elites, rather than common people. The scene of using captives for target practice was another invention of the filmmakers.

The film also erroneously placed the end of the story in 1492, with the arrival of the Spaniards. In fact, the Classic Maya civilization (AD 250–900) collapsed in the 8th century AD.[14] When the Spaniards arrived in 1502 (not 1492—Columbus did not reach Central America until his fourth voyage), the Mayans had long since abandoned most of their large cities and returned to subsistence agriculture. This historical fact has baffled historians, archeologists, and anthropologists for decades, and it remains a mystery to this day. The Post-Classic Period (AD 950–1539) was marked by a substantially reduced developed area, as the population shifted to the northern lowlands and highlands of the Mayan territory. Rather than sticking to facts, the makers of *Apocalypto* meshed together two distinct Mayan eras.

The film's cast was made up completely of Native American actors from the United States, Mexico, Canada, and Guatemala. The cast included Rudy Youngblood (Jaguar Claw); Dalia Hernández (Seven); Itandehui Gutiérrez (Wife); Jonathan Brewer (Blunted); Mayra Serbulo (Young Woman); Morris Birdyellowhead (Flint Sky); Carlos Emilio Báez (Turtles Run); and Israel Contreras (Smoke Frog), among many others.

The film uses the language of the Yucatec Mayan. The film was shot on location in Catemaco, San Andrés Tuxtla, and Paso de Ovejas, Veracruz, in Mexico. Additional scenes were filmed at El Petén, Guatemala.

Apocalypto had an estimated budget of $40 million and grossed domestically $164.5 million when adjusted for inflation.[15]

Skins (2002, Starz!)

Perhaps the darkest film made in the United States about Native Americans is *Skins*, which was directed by Native American Chris Eyre. Whereas Eyre's earlier *Smoke Signals* tended to use humor to portray the harsh conditions in the reservation, *Skins* was uncompromising.

The screenplay was written by Jennifer D. Lyne and Adrian C. Louis (based on his novel of the same name). Louis (b. 1946) is of mixed ancestry: white and Lovelock Paiute. He was born in Nevada but now lives in the Pine Ridge Reservation in South Dakota. He is both a poet and a novelist.

The term *skins* is the slang word that a new generation of Native Americans use for each other. The film was shot almost entirely within the Pine Ridge Reservation in South Dakota, site of the Oglala Nation.

Both the novel and the film are set in the fictional Beaver Creek Indian Reservation, located in South Dakota. The film's narrative involves the relationship between two brothers. One, Mogie (Graham Greene), is a Vietnam veteran who is physically and psychologically traumatized by the war. Following his return from combat, he becomes an alcoholic and experiences severe social dysfunctions. His younger brother, Rudy Yellow Dog (Eric Schweig), is a tribal policeman who is himself a recovering alcoholic and angry about the dire poverty in the reservation.

Rudy manifests his societal outrage by masquerading as a masked vigilante at night, targeting a white-owned liquor store and drug-addicted young men who are corrupting other youths. It isn't until his older brother dies of severe diabetes that Rudy realizes that Mogie loved him unconditionally and both were struggling in different ways to make the lives of their people better. When Rudy goes to pour paint over the four presidential statutes at Mount Rushmore, built on stolen Oglala land, he sees the spirit of his deceased brother on the way back to the reservation.

Skins is a hard-edged film that captures the grinding poverty, despair, and lingering hard-to-manage hope that still pervades in native communities. Director Chris Eyre documents the hard truths and ravages of a people who have been marginalized and oppressed for so long. There is no romanticized image, but rather a depiction of the struggle of everyday life for native people, their tarnished lives and dreams, and their attempts to cling to their culture. Both Graham Greene and Eric Schweig give remarkable performances. Others in the cast (Gary Farmer, Gil Birmingham, Elaine Miles, Noah Waits, and Lois Red Elk, among others) provide convincing performances as well.

Skins won the 2002 Tokyo International Film Festival Best Actor award for Grahame Greene; the First Americans in the Arts Best Director award for Chris Eyre; and the 2003 PRISM award for Best Theatrical Feature Film. It received generally excellent reviews but limited distribution. Roger Ebert, in the *Chicago-Sun Times* (October 18, 2002), wrote, "Graham Green achieves the difficult task of giving a touching performance even though his character is usually drunk.... To see this movie is to understand why the faces on Mount Rushmore are so painful and galling to the first Americans. The movie's final image is haunting."[16]

The Other Conquest/La Otra Conquista (2000, Arenas Entertainment)

The most important Mexican film in recent years to focus on native history was *The Other Conquest/La Otra Conquista*, which explored the religious and psychological conquest perpetrated by Spanish conquistadores against Mexican native peoples. The film was directed by Mexican filmmaker Salvador Carrasco and produced by renowned opera singer Placido Domingo. The film featured two languages: Náhuatl and Spanish. (It was actually released in Mexico in 1998; two years later, it came to the United States.)

The narrative is set in 1520, one year after the conquest of Tenochtitlán, the capital city of the Aztecs. The film begins with the Spanish massacre of Aztecs by the huge temple of Tenochtitlán. One survivor is Topilzin (Damián Delgado), an illegitimate son of the Moctezuma, the deceased Aztec emperor. When Topilzin awakens amid the piles of corpses and blood, he finds himself surrounded by a different language, religion, customs, and people. He is taken prisoner and later presented to Hernán Cortés (Inaki Airra). The infamous conquistador places him under the tutelage of Friar Diego (José Carlos Rodríguez). The friar is ordered to convert Topilzin and make him a Christian. Topilzin, in turn, struggles from within to maintain his identity and culture.

La Otra Conquista won numerous awards, including an Ariel (Mexico's equivalent of an Academy Award) for Best First Work (Mejor Opera Prima) for Salvador Carrasco and the 1999 San Antonio Cine Festival Special Jury Award (Salvador Carrasco), among others.

Carrasco noted, "These were sophisticated civilizations. There must have been resistance to the conquest. I'm sure there were people who struggled to preserve their cultural identity, their beliefs and their ideas. And yet I was being taught as the opposite. That was very troubling."[17] Carrasco also commented on the topic of the Mexican national identity: "We look at ourselves in the mirror and it's like, 'Who am I? Where do we come from? How come on the one hand we have dark skin and on the other we speak Spanish?' Sometimes we feel indigenous, sometimes we deny our indigenous roots."[18]

La Otra Conquista is an excruciating film to watch as a Native American. The Spanish conquest of Mexico is still an open wound in the Mexican/Native American psyche. The film is brutal and uncompromising, like all conquests are. It explores the harsh and profound conquest of the mind through religion and culture. The film's attention to detail and locales brings to life the Aztec world at the time of the conquest. It is a deeply moving experience to remember and reflect on this momentous event in Mexican history.

The performances from the Mexican Native American actors, especially Damián Delgado as Topilzin and Elipidia Carrillo as Tecuichpo, are extraordinary. Other members of the cast include Guillermo Ríos (Alanpoyatzin), Zaide Silvia Gutiérrez (Beata Conversa), and Lourdes Villareal (Cihuacóatl), among others.

La Otra Conquista was made over a period of some seven years, due to the difficulty in acquiring sufficient funding. The film was shot in various historic sites in Mexico: Xochimilco (the surviving area of Lake Texcoco) and Coyoacán in Mexico City; Tepoztlán and Tlayacapan in Morelos; and the Grutas de Cacahuamilpa in Guerrero. In the end, despite the difficulties, the film proved to be a critical and commercial success.

Imprint (2007, Linn Prods.)

The film *Imprint* is a unique supernatural thriller set in the Pine Ridge Reservation in South Dakota. It explores the power of history and culture upon the lives of individuals and what they decide to do in their lives. The film was directed by Michael Linn and written by Linn and Keith Davenport.

The narrative focuses on a young Lakota attorney, Shayla Stonefeather (Tonantzín Carmelo). She resides in Denver, Colorado, where she prosecutes a young Lakota for murder. The defendant is found guilty by a mostly white jury. This ruling angers the native community, as they feel that there has been a gross miscarriage of the justice. The high-profile case brings Shayla much publicity, as well as denouncement by the native community. Her white boyfriend, Jonathan Freeman (Cory Brusseau), is an ambitious politician, anxious to make a name for himself and run for public office. Soon after the end of the trial, Shayla is informed that the young defendant was killed during an escape attempt.

Shayla and Jonathan leave to visit her parents at the Pine Ridge Reservation. She finds her father, Sam Stonefeather (Charlie White Buffalo), slowly dying from a stroke, and her mother, Rebecca, hard pressed to care for him. Jonathan leaves the next day, but Shayla stays for several days. She experiences supernatural visions and hallucinations but is unable to understand what is going on.

She meets a Lakota medicine man (Dave Bald Eagle) at the Wounded Knee cemetery. He advises her to listen to the cries and laments of the spirits. However, she has become so acculturated to Euro-American culture that she is unable to understand. She also continues to believe that her father murdered her brother, Nathaniel, who disappeared two years earlier. She finds her brother's motorcycle hidden in a shed and assumes that her father's stroke was a result of his murder.

Shayla is reconnected with Tom Greyhorse (Michael Spears), a former boyfriend and now a tribal policeman. When her father dies, she realizes that her boyfriend Jonathan paid a witness to testify against the young Lakota defendant and have him convicted, thus currying favor with the state governor. She is also reunited with her lost brother Nathanial (Tokala Black Elk), causing her to realize her error in assuming her father's guilt. She finally understands that the supernatural events were related to the spirit of the young Lakota boy who was killed.

At the end of the film, Jonathan tries to kill Shayla because he fears that she will report him to the authorities. However, he dies accidently in the process. Afterward, Shayla goes to a hill overlooking the Pine Ridge Reservation and experiences an epiphany of consciousness. She finally realizes that her work is here, with her people.

Imprint is an evocative and an emotionally overwhelming film that combines Native American culture with supernatural elements. It also brings home the point of how, in the process of acquiring professional success in the white world, traditional culture and traditions are sometime lost. There are excellent performances by Tonantzín Carmelo as Shayla, Michael Spears as Tom Greyhorse, Dave Bald Eagle as the medicine man, and Charlie White Buffalo as Sam Stonefeather. Carla-Rae is a standout as the resolute and strong-willed mother, Rebecca Stonefeather.

Imprint received numerous awards, including the American Indian Film Festival awards for Best Film, Best Actress (Tonantzín Carmelo), and Best Supporting Actress (Carla-Rae). It also won the Cherokee Film Festival Best Film award and the South Dakota Film Festival Best Film award.

Black Cloud (2004, High Maintenance Films)

Black Cloud is a boxing film set against the background of the Navajo Nation. It was directed and written by former actor Rick Schroder (who also has a small role in the film). It is perhaps the first U.S. film to feature a Native American protagonist in a boxing drama.

The narrative focuses on Black Cloud (Michael Spears), a young amateur boxer in the Navajo Reservation, who aspires to win boxing glory for his native people. However, he is consumed by the alcoholism in his family, his mixed blood, and the rampart poverty in which he lives. His trainer, Bud (Russell Means), puts up with his flaws because he sees a little of himself from when he was young. Bud continues to motivate Black Cloud in his boxing career.

Black Cloud's anger almost destroys his relationship with his girlfriend Sammi (Julia Jones). It also worsens his conflict with Sheriff Cliff Powers (Tim McGraw) and results in a physical confrontation with Sammi's former boyfriend and the father of her child, Eddie (Ricky Schroder), who is a bigot and prone to violence.

Black Cloud takes a long retreat into the solitude of the reservation, where his grandfather (Saginaw Grant) becomes his guide in healing his anger and reconnecting to his cultural roots. After several months, Black Cloud returns a changed person and a refocused boxer. He wins an important boxing tournament that makes him eligible to compete in the Olympics. He improves his relationship with his girlfriend, and they finally understand that they have each other when it comes to facing the challenges of the future.

Black Cloud is a unique film in many ways. It is a coming-of-age narrative set in the context of a contemporary native reservation. In addition, it offers a fascinating view of the struggles of young boxers who aspire to compete in the Olympics and beyond. Michael Spears is excellent as the angry and talented pugilist and has all the physical requirements to play a boxer realistically. Too many times, actors have been terribly unconvincing as boxers (i.e., Will Smith, Antonio Banderas, etc.). Here, Spears was trained by the legendary boxing coach Jimmy Gambina to really be a boxer, possesses real talent, and very convincing in the actual boxing scenes.

The supporting cast could not have been better. Most of them are real Native American actors; activist-turned actor Russell Means as the boxing coach; Julia Jones as his girlfriend; Saginaw Grant as Grandpa; and Nathanial Arcand as his friend Jimmy. Country singer Tim McGraw as the Sheriff; and Rich Schroder as Eddie turn in fine performances. The spiritual beauty and magnificence of the Navajo Nation locales provide an exhilarating setting for the narrative.

The film received generally good reviews. The film won the 2004 First Americans in the Arts award for Best Actress (Julia Jones); the 2004 Nashville Film Festival President's award (Ricky Schroder); and the 2004 Phoenix Film Festival Best Ensemble Acting award.

Flags of Our Fathers (2006, Warner Bros.)

Flags of Our Fathers is one of the few mainstream films to depict a significant Native American character. In this case, it was Ira Hayes (1923–1955), a Pima and U.S. Marine who helped raise the flag at the Battle of Iwo Jima during World War II.

This film was directed, scored, and co-produced by Clint Eastwood (the other producers included Steven Spielberg and Robert Lorenz). The screenplay was based on the book of the same name written by James Bradley and Ron Powers, adapted for the screen by William Broyles, Jr., and Paul Haggis.

Flags of Our Fathers focuses on the U.S. perspective of the Battle of Iwo Jima during February and March 1945. Later in 2006, Eastwood directed and released a companion feature titled *Letters from Iwo Jima*, which told the Japanese side of the story. Like its predecessor, the latter film garnered excellent reviews and turned out to be an even bigger box-office success (especially in Japan).

The narrative of *Flags of Our Fathers* primarily revolves around three U.S. soldiers: Navy Corpsman John "Doc" Bradley (Ryan Phillippe), Marine Private First Class Ira Hayes (Adam Beach), and Private First Class Rene Gagnon (Jesse Bradford). After receiving combat training at Camp Tarawa in Hawaii, the 5th Marine Division is sent to invade the volcanic island of Iwo Jima, where the Japanese have dug in. There the newly trained Marines witness the utter horrors of war: the death of comrades, decomposed bodies, brutal combat, and inhumanity on both sides.

After reaching Mount Suribachi, a platoon is ordered to climb the mountain and plant the U.S. flag. However, Secretary of the Navy James Forrestal, who sees the raising of the flag as he disembarks from his ship, demands the flag for himself as a keepsake. As a consequence, another group is sent to Mount Suribachi to put up another flag. Doc, Ira, Rene, and three other Marines are photographed by a war reporter Joe Rosenthal, resulting in the iconic image.

Later, Doc, Ira, and Rene (as the only survivors of the group) are sent on a war bonds tour on the mainland. However, the war drive takes its toll on the three men, especially Ira, who begins to drink heavily and is stricken with survivor's guilt. He is discriminated against by most people he meets and referred to as "chief." The top brass consequently return him to active service, and the war bond drive continues with Doc and Rene.

After the war, the three veterans meet one more time as part of an event for the United States Marine War Memorial in Washington, D.C., but eventually they lose track of each other. Ira returns to the reservation and drinks himself to death. Rene tries to build a business career that had been encouraged during the war drive but ends his life working as a janitor. However, Doc becomes a successful businessman after buying a funeral home. In 1994, as he is dying, Doc tells his story to his son, James Bradley (who goes on to co-write a book with Ron Powers).

Flags of Our Fathers received mostly positive reviews, although it failed to become a big box-office success. Roger Ebert of the *Chicago Sun-Times* (November 29, 2006) noted, "But the most complex and tragic figure is the American Indian Hayes, who America wanted to be a hero, but not an American: he is routinely addressed as 'chief,' is refused service at a bar because he is not white, is condescended by dignitaries.... Adam Beach's performance is the most memorable in the film."[19] Todd McCarthy in *Variety* (October 11, 2006) wrote, "Given this dramatic arc, Hayes' story becomes the heart of the movie, and Beach, who previously played a Native American in the Pacific campaign in '*Windtalkers*,' unquestionably takes the acting honors with it, delivering a full sense of the narrator's pain and entrapment in an absurd situation."[20]

Flags of Our Fathers was listed in the *National Board of Review* as one of the ten best films of 2006. The film was nominated for two Academy Awards: Best Sound (John T.

Adam Beach as Ira Hayes in Clint Eastwood's *Flags of Our Fathers* (2006, Warner Bros).

Reitz, David E. Campbell, Gregg Rudloff and Walt Martin) and Best Sound Editing. However, Adam Beach, who received the best reviews, was not even nominated for a well-deserved Best Supporting Actor Oscar nomination.

Into the West (2005, DreamWorks TNT miniseries)

Into the West was an ambitious television project that documented the history of two families—one Native American and the other Euro-American—during the westward expansion of the United States during the 1800s. Native actors in the mini-series included Iren Bedard, Gil Birmingham, Tonantzín Carmelo, Sheila Tousey, Russell Means, Michael Spears, and Eric Schweig. *Into the West* was nominated for several awards. It won the 2006 First Nations in the Arts awards for Outstanding Performance in a TV Movie/Special (Lead) (Zahn McClarnon); Outstanding Supporting Actor (Tyler Christopher); Outstanding New Performance by an Actor in a Film (Nakotah LaRance); and Outstanding Actress Performance (Lead) (Tonantzín Carmelo).

A Thousand Roads (2005, NMAI)

A Thousand Roads is a short film commissioned by National Museum of the Native American (located in Washington, D.C.). The film is only 40 minutes in length and showcases the contemporary life of native peoples in the Americas. It was directed by Chris Eyre and produced by Sonya Gay Dorn, Barry Clarke, and Scott Garen.

The film depicts one day in the lives of four Native Americans: The first segment involves a Mohawk woman (Candice Costello) who is a stressed-out and culturally disoriented stockbroker on Wall Street. The second segment is set in Alaska, where Dawn, an Inuit, is sent to visit her grandparents. There she discovers her cultural homeland. The third segment is set in the Navajo Reservation, where Johnny Shee (Jeremiah Bitsui) is caught up in the gang life. The last segment is set in Perú, where a curandero/shaman (Honorato Nanatay), a Quechua, sets out on a failed journey to cure a patient.

A Thousand Roads was provided with a moving and poetic narration by John Trudell, who at the end comments, "Though we journey down a thousand roads, all roads lead home." Claudio Miranda did the stunning cinematography, and the film was accompanied by a variety of native music.

This film is an evocative rendition of a mosaic of Native American experiences, their hopes and dreams, as well as their unending struggle to maintain their precious native roots, culture, and spirituality. *A Thousand Roads* is available on DVD.

NATIVE AMERICAN FILM STARS AND FILMMAKERS

Gil Birmingham

Gil Birmingham is a Native American actor who has been working on his craft for several decades, though he only came into prominence in the 2000s. He was born on July 13, 1953, in San Antonio, Texas. He is of Comanche ancestry.

Birmingham obtained a bachelor of science degree at the University of California School of Policy, Planning and Development. He later worked as petrochemical engineer before he turned to acting as a profession.

He made his acting debut in the television show *Riptide* in 1986. His first film role came in *House II: The Second Story* in 1987 (New World). His film credits include *The Doe Boy* (2001, Vozza Prods.); *Skins* (2002, Starz!); *End of the Spear* (2005, Rocky Mountain Pictures); and *No Man's Land: The Land of the Reekers* (2008, Lionsgate).

In 2008, Birmingham was cast in the role of Billy Black in *Twilight* (Summit). The film was a romantic fantasy, based on a popular novel of the same name by Stephanie Meyer. It was hugely popular, and four more installments followed: *The Twilight Saga: New Moon* (2009, Summit); *The Twilight Saga: Eclipse* (2010, Summit); *The Twilight Saga: Breaking Dawn—Part 1* (2011, Summit); and *The Twilight Saga: Breaking Dawn—Part 2* (2012, Summit).

Birmingham's most recent film credits include *The Lone Ranger* (2013, Disney); *Hell and High Water* (2016, Lionsgate); *The Space Between Us* (2017, Huayi Bros.); and *Transformers: The Last Knight* (2017, Paramount). His television credits include *Falcon Crest*, *Buffy the Vampire Slayer*, *Night Man*, *House of Cards*, *Vegas*, *The Mentalist*, *Charmed*, and *Yellowstone*, among others.

Tonantzín Carmelo

One of the most notable native actresses to emerge in the new millennium was Tonantzín Carmelo. In Aztec history, Tonantzín was the name of the mother goddess; it is a common name today among the Nahuas people of central Mexico.

Carmelo's ancestry stems from the Kumeyaay and Tongova people of southern California on her mother's side. She grew up performing in a Native American group organized by her mother, Virginia Carmelo. While attending at UC Irvine, she studied acting and has numerous theater credits.

Carmelo made her film debut in *King Rikki* in 2002 (Mistral Pictures). Since then, her films have included *Imprint* (2005, Linn Prods.); *Unearthed* (2007, Cold Iron Pictures); *We Shall Remain* (2009, PBS); *Shouting Secrets* (2011, Joker Film Prods.); *The Activist* (2014, Media in Sync); *Child of Grace* (2014, Stenman Prods.); *Entertainment* (2015, Autumn Prods.); and *Medicine Man* (2017, ABS). For her role in the film *Imprint*, she was honored with the 2007 American Indian Film Festival Best Actress award.

Carmelo's television credits include *Dragnet*, *CSI: Miami*, *Dark Blue*, *Freedom Riders*, *American Dad*, *Z Nation*, and *Teen Wolf*. In 2005, she co-starred in the television miniseries *Into the West*. She has also done voicework for several video games: *Dead Space* (2008), *Shawdowheart* (2009), *The Crew* (2014), and *Lego Marvel's Avengers* (2009).

Candice Costello

Candice Costello is a Native American actress who made her film debut in *Coyote Waits* in 2003 (PBS) opposite Adam Beach and Wes Studi. Since then, her films have included *A Thousand Roads* (2005, NMAI); *Not Forgotten* (2009, Skyline); *The Dry Land* (2010, Maya Entertainment); *Jacob* (2011), a film short; *Moses on the Mesa* (2013, Films by Giants), a film short; *I Am a Weapon* (2016), a film short; and *The Longest Sun* (2017), a film short. In 2011, she also worked as film grip in the short film *Opal*.

Stuart Proud Eagle Grant

Stuart Proud Eagle Grant is a Native American actor who works in both film and television. He was born on January 26, 1946, in McCook, Nebraska. He is of Lakota ancestry.

Grant made his television acting debut in the series *Bagdad Café* in 1991. He made his film debut in *Hot Shots! Part Deux* (1993, 20th Century–Fox). His other film credits include *Geronimo: An American Legend* (1993, Warner Bros.); *Wagons East* (1993, Carolca Pictures); *3 Ninjas Knuckle Up* (1995, Sheen Prods.); and *Switchback* (1997, Paramount). His television credits include *Follow the River*, *The Cherokee Kid*, *Murder, She Wrote*, and *South by Southwest* (a 1997 TV film).

Michael Greyeyes

Michael Greyeyes is one of several Native Americans who began working in films and television in the 1990s and built up a long career thereafter. He was born on June 4, 1967, in Qu'Appelle Valley, Saskatchewan, Canada. His ancestry is Plains Cree and derives from the Muskeg Lake First Nation in Saskatchewan on his father's side; his mother was from the Sweetgrass First Nation, also from Saskatchewan.

Greyeyes made his television debut as Juh in the TNT television film *Geronimo* in 1993. His films include *Dance Me Outside* (1994, Cineplex); *Crazy Horse* (1996, Turner), a TV film; *Stolen Women, Captured Hearts* (1996, CBS), a TV film; *True Women* (1997, Hallmark), a TV film; *Smoke Signals* (1998, Shadow Catcher); *Race Against Time* (2000, TNT), a TV film; *Sunshine State* (2002, Sony); *The New World* (2005, New Line Cinema); *Woman Walks Ahead* (2017, Bedford Falls Co); and *Blood Quantum* (2019, Prospector Films), among others.

Greyeyes has played two of the most famous Native American leaders in U.S. history: Crazy Horse (in a television film) and Sitting Bull (in the film *Woman Walks Ahead* [2017, Direct TV]). The latter film tells the story of Catherine Weldon (Jessica Chastain), a widowed painter who in the 1880s traveled to South Dakota to paint the legendary Sitting Bull. Greyeyes said about Sitting Bull, "He was politically very astute. He understood people, he understood the cost of war and he had witnessed destruction and illness. So all these notes that we had in the script told me right away that I was looking at a landmark portrayal."[21] In reference to the casting of indigenous actors in indigenous roles, he commented, "Casting Native people in Native roles should be a no-brainer. First of all, we're bringing in a certain kind of culture, social, political knowledge that we grow up with—that's our life experience. Our personal histories can help elevate writing and shift it to transform it from something that's stereotypical into something that's more three-dimensional."[22]

His numerous television appearances include *Promised Land*; *Dr. Quinn, Medicine Woman*; *Millennium*; *The Magnificent Seven*; *Walker, Texas Ranger*; *Charmed*; *Myth Quest*; *The Jury*; *True Detective*; *American Gods*; and *Freedom Riders*, among others. Greyeyes is also a dancer, scholar, and director, and he was a founding member of the Signal Theatre.

Carla-Rae (Holland)

Carla-Rae is a Native American actress of Mohawk-Seneca and French-Canadian ancestry. She was born in 1963 and has a diverse professional background: model, stage actress, television actress, and film actress.

She made her film debut in the Chris Eyre–produced film *Imprint* (2007, Linn Prods.), in which she played Rebecca Stonefeather, the mother of Tonantzín Carmelo's character. For this role, Carla-Rae was honored with the 2007 American Indian Film Festival Best Supporting Actress award.

On television, her credits include *New Amsterdam*, *Freedom Riders*, and *Scoundrels*. Her films include *Taking Chance* (2009, HBO), a TV film; *We Shall Remain* (2009, PBS); and *The Sharman and the Escapee* (2017, Quixotic Prods.), a short film.

She married Ricky Holland in 1981; together they had two children. They are now divorced.

Julia Jones

Julia Jones was born on January 23, 1981, in Boston, Massachusetts. She is of mixed ancestry: Chickasaw, Choctaw, and African American. She began studying at the Boston Ballet School at the age of four and started performing in commercials and theater at the age of eight. She is a graduate of the Boston Latin School and Columbia University.

Jones has modeled for such well-known labels such as The Gap, Esprit, Levi's, and L'Oreal.

She made her film debut in *The Look* in 2003. She also played Sammi, the girlfriend of the angry Navajo boxer played by Eddie Spears in *Black Cloud* (2004, High Maintenance). For this role, she was honored with the Best Actress award in 2004 by the First Americans in the Arts.

Starting in 2010, Jones was cast in three films of the *Twilight* franchise: *The Twilight Saga: Eclipse* (2010, Summit); *The Twilight Saga: Breaking Dawn—Part 1* (2011, Summit); and *The Twilight Saga: Breaking Dawn—Part 2* (2012, Summit). Her other films include *Hell Ride* (2008, Dimension Films); *Three Priests* (2008, Gum Spirits); *Jonah Hex* (2010, Warner Bros.); *California Indian* (2011, Against the Wind Prods.); *Missed Connections* (2012, Gables Entertainment); *Winter in the Blood* (2012, Ranchwater Prods.); *The Ridiculous Six* (2015, Happy Madison Prods.); *Wind River* (2017, Acadia); *High School Lover* (2017, Elysium Bandini); *Hard Powder* (2018, Studio Canal); and *Angelique's Island* (2018, Circle Blue).

Her television credits include *ER*, *In Plain Sight*, *The Thanksgiving House*, and *Longmire*. In 2009, she performed with Culture Clash production at the Mark Taper Forum in Los Angeles *Palestine, New Mexico*.

Georgina Lighting

Georgina Lighting is a Native American director, writer, producer, and actress. She was born in Edmonton, Alberta, Canada, in 1964. She is of the Samson Cree Nation and moved to Los Angeles in order to pursue an acting career.

She made her film debut in *Yellow Wooden Ring*, a film short, in 1998. Her other film credits include *Pocahontas II: Journey to a New World* (1998, Disney), as "additional voice"; *My Brother* (1999, AFI), a film short; *Backroads* (2000, Off Line); *Johnny Greyeyes* (2000, Nepantla Films); *Christmas in the Clouds* (2001, Random Ventures); *Cowboy Up* (2001, Code); and *Dreamkeeper* (2003, Hallmark), a TV film. Her television appearances include *Blackstone*; *The West Wing*; *Auf Wiedersehen, Pet*; and *Walker, Texas Ranger*.

In 2008, Lighting became the first Native American female film director with *Older Than America* (MPI), which she also wrote and in which she played the leading role.

Bramscombe Richmond

Bramscombe Richmond is a character actor and stuntman who can claim a mixture of different ethnicities: English, French, Spanish, Native American, Native Hawaiian, and French Polynesian. He was born Bramscombe Leo Charles Richmond on August 8, 1955, in Los Angeles, California.

Richmond has often been cast as evil villains or amiable good guys. He made his film debut in *Two-Minute Warning* (1976, Universal). Other films include *Rollercoaster* (1977, Universal); *MacArthur* (1977, Universal); *Star Trek III: The Search for Spock* (1984, Paramount); *Best Seller* (1987, Hendale); *License to Kill* (1989, MGM/United Artists); *The Scorpion King* (2002, Universal); *Black Cloud* (2004, High Maintenance); and *Kuleana* (2017, Hawaii Cinema), among many others. He has also made numerous appearances on television: *Chicago Med*; *Roadies*; *Hawaii Five-O*; *Eyes*; *Desperate Housewives*; *Tremors*; *Walker, Texas Ranger*; and *Nash Bridges*, among others.

Eddie Spears

Eddie Spears is a Native American actor. He was born Edward Spears on November 29, 1982, in Chamberlain, South Dakota, on the Lower Brule Indian Reservation. He is a member of the Kul Wicasa Oyate Lakota tribe. He began acting as an adolescent. (His older brother, Michael Spears, is also an actor.)

Eddie Spears made his film debut at the age of ten in the television film *Geronimo* (1993, TNT). In 2004, he was cast in the title role of *Black Cloud* (High Maintenance) as a young Navajo boxer. Both Spears and the film earned wide acclaim. His other film credits include *The Slaughter Rule* (2002, Solaris); *Dreamkeeper* (2003, Hallmark), a TV film; and *Edge of America* (2003, Showtime); *Into the West* (2005, DreamWorks), a TV mini-series; *Bury My Heart at Wounded Knee* (2007, HBO), a TV film; *Comanche Moon* (2008, CBS Paramount), a TV mini-series; *Yellow Rock* (2011, Black Elk Prods.); *Guns, Girls, and Gambling* (2012, Freefall Films); *Bone Tomahawk* (2015, Caliber Media); *The Red Man's View* (2018, Biograph); and *Second Sunrise* (2018, Red Nation Films).

His television credits include *Hell on Wheels*, *Sleepy Hallow*, *Z Nation*, and *Longmire*. He also provided his voice for the animated film *White Fang* in 2018.

Rudy Youngblood

Rudy Youngblood is a Native American actor, artist, dancer, and musician. He was born Rudy Gonzalez in Belton, Texas, and is of Yaqui, Cree, and Comanche ancestry. He has two younger sisters.

Youngblood began working at an early age in construction. In high school, he excelled in track and field, as well as boxing. Upon graduation, he was accepted at several universities and offered Fulbright scholarships. However, he chose to become a dancer with the American Indian Dance Theatre.

He made his film debut in *Spirit: The Seventh Fire* (2005, Purple Union Co.), playing the role of the Warrior Protector. At a general casting call, Youngblood met actor-director

Mel Gibson. To his utter surprise, he was given the leading role of Jaguar Paw in *Apocalypto* (2006, Icon). In preparation for the role, he studied the Yucatec Maya language. The film proved to be a critical and commercial success.

Youngblood's other films include *Beatdown* (2010, Americana Films); *Wind Walkers* (2015, Iron Circle Films); *Shepherd's Blade* (2015, JLE Cinema), a film short; *Crossing Point* (2016, Conflict Pictures); *Attrition* (2018, Grindstone); and *Glechschaltung* (2018, Masch). His television appearances include *Amnesia* and *American Mythos*.

13

The Return to Invisibility (2011–Present)

The period of 2010 to the present marked a return to invisibility for Native Americans, both in film and in the media, as well as in real life. However, indigenous people remained vibrant, active, and committed to exercising agency over their communities and within their lives.

On Friday, January 20, 2017, Donald Trump was inaugurated as president of the United States. Prior to this event, the departing president, Barack Obama, had dashed the hopes of millions of Native Americans when he refused to pardon Leonard Peltier, age 70, who had already served more than forty years in prison following a universally recognized controversial trial.

After his inauguration, Trump promptly issued an executive order (on January 20, 2017) to continue the Dakota Access Pipeline (a 1,172-mile-long underground pipeline) from North Dakota to Texas. The pipeline was opposed by numerous indigenous tribes, environmentalists, and other groups due to the potential impact on the water, pollution of surrounding land, and other concerns. The opposition by indigenous tribes made headlines throughout the world.

Trump began his presidency by insulting Mexicans as "rapists" and "criminals." Soon thereafter, he went on to insult every other minority community (i.e., African Americans, Muslims, etc.) as well. Women were a constant target of his tirades. Trump also proceeded to double down on implementing increasingly harsh immigration policies, especially in relation to Mexican and Central Americans. Neither government officials nor the media appeared to remember that these people were the original residents of the continent.

The Trump presidency has given rise to one of the most divisive, disturbing, and controversial eras in recent U.S. history, which shows no signs of ending anytime soon.

NATIVE AMERICAN FILM IMAGES IN THE 2010S

During the decade of 2011–2020, relatively few Native American–themed films were made. Indigenous actors likewise became an endangered species.

Crooked Arrows (2012, Sports Studio) is an offbeat film about the efforts of Native American lacrosse team competing against white, upper-crust schools in the Northeast.

Loren King, in the *Boston Globe* (May 29, 2012), wrote, "The story is unique and engaging enough to transcend the uplifting sports-underdog formula."[1]

The film *Winter in the Blood* (2013, Kino Lorber) was produced by native writer Sherman Alexie and directed by Alex and Andrew J. Smith. The story is set in Montana and focuses on the ordinary life of a Native American community. The native cast included Chaske Spencer, Julia Jones, Gary Farmer, and Michael Spears, among others. The film was based on the novel *Winter in the Blood* (1974) by native author James Welch. Sherman Alexie was asked by William O'Connor in *The Daily Beast* about the sense of loss that runs throughout the film, and he stated, "I think it is absolutely a part of our culture. I think loss is in our DNA by now—every song, every feeling, every story is infused with that. Even though we live on reservations often, they're often in places where we never actually lived....We're a colonized people."[2]

Representative Films

César Chávez (2014, Pantellon Films)

César Chávez (1927–1993) was a Mexican Native American born in Yuma, Arizona. He and his family were migrant farm workers who faced rampant racism, exploitation, and harsh working conditions (including pesticide-ridden fields). As an adult, Chávez became of the most revered labor rights and civil rights leaders in the United States. Along with Dolores Huerta, he co-founded the United Farm Workers union in the 1960s. Chávez inspired millions of impoverished farm workers with his nonviolence and spirituality. In motivating his fellow workers, he made use of two powerful Mexican Native American symbols: the Aztec eagle and the *Virgen de Guadalupe*.

Making a film about César Chávez proved difficult. Hollywood studios were unwilling to provide funding to make a film about the best-known Mexican Native American, showing little interest in the subject (and even some disdain). In the end, the $10 million budget was raised through Mexican capital. The film was shot in the northern Mexican state of Sonora and directed by Mexican director-producer Diego Luna (this project marked Luna's first English-language film). The screenplay was written by Keir Pearson, who had previously been nominated for an Academy Award for Best Screenplay for the film *Hotel Rwanda* in 2004.

A major aspect of the film was Chávez's early efforts in California to organize more than fifty thousand farm workers (the vast majority of them Mexican, but also some Filipino workers), including Mexican *braceros* (in Spanish, "one who works with their arms"). The *bracero* program was started on August 4, 1942, in order to import Mexican agricultural laborers due to the labor shortage in the United States during World War II. Thereafter, growers used this program to ensure a steady supply of cheap laborers who could not legalize their status or unionize and who returned to Mexico once the harvest season was over. As a result, the efforts to organize farm workers often pitted two groups of farm workers—documented and undocumented—against one another. It was not until 1964, when the *bracero* program ended, that Chávez, Huerta, and others were finally able to more be effective in founding and organizing the United Farm Workers (UFW) union.

César Chávez depicted the difficulty involved in organizing agricultural workers who had been marginalized, brutalized, and exploited for generations. It culminated in the Grape Boycott (1965–1971) and Salad Bowl Strike (August 23, 1970–March 26, 1971), which was the largest farm worker strike in U.S. labor history. The efforts of the UFW resulted in the passage of the landmark California Agricultural Relations Act (CARA), which became law in 1975, thus legalizing collective bargaining for farm workers, which had been ignored by the federal National Labor Relations Act (NLRA) of 1935.

This film documents the evolution of César Chávez as a community activist and organizer, including his human flaws and his labor strategies, as well as the rising political consciousness of farm workers and the impact on the world labor movement. It captures the spirit, hope, and passion of a momentous time in Mexican American history. Such things are hard to convey to another generation, especially to white audiences. However, this film serves as a window into a pivotal time in both Chicano and labor history. The three leads—Michael Peña, America Ferrara, and Rosario Dawson—are especially moving, authentic, and transforming.

Mexican American actor Michael Peña was cast as César Chávez. His father (a former farm worker) reportedly wept with joy when his son was cast in the role. America Ferrara played César's wife Helen Chávez, an equal partner in the building of the labor union; Rosario Dawson played Dolores Huerta, the co-founder of the union; John Malkovich played the powerful grower Bogdanovich Senior; and Jacob Vargas played Chávez's younger brother Richard.

The state of Sonora, in Mexico, was chosen as the filming location due to its similarity to California in the early 1960s. Much of the film was shot among the vineyards; parts were also filmed in the city of Hermosillo. In addition, a dialect coach taught actors how to speak with a Chicano intonation.[3]

The film received mixed reviews. Bill Zwecker, in the *Chicago Sun-Times* (March 27, 2014), wrote, "A solid and mostly successful attempt to introduce this important labor leader and civil rights activist to younger audiences, while reminding older folks of the impact Chávez had on this country."[4] Claudia Puig, in *USA Today* (March 27, 2014), noted, "Not only powerful but timely, given divided attitudes toward immigration and unionization."[5] Ben Sachs, in the *Chicago Reader* (March 27, 2014), stated, "Michael Peña is particularly impressive in the lead, resisting the obvious temptation to make Chávez larger than life. Diego Luna, a fine actor himself, directed, grounding the story in earthy, authentic-seeming detail."[6] The Mexican American community, which had waited decades for a film about a genuine hero, embraced the film, heart and soul.

Due to the film's limited budget and publicity, *César Chávez* did only modest business at the box office. However, for Mexican Americans and Native Americans, the film proved extremely popular, especially in schools.

The Lone Ranger (2013, Disney)

During the leadup to the release of *The Lone Ranger* in 2013, there were hopes that at long last the famous character of Tonto (the sidekick of the Lone Ranger) would be redeemed in a portrayal that would grant him some dignity and integrity. However, as usual, Hollywood chose to repeat the past in pursuit of the all-mighty dollar.

Given that the name Tonto means "dumb" or "stupid" in Spanish, the entire premise of *The Lone Ranger* (an old workhorse in Hollywood films) does not come across as very promising. The original story and characters were created by George W. Trendle and

Fran Striker. The Lone Ranger first appeared on radio in Detroit in 1934, airing on a radio station owned by Trendle. The radio shows were written by Striker. Later, the radio show was further popularized by books, written mostly by Trendle and Striker.

After *The Lone Ranger* became a popular staple in comic books, Republic Pictures released two film serials: *The Lone Ranger* (1938), which had fifteen chapters, starring Lee Powell as the Lone Ranger and native actor Chief Thundercloud as Tonto; and *The Lone Ranger Rides Again* (1939), which also had fifteen chapters. Thundercloud reprised his role as Tonto for the second serial, but Powell was replaced by Robert Livingston. Both products were filled with impressive action scenes (often performed by some of the greatest stuntmen of the era, like Yakima Canutt and David Sharpe) and proved enormously popular.

Between 1949 and 1957, *The Lone Ranger* aired on television in half-hour episodes. The Lone Ranger was played by Clayton Moore, and Tonto was played by native actor Jay Silverheels. Both actors reprised their roles in two feature films: *The Lone Ranger* (1956, Warner Bros.) and *The Lone Ranger and the Lost City of Gold* (1958, Warner Bros.). More than twenty years later, a new film, *The Legend of the Lone Ranger* (1981, ITC), was released. In this version, native (Yaqui) actor Michael Horse played Tonto, and Klinton Spilsbury played the famous masked man. In 2003, Warner Brothers released a television show titled *The Lone Ranger* as a pilot for a prospective series. Michael Murray played the ranger, while native actor Nathaniel Arcand was Tonto.

The 2013 film version of *The Lone Ranger* was written by Terry Rossio, Justin Haythe, and Ted Elliott. They reworked some of the original story as first written by George W. Trendle and Fran Striker. The narrative of the film is set in 1933 and involves a boy whose hero is the Lone Ranger. At a San Francisco fair, the boy meets an aged Tonto (of Comanche ancestry), who tells him his life story.

In 1869, Tonto is riding the transcontinental railroad. The train also carries an outlaw named Butch Cavendish, who is being taken to his execution. Butch was captured by Dan Reid, a Texas Ranger. However, Cavendish's gang derails the train and rescues Butch. Tonto is jailed as a suspected member of the gang. Later, the Cavendish gang ambushes a group of Texas Rangers (including Dan Reid, as well as his younger brother John) who are pursuing them. Butch kills Dan and then consumes his heart as revenge.

In the meantime, Tonto has escaped from jail; he finds the dead rangers and buries them. At this point, a white spirit horse brings John Reid back to life, and he becomes a "spirit walker." Later, Tonto informs Reid that he can no longer be killed. Tonto then gives Reid a silver bullet made from Texas Ranger badges and advises him to use it on Cavendish (whom Tonto believes is a mythological beast called a *wendigo*). He also informs Reid that Collins, one of the rangers, betrayed the men who were ambushed. Reid subsequently dons a mask to hide his identity and makes a pact with Tonto to dedicate their lives to capturing the fugitives. The pair become known as the Lone Ranger and Tonto throughout the West.

The casting for this film proved problematic. Johnny Depp, who was riding high on several years of box-office hits, was cast as Tonto. Depp, an actor of talent and stature, claimed that he had Native American roots.[7] In playing the role of Tonto, a Comanche, Depp opted for wearing a dead bird on top of his head without any cultural basis for doing so. (In fact, an actor who had played the shaman in the film *A Man Called Horse* had worn the same dead bird, again without the slightest evidence of cultural context or authenticity.) Native American actors were cast in small parts: Saginaw Grant (Chief Big

Bear); David Midthunder (Fuller's Native American scout); Gil Birmingham (Red Knee); Loren Anthony (a Comanche warrior); and Malachi Tsoodle-Nelson (Red Knee's young warrior), among others.

The film faced adversity and problems almost from the very beginning. Instead of keeping the essential story and embellishing it with an updated vision, the producers proceeded to cram the narrative with special effects and unnecessary subplots. The result was a convoluted, confusing, and overworked plot that pleased no one. Delays and other mishaps ballooned the budget to some $225–250 million (though in fact the film cost even more to make). *The Lone Ranger* grossed, worldwide, some $260.5 million,[8] making it one of the most notorious film failures of all time. One redeeming feature, however, was the stunning cinematography by Bojan Bazelli of such places as Monument Valley, in the Four Corners region; Moab, Utah; Creede, Colorado; and Cimarron State Park, New Mexico.

Reviews of the film were predictably negative. Kenneth Turan, in the *Los Angeles Times* (July 3, 2013), wrote, "Not even Johnny Depp can rescue this unappealing 'Lone Ranger.'"[9]

The Ridiculous Six (2015, Happy Madison Prods.)

The Ridiculous Six is a comedy western headlined by Adam Sandler and distributed by Netflix. The film was directed by Frank Coraci and co-written by Adam Sandler and Tim Herlihy. The narrative focuses on six men who discover that they have the same father, bank robber Frank Stockburn (Nick Nolte).

Vincent Schilling, writing in the *Indian Country Media Network*, reported on April 23, 2015, that "a dozen Native actors and actresses, as well as the Native cultural advisor, left the set of Adam Sandler's newest production, *The Ridiculous Six*" to protest the demeaning portrayals of Apaches, especially those of native women.[10] A Netflix representative stated, "The movie has ridiculous in the title for a reason: because it is ridiculous. It is a broad satire of Western movies and the stereotypes they popularized."[11]

The film was budgeted at $60 million. It received negative film reviews and was a notable commercial flop.

Hostiles (2017, Entertain. Studios)

Hostiles is a western that focuses on dying Native American leader's journey back to his homeland. It was directed by Scott Cooper, who also wrote the screenplay (based on a manuscript by Donald E. Stewart). Native Americans in the cast included Wes Studi, Adam Beach, David Midthunder, Gray Wolf Herrera, Xavier Horsechief, Q'orianka Kilcher, Tanaya Beatty, Makayah Crowfoot, and Sharon Anne Henderson, among others.

The narrative is set in 1892, at the end of the so-called Indian Wars. An U.S. Army captain, Joseph J. Blocker (Christian Bale), sets out to return a dying Chief Yellow Hawk (Wes Studi) to his homeland. He anticipates obstacles along the way.

Hostiles is a well-meaning effort to summarize the legacy of the so-called Indian Wars. However, this film is yet another narrative that seen through the eyes of a burned-out white soldier, a man who has outlived his usefulness. Captain Joseph Blocker is like the character of Ethan Edwards in John Ford's *The Searchers* (1956, Warner Bros.). Blocker cannot fully let go of his hatred for Native Americans, and he is psychologically unable to adjust to a new era. He sees the devastation that the genocidal wars have brought upon native people, but he cannot come to terms with his own personal pangs of guilt. The native characters who populate the film are only framed within his own perspective.

Hostiles received mixed reviews. A. O. Scott, in the *New York Times* (December 21, 2017), wrote, "It is unlikely to escape notice that this is yet another tale of a white man's conscience, which uses Yellow Hawk and his children and grandchildren as vehicles for Blocker's awakening. Whether this awakening is complete and whether the film's final notes of absolution are fully earned are matters worth arguing about."[12]

The film was shot in Arizona, Colorado, and New Mexico. It was budgeted at $39 million and grossed $28.4 million by February 2018.

Roma (2018, Netflix)

Just before this book went to press, a comet of hope brightened the Hollywood firmament when Mexican actress Yalitza Aparicio became the first indigenous woman ever to be nominated for an Academy Award for Best Actress for the Mexican film *Roma*, released in 2018 through Netflix. In the film, Aparicio played an indigenous domestic worker employed by a Euro-Mexican family in the upscale Roma neighborhood in Mexico City during the 1970s. Although Aparicio did not win the award, she nonetheless made history. The film went on to earn director Alfonso Cuarón the Oscar for Best Director, as well as the Academy Award for Best Foreign Film.

Aparicio was born in Mexico's southern state of Oaxaca. She belongs to the Mixtec people (on her father's side) and the Triqui (though her mother).

14

Looking Back and Looking Forward

The images, perceptions, and attitudes about Native Americans were originally constructed more than five hundred years ago with the arrival of Europeans in the Americas in 1492. The newcomers' impressions of indigenous peoples (however biased and erroneous such ideas might have been) were cataloged and disseminated through the logs of explorers and seamen, diaries of conquistadores and clergy, government documents and church records, personal correspondence and newspapers, books and plays, Wild West shows, and, finally, motion pictures. The essence of these images was that native people were soulless savages, cruel and barbarous, backward and uncivilized. In the end, these perceptions were used to justify the wholesale appropriation of the entire continent and the annihilation of Native Americans.

The first U.S. film images of native people were created in the late 1800s. Most of these early films were anthropological in nature, for some believed that these primitive people were a vanishing race and that a record should be made for posterity and science. Thereafter, movies in the United States became a huge money-making industry. Later, the nation documented its expansion across the continent in cinema. Motion pictures were a convenient art form through which to celebrate the history of the nation and educate citizens about their country's past. (It was also a way to profit from that history.)

Inevitably, the history of the United States in movies was a visual catharsis of its own contradictions and social stresses. In film, both Manifest Destiny and genocide were depicted as a Darwinist metaphor of "the survival of the fittest." A filmic mythology was invented that justified all misdeeds and celebrated the "exceptionalism" of the nation.

It has now been more than one hundred years since the beginning of motion pictures in the United States. And while some of the mythology of Manifest Destiny and the "winning of the West" has receded, many people still cling to the myths perpetuated by motion pictures.

It is this writer's hope that the nation will finally come to terms with its authentic history. It is time to acknowledge the true past and present of Native Americans and to discard the mythologies of Manifest Destiny and westward expansion. Only then can the truth make us free.

Let us begin.

Chapter Notes

Acknowledgments

1. Angel R. Oquendo (1998). "Re-Imagining the Latino/a Race," *The Latino/a Condition: A Critical Reader*, Richard Delgado and Jean Steancicic, eds. New York: New York University Press, p. 63.
2. Suzanne Oboler (1998). "Hispanic: That's What They Call Us," in Delgado and Stefanic, eds., p. 4.

Introduction

1. Means, Russell and Marvin J. Wolf (1995). *Where White Men Fear to Tread: The Autobiography of Russell Means*. New York: St. Martin's Griffin, p. 239. The Mexican government for example, defines "*indios*" or "*indigenas*" only as those living in traditional way of life (i.e., religion, language, etc.). Thus, the Mexican census indicates that only 14.86 percent of its 115,000,000 (2015) population is Native American. However, the reality is that today Mexico continues to have the largest Native American population in the world. Native American leader and activist Russell Means wrote in his autobiography, "We Lakota thought of Mexicans as just another kind of Indian people who spoke a different language."
2. Dunbar-Ortiz, Roxanne (2014). *An Indigenous Peoples' History of the United States*. Boston: Beacon Press, p. 115.
3. Ibid., p. 116.

Chapter 1

1. Stannard, David E. (1992). *American Holocaust: The Conquest of the New World*. New York: Oxford University Press, pp. 57–61. The Europe of the 11th, 12th, 13th, 14th, and 15th centuries was one beset by plagues; witch burnings; the Spanish Inquisition; religious intolerance, widespread slavery, and peasant peonage. Persistent warfare raged throughout Europe. For example, the One Hundred Years War (1337–1453), was a conflict fought between the Kingdom of England and the Kingdom of France. The Thirty Years' War (1618–1648), was fought in Central Europe is said to have resulted in at least eight million deaths. In addition, religious wars raged almost continually across Europe. The best known were the Crusades against Islam: the First Crusade (1095–99) to the 9th Crusade (1271–72).
2. Dunbar-Ortiz, Roxanne (2014), p. 17.
3. Josephy, Alvin M. (1994), *500 Nations: An Illustrated History of North American Indians*. New York: Alfred A. Knopf, p. 64.
4. Flores, Antonio. *How the U.S. Population Is Changing*. September 18, 2017. *PEW Research Center*. In 2016, the Latino population was listed as nearly 58 million; and accounted for 18 percent of the nation's population. Latinos have been the nation's largest minority for more than a decade. The Mexico-origin population accounted for 63.3 percent (or 36 million) of the nation's Latino population in 2015. In summary, the assumption that the Native American population is only 0.8 percent of the nation's Native American demographics is incorrect.
5. Dunbar-Ortiz, p. 18.
6. Josephy, Alvin M. (1994). *500 Nations: An Illustrated History of North American Indians*. New York: Alfred A. Knopf, p. 64.
7. Ibid.
8. The name Inca referred to the ruling family of the empire. However, the Spanish mistakenly used the name as an ethnic term for Quechua-speaking people that made up the entire Inca Empire.
9. Coe, Michael D. (1984). *Mexico*. London: Thames and Hudson, p. 68.
10. Stannard, David E. (1992), *American Holocaust: The Conquest of the New World*. Oxford: Oxford University Press, p. 95. The actual number of Spanish who lived in the Americas was relatively small, compared to the tens of millions of Native Americans. As a consequence, Mexico and several countries in the Americas remain indigenous-majority nations. Stannard noted, "By the time the sixteenth century had ended perhaps some 200,000 Spaniards had moved their lives to the Indies, to Mexico, to Central America, and points further to the south."
11. *Northwest Land Ordinance of 1787*.
12. Drinnon, Richard (1980). *Facing West: The Metaphysics of Indian-Hating and Empire-Building*. Minneapolis: University of Minnesota Press, p. 331.
13. Deloria, Vine, Jr., and Raymond DeMallie (1999). *Documents of Indian Diplomacy: Treaties, Agreements, and Conventions, 1775–1979*. Norman: University of Oklahoma Press.
14. Dunbar-Ortiz, Roxanne (2014). *An Indigenous Peoples' History of the United States*. Boston: Beacon Press, p. 142.
15. Ibid., p. 40.
16. Resendez, Andres (2016). *The Other Slavery: The Uncovered Story of Indian Slavery in America*. Boston: Houghton Mifflin Harcourt.
17. *The American Experience: We Shall Remain*

(2009). PBS. At his deathbed, Geronimo is reputed to have told his nephew that he regretted having surrendered, "I should have never surrendered. I should have fought until I was the last man alive." Despite numerous entreaties by the Apache Nation for many years, the U.S. Government has refused to transfer Geronimo's remains to his people.

Chapter 2

1. The groundbreaking research of Native American film images that has been undertaken by such scholars as Angela Aleiss and M. Elise Marubbio has been an important contribution to this field.
2. Marubbio, M. Elise (2009). *Killing the Indian Maiden: Images of Native American Women in Film.* Lexington: The University Press of Kentucky, p. 14.
3. Aleiss, Angela. "Community Comment: Maidens of Hollywood: 'Pocahontas' is the pure expression of filmmakers' fantasies about Indian women." *Los Angeles Times,* June 24, 1995.
4. Marrubbio, M. Elise (2009). *Killing the Indian Maiden,* p. 16.
5. Aleiss, Angela (2005). *Making the White Man's Indian: Native Americans and Hollywood Movies.* Westport, CT: Praeger, p. 84.

Chapter 3

1. Aleiss, Angela (2005). *Making the White Man's Indian: Native Americans and Hollywood Movies.* Westport, CT: Praeger, p. 2.
2. *The Redman's View* film is available on You Tube.
3. The re-discovery of *In Old California* has revised the long-held belief that DeMille's *The Squaw Man* (1914) was the first film shot in Hollywood.
4. Aleiss, Angela (2005). *Making the White Man's Indian: Native Americans and Hollywood Films.* Westport, CT: Praeger, p. 23.
5. DeMille, Cecil B., and Donald Hayne, editor (1959). *The Autobiography of Cecil B. DeMille.* Englewood Cliffs, NJ: Prentice Hall, p. 71.
6. Aleiss, Angela (2005). *Making the White Man's Indian: Native Americans and Hollywood Movies.* Westport, CT: Praeger.
7. DeMille, p. 89.
8. See: Sara Orenstein (2005), "Void for Vagueness: Mexicans and the Collapse of Miscegenation Law in California," *Pacific Hist. Rev.* 74, 367–368. The case involved Andrea Lopez, a Mexican women, and Sylvester Davis, an African American. Perez listed herself as "white" in the marriage license with the County Clerk of Los Angeles; and Davis listed himself as "Negro." Both of the plaintiffs were Catholics. Under California law, Mexicans were classified as "white" because of the Spanish colonization. The County clerk W. G. Clark denied the issuance of the marriage license because under California Civil Code, Section 69, which stated, "No license may be issued authorizing the marriage of a white person with a Negro, mulatto, Mongolian or member of the Malay race." At the end, the California ruled that the anti-miscegenation laws violated Fourteenth Amendments "due process" and "equal protection of the laws." It also stated that the California statute violated the religious freedom of the plaintiffs because they infringed on their rights of in the Catholic sacrament of marriage.

9. Aleiss, Angela (May 2013). "Who Was the Real James Young Deer?" *Bright Lights Journal.*
10. Aleiss, Angela (February 24, 2014). "100 Years Ago: Lillian St. Cyr, First Native Star in Hollywood Feature Films." *Indian Country.*
11. Aleiss, Angela (May 2013). "Who Was the Real James Young Deer?" *Bright Lights Journal.*
12. *Ibid.*

Chapter 4

1. Black, George (1988). *The Good Neighbor Policy.* New York: Pantheon Books.
2. *Variety.* November 21, 1913.
3. Wlaschin, Ken (1989). *The World's Great Movie Stars: The International Years.* New York: Hill & Wang, p. 3.
4. The Spirit Lake Massacre occurred during March 8–12, 1857, in northwestern Iowa. It was led by Inkapaluta, leader of a dissident band of Santee Lakota (Sioux). Other bands that made up the Lakota in the region were the Sisseton and Wahpeton. They were supposed to be given annual annuities by the U.S. government according to the *Traverse des Sioux and Mendota 1852,* in exchange for the lands they had been forced to give up. However, the government repeatedly failed to pay the annuities in a timely manner. The harsh winter of the years 1856–57 aggravated the conditions of the Sioux (Lakota) band and reduced them to begging for food. The rising numbers of Euro-American settlers into the area drastically reduced the yield of hunting. Tensions between Native Americans and Euro-American settlers were stretched to the breaking point.
   At that point, Inkpaduta led some 14 warriors against the white settlement in northwestern Iowa, in retaliation of the murder of his brother Sidominadotah, and that of his family by Henry Lott. Inkpaduta and his warriors killed an estimated 40 white settlers and took four young women as captives. In 1862, the Sioux Uprising took place after thousands of Sioux (Lakota) starved, as white settlers continued to take prime farming land. According to all reliable evidence, Sitting Bull never took part in the Spirit River Massacre of 1857. See: *The Sioux Uprising of 1862* by Kenneth Carley. St. Paul: Minnesota Historical Society Press, 1976.
5. Dunbar-Ortiz, Roxanne (2014). *An Indigenous Peoples' History of the United States.* Boston, MA: Beacon Press, p. 22.
6. Roberts, David (2004). *The Pueblo Revolt: The Secret Rebellion That Drove the Spanish out of the Southwest.* New York: Simon & Schuster, p. 27.
7. *Variety.* October 2, 1925.
8. Nolley, Ken (1999). "The Representation of Conquest: John Ford and the Hollywood Indian, 1939–1964." In Rollins, Peter C., and John E. O'Connor, eds. *Hollywood's Indian: The Portrayal of the Native American in Film.* Lexington: The University Press of Kentucky, p. 73.
9. *New York Times.* August 29, 1924.
10. National Registry. Library of Congress, 2011.
11. Madley, Benjamin (2017). *An American Genocide: The United States and the California Indian Catastrophe, 1846–1873.* New Haven, CT: Yale University Press, p. 347.
12. Hall, Mordaunt. *New York Times,* May 28, 1928.
13. Dunbar-Ortiz (2014), p. 65.
14. Mordaunt Hall. *New York Times,* January 29, 1929.

15. *Photoplay*, July 1922.
16. *Photoplay*, April 1923.
17. *Photoplay*. March, 1926.
18. Ramón, David (1997). *Dolores Del Río, Volúmen 1: Un cuento de Hadas*. Mexico City: Editorial Cio, pp. 51–52.
19. Golden Silents website. Accessed April 11, 2018.
20. *Los Angeles Herald-Examiner TV Weekly*, November 8–14, 1964.
21. Ibid.
22. *New York Times*, November 1, 1968.
23. López, Ana M. (1993). "Are All Latinas from Manhattan?" In John King, Ana M. Lopez and Manuel Alvarado, eds. *Mediating Two Worlds: Cinematic Encounters in the Americas*. London: British Film Institute, p. 71.
24. Woll, Allen L. (1977). *The Latin Image in American Film*. Los Angeles: UCLA Latin American Center Publications, University of California, p. 71.

Chapter 5

1. See: Balderama, Francisco E., and Raymond Rodriguez (2006). *Decade of Betrayal: Mexican Repatriation in the 1930s*. Albuquerque: University of New Mexico Press.
2. Hall, Mordaunt. *New York Times*. November 2, 1930.
3. Hall, Mordaunt. *New York Times*. May 20, 1930.
4. Birchard, Robert S. (2004). *Cecil B. DeMille's Hollywood*. Lexington: The University Press of Kentucky, p. 249.
5. Hall, Mordaunt. *New York Times*. September 19, 1931.
6. Feaster, Felicia. Turner Movie Classics website. Accessed August 3, 2017.
7. Hall, Mordaunt. *New York Times*. November 25, 1932.
8. O'Connor, John E. (1980). *The Hollywood Indian: Stereotypes of Native Americans*. Trenton: New Jersey State Museum.
9. *Variety*. January 2, 1934.
10. Hall, Mordaunt. *New York Times*. November 15, 1933.
11. *Variety*. May 3, 1939.
12. Nugent, Frank S. *New York Times*. October 7, 1936.
13. Ibid.
14. *Variety*. April 26, 1939.
15. Ibid.
16. Quinn, Anthony, and Daniel Paisner (1995). *One Man Tango*. New York: Harper Collins, pp. 9–10.
17. Ibid., p. 10.
18. Ibid., p. 13.
19. Ibid., p. 72.
20. Ibid., pp. 123–124.
21. Ibid., p. 129.
22. DeMille, Cecil B., p. 352.
23. Quinn, Anthony and Daniel Paisner, p. 155.
24. Ibid., p. 187.
25. Ibid., p. 193.
26. Ibid., p. 109.
27. Ibid., pp. 238–239.
28. Rovin, Jeff (1976). *The Films of Charlton Heston*. Secaucus, NJ: The Citadel Press, p. 98.
29. Quinn, Anthony and Daniel Paisner, p. 267.
30. Ibid., p. 269.
31. Ibid., p. 342.
32. Ibid., p. 343.
33. Ibid., p. 344.
34. *Los Angeles Times*. January 3, 1994.
35. *Los Angeles Times*. January 3, 1994.
36. "Indian Thorpe In Olympiad; Redskin from Carlyle Will Strive for Place on American Team." *New York Times*. April 28, 1912.
37. Buford, Kate (2010). *Native Son: The Life and Sporting Life of Jim Thorpe*. Lincoln: University of Nebraska Press, p. 292.
38. "Thorpe Has Cancerous Growth." *New York Times*, November 10, 1951.

Chapter 6

1. See: Berstein, Alan (1999). *American Indians and World War II: Toward a New Era in Indian Affairs*. Norman: University of Oklahoma Press.
2. See: Ulrich, Roberta (2010). *American Indian Nations form Termination to Restoration, 1953–2006*. Lincoln: University of Nebraska Press.
3. Nixon, Richard. "Special Message to the Congress on Indian Affairs." July 8, 1970.
4. Reagan, Ronald. "American Indian Policy Statement," January 24, 1983.
5. Marrubbio, M. Elise (2009). *Killing the Indian Maiden*, p. 116.
6. O'Connor, John E. (1999). "The White Man's Indian: An Institutional Approach." In Rollins, Peter C., and John E. O'Connor, eds. *Hollywood's Indian: The Portrayal of the Native American in Film*. Lexington: The University Press of Kentucky, p. 34.
7. *Variety*. November 7, 1941.
8. Crowther, Bosley. *New York Times*. June 25, 1948.
9. Crowther, Bosley. *New York Times*. November 18, 1949.
10. Nugent, Frank S. *New York Times*. March 8, 1940.
11. Ultimate Movie Rankings website. Accessed May 24, 2018.
12. Marubbio, M. Elise (2006). *Killing the Maiden: Images of Native American Women in Film*. Lexington: The University Press of Kentucky, p, 123.
13. Box Office Mojo. Accessed August 9, 2018.
14. *Variety*. October 23, 1940.
15. Crowther, Bosley. *New York Times*. October 11, 1947.
16. Ultimate Movie Ranking. Accessed January 9, 2018.
17. Marubbio, M. Elise (2006). *Killing the Indian Maiden: Images of Native Women in Film*. Lexington: The University Press of Kentucky, p. 115.
18. *Doña Marina* or *La Malinche* is said to have lived from 1496 or 1501 to 1529. She was one of 20 women slaves given to Córtes by the native leaders of Tabasco in 1519. She gave birth to the first son of Córtes, Martín, who some consider to be one of the first *mestizos* in the Americas. Some modern Mexican feminists see her as the scapegoat for the Spanish conquest. She is seen by some as been blamed for the fall of the Mexico, in a similar way that Eve is blamed (instead of Adam) for the expulsion from the Garden of Eden.
19. Two of the actors in *Captain from Castile* were embroiled in the politics of the House Un-American Activities Committee. The highly respected character actor Lee J. Cobb (1911–1976), who played the role of Juan Garcia, was accused of being a Communist in 1951

before HUAC, by actor Larry Parks. Cobb refused to testify when he was called before the committee. However, in 1953, after being blacklisted for two years, he became a "friendly witness" and named 20 persons as being members of the Communist Party. The character actor Marc Lawrence (1910–2005) who played the role of Corio), one of the mutineers against Cortez, was called before HUAC in 1951. He named names, among them Sterling Hayden, Keren Morley, Larry Parks, and others. Nonetheless, Lawrence was blacklisted and left for Europe to make films. He did not appear in U.S.-shot films until the 1970s.

20. *Ultimate Movie Rankings*. Accessed March 12, 2018.
21. *Variety*. November 26, 1947.
22. Barnes, Howard. *New York Herald*. November 26, 1947.
23. *Variety*. June 25, 1947.
24. *Cue*. September 6, 1947.
25. *The Hollywood Reporter*. June 23, 1947.
26. Crowther, Bosley. *New York Times*. April 20, 1944.
27. O'Hara, Maureen, and John Nicolletti (2004). '*Tis Herself: A Memoir*. New York: Simon & Schuster.
28. *Ultimate Movie Rankings*. Accessed August 9, 2018.
29. Davis, Ronald L. (1991). *Hollywood Beauty: Linda Darnell and the American Dream*. Norman: University of Oklahoma Press, p. 10.
30. *Ibid*., p. 12.
31. Crowther, Bosley. *New York Times*. February 7, 1946.
32. The Mexican Revolution (1910–1920) overthrew the longstanding dictatorship of Porfirio Díaz and sought to bring about land reform, social justice, and to curb the power of the Catholic Church. A series of counter-revolutions in the following years led by Victoriano Huerta, Venustiano Carranza, and Alvaro Obregón ultimately resulted in less radical changes in Mexican society. The indigenous and mestizo poor and marginalized had pinned their hopes in the mestizo Francisco "Pancho" Villa from the northern state of Chihuahua; and the Native American leader Emiliano Zapata from the southern state of Morelos. However, both were assassinated by the counter-revolution.
33. Katz, Ephraim (1994). *The Film Encyclopedia*. New York: HarperCollins, p. 444.

Chapter 7

1. The Louisiana Purchase in 1803 by President Thomas Jefferson involved the acquisition of some 822,000 square miles. The United States paid 15 million francs, along with the cancellation of France's debts. The title to the area by the French and the actual purchase by the United States is fraught with legality, in light of the millions of Native Americans living in the large area and the non-existent acquiescence to such title of land in the first place.
2. President Thomas Jefferson initially believed Native Americans as "equal to the white men." During his Presidency, he talked about the assimilation of indigenous peoples. However, beginning in 1803, however, his private letters manifested a policy of removal.
3. The Native American woman Sacajawea (1788–1812), of Shoshone ancestry, has become the cause of controversy by some. Some indigenous people see her as a sellout of her people or as a victim of European opportunism. Like Dona Marina and/or La Malinche; Sacajawea is vilified by some and honored by others.
4. *New York Times*. November 10, 1950.
5. *Los Angeles Daily News*. October 31, 1950.
6. *Fortnight*. October 30, 1950.
7. *Focus on Film*. Autumn 1972.
8. *Variety*. June 15, 1950.
9. *Film Daily*. June 14, 1950.
10. *The Hollywood Reporter*. June 12, 1950.
11. Katz, Ephraim (1994). *The Film Encyclopedia*. New York: HarperCollins, p. 331.
12. *New York Times*. January 2, 1953.
13. Eliot, Marc (2017). *Charlton Heston: Hollywood's Last Icon*. New York: HarperCollins, p. 68.
14. *Ibid*.
15. Ultimate Moving Ranking website. Accessed January 17, 2018.
16. Crowther, Bosley. *New York Times*. March 1, 1956.
17. Crowther, Bosley. *New York Times*. November 26, 1954.
18. Crowther, Bosley. *The New York Tines*. April 28, 1955.
19. Ultimate Movie Ranking website. Accessed January 17, 2018.
20. Nash, Jay Robert, and Stanley Ralph Ross (1987). *The Motion Picture Guide*. Chicago: Cinebooks, pp. 2789–2790.
21. *Variety*. March 13, 1956.
22. *Los Angeles Times*. March 13, 1956.
23. *The Hollywood Reporter*. March 13, 1956.
24. *Rolling Stone*. July 10, 1993.
25. *Reader*. June 25, 1993.
26. Thompson, Howard H. *New York Times*. May 10, 1952.
27. *Ultimate Movie Rankings*. Accessed January 19, 2018.
28. See: Madley, Benjamin (2017). *An American Genocide: The United States and the California Indian Catastrophe, 1846–1873*. New Haven, CT: Yale University Press.
29. Miranda, Deborah A. "To Some in California, Founder of Church Missions is Far from Saint." *New York Times*. January 21, 2015.
30. Crowther, Bosley. *New York Times*. October 8, 1955.
31. *Ultimate Movie Rankings*. Accessed January 20, 2018.
32. Friedrich, Otto (1986). *City of Nets*. New York: Harper & Row, p. 168.
33. Alexander, Linda J. (2008). *Reluctant Witness: Robert Taylor, Hollywood and Communism*. Swanborn, South Carolina: Tense Publishing LLC. According to Alexander, "He [Robert Taylor] was caught in a web. If he wanted to keep his career, his elevated place in Hollywood, and the lifestyle to which he had become accustomed, Bob had to magnify his position as a patriotic countryman. He had to make very clear his place as a 'company man' for Louis B. Mayer [the MGM chief]," p. 233.
34. Crowther, Bosley. *New York Times*. January 19, 1950.
35. *Los Angeles Times*. July 22, 1954.
36. *Variety*. June 30, 1954.
37. Kazan, Elia. *A Life* (1988). New York: Alfred A. Knopf, p. 427.
38. *Saturday Review*. April 5, 1972.
39. *Saturday Review*. April 5, 1972.
40. Quinn, Anthony, and Daniel Paisner. *One Man Tango*, New York: HarperCollins, p. 209.

41. *Time.* February 11, 1952.
42. Thomas, Tony (1973). *The Films of Marlon Brando.* Secaucus, NJ: Citadel Press, p. 36.
43. Cooper, Jeanne, and Lindsay Harrison (2002). *Not Young, Still Restless: A Memoir.* New York: HarperCollins, p. 2.
44. Garner, James, and Jon Winokur (2011). *The Garner Files: A Memoir.* New York: Simon & Schuster, pp. 3–4.
45. Author interview with Lupita Tovar, January 13, 1998.
46. LoBianco, Lorraine. "Woody Strode Profile." Turner Classic Movies website. Accessed February 5, 2018.
47. *Ibid.*

Chapter 8

1. President John F. Kennedy Inaugural Address. January 1961,.
2. See: Frayling, Christopher (2006). *Spaghetti Westerns: Cowboys and Europeans from Karl May to Sergio Leone.* London: I.B. Tauris.
3. Bogdanovich, Peter. "The Autumn of John Ford." *Esquire Magazine.* April 1964.
4. *Motion Picture Herald.* November 11, 1964.
5. *Los Angeles Times.* December 21, 1964.
6. Mirisch, Walter (2008). *I Thought We Were Making Movies, Not History.* Madison: University of Wisconsin Press. pp. 160–161.
7. Crowther, Bosley. *New York Times.* December 26, 1963.
8. Edward Dmytryk was one of the Hollywood Ten in 1947, Hollywood filmmakers who refused to testify before the House un-American Activities Committee (HUAC); and who were subsequently blacklisted and serve time in prison. However, in 1951, Dmytryk reversed himself, and became a friendly witness naming names before HUAC. He saved his career and went on to make several notable films in diverse genres: *The Caine Mutiny* (1954, Columbia); and *Raintree Country* (1957, MGM), among others. However, his testimony before the HUAC committee cast a cloud over him for the rest of his film career.
9. Archer, Eugene. *New York Times.* July 27, 1961.
10. Ultimate Movie Ranking website. Accessed March 23, 2018.
11. Alden, Robert. *New York Times.* January 16, 1966.
12. Quirk, Lawrence J. (1975). *The Films of Robert Taylor.* Secaucus, NJ: The Citadel Press, p. 184.
13. *New York Times.* June 16, 1966.

Chapter 9

1. Means, Russell, and Marvin J. Wolf (1995). *Where White Men Fear to Tread: The Autobiography of Russell Means.* New York: St. Martin's Griffin, p. 265.
2. *Ibid.,* p. 261.
3. On June 26, 1975, two FBI agents, Roland A. Williams and Jack R. Coler; and one Native American, Joseph Stuntz, were killed in a shootout at the Pine Ridge Reservation. The federal government began a massive search in order to arrest several AIM members. Subsequently, Leonard Peltier, one of the members of AIM, was extradited from Canada, and put on trial for the death of the two federal agents. Nobody was ever charged for the death of Joseph Stuntz. The trial was controversial, and it made news across the world. In 1977, Peltier was convicted of first-degree murder. At the end, Peltier was found guilty and sentenced to two consecutive life terms. As of 2018, Peltier is imprisoned at the Coleman Federal Correctional Complex, in Coleman, Florida. On January 18, 2017, two days before his term ended, President Barack Obama denied Peltier's application for clemency. As of February 2018, Peltier has completed 43 years in prison. The case of Leonard Peltier continues to be seen in Native American communities as a miscarriage of justice.

Numerous films, songs, articles, and books have been written about the case and the surrounding events. See:

Banks, Dennis (2004). *Ojibwa Warrior: Dennis Banks and the Rise of the American Indian Movement.* Norman, OK: University of Oklahoma Press.

Matthiessen, Peter (1991). *In the Spirit of Crazy Horse.* New York: Penguin Books.

Means, Russell, and Marvin J. Wolf (1995). *Where White Men Fear to Tread; The Autobiography of Russell Means.* New York: St. Martin's Griffin.

Peltier, Leonard (1999). *Prison Writings: My Life Is a Sun Dance.* New York: St. Martin's Griffin.

4. *Re-Member* (2018). Pine Ridge Reservation. Pine Ridge, South Dakota. The poverty rate is 53.75 percent, and the school drop-out rate is 70 percent.
5. Thompson, Howard. *New York Times.* January 1, 1971.
6. *Ibid.*
7. ICMN Staff. Indian Country Media Network. December 12, 2013. Accessed February 7, 2018.
8. Tom Laughlin Official Website. Accessed February 7, 2018.
9. Crowther, Bosley. *New York Times.* August 19, 1967.
10. Thompson, Howard. *New York Times.* July 29, 1971.
11. Canby, Vincent. *New York Times.* November 14, 1974.
12. *CNN Showbiz Tonight.* 1995.
13. Hartke was unsuccessful in obtaining Democratic nomination for the Presidency in 1972. In 1994, he pleaded guilty to misdemeanor election fraud.
14. Waxman, Sharon. "Billy Jack Is Ready to Fight the Good Fight Again." *New York Times.* June 20, 2005.
15. Sachs, Ben. *The Chicago Reader.* August 1, 2013.
16. Ultimate Movie Rankings. Accessed February 7, 2018.
17. *New York Times.* April 30, 1970.
18. Means, Russell, and Marvin J. Wolf (1995). *Where White Men Fear to Tread: The Autobiography of Russell Means.* New York: St. Martin's Griffin,, pp. 189–190.
19. Ebert, Roger. *Chicago Sun-Times.* August 19, 1976.
20. *TV Guide.* Accessed February 14, 2018.
21. *Variety.* December 1, 1974.
22. *The Master Gunfighter* DVD. Special Features. Accessed February 26, 2018.
23. *Films and Filming.* March 1970.
24. *Time.* February 2, 1970.
25. *Playboy.* November 1970.
26. *Variety.* August 17, 1970.
27. *Hollywood Reporter.* August 12, 1970.
28. *New York Times.* September 30, 1970.
29. *Variety* (May 17, 1971).
30. *Los Angeles Times* (July 19, 1972).
31. Brando, Marlon, and Robert Lindsey (1994). *Brando: Songs My Mother Taught Me.* New York: Random House, p. 381.

32. *Ibid.*, p. 404.
33. *Los Angeles Times* (September 24, 1978).
34. *Los Angeles Times* (June 5, 1994).
35. *Ibid.*
36. *Los Angeles Times*. September 24, 1978.
37. *TV Guide.* November 11, 1989.
38. *Ibid.*
39. *Los Angeles Times.* June 5, 1994.
40. *Ibid.*
41. *TV Guide* (November 11, 1989).
42. *Ibid.*
43. *Ibid.*

Chapter 10

1. Elipidia Carrillo (born 1961), is a Mexican Native American actress. She was often typecast as young and uprooted indigenous Mexican and/or Latin American women, a victim of the cotemporary political upheavals in the American continent. See: Frank Javier Garcia Berumen (2014). *Latino Image Makers of Hollywood: Performers, Filmmakers and Films since the 1960s.* Jefferson, NC: McFarland, pp. 157–160.
2. Canby, Vincent. *New York Times.* January 29, 1982.
3. Berumen, Frank Javier Garica (2014), pp. 139–141.
4. Ebert, Roger. *Chicago Sun-Times.* November 11, 1983.
5. Benson, Shiela. *Los Angeles Times.* November 14, 1986.
6. Kempley, Rita. *Washington Post.* November 14, 1986.
7. Maslin, Janet. *New York Times* March 13, 1981.

Chapter 11

1. *Los Angeles Times.* April 1, 1991.
2. *Boston Globe.* March 3, 1999.
3. King. Susan. *Los Angeles Times.* April 28, 2015.
4. "The Pocahontas Myth—Powhatan Renape Nation—the real story, not Disney's Distortion." Powhatan. org. July 5, 2013.
5. Aleiss, Angela. "Community Comment: Maidens of Hollywood: 'Pocahontas' is the pure expression of filmmaker's fantasies about Indian women." *Los Angeles Times*, June 24, 1995.
6. *Variety.* November 1, 1990.
7. *Newsweek.* November 19, 1990.
8. *Chicago Sun-Times.* November 9, 1990.
9. Means, Russell, and Marvin J. Wolf (1995). *Where White Men Fear to Tread: The Autobiography of Russell Means.* New York: St. Martin's Press, p. 513.
10. Ultimate Movie Ranking website. Accessed March 24, 2018.
11. "Polémico filme de Mel Gibson." *El Pais.* December 11, 2006. Accessed March 7, 2018.
12. Mexico's Golden Age of Cinema (1930s to 1960s) had declined due to several factors: the passing of the great Mexican film stars; the proliferation of television; the film market takeover of Hollywood films; the 1994 Mexican recession; and the purveyors of cheap and violence-prone scores of simple-minded films from the 1970s to the early 1990s.
13. *Washington Post.* May 22, 1992.
14. Maslin, Janet. *New York Times.* February 15, 2005.
15. Turan, Kenneth. *Los Angeles Times.* September 6, 2014.
16. Kempley, Rita. *Washington Post.* September 25, 1992.
17. Ebert, Roger. *Chicago Sun-Times.* September 25, 1992.
18. Means, Russell, and Marvin J. Wolf, p. 516.
19. *Ibid.*, 517.
20. Ultimate Movie Rankings website. Accessed February 27, 2018.
21. *Men with Guns* Press Kit (Sony Pictures, 1998).
22. *The Hollywood Reporter.* September 15, 1997.
23. *New York Times.* March 6, 1998.
24. Cobb, Amanda J. "This Is What It Means to Say Smoke Signals: Native American Cultural Sovereignty." In Rollins, Peter C., and John E. O'Connor. *Hollywood's Indian: The Portrayal of the Native American in Film,* p. 224.
25. Sterngold, James. *New York Times.* June 21, 1998.
26. *The Observer.* "A gifted barbarian in the hills." March 20, 1994.
27. Ebert, Roger. *Chicago Sun-Times.* December 10, 1993.
28. Howe, Desson. *New York Times.* December 10, 1993.
29. Maslin, Janet. *New York Times.* April 3, 1992.
30. "Dr. Evan Adams Named Chief Medical Officer of First Nations Health Authority." *Native News Online.* November 17, 2014.
31. *Daily Kos*, February 1, 2012.
32. Banks, Dennis, and Richard Erdoes (2004). *Ojibwa Warrior: Dennis Banks and the American Indian Movement.* Norman: University of Oklahoma Press, p. 360.
33. Miranda, Carolina A. "Q&A with Adam Beach." *Time.* February 2, 2007.
34. *Ibid.*
35. Peralta, Eyder. "Russell Means, Indian Activist and Actor Dies." *New York Times*, October 22, 2012.
36. "Longtime Indian Activist Russell Means Dies at 72." *ABC News.* October 23, 2012.
37. Means, Russell, and Marvin J. Wolf, p. 535.
38. Tony Baltazar and his wife, had a son, who developed and succumbed to a strange blood disease in 1995. Baltazar was had been a professional boxer (1979–1992). Later, Baltazar started a foundation to help kids with the disease.
39. "Sheila Tousey." Stockbridge-Munsee Community Band of Mohican Indians. Retrieved May 3, 2027.
40. "Remembering the Life and Legacy of John Trudell." *Indian Country Today Media Network*, December 8, 2015.
41. *Trudell* (2007). Appaloosa Pictures.

Chapter 12

1. Archibold, Randal C. "Arizona Enacts Stringent Law on Immigration." *New York Times*, April 23, 2010.
2. Santa Cruz, Nicole. "Arizona Bill Targeting Ethnic Studies Signed into Law." *Los Angeles Times*, May 12, 2010.
3. Ravitch, Diane (2014). *Reign of Error: The Hoax of the Privatization Movement and the Danger to America's Public Schools.* New York: Alfred A. Knopf, p. 4.
4. 2010 U.S. Census.
5. 2010 U.S. Census.

6. 2010 U.S. Census. The U.S. Census did not include the 29.3 million Mexicans (who are indigenous people) living in the United States, or remotely connect them to the "Native American" population.
7. *Screen Actors Guild Report 2009.*
8. Ebert, Roger. *Chicago Sun-Times.* June 14, 2002.
9. Meister, Erin. *The Boston Globe.* March 10, 2006.
10. Heffernan, Virginia. *New York Times.* May 25, 2007.
11. Global Heritage Fund. November 2, 2007.
12. Sperling, Nicole. *The Washington Post.* December 15, 2006.
13. Scott, A.O. *New York Times.* December 8, 2006.
14. Martin, Simon, and Nikolai Grube (2000). *Chronicle of the Maya King and Queens: Deciphering the Dynasties of The Ancient Maya.* London: Thames & Hudson, p. 9.
15. Ultimate Movie Rankings. Accessed February 23, 2018.
16. Ebert, Roger. *Chicago Sun-Times.* October 18, 2012.
17. O'Leary, Devin D. "The Other Conquest Conquers America: An Interview with writer/director Salvador Carrasco." *Alibi.* May 3–9, 2007, Volume 16, Number 18. Accessed March 8, 2018.
18. *Ibid.*
19. *Chicago Sun-Times.* November 29, 2006.
20. McCarthy, Todd. *Variety.* October 6, 2006.
21. Kaufman, Amie. "It's the role of a lifetime." *Los Angeles Times.* June 24, 2018.
22. *Ibid.*

Chapter 13

1. King, Loren. *Boston Globe.* May 29, 2012.
2. O'Connor, William. *The Daily Beast* (August 22, 2014). Accessed on March 2, 2018.
3. Wilkinson, Tracy. "Diego Luna's Cesar Chavez Movie Marches in México." *Los Angeles Times.* July 1, 2012.
4. Zwecker, Bill. *Chicago-Sun Times.* March 27, 2014.
5. Puig, Claudia. *USA Today.* March 27, 2014.
6. Sachs, Ben. *Chicago Reader.* March 27, 2014.
7. "Depp Trying to Right the Wrongs of the Past with Tonto." *Indian Country Media Network.* June 10, 2013.
8. Graser, Mark. "Disney, Bruckheimer, see 'The Lone Ranger' as a new Genre-Bending Superhero." *Variety.* July 7, 2003.
9. Turan, Kenneth. "Lost on the plains." *Los Angeles Times.* July 3, 2013.
10. Schilling, Vincent. Indian Country Media Network. April 23, 2015.
11. Bradley, Laura. "Adam Sandler is awful and it's all our fault." *Slate.* April 26, 2015.
12. Scott, A.O. *New York Times.* December 21, 2017.

Bibliography

Aleiss, Angela (2005). *Making the White Man's Indian: Native Americans and Hollywood Movies.* Westport, CT: Praeger.

Banks, Dennis, and Richard Erdoes (2004). *Ojibwa Warrior: Dennis Banks and the Rise of the American Indian Movement.* Norman: University of Oklahoma Press, 2004.

Barnett, S.M., ed. (2011). *Geronimo: the True Story of America's Most Ferocious Warrior.* New York: Skyhorse Publishing.

Bataille, Gretchen M., and Charles L.P. Silet (1980). *The Pretend Indians: Images of Native Americans in Movies (1980).* Ames: The Iowa State University Press.

Bernstein, Alison R. (1999). *American Indians and World War II: Toward a New Era in Indian Affairs.* Norman: University of Oklahoma Press.

Berumen, Frank Javier García (2001). *Ramon Novarro: The Life and Films of the First Latino Hollywood Superstar.* New York: Vantage Press.

_____ (2003). *Brown Celluloid: Latino/a Icons and Images in the Hollywood Film Industry Volume I (1894–1959).* New York: Vantage Press.

_____ (2014). *Latino Image Makers in Hollywood: Performers, Filmmakers and Films since the 1960s.* Jefferson, NC: McFarland.

Brando, Marlon, and Robert Lindsey (1994). *Brando: Songs My Mother Taught Me.* New York: Random House.

Brown, Dee (1970). *Bury My Heart at Wounded Knee.* New York: Henry, Holt, & Co.

Buford, Kate (2010). *Native American Son: The Life and Sporting Life of Jim Thorpe.* Lincoln: University of Nebraska Press.

Buscombe, Edward (2006). *'Injuns! Native Americans in the Movies.* London: Reaktion Books.

Cooper, Jeanne, and Lindsay Harrison (2012). *Not Young, Still Restless: A Memoir.* New York: HarperCollins.

Cummings, Denise K. (2011). *Visualities: Perspectives on Contemporary American Indian Film and Art.* East Lansing: Michigan State University Press.

Davis, Ronald L. (1991). *Hollywood Beauty: Linda Darnell and the American Dream.* Norman: University of Oklahoma Press.

DeMille, Cecil B., and Donald Hayne, ed. (1959). *The Autobiography of Cecil B. DeMille.* Englewood Cliffs, NJ: Prentice Hall.

Dunbar-Ortiz, Roxanne (2007). *Roots of Resistance: A History of Land Tenure in New Mexico.* Norman: University of Oklahoma Press.

_____ (2014). *An Indigenous People's History of the United States.* Boston: Beacon Press.

Fitzgerald, Michael Ray (2013). *Native Americans on Network TV: Stereotypes, Myths, and the Good Indian.* New York: Rowman & Littlefield.

Fixico, Donald Lee (1986). *Termination and Relocation: Federal Indian Policy, 1945–1960.* Albuquerque: University of New Mexico Press.

Frayling, Christopher (2006). *Spaghetti Westerns: Cowboys and Europeans from Karl May to Sergio Leone.* London: I. B. Tauris.

Garner, James, and Jon Winokur (2011). *The Garner Files.* New York: Simon & Shuster.

Garroutte, Eva Marie (2003). *Real Indians: Identity and the Survival of Native America.* Berkeley: University of California Press.

Hearne, Joanna (2012). *Smoke Signals: Native Cinema Rising.* Lincoln: University of Nebraska Press.

Higler, Michael (1986). *The American Indian in Film.* Metuchen, NJ: Scarecrow.

Howe, LeAnne, ed. (2012). *Seeing Red—Hollywood's Pixeled Skins: American Indians and Film.* East Lansing: Michigan State University Press.

Josephy, Alvin M (1980). *500 Nations: An Illustrated History of North American Indians.* New York: Knopf, Reprint edition, 1998.

Katz, Ephraim (1979). *The Film Encyclopedia.* New York: Perigree Books.

Kilpatrick, Neva Jacquelyn (1999). *Celluloid Indians: Native Americans and Film.* Lincoln: University of Nebraska Press.

Madley, Benjamin (2017). *An American Genocide: The United States and the California Catastrophe, 1846–1873.* New Haven, CT: Yale University Press.

Marill, Alvin H. (1975). *The Films of Anthony Quinn.* Secaucus, NJ: The Citadel Press.

Marubbio, M. Elise (2013). *Native Americans on Film: Conversations, Teaching, and Theory.* Lexington: The University Press of Kentucky.

Matthiessen, Peter (1980). *In the Spirit of Crazy Horse.* New York: Penguin Books.

Means, Russell, and Marvin J. Wolf (1995). *Where White Men Fear to Tread: The Autobiography of Russell Means.* New York: St. Martins Griffin.

Mihesuah, Devon A. (2009). *American Indians: Stereotypes & Realities.* Atlanta: Clarity.

Mills, Billy, and Nicholas Sparks (1990). *Wokini: A Lakota Journey to Happiness and Self-Understanding.* Carlsbad, CA: Hay House.

O'Connor, John E. (1980). *The Hollywood Indian: Stereo-

types of Native Americans. Trenton: New Jersey State Museum.
Peltier, Leonard (1999). *Prison Writings: My Life Is My Sun Dance*. New York: St. Martin's Griffin.
Portilla, Miguel Leon (2006). *The Broken Spears: The Aztec Account of the Conquest of Mexico*. Boston: Beacon Press.
Quinn, Anthony, and Daniel Paisner (1995). *One Man Tango*. New York: HarperCollins.
Quirk, Lawrence J. (1975). *The Films of Robert Taylor*. Secaucus, NJ: The Citadel Press.
Rahega, Michelle H. (2013). *Reservation Reelism: Redfacing, Visual Sovereignty, and Representations of Native Americans in Film*. Lincoln: University of Nebraska Press.
Roberts, David (1993). *Once they Moved Like the Wind: Cochise, Geronimo and the Apache Wars*. New York: Simon & Schuster.
_____. *The Pueblo Revolt: The Secret Rebellion That Drove the Spaniards Out of the Southwest*. New York: Simon & Shuster.
Rollins, Peter C., and John E. O'Connor, eds. (2003). *Hollywood's Indian: The Portrayal of the Native American in Film*. Lexington: The University Press of Kentucky.
Rovin, Jeff (1977). *The Films of Charlton Heston*. Secaucus, NJ: The Citadel Press.
Schweninger, Lee (2013). *Imagic Moments: Indigenous North American Film*. Athens: University of Georgia Press.
Singer, Beverly R. (2001). *Wiping the War Paint Off the Lens: Native American Film and Video*. Minneapolis: University of Minnesota Press.
Stannard, David E. (1993). *American Holocaust: The Conquest of the New World*. Oxford, England: Oxford University Press.
Stuart, David E. (2000). *Anasazi America*. Albuquerque: University of New Mexico Press.
Thomas, Hugh. *Conquest: Moctezuma, Cortes, and the Fall of Old Mexico* (1993). New York: Simon & Schuster.
Thomas, Tony (1990). *A Wonderful Life: The Films and Career of James Stewart*. New York: The Citadel Press.
Ulrich, Roberta (2010). *American Indian Nations from Termination to Restoration, 1953–2008*. Lincoln: University of Nebraska Press.
Willis, John. *Screen World 1949–1994* (1994). New York: Crown Publishers.

Index

Aaron, Victor 217–218
Acker, Jean 41
Acosta, Rodolfo 98, 114–115, 139
Across the Wide Missouri (1951, film) 11, 12, 126
Adams, Evan 13, 215–216, 219–220, 297
Aherne, Brian 78
Alcatraz Island takeover 172, 235
Aldrich, Robert 147, 181–182
Aleiss, Angela ix, 17
Alexie, Sherman 13, 208, 215–216, 220–221, 255
Allende, Salvador 171
Ambush (1950, film) 144–145
Ameche, Don 73
America (term) 5–8
America (1924, film) xi, 32
American Indian Movement (AIM) 171–173, 235
Anasazi 6, 36
Annie Oakley (1935, film) 61
Apache 6, 7, 8, 12, 217–218
Apache (1954, film) 12, 43, 125, 145–147
Apache Trail (1942, film) 99
Aparicio, Yalitza 259
Apocalypto (2006, film) 241
Apted, Michael 212, 218–219
Arcand, Nathaniel 207–208, 221–222, 245
Armendariz, Pedro 47–48, 100, 119–120
Arrowhead (1953, film) 126
The Aryan (1916, film) 23
Atanarjuat: The Fast Runner (2001, film) 239
Aztecs 6, 210–211, 243–244
Aztlan 210–211

Baker, Carroll 159, 164–165
Bald Eagle, Dave 244
Banks, Dennis x, 22–223
Barthelmess, Richard 10, 68–69
The Battle of Apache Pass (1952, film) 141–142
Battle of Elderbush Gulch (1914, film) 20
Baxter, Warner 38, 65
Beach, Adam 13, 207, 215–216, 223–224, 239, 240, 246–248, 258
Bedard, Irene 13, 215–216, 224
Behold My Wife! (1934, film) 61
Ben-Hur (1925, film) 49
Bergen, Candice 186–187
The Big Trail (1930, film) 62–63, 71
Big Tree, Chief John 23–24
Billy Jack (1971, film) 174, 176, 177–178
Billy Jack films 176–181
Birmingham, Gil 248–249
The Birth of a Nation (1915) 18
Black Cloud (2004, film) 240, 245–246
Black Gold (1947, film) 11, 86, 98, 99, 112–113
Black Robe (1991, film) 206
Blackfeet 6, 11
The Blackfeet Halfbreed (1911, film) 19
Blazing the Trail (1912, film) 19
Blue, Monte 41–43, 71, 72, 77, 98, 107, 129, 145–146
boarding schools (Indian) 8
Boardman, Eleanor 64–65
The Border (1985, film) 198, 199
Bow, Clara 10, 33, 68
Bramcombe, Richard 252
Brando, Marlon 86–87, 148–149, 191, 240
Braveheart (1925, film) 33, 34–35
Broken Arrow (1950, film) 11, 125, 131–133
Broken Lance (1954, film) 12, 126
Broken Rainbow (1985, documentary) 198
Bronson, Charles 175–176
Brynner, Yul 161
The Buccaneer (1958, film) 88
Buck and the Preacher (1971, film) 174
Buffalo Bill (1944, film) 99, 113–114
Buffalo Bill Cody Wild West Show 79
Buffalo Child Long Lance, Chief 64
Bureau of Indian Affairs (BIA) 16; takeover 172

Bury My Heart at Wounded Knee (2007, film) 240
Bush, Pres. George W. 237–238

Cabot, Bruce 75
California 6, 38–39
California Indians 34
Call Her Savage (1932, film) 10, 11, 61–62, 67–68
Caltett, Juan Mora 210–211
Captain from Castile (1947, film) 99, 110–112, 121, 210, 211
Cárdenas, Lázaro 78
Cardinal, Tantoo 13, 224–225
Carewe, Edwin 39, 43, 45–46
Carmelo, Tonantzin 13, 244–245, 249
Carrasco, Salvador 243–244
Carrera, Barbara 184–186
Carrillo, Elipidia 198, 199, 244
Carson, Kit 36, 37, 98–99
Carter, H.P. 63
Carter, Pres. Jimmy 171
Castañeda, Movita 149, 152–153
Cat Ballou (1965, film) 158
Celluloid Princess Representation 9, 10
Centennial (1979, mini-series) 193
A Century of Dishonor (book) 34
Cesar Chavez (2014, film) 255–256
Chandler, Jeff 11, 128, 131–133, 141–142, 143
Chaplin, Charles 22, 32
Chato's Land (1972, film) 174
Chavez, Cesar 88–89, 191
Cherokee 6, 16, 52
Cheyenne 13, 159–161
Cheyenne Autumn (1964, film) 13, 48, 158, 159–161
Chicano Movement 88–89
Choctaw 6, 16
Chorre, Gertrude 45, 61
Chorre, Marie 81, 98
Chorre, Sonny 81–82, 98
Cimarron (1931, film) 61, 65–66
Cisco Kid series 84
citizenship (Indian) 8
Clinton, Pres. Bill 237

Index

Cochise 11, 102, 131–133, 141–142, 143
Cody, Buffalo Bill 113–114
Cody, Iron Eyes 26–27
Colorado Territory (1949, film) 99–100
Columbus 6, 205
Comanche 6, 240
Comanche Moon (2008, film) 240
Connery 162–163
Cooper, Gary 56, 71, 85, 106–108, 127, 128
Cooper, James Fennimore 74, 212–213
Cooper, Jeanne 129, 149–150
Cooper, Scott 258
Costello, Candice 248, 249–250
Costner, Kevin 13, 206, 208–210
Cortes, Hernando 6, 110–112
The Covered Wagon (1923, film) 32
The Cowboys (1972, (film) 193
Crazy Horse 44, 101, 136–137, 174–176, 250
Creeks 6, 16
Cristal, Linda 163–164
Crooked Arrows (2012, film) 254–255
Crosland, Alan 69
Curtis, Charles 8
Curtis, Tony 166
Curtiz, Michael 134
Custer, Gen. Armstrong 71, 99, 100–101
Custer's Last Fight (1912, film) 19

Dakota Access Pipeline 254
Dances with Wolves (1990, film) 13, 16, 206, 208–210, 228
Dark Cloud 24
Dark Cloud, Beulah 25
The Dark Wind (1991, film) 206
Darkfeather, Princess Mona 19, 27
Darnell, Linda 98, 99, 109–110, 114, 116–117
Daughters of the West (1949, film) 100
Daves, Delmer 133
Dawes Act of 1887 (Dawes Severalty Act) 16
De Córdova, Arturo 57, 59
De Coronado, Francisco Vázquez 36
De las Casas, Bartolomé 6
Delgado, Damián 207, 214, 225–226j, 243–244
Del Rio, Dolores 10, 13, 32, 38–39, 43, 45–48, 50, 59, 98, 119–120, 159–161
DeMille, Katherine 11, 73, 86, 90, 112–113
Demillo, Cecil 10, 11, 18, 20–22, 24, 34, 35, 64–65, 70–72, 85–86, 88, 99, 106–108
Depp, Johnny 257–258
Destry Rides Again (1939, film) 71
The Devil Horse (1926, film) 33
Devil's Doorway (1950, film) 125, 129–131, 131–133

Dieterle, William 77
A Distant Trumpet (1964, film) 157
Dix, Richard 10, 35–37, 40–41, 65
Dmytryk, Edward 162
Dodge City (1938, film) 61, 71
Drum Beat (1954, film) 126
Duel at Diablo (1966, film) 158–159, 166–167
Duel in the Sun (1946, film) 11, 98, 99, 104–106
Dunbar-Ortiz, Roxanne ix
Dunne, Phillip 212
Dupea, Tatzumbia 98, 107–108

Earp, Wyatt 23, 108–110
Eastwood, Clint 246–248
Edison, Thomas 17
Ejército Zapatista de Liberación Nacional (EZLN) 205
The Emerald Forest (1985, film) 198
The End of the Trail (1932, film) 67
Eskimo (1931, film) 62, 70
The Exiles (1961, film) 157
Eyre, Chris 13, 215–216, 219, 226, 239, 240, 242–243, 248

Fairbanks, Douglas 22–23, 54, 56
Fallen Angel (1945, film) 117
The Far Horizons (1955, film) 11–12, 126
Farmer, Gary 13, 226–227
Farrow, John 138–139
Ferber, Edna 65
Fernandez, Emilio "Indio" 47–48, 98, 115, 118–121
Field, Shirley Anne 162
The Fighting Cowboy (1933, film) 61
Figueroa, Gabriel 47
First Continental Meeting of indigenous Peoples 205
Five Civilized Tribes 15
Flags of Our Fathers (2006, film) 223, 240
Flaherty, Robert J. 32
Flap (1970, film) 173–174
Flynn, Errol 100–101
For the Squaw (1911, film) 18
Ford, John 13, 32, 33, 37–38, 48, 62, 73–74, 99, 100, 102–103, 125, 139–140, 159–161, 163–164
Fort Apache (1948, film) 99, 102
French & Indian War 6–7
Frontier Fury (1943, film) 99
Fuller, Samuel 140–141

Gable, Clark 11, 12
Galilea, Annie 14, 227
Garcia, Stella 188–190
Garfield, John 78
Garner, James 129, 150–151, 166–167
Garroutte Eva Marie ix
The Gaucho (1927, film) 23, 56
General Custer and the Little Big Horn (1926, film) 34

George, Chief Dan 187–188, 202
Geronimo 7, 23, 37, 74, 77, 131–133, 157, 217–218
Geronimo (1939, film) 77
Geronimo (1962, film) 157
Geronimo (1993, film) 217–218
Gibson, Hoot 99
Gibson, Mel 241–242
The Godfather (1972, film) 191
The Good Neighbor Policy 77
Grant, Rodney 219–210
Great Depression 60
The Great Train Robbery (1903, film) 17
Greene, Graham 13, 207, 208, 209–210, 218, 227–228, 239, 241–242
Grey, Zane 35
Grey Owl (1999, film) 14, 207
Greyeyes, Michael 250
Griffith, David Wark 18, 22–23, 32, 39, 42, 56
Guarani 201–202

The Half-Breed (1916, film) 22–23
The Half Breed's Courage (1911, film) 19
Harris, Richard 182–184
Hart, William S. 23
Hayes, Ira 165–166
Heston, Charlton 12, 88, 134, 188
Hickok, Wild Bill 70–71, 174–176
Hidalgo (2004, film) 240
Hill, Walter 218
His Squaw (1912, film) 20
Hispanic (term) x
The Homestead Act of 1862 66
Hondo (1953, film) 126, 138–139
Horse, Michael 190, 257
Hostiles (2017, film) 258
The Hour of Reckoning (1914, film) 20
House Made of Dawn (1972) 174
House Un-American Activities Committee (HUAC) 97–98, 124–125, 144–145, 147–148
How the West Was Won (1962, film) 157, 164–165
Huerta, Dolores 255–256

Imprint (2007, film) 3, 240, 244–245
In Old California (1910, film) 18
Incident at Oglala (1992, film) 206, 211–212, 235
Inda, Estela 111–112
Indian (term) xi
Indian Actors Association 62
Indian Appropriations Act of 1889 66
Indian Citizenship Act (1924) 8
The Indian in the Cupboard (1995, film) 207
Indian Paint (1965, film) 158
Indian Self-Determination Act (1975) 8
Indian treaties 7
Indian Wars 6–7, 8

Indian Women film representation 9 15, 17–18
Into the West (2005, film) 248
The Iron Horse (1924) 32, 33, 37–38
Island of Blue Dolphins (1964, film) 158, 168

Jackson, Helen Hunt 10, 18, 38, 45, 72
Jeremiah Johnson (1972, film) 174
Jesse James (1939, film) 71, 72
Jim Thorp—All American (1952, film) 93, 127, 134–135
Joe Kidd (1972, film) 189–190
Joffe, Roland 201–202
Johnny Tiger (1966, film) 159, 167–168
Johnson, Noble 23
Jones, Jennifer 11, 106
Jones, Julia 251
Journey Through Rosebud (1972, film) 174
Juarez (1939, film) 61, 77–79
Juárez, Benito 77–79
Jurado, Katy 12, 128, 129

Kaye, Celia 168
Kazan, Elia 86–87, 147–149
Kennedy, Pres. John F. 156–157
King, Henry 71, 72, 110
Kings of the Sun (1963, film) 157, 161–162
Kit Carson (1940, film) 98–99
Knox, Henry 7

La Farge, Oliver 77
Lakota 6, 208–210
Lancaster, Burt 12, 128, 134–135, 145–147, 181–182
La Roque, Rod 34, 45
The Last Hunt (1956, film) 125, 135–136
The Last Movie (1971, film) 188
The Last of the Mohicans (1826, novel) 74–75, 212–213
The Last of the Mohicans (1936, film) 37, 61, 74–75
Last of the Mohicans (1992, film) 212–213
The Last Roundup (1947, film) 100
Latino (term) x
Laughing Boy (1934, film) 11, 51, 62, 69, 75–77
Laughlin, Tom 174, 176–181, 184–186
The Law Rides Again (1944, film) 99
Lederman, D. Ross 67
The Legend of the Lone Ranger (1981, film) 257
Legend Walks Woman (1982, film) 198
The Light at the End of the Forest (1958, film) 128
Lighting, Georgina 240, 251–252
Little Big Man (1970, film) 188
Little Sky, Dawn 192

Little Sky, Eddie 192–193
Lo, the Poor Indian (1910, film) 19
Lombard, Karina 228–229
The Lone Ranger (1938, film serial) 257
The Lone Ranger (1956, film) 257
The Lone Ranger (2013, film) 256–258
The Lone Ranger and the Lost City of Gold (1958, film) 257
Lone Ranger & Tonto characters 122–123, 254–256
The Lone Ranger Rides Again (1939, film serial) 257
Long Lance, Buffalo Child 27–28
Luke, Jorge 181–182
Luna, Diego 255–256
Lust for Life (1956, film) 88

Mala, Ray 70, 83–84, 98
Malinche, La 111–112
A Man Called Horse (1970) 182–183
The Man Who Shot Liberty Balance (1962, film) 2
Manifest Destiny 7, 8, 12, 13
Mann, Anthony 129–131
Mann, Delbert 165
Mann, Michael 212–213
Many Treaties, Chief 98, 115–116
Margo (Maria Marguerite Guadalupe Teresa Bolano Castillo y O'Donnell) 151–152
Márquez, María Elena 11, 12
Marrubio, M. Elisa ix, 9–10, 84
Marshall, George 134, 164
Martin, Chris-Pin 84
Martinez, A 193–195
Massacre (1912, film) 19, 61
Massacre (1934, film) 10–11, 68–69, 75
Massai 145–147
Mature, Victor 109–110, 137
Maverick (1994, film) 208
Mayan genocide 206
Mayans 5–6, 161–162, 206, 241–242
Mayo, Virginia 100
McCoy, Tim 67
McCrea, Dusty 203–204
McCrea, Joel 71–72, 114
McDonald, Joseph Patrick "Joe" 161
The McMasters (1970, film) 173
Means, Russell ix, 172, 212–213, 229–230, 239, 245–246
Men with Guns (1997, film) 207, 213–215
Mendez v. Westminster (1947) 124–125
Menominee Restoration Act (1973) 172
Mexican-American War 8
Mexican Greaser films 23
Mexican Repatriation 45, 50
Mexican Spitfire films 57–58
Mexico 5–6
Mills, Billy 198, 200–201

The Mission (1986, film) 201–202
Moctezuma 211
Momaday, N. Scott 174
Monroe Doctrine 78
Montiel, Sarita 12, 127, 140–141
Moore, Clayton 122–123, 257
The Mountain Man (1980, film) 198
Muni, Paul 78
My Darling Clementine (1946, film) 99, 108–110, 117

Naked in the Sun (1957, film) 126
Nanook of the North (1922, film) 32
National League for Justice to American Indians 62
Naranjo, Ivan 204
Nava, Gregory 198
Navajo 6, 96
Navajo (1952, film) 126–127
Navajo Joe (1966, film) 158
Navajo Code Talkers 96, 239–240
Nelson, Ralph 166, 186–187
Newman, Joseph M. 165
Nicholson, Jack 198, 199
Nixon, Pres. Richard M. 96, 172
El Norte (1984, film) 198
North American Free Trade Agreement (NAFTA) 205
North of 36 (1924, film) 32
Northwest Mounted Police (1940, film) 99
Northwest Passage (1940, film) 99, 103–104
Novarro, Ramon 11, 32, 45, 48–52, 69, 75–76, 88, 98, 119

Obama, Pres. Barack 2–3
O'Brien, George 37, 158, 160
Office of Indian Affairs (Bureau of Indian Affairs) 16
O'Hara, Maureen 114
Ojibway 63–64
Oklahoma Land Rush (1889) 66
Older Than America (2008, film) 240
One Flew Over the Cuckoo's Nest (1975) 174, 195–196
100 Rifles (1969, film) 13, 14, 159
The Other Conquest/La Otra Conquista (2000, film) 239, 243–244
The Outlaw Trail (1944, film) 99
The Outsider (1961, film) 157, 165–166

The Pagan (1929, film) 50
Paget, Debra 11, 13, 131–133, 136
Palomino, Carlos 208, 218, 230–231
Pathé (Pathe Freres) studios 17
Pathfinder (2007, film) 240
Peck, Gregory 104–106
Peltier, Leonard ix, 210–211
Pena, Michael 256
Peters, Jean 12, 86–87, 111, 128, 146, 147–148

Phillips, Lou Diamond 200–201, 206
Pickford, Mary 18, 22
Pierre of the Plains (1944, film) 37
Pine Ridge Oglala Reservation (South Dakota) 8, 13, 211–212, 218, 242–243, 245–246
The Plainsmen (1936, film) 61, 70–71, 85
Pocahontas 207
Pocahontas (1995, animated film) 207
Power, Tyrone 110–112, 123
The Prisoner of Zenda (1922, film) 49
Proclamation of 1763 7
Pueblo people 36, 40–41
Pueblo Revolt (1680) 37

Quinn, Anthony 11, 52, 71, 84–90, 98, 101, 112–113, 114, 128, 144, 147–149, 173–174

Rae, Carla Holland 245, 250–251
Ramona (novel, 1884) 10
Ramona (1910, film) 10, 18–19
Ramona (1916, film) 10, 39
Ramona (1928, film) 10, 33, 38–39, 46
Ramona (1936, film) 10, 39, 72–73
Ramos, Nick 203, 204
Reagan, Ronald 89, 96–97, 197
Red Crow, Floyd 209–210
The Red Girl and the Child (1910) 17
The Red Man and the Child (1908, film) 18
The Red Man's View (1909, film) 18
Redfearn, Linda 168–169
Redford, Robert 13
Redskin (1928, film) 10, 33, 39–41
Requiem for a Heavyweight (1962, film) 89, 157
Retorno a Aztlán/Return to Aztlan (1991, film) 210–211
Return of a Man Called Horse (1976) 183–184
The Ridiculous Six (2015, film) 258
Rio Grande (1950, film) 100, 103
Rios, Elvira 74, 91–92
Roberts, Marguerite 145
Rogers, Robert 99, 103–104
Rogers, Will 52–54, 127–128, 153
Rogers, Will, Jr. 153
Roland, Gilbert 10, 32, 57, 68, 78, 84, 159
Roma (2018, film) 259
Romancito, Richard 195
Romero, Cesar 84
Romero, Ned 169
Rooster Cogburn (1975, film) 195
Ruggles, Wesley 65
Run of the Arrow (1957, film) 12, 125, 140–141
Running Brave (1983, film) 198, 200–201

Sacajawea 126
Sacheen Littlefeather 190–192, 240
Safinia, Farhad 241–242
St. Cyr, Lillian (Red Wing) 20–22, 25–26, 29–30
St Cyr, Vince 166, 169–170
Salvador (1986, film) 198
Sampson, Will 175–176, 195–196
Sandinistas 171
Sandino, Augusto Cesar 31
Sandler, Adam 258
The Savage (1952, film) 126 134
Sayles, John 213–215
The Scalphunters (1968, film) 159
The Scarlet West (1925, film) 33
Shadow of the Hawk (1976, film) 188
Schertzinger, Victor 39
Schroder, Rick 245–246
Schweig, Eric 212–213, 231, 242–243
Scott, Randolph 75
The Searchers (1956, film) 125, 139–140
Seguin (1981, film) 193
Seitz, George 37, 74
Self-Determination and Education Assistance Act (1973) 96–97
Seminole 6
Serra, Father Junipero 144
The Seven Cities of Gold (1955, film) 143–144
sexualized maiden representation 9–10
Shalako (1968, film) 160, 162–163
She Wore a Yellow Ribbon (1949, film) 99, 102–103
The Silent Enemy (1931, film) 62, 63–64, 79, 82
Sitting Bull 34, 136–137
Sitting Bull (1954, film) 136–137
Sitting Bull and the Spirit Lake Massacre (1927, film) 34
Silverheels, Jay 62, 98, 110–112, 123–125, 131–133, 257
Sioux War Dance (1894, film) 17
Skins (2002, film) 239, 242–243
Sloane, Paul 77
Smoke Signals (1998, film) 13, 215–216, 220, 221, 223
Society of American Indians 62
Soldier Blue (1970, film) 186–187
Spears, Michael 232, 245–246
Spotted Elk, Mollie 82
Squanto: A Warrior's Tale (1994, film) 207
The Squaw Man (1914, film) 10, 18, 20–22, 25
The Squaw Man (1918, film) 10
The Squaw Man (1931, film) 10, 62, 64–65
The Squaw's Mistaken Lover (1911, film) 18
Stagecoach (1939, film) 61, 71, 73–74
Standing Bear, Chief 43–44

Standing Bear, Luther 62
Steele, Bob 33, 99
Steinbeck, John 149
Stevens, Charles 23, 37, 54–55, 71, 98, 110, 145, 166
Stewart, James 11, 131–133, 163–164, 164–165
The Story of Will Rogers (1952, film) 127–128
La Strada (1954, film) 87
Striker, Fran 257
Strode, Woody 153–155, 163
Strongheart, Nipo T. 35
Stuart Proud Eagle Grant 250
Studi, Wes 207, 217–218, 232–233 239, 258–259
Susanna of the Mounties (1939, film) 61

Tarahumara 6, 85, 98
Taylor, Robert 128, 129–131, 135–136, 145, 159, 167–168
Taza 142–143
Taza, Son of Cochise (1954, film) 142–143
television 125
Tell Them Willie Boy is Here (1969, film) 13, 159
Tenochtitlan 6
termination policy 96–97
They Died with Their Boots On (1942, film) 99, 100–101
The Thief of Bagdad (1924, film) 23
Thirteen Colonies 7
Thompson, J. Lee 161–161
Thorpe, Jim 92–94, 98, 127, 134–135
A Thousand Roads (2005, film) 126, 240, 248
Thrush, Michelle 233
A Thunder of Drums (1961, film) 157, 165
Thundercloud, Chief 77, 80, 99, 257
Thunderheart (1992, film) 13, 207, 218–219, 235, 236
Tonka (1958, film) 128
Tootoosis, Gordon 233–234
Tousley, Sheila 207, 219, 234–235
Tovar, Lupita 32, 119
Tracy, Spencer 12, 103
Trail of Broken Treaties caravan 172
Treasure of the Sierra Madre (1948, film) 99
Trender, George W. 257–258
Triumphs of a Man Called Horse (1983, film) 184
Trooper Hook (1957, film) 126
Trudell (2005, film) 235
Trudell, John 207, 234–236, 240
Trump, Pres. Donald 254
Two Rode Together (1961, film) 163–164

Ulzana (Apache warrior) 181–182, 217–218

Ulzana's Raid (1972, film) 147, 182–183
Unconquered (1947, film) 99, 107–108
Union Pacific (1939, film) 61
United States 7

Valentino, Rudolf 49
Van Dyke, W.S. 70, 75–76
The Vanishing American (1925, film) 33, 34, 35–37, 54
Velez, Lupe 11, 23, 32, 55–59, 64–65, 69, 75–76
Vera Cruz (1954, film) 126, 127
Vidor, King 103, 106
Villa, Pancho 85
La Virgen Que Forjo Una Patria (1942, film) 50, 51
Viva Zapata! (1952, film) 86–87, 125, 128, 147–149

Walk the Proud Land (1956, film) 126
Walsh, Raoul 62, 99, 100
War Party (1988) 200
Washington, George 7
Wayne, John 62, 73–74, 102–103, 138–140, 164

Webb, James R. 161, 165
Webb, Richard D. 143
Welch (Tejeda), Raquel 13, 14, 198
Wellman, William 113–114
Wells Fargo (1937, film) 61
Wendkos, Paul 167
When the Legends Die (1972, film) 174
The White Dawn (1974, film) 174
White Eagle, Chief 44, 80–81, 98
White Feather (1955, film) 12–13, 126
White Horse, Chief 81
White Buffalo, Charlie 244
The White Buffalo (1977, film) 174–176
The White Man Takes a Red Wife (1910, film) 19
White Shadows of the South Seas (1928, film) 42
Windtalkers (2002, film) 239
Windwalker (1981, film) 198, 202–203
Winter in the Blood (2013, film) 255
Women Walks Ahead (2017, film) 250

Wong, Anna May 23
Wood, Sam 144–145
World War II and Native Americans 95–96
Wounded Knee incident (1975) 173
Wounded Knee massacre (1890) 8
Wounded Knee siege (1973) 172–173, 190–191

Yaqui 6, 13
The Yaqui Girl (1910, film) 18
Yellow Robe, Chauncey 63–64, 79
Young, Loretta 73
Young Deer, James Gordon 17–18, 25, 28–30
Young Guns (1998, film) 199–200
Youngblood, Rudy 241–242, 252–253
Yowlachie, Chief 44–45

Zapata, Emiliano 128 147–149
Zorba, the Greek (1964, film) 89–90

www.ingramcontent.com/pod-product-compliance
Ingram Content Group UK Ltd.
Pitfield, Milton Keynes, MK11 3LW, UK
UKHW050540150426
5217IPUK00026B/2008